POTTER ADDITION

SOCIAL INSTITUTIONS AND SOCIAL CHANGE
An Aldine de Gruyter Series of Texts and Monographs
EDITED BY
Michael Useem • James D. Wright

POTTER ADDITION
Poverty, Family, and Kinship in a Heartland Community

DAVID L. HARVEY

ALDINE DE GRUYTER
New York

About the Author

David L. Harvey is currently an Associate Professor of Sociology at the University of Nevada, Reno, where he teaches sociological theory, family and kinship, and the sociology of the community. Over the last twenty-five years his research interests have spanned the areas of critical theory, the measurement of subjective reification, critical political economy, dissipative systems theory, and studies in poverty and the culture of poverty.

Copyright © 1993 Walter de Gruyter, Inc., New York
All rights reserved. No part of this publication may be reproduced or transmitted in any form or by any means, electronic or mechanical, including photocopy, recording, or any information storage or retrieval system, without permission in writing from the publisher.

ALDINE DE GRUYTER
A division of Walter de Gruyter, Inc.
200 Saw Mill River Road
Hawthorne, New York 10532

This publication is printed on acid-free paper ∞

Library of Congress Cataloging-in-Publication Data
Harvey, David L., 1936–
    Potter addition : poverty, family, and kinship in a heartland
community / David L. Harvey.
        p.   cm. — (Social institutions and social change)
    Includes bibliographical references and index.
    ISBN 0-202-30441-8 (alk. paper). — ISBN 0-202-30442-6 (pbk. :
alk. paper)
        1. Middle West—Rural conditions—Case studies.   2. Rural
families—Middle West—Case studies,   3. Rural poor—Middle West—
Case studies.   4. Kinship—Middle West—Case studies.   I. Title.
II. Series.
HN79.A14H37   1993
305.5'69'0977—dc20   92-22422
                                                                CIP

Manufactured in the United States of America

10 9 8 7 6 5 4 3 2 1

Contents

Acknowledgments

Any work this long in the making encounters many obstacles and incurs innumerable debts. This work is no exception; it has somehow survived the trials and joys of two marriages, a divorce, a house fire that destroyed a partially completed manuscript, and the questionings of a precocious teenage daughter. Running in tandem with these tribulations has been a long string of kindnesses and an unending river of support and encouragement from many quarters. While I cannot thank all those students, friends, and colleagues who have contributed to the realization of this work, I would like to thank a few who have shaped its final outcome.

I would first like to acknowledge my intellectual debt to Professor Bernard Farber of Arizona State University and Professor Michael Lewis of the University of Massachusetts. Their enduring influence and ideas are scattered throughout these pages. My wife, Elizabeth Safford Harvey, has been both an affectionate helpmate and source of insight. The daughter of a Nevada rancher and a long-time resident of Nevada's "cow counties," who worked for several years at a local food pantry, she has shown me afresh that while poverty's faces change from one generation to the next, the way in which one lives that poverty remains relatively constant.

I have also been fortunate to be in an institutional setting that has provided me with wise and generous friends. Professor Michael Brodhead has given me the benefit of the historian's perspective on America's heartland and its poverty. Professor Michael Reed gave freely of his time, reading and discussing the manuscript and commenting extensively on the economic chapters. Professor Edward Royce of the Department of Sociology at Rollins College commented on several drafts of this work and contributed significantly to its rewriting. The criticisms of Professors Karl Kreplin and Robert Dunn concerning the organization of this work proved invaluable. I would also like to thank the members of my own department for their support and tolerance throughout the history of this project.

I am especially indebted to two women who labored long and hard on this manuscript. First, Mrs. Sharon Cook spent many long and tedious hours transcribing the taped interviews that I collected during my field-work. Putting them into a readable form has significantly eased my efforts. Second, Mrs. Lilika Newman not only typed, but profusely cri-tiqued early drafts of this work. Her skills as an editor and her growing concern for the people she came to know in the course of working on this manuscript have enriched it appreciably. I would also like to thank Miss Denise Schaar and Peggy Hart for typing portions of later versions of this manuscript.

I would be remiss if I did not acknowledge the people at Aldine de Gruyter for their kindness and professional contributions. I would like to thank Professor Joel Best, who reviewed the manuscript and recom-mended that Aldine de Gruyter give it serious consideration. Executive editor Richard Koffler has offered valuable advice and encouragement throughout this process, while managing editor Arlene Perazzini has shown generosity and good humor in overseeing the complex process of editing and preparing the manuscript for publication. Finally, Mike So-la's painstaking copyediting of the manuscript has contributed enor-mously to its coherence and readability.

The deepest debt of all, hovever, goes to the people of Potter Addi-tion. They took my wife and myself in hand, befriended us, and shared their lives with us for a brief time. They showed me all the virtues, foibles, and flaws that men and women display under pressure. Their lives testified to the fact that people can face chronic material need and do so with grace, dignity, and a wicked sense of humor. Above all else, they showed me how to retain one's fragile humanity in difficult times. This book is their story and a partial repayment for their having "taught the teacher." To them I dedicate this work.

1

First Impressions and Second Thoughts

In the spring of 1966 it was first suggested that I undertake this study. The War on Poverty was by then in its first flowering and there was still hope that we might escape Viet Nam relatively unscathed. Money for poverty research was suddenly available and it was my good fortune to be working for a multidisciplinary research institute that was renowned for its ground-breaking work on educating marginal populations. Funding had been found for developing programs that would meet the educational needs of poor children, and in keeping with the multidisciplinary nature of the institute, sociologists and psychologists would be expected to make their contribution. It would be the job of the sociologists to identify the institutional and community-based factors that contributed to the educational burdens of poor children.

To this end I was asked by Bernard Farber and Michael Lewis, the principal investigators directing the sociological part of this research, to take part in a three-pronged study of poverty in the city of Grand Prairie. Farber would use survey research techniques to investigate class-specific differences in kinship patterns. Lewis would study the large black community that had flourished in the North End of Grand Prairie since the 1860s, tracing the roles that racial oppression and class-based inequality played in generating black poverty. I would undertake a participant-observer study of Potter Addition, a notorious "hillbilly slum" located on the rural-urban fringe of Grand Prairie.

Because of my working-class background and border state origins, Farber and Lewis thought that I would be a natural for this project. I was less enthusiastic. I was reluctant to abandon my antiwar activities and even more chary about taking money from a government that was each day becoming more and more vicious in implementing its foreign policy. Moreover, I was still not at peace with my origins and my father. He had been dead for two years, and I had been alienated from him for more than a decade before his death. Living in Potter Addition would dredge up memories of my father and force me to confront our relationship. I was not sure I was yet up to that. There was also the issue of coming to grips with my own class origins: of facing once more my youthful marginality; of exhuming the scarring experiences and unresolved ambivalence from which I had become increasingly insulated during my years in the university. Surely participant-observer research in Potter Addition would reopen old wounds and force me to relive things that I had so artfully avoided thinking about for more than a decade.

Before giving an answer, I wanted to visit Potter Addition and see what I was getting into. Thus, I drove to the edge of Grand Prairie, to a place called Four Corners, where Speer Avenue and State Route 111 intersect. I turned left on Route 111 and drove past a series of small businesses housed in a set of unremarkable buildings. A half mile beyond Four Corners the highway passed over a littered, steep-banked drainage ditch that contained only a trickle of water. On the north bank of the ditch a graveyard extended a quarter mile up the highway. Huge elms and a high hedge running its full length gave it a dark, cavernous appearance. At the far end of the cemetery a small country road, Banks Avenue, intersected Route 111.

On the other side of Banks Avenue stood a cluster of blighted businesses: a group of white, two-storied "tourist cabins," a flower shop, and an auto repair business. The buildings' disrepair communicated the economic despair and marginality of their owners. The cabins could have appealed to only the most destitute of travelers, while the florist shop, with the freshness and beauty of its flowers, seemed out of place. Some distance down the highway, I saw Spooner Road and the abandoned brick schoolhouse that I had been told would mark the intersection of Spooner Road and Route 111. When I got to the intersection, I turned onto Spooner Road. Its blacktopped surface was already sticky from the unseasonably hot sun. I saw no structures on the north side of the road, save the old schoolhouse. A field of golden-hued, red winter wheat, beginning to droop under its ripening burden, stretched a mile or so to the raised embankment of a cloverleaf, which joined Route 111 to the new interstate. A half mile down Spooner Road, on the right, stood an incongruous grove of pine trees. You might have mistaken the stand for a nursery, until you were full upon it and saw the large, white, two-storied house standing in the middle of the pines. Grand in scale, yet prosaically sensible in its midwestern sobriety, it was the residence of an agronomy professor, as I later learned. I would hear it said more than once during my stay in Potter Addition that he had planted his full acre in trees to dissociate his home from the blight of Potter Addition.

Some vacant land separated the pine grove from a white house that had originally been a church. Its bell-less steeple signaled it had once been a house of God, while the swing set in a trampled yard barren of grass testified that it was now a residence. Past another gap of unused land, I got my first glimpse of Potter Addition.

Instead of turning onto Potter Avenue and entering the community, however, I continued down Spooner Road, past the two intersecting streets that gave Potter Addition its skeletal, rectangular outline, and out a short distance into the country. On my first pass I had noticed only the huge, arching trees. Most were three feet or more in diameter, rising in Gothic curves of green, gray, and sun-reflected gold to form a cooling haven for the houses below. I turned around and retraced my path. This time I would attend more carefully to the houses. The six or seven dwellings were a bit rundown. Two were covered with the heavy, red-brick tar paper that had been popular before the advent of aluminum siding. One house had a lean-to, which obviously was not part of the original structure, attached to its back wall. Perhaps it had been built to give a daughter who had come of age some small measure of privacy from her brothers. Another house, sitting far back on a lot overgrown with weeds, looked more ramshackle than the rest. While clearly not suburban housing, these were by no means the slum dwellings I had been told to expect. Marginal at best, they were no different from those found in most midwestern hamlets with populations of under two thousand. In the Midwest such dwellings usually were occupied by solid, small-town "working-class" families.

Turning onto Potter Avenue, I saw a well-kept trailer. A high aluminum awning ran its full length, and its yard was surrounded by a low cyclone fence. The yard was covered with a well-raked, thumb-sized schist that glistened in the sun. The concrete slab that served as a driveway was decorated with potted plastic flowers. Tacky perhaps, but not slummy; its clones could be found in any number of Sun Belt retirement villages. Across the street was a well-tended vegetable garden, about one eighth of an acre in area. Its corn and tomatoes were already well along for that time of year. South of the garden stood a shabby gray trailer. Two junk autos parked in front of it established what would become a leitmotif for the entire community. South of the trailer, about twenty feet from the road, was an ugly but functional firehouse. Built of cinder blocks and capped with an oddly pitched roof, it housed two fire trucks. Later I learned it had a "clubhouse" in the back, which was used for various community social functions.

Past the firehouse was a series of homes resembling suburban tract housing. Across the street stood a row of older homes, all in need of paint and minor repairs. Again, peppered across the landscape were more junk cars. Some were up on concrete blocks, while others sat on the ground in various stages of cannibalization. Groups of men and teenagers, engrossed in "shade tree diagnostics," clustered around two of the cars. Further south, on the west side of Potter Avenue, I spied the first real shack. It showed no trace of paint on its bare-board exterior, and its window screens, peeling back at the corners, looked like earmarked pages in a book. The roof, shingled in random colors, sagged in the middle. Images of my short stay in Appalachia came to mind. South of the shack someone had recently assembled a prefab redwood garage. A door and a square window had been inserted where the overhead door should have hung. Wood scraps in the yard and the absence of curtains on the window suggested that no one had yet moved in.

Two doors down from the garage, on the left, was a large all-metal warehouse. To the right, lodged between two junkyards and set well back from the road, was Betty's Market. The northernmost yard appeared defunct, while the other, Bull Gomes's garage and junkyard (judging from the number of cars parked on the west apron of the road), was a thriving concern. Gomes's establishment was housed in a giant, wooden, boxlike structure, which was covered with a nondescript tar paper–like material. Next to it sat a large Quonset hut in which, I later learned, Gomes lived and rented apartments. In back of the garage, extending the full length of the one-and-one-half-acre lot, was the junkyard. I surmised this was the place that produced the occasional columns of black smoke from burning cars that I had noticed on my trips to Farmer City. The junkyard's autos and parts had, over time, spread to the front of the garage and apartment house.

The road here passed over the crest of a low ridge. The autos, the columns of trees, and the small garden plots were still everywhere. I saw the first visible signs of livestock being raised in the back of one of the properties. The area's visage had shifted: nothing dramatic, more a change of mood than of tangible substance. There was still a mix of shanties and better kept, more proper dwellings, but the shanties, many deserted, now preponderated. There seemed to be more trailers at this end of the community, and the shacks here were smaller and looked more despairing. The houses were seedy in appearance. One trailer, circa 1940, had a cancerous wooden attachment built onto its front. Next to the trailer was a small building resembling a child's playhouse. In front of it sat an ancient gentleman petting a black and white mongrel. Here, finally, was the "rural slum" I had heard so much about.

At the end of Potter Avenue I turned left onto the road into which it emptied and glanced at the street sign—Banks Avenue. It was the street I had passed earlier on Route 111. There was, it seemed, a more direct route to Potter Addition. After turning, I spied yet a third, and then a fourth junkyard. The lots were deeper than those on Potter Avenue. They contained as many as four or five structures, often arranged in files of two or three houses each. It was all but impossible to determine if those houses set deepest on the lots were inhabited. Besides looking at the housing, I was now forced to watch out for children. The street suddenly contained fifteen or twenty youngsters, riding bikes and driving homemade go-carts. Some children were clustered about talking, while others were off on their own, playing and "popping wheelies" on their bicycles.

Suddenly I was at the end of Banks Avenue. At a second cluster of businesses it had turned in elbow fashion, veered north, and become North Star Avenue. Some one hundred feet or so from where I sat, a graveled, two-lane path stretched south from the intersection of North Star and Banks. After running first between a junkyard and a row of houses, it degenerated into two ruts overgrown with weeds, and finally disappeared into a thick, second-growth foliage that grew on the edge of the drainage ditch I had crossed earlier on Route 111.

I turned left onto North Star, drove twenty feet, and came to a sudden halt. On the left were two boxcars set flush against each other. These were people's homes! It was a scene from a work of fiction. The name Rose of Sharon came to mind: Rose of Sharon, lying on that filthy floor with the dead Moses set adrift in the flooding irrigation ditch; her people without salvation; Rose of Sharon clutching the dying old man to her breast.

As the son of an itinerant pipefitter I was no stranger to lean times. In my youth I had seen my parents periodically dodging creditors and collection agencies. These experiences had not, however, steeled me to accept the poverty I now confronted. I could grasp the abstract poverty I encountered in books, or heard in the depression stories that my mother and father told me—tales of hard times tinged by a dread of their imminent return—but this was different. On that bright near-summer day in 1966, I was not prepared to find dark remnants of the 1930s. Coming over the crest of the ridge, I had entered the world of James Agee's *Let Us Now Praise Famous Men*, a world of poverty and despair that had been memorialized by the photographers and artists of the Farm Security Administration.

Those first impressions of Potter Addition, though altered by fifteen months of participant-observation and by twenty years of reflecting on those images, have never left me. The period of actually living in the community was one of reeducation. The people of Potter Addition took my family into their homes and tutored me in the subtleties and nuances of living on the edge. I lived with them, worked in their youth club, joined in their community activities, and shared (as much as any outlander in a tight little community ever can) their lives, joys, and sorrows. I collected some eight hundred pages of field notes and almost one hundred hours of taped interviews during my stay. In those interviews the "teacher was taught" by his friends and neighbors.

The conditions of that reeducation were not always scientifically controlled. The atmosphere was saturated with personal politics and endless ideological confrontation. Continuous attempts were made by a proud community to propagandize my wife and me, as it sought to defend itself against being negatively stereotyped as a latter-day Hooverville. Residents often tried to deny the very poverty through which they and I daily walked. At other times, when denial seemed fruitless, they sought to soften my interpretation of their poverty. At every opportunity prideful people defended themselves against the "lies" that outsiders daily spun.

During my fieldwork I never felt "off stage," was never able to relax fully, and only seldom escaped the constant efforts of the people to shape my research. In the context of this protracted struggle I developed my ideas about the community and how it operated. I cannot assure the reader, even now, that my "scientific vision" has remained untouched by the negotiated meanings and passions that emerged during my fieldwork. Nor is it devoid of the unsettled personal accounts I have already mentioned. I took them with me into the community and, as part of me, they entered into the ethnographic record. In Potter Addition I made friendships and associations that were more familylike than professional. I was permanently influenced by the community, even as I undoubtedly must have changed it in the very act of studying it. As in all participant-observer encounters, I became as much a part of the data as those whom I studied. The ghosts and shadows of that personal struggle are interwoven into the fabric of this work, as are the academic polemics and politics that surrounded the antipoverty movement in the 1960s.

The public issues of three decades reverberate throughout this work. Having never been resolved, they haunt our consciousness. Much has changed in the three decades since I first visited Potter Addition. The nation's call to conscience and social justice was consumed in the crucible of Viet Nam. We have paid dearly for that flaw in national character. The great issues of the 1960s—poverty, racism, and the war— have been submerged in a sea of reaction and willful social amnesia. Still, they are part of our unfinished agenda. In the late 1960s there was a turning point, a moment when the panic over violence in America led to calls for a moratorium on combating social injustice. Walter Miller, a scholar whose reputation for understanding the poor and combating poverty could never be doubted, by 1968 could write in both frustration and apprehension:

The immediate proposal is this: that all federal agencies, and all agencies within the orbit of federal influence, be advised forthwith to terminate the practice of using, in speech, reports, legislative proposals, and all other documents, the major terms of the Poverty Ideology—particularly such terms as "the poor," "the power structure," "the ghetto," "denial of opportunity," "deprivation" and "alienation." This proposal assumes first that the conceptualization underlying these terms provides a major incentive for domestic violence in that it justifies a policy of revenge for past and present injustices, and second that it promotes a dangerously divisive image of the United States as comprising two irreconcilable warring camps: the exploited and the exploiters. Even those who remain unconvinced of the validity of these assumptions might see fit to support this measure on the grounds that it can be implemented at little cost relative to the benefits that could accrue if the assumptions are valid.

The long-term proposal is that an appropriate and adequately supported agency, in or out of government, deliberately and systematically undertake the development of a conceptual formulation that can serve as a sound basis for national policy with respect to low status populations in the United States. As already mentioned, many feel that the diversion of national attention and resources to Asian warfare has seriously impeded efforts to accommodate pressing domestic problems; this diversion could be turned to advantage if it were conceived as a temporary lull that provides an opportunity to prepare the groundwork for a revitalized postwar renewal of these efforts. Most important, it affords an opportunity to remedy one of the most critical defects of the War on Poverty—the absence of an adequate conceptual rationale. (Miller 1968, p. 304)

With an irony and vengeance befitting *The Monkey's Paw*, Miller and many other liberal scholars obtained their lull. By the 1970s, that lull became benign neglect as the issues of race and poverty were replaced by new, seemingly more urgent social problems. Class-based social problems gave way in the public consciousness to environmentalism, the struggle to legitimate alternative life-styles, and the frantic flight toward renewed conspicuous consumption. The 1980s saw the circle completed. With the rebirth of the old mean-spiritedness, America's poor were once more stigmatized and became—in the popular mind— the source of their own degradation.

Intellectual styles also shifted during this thirty-year period.[1] In the 1960s many poverty researchers studied poverty "from the bottom up." Descriptions of who the poor were, their subculture, and the structural regularities of their everyday life became integral parts of poverty's problematic. Works such as Herbert Gans's (1962) *The Urban Villagers*, Elliot Liebow's (1967) *Talley's Corner*, and Oscar Lewis's (1966) *La Vida* are today classics of this genre. Each attempted in its own way to look beyond the statistics and grasp poverty as a lived, everyday experience.

But there was more to studying poverty from the bottom up, for while poverty research was expected to make policy recommendations, many sociologists and anthropologists went beyond mere programs of amelioration. Rejecting the "cultural deprivation" paradigm as a paternalistic misunderstanding of what living poor actually entailed, many began to argue that poverty's subculture was more than an aggregation of individual deficiencies and "negative" cultural traits. Scientists of a progressive orientation argued that poverty's subculture and the ethnic diversity so often associated with it warranted protection and preservation as valued life forms. They maintained that the path to security need not be paved with embourgeoisification. The idea that the poor had a right to codetermine politically their own future and, if they so chose, to preserve valued family patterns and cultural orientations became a major source of friction between liberal scholars and their New Left progeny.

During the 1970s a major political and intellectual shift occurred as social agendas were altered to reflect the diminished expectations of an increasingly apprehensive nation. Poverty was redefined as primarily an economic and technical problem. It was approached "from the top down," and the poor became little more than a faceless, bureaucratically administered, client population. They were united by a single, abstract statistical trait: all those who lived below a politically manipulated "poverty line" (Orshansky 1965; Rodgers 1982, pp. 14–49). Talk of "self-determination" and "maximum feasible participation" was abandoned and replaced with purely administrative preoccupations. A class of alleged social superiors once again assumed the ego-inflating, bourgeois mantle of caretakers. By the 1980s the final step had been taken: The poor had been safely criminalized once again, becoming objects of either fear or contempt, and in some cases, both.

The research reported here spans these academic and political changes. It began during a period of progressive resurgence and political hope. It was completed at the ebb of that progressive ideology. Thus, it reflects both my early commitment to doing politically relevant sociology from below and the chastening realization that after two decades of reaction and retrenchment, such research has done little to ease the lot of the poor. To this extent, this book is permeated with "politics": the shifting political lessons of three decades, the undiminished commitments of the writer, and, finally, the subtle politics of fieldwork in which a community struggles to shape ideologically what will be written about it. Knowing this, I have tried to dampen my advocacy for those with whom I lived and worked. At the same time, I have refused to depict the people of Potter Addition as either pathological or in need of extended apologetics. There is no need to hide "warts" or to soft-pedal the unsavory aspects of life at the bottom. Since leaving Potter Addition I have encountered more predatory and pathological forms of humanity: used-car salesmen and university administrators, to mention but two.

There are three reasons that I now write about Potter Addition: First, the people of Potter Addition deserve to have their story told. There is drama, heroism, and grim, life-sustaining humor in their struggles. Second, I want to preserve for the record the particular experience of a lower-class fraction that has been relatively neglected by sociologists: poor, nonethnic whites who within the last two generations or so have been driven from the land.[2] Finally, the ethnographic details recorded here serve as a pretext for theoretically exploring the structure of poverty and its subculture. Combining ethnographic description and theoretical analysis, I hope to penetrate the gritty empirical details of living poor and expose the real structures that generate the everyday life of poverty. Despite the age of the field record, the economic and kinship analyses contained herein are far from dated. The processes of deindustrialization and the so-called feminization of poverty, especially among black women, to be sure, are *new sources* of poverty. But for all the shifting in poverty's demographic profile, living poor has changed little in the past few decades. The anxiety of economic uncertainty is still the hallmark of poverty-induced life-styles. If we have a more developed critical understanding of the economics of poverty—both the new and the old—we have not advanced our understanding of the inner parameters of what it means to live poor.

I. PLAN OF THE BOOK

This work employs ethnographic description and structural analysis to reconstruct the world of family, kinship, and poverty in an American heartland community. As is the practice in studies such as this, every attempt has been made to preserve the anonymity of the community, its people, and the resource persons who worked with me on an everyday basis. Consequently, I have called this community Potter Addition, though that is not its real name. Similarly, Grand Prairie and Clay County are pseudonyms, as are the proper names I use throughout. In some instances it has been necessary to alter certain biographical or ethnographic details in order to protect the privacy of Potter Addition and its people. In doing so, however, I have taken care not to alter the substance or meaning of the sociological narrative itself.

With these minor exceptions then, what follows is a faithful account of Potter Addition and the struggle of its people to retain their dignity in the face of enormous odds. The work itself is divided into five sections. The first consists of this introductory chapter and a theoretical chapter in which I develop a model of poverty that integrates elements of critical Marxism, cultural ecology, and Oscar Lewis's (1964, 1966) culture of poverty concept. The essence of this model lies in the premise that poverty is imposed upon the poor from above, and that those who live in poverty occupy a "class niche" whose radical uncertainty makes future planning all but impossible. Moreover, the culture of poverty is not portrayed as being pathological. It is seen instead as a reasoned set of responses that allows the poor temporarily to finesse poverty's chaotic class niche.

The second section establishes the stage upon which family life and kinship activity actually unfold in Potter Addition. It describes the ecological and material foundations of life of Potter Addition: the ecology, history, and physical layout of the community, its everyday work life and occupational subculture, its leisure time pursuits and the ideological uses to which leisure is often put, and finally the consumption practices that the poor daily use to stabilize their economic environment. At each step of the discussion the concept of variable class environments is used to demonstrate the underlying social logic that orders the material and ecological foundations of life in Potter Addition.

The third section analyzes the structure and dynamics of lower-class family life. It consists of two chapters. The first describes lower-class family roles and their evolution, while the second analyzes a particular type of lower-class family: a female-dominated set of households that I will call the *uxoricentric family*. The last two sections are devoted to a consideration of the dynamic contradictions that animate lower-class kinship. The fourth section explores the impact that economic uncertainty has upon the material foundations of lower-class descent groups. It analyzes the strains and contradictions that poverty introduces into the relations between the households that make up lower-class descent formations. The fifth section deals with the moral interior of kinship and focuses on how personal identities and kinship roles are socially constructed.

I conclude this study with an epilogue and a summary chapter. In the epilogue I describe Clay County, Grand Prairie, and Potter Addition as they exist today. I report how things have changed and how they have remained the same—especially how Potter Addition's poverty has evolved during the intervening twenty-five years. In the summary chapter I review the major motifs developed in this work and suggest their relevance for the present poverty debate. With this overview in mind, let us turn to the issues of class, the capitalist mode of production, and the structural genesis of modern poverty.

2

The Social Reproduction of Poverty

Do the poor produce their own poverty? This question more than any other split the antipoverty movement of the 1960s. For conservatives, the answer was yes. How else could the free enterprise system be absolved of blame? How else could the simultaneity of chronic poverty and massive wealth be rationalized, unless the poor were shown to be the authors of their own fate? For New Deal liberals of the Kennedy and Johnson eras, the answer was a *qualified* yes. How else could one defend the social programs of welfare capitalism from the attacks of the right, while simultaneously advocating systemic reforms that could make American society more just? For the New Left, disenchanted with a sclerotic labor movement and a co-opted working class, the answer was a resounding no. Minorities and the poor were not just an oppressed group for whom justice was long overdue, they were a vehicle for social renewal. To suggest that the poor somehow cooperated in their economic exploitation and cultural oppression was to commit the intellectual crime of blaming the victim.

These positions still haunt discourses on poverty. Their echoes reverberate in the renewed debates of the 1990s. Those on the right still justify their policy of malign neglect by claiming that the poor cause their own poverty. Liberals, even after suffering a series of reverses in the War on Poverty, still demand an agenda of expanded social entitlements.[1] And the Left, though largely in disarray, continues to insist that poverty can be eliminated if and only if the productive structures of capitalism itself are radically altered. None of these positions have fared that well over the last three decades. Each has been chastened as much by its irony-laden victories as it has by its unanticipated defeats.

Despite their checkered history and the virtual stalemate in which they now find themselves, I believe each position has something to contribute to the analysis of poverty. Once the ideological denial and assigning of blame that have characterized this three-cornered debate are put aside, it is possible to appropriate elements from each that will aid our understanding of modern poverty. In this volume, I will synthesize elements of all three positions. Modern poverty will be treated first and foremost as a problem endemic to capitalist economic organization. At the same time, the role that the poor themselves play in reproducing their poverty will be explored.

Poverty results as a logical consequence from the way in which capital structures the production of commodity wealth. The capitalist system requires an industrial reserve army of unemployed and underemployed persons to sustain itself. The men and women who make up this army are condemned to idleness for long periods of time so that the system can operate more efficiently. Forced to live on the edge and excluded from a stable means of subsistence, these economically superfluous individuals lead lives of material and social uncertainty. The dual factors of chronic material need and the social uncertainty it engenders form the crucial benchmarks of modern poverty.

At the same time, the poor play an active role in determining the empirical contours of their poverty. That is, in response to their economic superfluity, the poor construct novel social and cultural forms that allow them to survive the rigors of living on the edge. Such constructions, however, carry within themselves a rich set of dialectical ironies. To the extent that the poor successfully cope with and adapt to their marginality, they also unintentionally reproduce the cultural dimensions of their poverty. Thus, while holding that the objective foundations of poverty originate in the economic contradictions of late capitalist society, I also hold that poverty has a cultural superstructure that is constructed by the poor themselves. While emerging from the material infrastructure of lower-class life, this superstructure is not reducible to the economics of superfluity alone. Instead, the culture of poverty possesses a relative autonomy from productive relations. The cultural productions of the poor draw heavily upon the various at-hand cultural materials and social conventions in which they, as a class, are immersed—the hegemonic customs and practices of the larger community. By constructing social relations that meet their special needs, the poor assemble a cultural superstructure of poverty that assumes different expressive forms in different locales. Moreover, the culture of poverty feeds back upon and overdetermines its economic foundations. This dialectical intertwining of poverty's material and cultural dimensions produces a rich set of complex structures, which give different, concrete cultures of poverty their distinguishing marks.

In this and later chapters, this *reproductive model of poverty* will be laid out in greater detail. It should be noted, however, that the reproductive model, while stressing the dialectics of poverty, will distance itself from the family of explanations that are bent on blaming the victim. While studying the role the poor play in reproducing their own poverty, we at no time presume that poverty's *structural genesis* is reducible to the conduct or folkways of the poor.

I. CONVENTIONAL AND CRITICAL PROBLEMATICS

Most sociological analyses appropriate poverty's *immediate appearance* but seldom go beyond it. Mistaking empirical symptom for systemic cause, sociologists usually define poverty as a transitory market malfunction, as a "circulatory illness." Poverty in this context is viewed as a mere paucity of resources. The poor do not have enough money, education, self-respect, or self-control to win their way into the middle classes. Conservative social scientists, for example, see the market as a benevolent, selective mechanism. It is the mysterious instrument of a higher wisdom that permits the talented, the constitutionally inept, and all those in between to seek their own "natural level." Because certain persons are intellectually inferior, criminal, lazy, morally lax, or sexually improvident, they are bad employment or investment risks and deservedly descend into poverty. Poverty and squalor thus become the objective indicators that confirm the higher wisdom of the free market.

Liberal social scientists invert this logic, but still view poverty as a market-mediated phenomenon. They argue that *due to their poverty*, lower-class persons are more susceptible to such social pathologies as mental illness, educational underachievement, criminal activity, and family breakup. The cure for such pathologies, they argue, is state-directed and state-financed programs that will eliminate the poor's economic dependence by making them productive citizens. This, for example, is Lewis Coser's (1969) message in his presidential address to the Society for the Study of Social Problems. He excoriates those social scientists who defend the culture of the poor, charging that they are unwittingly sabotaging the cause of the very people they claim to help. Insofar as the cure for modern poverty is occupational mobility, defense of the cultural practices of the poor is a defense of the very pathologies that block their upward mobility. Progressives are thus erecting ideological barriers to mobility, and hence perpetuating existing class arrangements. Such misguided value relativism, Coser argues, works unwittingly to "keep the lower class in their place" (Coser 1969, p. 264). If the poor are to throw off the stigma of social and economic dependency (Coser 1965; Simmel 1965), they must abandon those dysfunctional cultural commitments that keep them from taking advantage of the technical and social opportunities offered them. In this context, Coser sin-

gles out for special criticism Walter Miller's (1958) work purporting to
show the inner logic and autonomy of lower-class culture:

> Although dysfunctional for achievement, as I argued earlier, lower-class
> life styles may indeed be functional for a society where opportunities for
> mobility, though allegedly open, are in fact restricted, and where an un-
> skilled labor force is needed. The situation is, however, very different in
> today's technological society. . . .
> It may well be true, as Miller claims, that the distinctive contributions
> that the lower classes have made in the past to the building of America
> could be made only through life styles that channeled lower-class males
> into rough, unskilled occupations. But the stark fact is that today such
> unskilled jobs tend rapidly to disappear. Modern society needs very few
> carriers of wood and drawers of water, and socialization patterns and
> styles of life that prepare men for such jobs, although they may have been
> 'functional' in the past, have now become dysfunctional. These life styles
> today do not even prepare men for the contributions about which Miller
> waxes so lyrically because there is no demand for them. Rather than being
> functional for maintaining a lower stratum for which there is much de-
> mand in the economy, these life styles now become increasingly maladap-
> tive to present-day technological society. . . .
> We have now come full-circle. The very characteristics of the lower class
> that have come in for so much high praise by liberal sociologists of good
> will, turn out upon inspection to help perpetuate for the lower classes and
> minorities the very degradation which liberals tend to deplore. (Coser
> 1969, pp. 269–70)

For social democrats such as Coser, the economic salvation of the poor
hinges on their willingness to abandon those values which impede their
assimilation into the mainstream. The idea that poverty might be generated by the systemic logic of capitalism is not seriously considered. In
the end, opposite ideological tendencies converge as liberals and conservatives alike seek, each on their own terms, a solution to poverty that
will preserve the class system while refining the efficacy of its sifting and
sorting mechanisms. Economic and social justice for both becomes a
matter of streamlining the class system, of refining its ability to retrieve
and reward that last scintilla of overlooked talent that might otherwise
be unjustly condemned to a life of poverty.

Insofar as these ostensibly opposed approaches divert attention from
the structural origins of poverty and focus on aspects of the offending
individual, both fail fully to confront poverty as a sociological reality.
Policy differences are eventually reduced to debates over which set of
measures can best winnow the deserving from the undeserving poor.
Despite their divergent rhetorics, the policy goals of liberals and con-

servatives alike are not the elimination of poverty as a social category, but making poverty individually just. Ultimately the goal for both sides is to make sure that only the "truly" untalented and undeserving remain under poverty's yoke.

Such programs do not eliminate poverty because they do not confront the structural sources of poverty itself. But why should poverty's institutional roots remain inaccessible to these reformers? The sociology of knowledge supplies us with a plausible explanation. The market problematic, like other effective ideologies, can explain its interpretive failures as easily as it can its successes. In this particular case, the market model's inability to identify poverty's *structural* origins is due to the fact that its analysis centers on *individuals and their aggregated conduct*. The failure of poverty amelioration schemes (like its successes) can therefore be laid at the doorsteps of the offending individuals themselves. Nurture-based solutions and "environmental enrichment" can only go so far (or so it is argued) in saving the poor from themselves. At some point all such schemes for self-improvement must run up against the stone wall of immutable natural limits.[2] Those not aided by the helping hand of their betters are then labeled either as constitutionally incapable of taking advantage of societal largess or as morally perverse. In either case, poverty's victimization becomes a self-inflicted wound, and the reformer is freed from further obligation. That was Malthus's ([1872] 1960) message nearly two hundred years ago, Arthur Jensen's (1969) message of two decades ago, and the point of Charles Murray's (1984) latest utilitarian parable.

To break out of this circular argument, we must begin by questioning the assumption that poverty is primarily a market-mediated phenomenon. We must turn our attention away from the sphere of commodity distribution and focus on the possibility that poverty is rooted in the historically specific, productive relations of capitalism itself. This leads us into the domain of Marxist political economy, and into a critical problematic that locates modern poverty in the historically specific contradictions of capital's productive relations.

The Marxist problematic assumes that before industrial capitalism's historical emergence, extremes of wealth and poverty had already existed. These earlier forms of poverty had been caused by the underdevelopment of society's technological forces and their inability to generate and distribute sufficient wealth. With the coming of industrial capitalism, however, this changed. By revolutionizing society's productive processes, capital created an undreamt of cornucopia of manufactured, commodity wealth. Yet this wealth was accompanied by an inexplicable and undiminished reservoir of poverty.[3] For the first time in history, the impoverishment of the producers became the sine qua non for the production of commodity wealth. Marx recognized this when he noted that with the advent of the capitalist mode of production wealth and poverty became *necessarily joined contradictions:*

> The antithesis between *lack of property* and property, so long as it is not comprehended as the antithesis of *labour* and *capital*, still remains an indifferent antithesis, . . . not grasped as a *contradiction*. It can find expression in this *first* form even without the advanced development of private property (as in ancient Rome, Turkey, etc.). It does not yet *appear* as having been established by private property itself. But labour, the subjective essence of private property as exclusion of property, and capital, objective labour as exclusion of labour, constitute *private property* as its developed state of contradiction—hence a dynamic relationship driven towards resolution. (Marx [1844] 1964, p. 132)

Marx showed that the simultaneous occurrence of wealth and poverty was part of the *essential productive dynamic* that animated capital's productive mode.[4] Capital in its competitive pursuit of profit systematically generated a surplus population—an "industrial reserve army."[5] Ironically labor's increased productivity rendered certain segments of the working class superfluous to the needs of production.

Marx identified two types of surplus populations: First, there were those *absolute surplus populations* formed when capitalist markets penetrated traditionally organized social formations.[6] In these instances, capital's reorganization of precapitalist productive modes had a devastating effect on traditional institutions and their division of labor. As production for profit increasingly undercut traditional fealties between patrons and their clients, the rights of the latter were politically abrogated, and the disinherited were thrown onto newly developing labor markets as free agents.[7] Abandoned to these markets, and often lacking the skills required to survive in an urban, industrial economy, many of the dispossessed were transformed into "the urban poor." This process has been graphically portrayed in E. P. Thompson's (1966) *The Making of The English Working Class.* He has shown how capitalism decimated an entire generation, rendering many traditional craftsmen wholly superfluous to the manufacturing process, so much so that many could not even tend the machines that had so recently displaced them.[8]

The second type of surplus population occurs in mature industrial systems. If absolute surplus populations are generated by conflicting productive modes, then *relative surplus populations* spring from the inner contradictions of a fully developed industrial capitalism. The genesis of relative surplus populations is found in the antagonistic relationship that capital establishes between workers and their machines. In advanced capitalist formations machines are *systematically* used to revolutionize worker productivity. This means that fewer workers can create ever greater masses of commodity wealth. Concomitantly, individual capitalists in their struggle to survive the rigors of ever-tightening markets replace pools of living labor with ever more sophisticated machinery. While the processes by which superfluous workers are created change as capital evolves, the renewal of an industrial reserve army remains a sine qua non of production. A permanent pool of unemployed or partially employed workers must be kept in readiness so that they can supply capital with labor power during expansionary periods of production. During nonexpansionary periods, they are required to "wait in the wings," until needed again.

This is the fundamental social contradiction of capital. In accordance with capital's productive logic, those men and women previously engaged in production, but who are now rendered superfluous by the increased productivity of the few, are stripped of their power to command steady wages. Unable to obtain a secure living otherwise, these unwanted workers join the ranks of the poor. While, as we have noted, there is a tendency for absolute surplus populations to be generated early on in the evolution of capitalism and for relative surplus populations to emerge only later, both occur side by side in mature social formations. Hitherto untapped pools of labor in advanced capitalist societies, "latent reserve armies," are carved out of existing populations. By razing traditional institutions, renegotiating existing role definitions, or redefining prior cultural commitments, capital continuously dismantles and reassembles different sectors of its institutional order in order to "spring loose" new categories of persons who until that moment would not normally have been defined as workers.

For example, the transformation of the American family and its role structure to meet the productive needs of capital has a long and complex history.[9] Beginning early on with the hiring of entire family units to labor in the textile mills of the East and the South, extending through the destruction of traditional immigrant families and their rigid sexual stereotypy, and ending with the dissolution of the so-called companionate family of five decades ago, first working-class and then lower-middle-class children and wives have been progressively "liberated," i.e., sent into the marketplace as low-paid, "free labor." In each case the structure and meaning of both sex and gender, not to mention the social protections and entitlements that such groups were periodically granted, have been renegotiated so that persons who had previously been defined as culturally disqualified from selling their labor on the open market could qualify as culturally legitimate workers.

The same process operates among our elderly. Three decades ago the elderly were generally assured that their old-age social entitlements were secure. Many are now forced to return to work in order just to keep up, or to avoid the catastrophe of medical indigence. Or, take those on welfare who are now required to perform "workfare" in order to help the state defray the social expense of their upkeep. This creation of new workhouses without walls is paradigmatic of the process by which new absolute surplus populations are created when institutional givens are suddenly redefined.

Despite the highly vaunted technological progress and the social streamlining of the workplace that separate the satanic mills and sweat shops of the preceding century from this century's "soulful corporation," there is a dark thread of continuity running through the history of industrial capitalism. The decimation of entire communities of cottage weavers (Thompson 1966; Calhoun 1982, 1983) finds its resonance in the destruction of the age- and sex-graded structures of American family life that has been going on for almost a century and a half. Each in its own context expresses capital's need periodically to redefine existing social contracts in order to renew the ranks of its reserve armies.

If the social and demographic composition of the industrial reserve army has changed since Marx's day, its coercive role in the class structure has remained fairly constant. The mere presence of the poor silently chastens the working class. It reminds the employed that they too can be replaced if they grow too strident in their demands. Concomitantly, if the conditions of ownership and control of productive capital have changed, the need for surplus workers to step forth during periods of economic expansion has not. And if political institutions have transformed the concrete expressions of class struggle, they have also institutionalized poverty as never before.

The role that industrial reserve armies play in dampening class conflict forms the dynamic backdrop against which I will interpret the poverty of Potter Addition. Before we can understand that role, however, we must take note first of certain developments that have recently altered the way in which reserve armies are structured. Chief among these changes is the development of a dual economy (Averitt 1968). The two major sectors of this dual economy are the *monopoly core* and *its periphery*. The monopoly core is made up of those bureaucratically organized firms that dominate the American economy. This core depends on the state's ability to politically moderate institutionally destructive levels of competition and regulate potential conflicts.

The peripheral sector, by contrast, is composed of small firms that fit the mold of the nineteenth-century entrepreneurial firm. Still subject to the classic discipline of the market and its anarchy, these firms are grounded in petit bourgeois cultural premises. They are usually organized around labor-intensive forms of production, work on small profit margins, and often operate as if they were the direct extension of the entrepreneur's charismatic personality and will.

Two types of labor correspond to these two forms of capital: the *primary labor force* of the core and the *secondary labor force* of the periphery. Workers in the primary sector are employed by capital-intensive firms. They are better trained, better educated, and often organized for their collective defense into unions. Generally they receive higher wages, have greater fringe benefits, enjoy relatively greater job security, and lead a more stable economic life than do other workers. By contrast, secondary workers are the mirror image of the core labor force. The former are employed either by small, peripheral capital, or they are only tenuously bound to firms situated in the core. They are usually semi-skilled or unskilled, inadequately schooled, poorly paid, and accrue few fringe benefits. Peripheral workers are rarely unionized, are subject to long stints of unemployment, and are bereft of the kind of economic security that workers in the primary sector usually enjoy. It is from the ranks of the secondary labor force that the poor more often than not are drawn.[10] As Ellwood (1988, pp. 81–127) has shown, these "working poor" are the most numerous and least cared for of the poor. They and the chronically unemployed members of the industrial reserve army make up a significant segment of the poor in America.

Despite changes in the social composition of the industrial reserve army, the basic structure and function of its poverty remain unaltered. Modern welfare institutions, for example, allow us to speak of a "social wage," which augments market wages (Piven and Cloward 1982). Redistributive mechanisms such as the social wage undoubtedly give class antagonisms an institutionalized political dimension that changes the conditions under which late capitalism has evolved. Such developments, however, do not eliminate the basic material contradictions that created the need for industrial reserve armies in the first place. In order to understand this, we need only look at the growing fiscal crisis of the Reagan and Bush administrations, their dismantling of welfare capitalism and its regulatory structures, and their attempts to restore an earlier, more overt form of class conflict, to realize that the principles and contradictions of capitalist production have not altered in their fundamentals.[11]

In sum, the spread of modern class conflict to society's superstructure represents the expansion of capital's constituting social contradictions into other institutional spheres. If, as Habermas (1975) maintains, this expanded search for solutions has moved beyond the economic base and transformed what was originally an economic contradiction into an unparalleled series of political, cultural, and motivational crises, the extension of that original crisis has not altered its basic economic origins. The brute economics of capital and the subsequent generation of surplus populations are still at the root of capital's continuing crises.

II. VARIABLE ENVIRONMENTS

Although poverty is generated by the systemic contradictions that mark all capitalist societies, these contradictions tell us little about poverty's everyday reality. We thus need a way of moving from the chronic tendency of capital to produce industrial reserve armies to the concrete particulars of Potter Addition's poverty. The neo-Marxist conception of class provides us with just such a bridge. While traditional Marxism usually treats class as an objective economic category, the neo-Marxist conception of class contains an additional subjective and cultural dimension. Some seven decades ago Georg Lukacs ([1922] 1971) showed that classes could be conceptually treated as *collective historical actors:* as "subjects" confronting specific social and economic environments. Beginning with this premise, we can treat each collective class-subject and its constituent members as occupants of an "ecological niche," so to speak. This ideal typical niche would consist of the material, economic, and institutional environments that circumscribe the social actions of the class actor that inhabits it.

Using such an ecological metaphor, each theoretically constituted class-subject can be identified by the resources that the class system legitimately allows it to appropriate from the total wealth of society. At the same time, classes can be identified by the structure of their social and material environments, and by the relations that the class-subject establishes between itself and its singular class niche.[12] This ecological model can be used to evaluate both the logic and the efficacy of class action by interpreting it in terms of the peculiar problems presented to each class by its own immediate niche. Every class—*lumpen proletariat*, "nonproductive" workers in large private bureaucracies, unionized proletariat, small shopkeepers, etc.—can be defined and differentiated empirically in terms of (1) the symbolic and material resources allocated to it; and (2) the singular political economic environment that it inhabits.

We can best grasp what such an environment is by adopting and modifying Amos Hawley's definition. In *Human Ecology* (1950), he defines environment not as mere physical habitat, but as the interactional product of the physical setting and the biotic community that lives off that habitat. An environment is a habitat that has been altered in the process of being occupied by a given biotic community. Concomitantly, a class environment would be a social niche that bears the characteristic markings of the class that inhabits it. Class environments, moreover, are actively *constructed* by classes in concert with other classes. The type of environment that a class constructs is a function of three things: (1) the economic and ideological materials that society places at its disposal, (2) the interactions a class establishes with other classes in the process of constructing its niche, and (3) the mode of production—the social totality whose reproductive needs and social contradictions regulate how each class reproduces itself and the contribution it makes to the reproduction of the social whole.

Extending the ecological metaphor one step further, we can posit that within this biotic community of classes there is a hierarchy in which one class, the "ecological dominant," organizes the entire community, and in so doing specifies the conditions under which the other classes, the "influents" in our model, operate. Because of the systemic interrelation of this community of classes and the hierarchy by which the dominant sets the conditions under which subordinate classes will exist, the social production of any one niche takes on a complex cast. Given the hegemonic domination of the ruling species/class, each class in reproducing itself and its niche reproduces, as a condition of its own immediate existence, the existing hierarchy, and thus its future subordination. In this way each influent class in its very subordination contributes to the character of the overall exploitative relations that regulate the class system as a whole.

It follows from this model that classes possess a dialectical character. The collective subject (the class) constructs an objective environment (the class niche) from the resources made available to it by the system as a whole. The niche's structure then provides a feedback to the class actor and confronts the actor with a set of complex challenges to which it must respond. In doing so, the structure delimits the social and economic possibilities within which everyday life operates. *A class and its niche are, therefore, correlative, codefining realities.* The reciprocal reproduction of each by the other means that, ideally, we can identify each class either by the structure of its niche or by the traditional criteria that sociologists have used to describe the class actor—its economic situation, its allotted status-honor, and its legitimate access to power. Each class is thus a unified field of subject and object; both the ideal typical class actor and its systemic niche are posited by the larger class configuration as part and parcel of the larger system's inner structure.

But what of the individual actors in this drama? Where do they fit into all of this? Class actors, as theoretically derived ideal structures are real, but exist concretely only in the organized interactions of living persons. Concomitantly, the motives, tactics, and goals of individuals in everyday class struggle are circumscribed (but by no means mechanically realized) by the ideal class actor and its situation. The class actor and the individual actor thus stand to each other as a social structure stands to its empirical object. The structure blocks out for the actor some implicit future goal by simultaneously opening up and delimiting biographical possibilities. The individual, on the other hand, is the material vehicle by which ideal class interests are actually worked out and realized in sociohistorical contexts. The collective class actor and the ideal niche that is its correlative constitute the objective situation in which flesh and blood persons actually operate.

Classes as collective personalities, with interests and consciousnesses of their own, are thus fabricated from the manifold lives of those individual actors who construct their biographical praxes from within the objective horizons of their class. The class actor and the individual are not coextensive, nor are they reducible to one another. The fate of the one neither totally subsumes nor dictates that of its counterpart. They are dialectically linked parts of a single whole so that each part only exists in and through the actions and limiting possibilities of its opposite.

We now have the means for examining how variable social and economic environments delimit the everyday conduct of the poor. Let us begin with the following five assumptions: First, stability and predictability, as long-term features of human existence, are preferable to uncertainty and chaos. Second, in any community of class actors, the dominant class will organize society and its resources so that it can maximize the predictability and stability of its particular niche. Third, the dominant class's success in constructing a predictable class environment for itself will be limited by the nature of the contradictions that drive the system, and by the fact that other classes are also striving to achieve the same predictability. Fourth, classes at the top will usually occupy the most stable niches, while those at the bottom will be forced to endure more unpredictable settings. Finally, the social distribution of predictable and stable life worlds is relative at best. In the capitalist mode of production, all classes live in a state of relative flux. Thus, order and certainty, even at the top, are tenuous, while chaos at the bottom is pandemic.[13]

The plausibility of these assumptions is revealed when we look at the professional classes that operate at the middle levels of management in the modern firm. These class fractions have at their disposal, *at least ideally*, the material resources and power necessary to stabilize their class niche. It has long been a tenet of modern theories of the capitalist firm that the structure of the large firm and the anarchy of the self-regulating market are incompatible. Market mechanisms severely limit the firm in its planning functions, its capital accumulation policies, and its ability to benefit fully from economies of scale. The solution to the firm's dilemma has been to use political power, where possible, to circumvent the market and thereby insulate itself from the anarchy of free enterprise. Once its labor markets are secured through the rationalizing structures of trade unions, and its capital markets are protected through price leadership and internal capitalization, it is safe to socialize the profit motive itself through internal bureaucratization. Consistent with the complexity of the large firm's division of labor and the fiduciary role its employees must play, the firm relies upon devices that prevent the reinstitution of market competition *within the firm* itself. The devices of office, tenure, and regular promotion based on length of service are but a few of the means used to facilitate the cooperative knitting of expertise and specialization into a harmonious apparatus. The firm ensures, in the ideal at least, the dampening of internal entrepreneurial zeal by providing its workers with the trade-offs of economic security and career stability.

The monopoly capitalist firm is only possible if it can secure for itself and its personnel such a stable environment. The individual expression of this internal stabilization is manifested in the concept of a career. Bureaucrats and professionals have careers, while others outside the firm only have jobs. Careers refer to the orderly unfolding of jobs in a logical and predictable trajectory over time (Wilensky 1961). To have a career is to be relatively certain that in so many years you will have moved up to a given position in the organization and will be able to count on making a certain income. Such personal certainty (again, ideally) is the hallmark of a stable social and economic niche and is only possible because the firm itself has politically secured economic markets and their noneconomic "externalities." While the occupational certainty of the career varies with one's position in the hierarchy, it is still the case that the controlled environment of bureaucratic enterprises generally makes the career trajectories of those associated with it more predictable.

The managerial class and its regulated niche coproduce one another. To have a career within this context is to occupy a class niche marked ostensibly by matter-of-fact stability and long-term predictability. The incumbent of such a niche engages in economic and occupational transactions without having consciously to attend to the small, everyday details. The niche, its operation, and its structure become a taken-for-granted reality to which the actor—living in a social space that is relatively unremarkable—seldom need attend. The class niche is just there, a stable infrastructure of unquestioned presuppositions, a "pretheoretic backdrop" against which the actor plays out the intentional details of his or her project. As an assemblage of tools and resources, the bureaucratic organization and its materials are always there at hand, so to speak, ready to be used when needed. The niche and its elements thus provide little resistance to the project currently absorbing the professional's energies. Even when some part of the niche breaks down, and the person is forced consciously to attend to its background and the way it operates, the wealth and structure of available resources make such ruptures short-run and minor in their consequences. The niche is itself relatively unproblematic because it is the life space of a relatively powerful and privileged class. Conversely, the class is the class it is largely *because* the niche it constructs, maintains, and daily inhabits is relatively predictable and unproblematic.

Poverty, by contrast, is typified by a dramatically different environmental niche. Its niche is characterized by radical flux and unpredictability. The economic life of impoverished households is a roller coaster ride between peaks of feast and valleys of famine. Erratic swings of material life and social fortune, long periods of desperate penny-pinching followed by euphoric bursts of "environmental plenty," are the sociological hallmarks of poverty. It is this unpredictability, not just a lack of resources, that generates the culture of poverty. *To be poor* is to lack resources; *to live in poverty*, however, means learning to live with *variable social and economic environments*.

The lower-class niche is so chaotic that its members experience their life space as one that constantly threatens to overwhelm them. Rent by rupture and fissure, the lower-class environment is perpetually plagued with crises and future uncertainty. Thus the impoverished cannot treat their niche as a taken-for-granted fact of everyday life. Since they do not have the power or the resources required to stabilize their niche, the people at the bottom must constantly attend and reattend to the disorder created by their niche's aperiodic tempos and willy-nilly rhythms. To live in poverty is to inhabit a social and economic life space that requires an eternal string of "beginnings again," and only seldom an incremental, cumulative "building upon." Persons living in variable niches must develop protocols for limiting the entropic inroads of variable environments.

Having neither the material resources nor the political power to transform their niche, the poor must devise ways to ride out or otherwise neutralize its unpredictable nature. In a world of continuous existential threat, long-term career goals are continuously set aside as necessities are secured and decaying environments once again pacified. The maximizing rationalities and the orderly career planning that structure the expectations of other classes are predicated upon the existence of relatively predictable environments and are not appropriate to lower-class life. Instead, given the lack of material resources and the unpredictability of their future availability, the lower class is lucky if it can *minimize* the losses it sustains during the periodic breakdowns of its life space. If one is to survive in a world that operates with little apparent rhyme or reason, then short-term, conservative tactics that seek stability replace the logics of growth and development. In such circumstances, success is measured in conservative terms as one tries to hold one's own and in one's ability to cut losses when disaster strikes.

III. THE CULTURE OF POVERTY AND VARIABLE ENVIRONMENTS

The *social structure* of poverty, as opposed to its political economy (which is imposed from above) is daily fabricated from below. Unable to eliminate their superfluity and hence escape their niche, the poor have little choice but to construct defenses that check everyday uncertainty. Successful gambits and countermoves are collected by each generation and passed on to the next as time-tested wisdom. Gleaned from a life of pain and struggle, these traditions are composed of practical truths that no amount of "book learning" can rival or reproduce. This accumulated wisdom is what Oscar Lewis called the "culture of poverty."[14]

Many of the traits that Lewis included in his culture of poverty model can be viewed as attempts made by the poor to stabilize their unpredictable class niche. Lewis maintained that the culture of poverty was not a mere residue that the poor gleaned from the folkways of other classes. Unwilling to trivialize the lives of those he studied, he chose to underscore the innovative and adaptive content of the culture of poverty. While rejecting a purely consensual and integrationist conception of the culture of poverty, he refused simultaneously to settle for a vulgar, economistic interpretation of poverty's superstructural elements. Lewis saw clearly the relative autonomy of poverty's cultural premises. While unequivocally locating the culture of poverty's origins in the capitalist mode of production, he recognized that once the culture of poverty was formed and became sedimented in the lives of the poor, economic amelioration could not, in and of itself, work its benign magic overnight. More time and effort would be required to combat poverty and its cultural elements than the quick-fix measures being proposed in the 1960s. He maintained, in fact, that in many instances, truly revolutionary measures might be required. Moreover, without unduly romanticizing the poor and their way of life, Lewis was not certain that economic reform could, or even should, be linked to genocidal programs of cultural uplift. He was too respectful of the poor and their values to treat either with such a cheap, paternalistic sleight of hand.

One problem in linking our reproductive model of poverty to the culture of poverty tradition is that Lewis himself never developed a formal statement of his paradigm. Seemingly more interested in mapping the empirical contours of poverty, he never took the time in the last hectic years of his life to formulate a definitive theoretical statement. We must, therefore, extrapolate from his ideas if we are to flesh out his model and link it to ours.

In synthesizing Lewis's work and the reproductive model of poverty I employ in this work, I have no intention of reducing the former to the latter, nor do I wish to construct a one-factor theory of the culture of poverty. The profusion of historical and regional differences in poverty's cultural content precludes any such simplistic project. Each concrete culture of poverty must be approached on its own terms. Further, each must be seen as possessing both endogenous and exogenous cultural elements. The endogenous content of poverty's culture is, of course, traceable to the structure of poverty's variable niche. Its exogenous content originates from without and is grounded in the larger social system of which the poor are a part. The fact that a concrete culture of poverty may contain some values that the poor share with other classes does not invalidate Lewis's original conception; in fact, it is difficult to understand how any class could avoid assimilating large portions of this culturally hegemonic content into its own premises and operations.

Yet if we treat the idea of variable environments as an ideal type and see Lewis's model as an unfinished theoretical project, then the two schemes can be synthesized without doing violence to either. Let us begin, then, by treating the variable lower-class niche as an "ecological mediation" between the objective class situation of the poor and the unique culture that they fabricate from their immediate class experience. Such an extrapolation is not all that foreign to Lewis's original intent, for instead of treating the culture of poverty as a heterogeneous aggregate of some seventy-odd traits (Lewis 1968), he believed that one could construct an analytic model that could order those traits into a coherent whole. He had already noted, for example, that many of the culture of poverty's key traits formed "clusters," and that these clusters, in turn, betrayed the outlines of larger clusters. The variable-environments model is thus but one way of identifying the structural principles around which such clustering takes place.

Following Lewis's lead, I have identified three distinct clusters in the culture of poverty: The first is rooted in the economic situation of the poor—in the material deprivation and economic uncertainties that typify their impoverished class niche. The second cluster consists of *instrumental* moves on the part of the poor that allow them to cope with the material shortfalls and uncertainties of their situation. The third is made up of the nonmaterial aspects of poverty's culture: the norms, ideals, sedimented practices, and structures of poverty proper.

When combined, these three clusters form something akin to Julian Steward's (1955) "cultural core"—a complex of material and nonmaterial cultural elements that are directly grounded in the productive life of the group. This cultural core mediates between the group's habitat and the purely symbolic regions of its culture. In discussing the concept of a cultural core, Steward writes:

> Elsewhere, I have offered the concept of <u>cultural core</u>—the constellation of features which are most closely related to subsistence activities and economic arrangements. The core includes such social, political, and religious patterns as are empirically determined to be closely connected with those arrangements. Innumerable other features may have great potential variability because they are less strongly tied to the core. These latter or secondary features are determined to a great extent by purely cultural-historical factors—by random innovations or by diffusion—and they give the appearance of outward distinctiveness to cultures with similar cores. (1955, p. 37)

In this work, we are dealing with class subcultures. Consequently, Steward's cultural core is the property of a class, not of a people. It mediates between the class-specific culture of a lower-class community, its class niche, and the larger social formation. Unlike Steward's cultural core, this core will possess a more fully elaborated set of "secondary features" and interclass cultural mediations. Even with these provisos, though, Steward's concept is an excellent heuristic device. The conception of a cultural core greatly facilitates the task of clarifying the structure of the culture of poverty.[15] When talking about the structure of poverty, we are in truth talking about the cultural core of poverty. This cultural core is itself surrounded by a penumbra of secondary cultural elements that are located in the concrete interaction of classes and the reproduction of the social formation as a whole. The concept of a class niche is thus grounded in Steward's seminal insights as to how a culture and its purely normative components are tied to the concrete, material life of the group. In the concept of a cultural core we have the necessary vehicle by which to link this work to that of Lewis's. Those elements of the culture of poverty that are grounded in the variable class niche of lower-class life form the cultural core of poverty.

As to the trait clusters themselves, the first deals with the material situation of the poor as such. It contains the following: low wages and income, underemployment and/or chronic unemployment, the constant pawning of possessions, the borrowing of money at usurious rates, poor housing, crowding, and, finally, the gregariousness that facilitates living with the stress of overcrowding (Lewis 1966). The second cluster consists of behavioral responses to the material factors enumerated in the first set of traits: the preponderant use of secondhand clothing and furniture, the "spontaneous" credit arrangements that develop from within the ranks of the poor themselves, the buying of small quantities of food (often several times a day), so-called present-time orientations, and the linked attributes of (1) an inability of the poor to plan for the future, (2) the alleged inability of the poor to defer gratification, (3) the supposed lack of impulse control, and (4) the inability of the poor to accumulate long-term savings. These two clusters are correlative in their content and correspond directly to Steward's cultural core.

Turning to the third cluster, the picture, as Steward suggests, becomes more complex. It contains the nonmaterial, idealistic elements of the culture of poverty. In this cluster we will find many norms, practices, and processes that do not originate in the social ecology of lower-class life. What Steward calls "random innovations" and "diffusions" now make their way into lower-class culture as the values and norms of local, hegemonic class fractions are taken over and adapted by the poor to meet their immediate needs. As the lower class socially constructs its niche, its members assimilate and rework for their own purposes many hegemonic precepts that are not of their own invention nor reflective of their objective class interests. Because we are dealing with a class subculture, and not an autonomous cultural entity, the culture of poverty can only be understood by referring to the common values and axioms that integrate the larger community of which the poor are a part.

The third cluster, then, is made up of a combination of class-specific and secondary ideological precepts. It consists of the psychological correlates of poverty: resignation, fatalism, low levels of personal aspiration, weak ego structures, and low levels of class consciousness.[16] To these traits can be added those individual feelings of helplessness, marginality, dependency, and inferiority that are generated by the person's chronic failure to manipulate his or her social situation successfully. Such negative forms of self-evaluation were, for Lewis, critical attributes to the culture of poverty [see Della Fava (1980) for a social-psychological model that attempts to explain how this occurs].

More is at work here, however, than the insular self-evaluations of the poor. Such "failure" usually occurs in an interactional context between classes. If failure is individual, it is still orchestrated in a social setting that has all the trappings of what Garfinkel (1955) calls a "degradation ceremony." If a preponderance of negative self-evaluations and self-images is "inherent" in the objective situation of the poor, their sensed inferiority is ritually dramatized and symbolically etched in the presence of their "social betters." It is this public dramatization of incompetence, not just objective failure, that is at the core of what Sennett and Cobb (1972) call "the hidden injuries of class." The individual learns of his or her incompetence not in isolation, but in periodic, dramatized enactments that are carried out in a public arena.

The fact that these secondary psychological traits have their origins and ongoing renewal in the mundane interaction between classes may account for their relative impermanence when compared to other elements of this third cluster. Lewis notes that under the auspices of revolutionary or nationalistic movements, many elements of the culture of poverty can be eliminated long before material poverty itself is rooted out. For example, Lewis saw in Castro's Cuba evidence of how a revolutionary élan might abolish, at least temporarily, the despair, self-victimization, and self-blame that poverty so often induces in its victims, even if it could not immediately remove the material bases of poverty. Lewis's point seems to be supported empirically by Kozol's (1978) description of Cuba's literacy campaign of recent decades.

If such psychological attributes can be dispatched by movements of political and social renewal, the same cannot be said of other elements in this third cluster. The organization of the family or the community, for example, if reproduced over several generations, can become socially sedimented and take on the trappings of tradition.[17] When such sedimentation occurs and becomes a socially functional attribute of poverty's culture, it takes more than a few years of sustained economic effort and the proving of untested promises from above to alter poverty's unique "cake of custom." If, as Lewis maintained, much of poverty's destructive consequences could be banished with a redistribution of wealth and institutional power, he also believed that the culture of poverty had a functional autonomy vis-à-vis the economic forces that first called it into existence.

These last and deepest levels of resistance to reform reside, I believe, in the social relations the poor construct as they cope with their variable class niche. This nonmaterial kernel of poverty's culture consists of the sedimented values and practices that form the social estates and family heritages of the poor. The power of these practices lies in both their practical efficacy and in the authoritative halo that socialization bestows upon intimate practices and beliefs. This kernel within the third trait cluster contains the following: a minimal level of social organization in poor communities—one that seldom transcends the extended family level of sociocultural integration, a verbal emphasis upon family solidarity, open cynicism as to public institutions and the motives of those who run them, provincialism and a strong adherence to anachronistic life-styles, and, finally, only partial integration into regional- and local-based social institutions. At one level, this last group of culture traits is the direct result of the cultural exclusion of the lower classes from "respectable" society. That is, many of these traits are not so much grounded in poverty's niche as they are part of the exclusionary mechanisms that reproduce the strict class boundaries of local and national social structures.

At the same time, provincialism and archaic preferences may be adaptive virtues. The caution, timidity, and social conservatism that they entail may be bred by the fragility and unpredictability of lower-class life. Indeed, discretion and rationality in such circumstances might well dictate protecting what one has, rather than aggressively expanding one's material or social status holdings. This conservative strategy of maintenance entails avoiding risky and novel encounters over which one has little or no control. It also demands staying with tried and true practices, often living a life of obsessive ritual so as not to lose everything because of a miscalculation concerning a stranger's motives. Insofar as such caution is a direct response to the lower-class niche, xenophobic, conservative, and even archaic cultural orientations may be logical outgrowths of variable environments.

Finally, there is the family. Lewis sees it as being marked by the following: conjugal instability and a high proportion of consensual unions, domestic relations that exhibit a matricentric bias, kinship systems structured along genealogically shallow lines of bilateral determination, descent groups that are characterized by intersibling conflict, and domestic arrangements that produce authoritarian personalities. The last half of this volume will consist of a detailed analysis of lower-class family and kinship. Our discussion of the relation between this aspect of poverty's cultural core and variable environments will thus be deferred until then.

This work's conception of the culture of poverty as cultural ecology is admittedly different from that offered by Oscar Lewis. Even as I have tried to remain faithful to his original intentions, I have also altered his conception. Such alterations are grounded in my desire to grasp the *dynamic principles* that underlie the trait lists Lewis so painstakingly assembled. This has meant going beyond ethnographic descriptions and implementing the next step in the development of a scientific model of poverty: the identification of the structures and contradictions that generate the trait clusters themselves. At the same time, I have not done violence to Lewis's original conception. His general depiction of the culture of poverty does not differ that much from the idea of a cultural core of poverty and its dynamic ecological underpinnings:

> The culture of poverty can come into being in a variety of historical contexts. However, it tends to grow and flourish in societies with the

following set of conditions: (1) a cash economy, wage labor and production for profit; (2) a persistently high rate of unemployment and underemployment for unskilled labor; (3) low wages; (4) the failure to provide social, political and economic organization, either on a voluntary basis or by government imposition, for the low-income population; (5) the existence of a bilateral kinship system rather than a unilateral one; and finally, (6) the existence of a set of values in the dominant class which stresses the accumulation of wealth and property, the possibility of upward mobility and thrift, and explains low economic status as the result of personal inadequacy or inferiority.

The way of life which develops among some of the poor under these conditions is the culture of poverty. It can best be studied in urban or rural slums and can be described in terms of some seventy interrelated social, economic and psychological traits. However, the number of traits and the relationships between them may vary from society to society and from family to family. For example, in a highly literate society, illiteracy may be more diagnostic of the culture of poverty than in a society where illiteracy is widespread and where even the well-do-do may be illiterate, as in some Mexican peasant villages before the revolution.

The culture of poverty is both an adaptation and a reaction of the poor to their marginal position in a class-stratified, highly individuated, capitalistic society. It represents an effort to cope with feelings of hopelessness and despair which develop from the realization of the improbability of achieving success in terms of the values and goals of the larger society. Indeed, many of the traits of the culture of poverty can be viewed as attempts at local solutions for problems not met by existing institutions and agencies because the people are not eligible for them, cannot afford them, or are ignorant or suspicious of them. For example, unable to obtain credit from banks, they are thrown upon their own resources and organize informal credit devices without interest.

The culture of poverty, however, is not only an adaptation to a set of objective conditions of the larger society. Once it comes into existence it tends to perpetuate itself from generation to generation because of its effect on the children. By the time slum children are age six or seven they have usually absorbed the basic values and attitudes of their subculture and are not psychologically geared to take full advantage of changing conditions or increased opportunities which may occur in their lifetime.

Most frequently the culture of poverty develops when a stratified social and economic system is breaking down or is being replaced by another, as in the case of the transition from feudalism to capitalism or during periods of rapid technological change. Often it results from imperial conquest in which the native social and economic structure is smashed and the natives are maintained in a servile colonial status, sometimes for many generations. It can also occur in the process of detribalization, such as that now going on in Africa.

The most likely candidates for the culture of poverty are the people who come from the lower strata of a rapidly changing society and are already partially alienated from it. Thus landless rural workers who migrate to the cities can be expected to develop a culture of poverty much more readily than migrants from stable peasant villages with a well-organized traditional culture. (Lewis 1966, pp. xliii–xlv)

This could very well serve as an extended definition of the cultural core of poverty. It does not commit itself to a single, inflexible trait list, one that even Lewis himself admits would not fit every community. Instead, the above passage points to the social, economic, and historical specificity of poverty. It links the culture of poverty to capitalism and its mode of production, even as it alludes to something akin to this work's reproductive paradigm. Lewis leaves little doubt as to where the causes of poverty ultimately reside, even as he opens up the possibility of viewing the lower class, its niche, and the culture it daily fabricates in dialectical terms.

The reproductive model of poverty developed here uses Steward's work on the cultural core as a means by which to link Lewis's work and my own. It is an attempt to join critical economic analysis and culture theory. My goal is to wed Steward's insights and those of Lewis, and in so doing to construct what Herbert Gans (1968) in another time and context called a "sociology of the underclass." Writing of Lewis's research and its bearing on the sociological study of poverty, Gans has observed:

Lewis's distinction between poverty and the culture of poverty is important, for it aims to separate different kinds of poverty and adaptations to poverty. His emphasis on alienation suggests, however, that this concept pertains more to belonging to an underclass than to being poor, while his identification of the culture of poverty with class-stratified, highly individuated societies suggests that, for him, the culture is an effect rather than a cause of membership in an underclass, even though he considers the culture of poverty to be a causal concept. The various traits of the culture of poverty that he describes are partly sociopsychological consequences, partly situational responses, and partly behavioral norms associated with underclass membership, but the major causal factor is the class stratified, highly individuated society. From a causal perspective, Lewis' concept is thus less concerned with culture than with the situational factors that bring about culture; it is less a culture of poverty than a sociology of the underclass. (1968, pp. 215–16)

This reading of Lewis's culture of poverty concept as a "sociology of poverty" is close to my own and places the entire culture of poverty problematic in a context that is compatible with Steward's cultural ecology paradigm. It is just such a sociology of poverty that I hope to construct in my study of Potter Addition.

3

Potter Addition

I. GRAND PRAIRIE

Potter Addition sits on the rural-urban fringe of Grand Prairie, the administrative seat of Clay County. A city of some one hundred thousand people, Grand Prairie is located in the heart of America's Corn Belt, at the northern focus of a fertile ellipse whose major axis runs some two hundred miles in a southwest to northeast direction. The northern third of that ellipse is cross-hatched by glacial moraines that were deposited on the land some ten thousand years ago. Today they appear to be little more than gentle land swells set in flat expanses of dark prairie loess. Farms are laid out along the surveyor's plats of township, section, and quadrant. From the air the rural lanes and fields form rectangles and squares that are inlaid with golds, yellows, greens, and blacks. Over and against this strict linear symmetry, numerous creeks and small streams have chiseled fingerlike patterns across the broad flatlands. Dense ribbons of oak, hickory, and chestnut crowd the creek banks, merging with second-growth saplings and heavy underbrush to form cooling retreats on hot summer days. In these naturally canopied places, the notion of finding one's way back to that "simpler America," the America of a century ago, seems momentarily plausible. Those living in the isolated farmhouses that dot Clay County's landscape still embrace the myths and promises of that golden, agrarian age. They abide by its canons and pass it on to their children. The agrarian myth is reaffirmed in the stubborn faith of a shrinking number of self-satisfied farm families, nurtured by their ownership of the land. The faith also hangs on in the small towns and hamlets. Weakened politically and losing ground demographically, the towns are still as much the potent adversary of the farmer as they are his ally. That much has not changed since Veblen

(1948, pp. 407–30) wrote his scathing denunciation of the rural small-town and its grasping opportunism. Still, farmer and small town entrepreneur share a sense of living in another land and working in another time.

At the center of this mixture of commercial myth and vulgar economic predation of the countryside is Grand Prairie. The city was once a thriving rail crossroads, and for a century the railroads dominated Grand Prairie's life. Local lawyers representing railroad interests formed an alliance with local bankers, land agents, a clique of parochial courthouse politicians, and a handful of rich farmers. Together they created a Republican party machine that dominated the life of Clay County for most of this century. Only in the late 1950s was its power sufficiently weakened that it was forced to make concessions to the more "culturally progressive" forces that had their center in the local Democratic party.

With the railroad's decline, the focal point of Grand Prairie's economic life shifted. By the mid-1960s the railroad and its shop facilities were in the last stages of being dismantled, and the railroads employed only a fraction of the workers they once did. By then, Grand Prairie was surviving by servicing the local university and its transient population. This is not to say that agricultural activity in the county had ceased to be a vital source of income for Grand Prairie, nor is it to ignore the burgeoning light industry that was beginning to transform the town, but in the midsixties, when I began my fieldwork, the university was a major source of employment for residents of Grand Prairie.

As it has benefited from the university's presence, it also has become its prisoner economically, so that a simmering, economic resentment has long exacerbated an ever-deepening town-gown schism. On the one side is the university, serving the regional manpower and research needs of large capital. Like most such progressive institutions in the heartland, it walks point for urban-based, monopoly capital and looks down on the bucolic and small-town parochialism that surrounds it. On the other side is the town, tenacious in its adherence to puritanical morality and dominated by the petit bourgeois culture that ties it to an earlier way of life. Not surprisingly, the university was a target of the red-baiting and witch-hunts of the 1950s. Many townspeople, in fact, still see it as a coven of communists, drug users, homosexuals, snobbish intellectuals, "snotty kids," and free love advocates. Yet both parties long ago learned that it was to their mutual financial benefit to coexist in compartmentalized silence.

II. THE ECOLOGICAL SETTING OF COMMUNITY

Potter Addition gets its name from Norman Potter, the land speculator who first subdivided its eighty acres and offered its parcels for public sale.[1] Advertising himself as a purveyor of prime land along the Rio Grande in Texas, Potter Addition's eighty acres were not the choicest properties in his portfolio. Natural history and a century of historical happenstance had already reduced the land's asking price. The land was originally part of a marshy tract located where Salt Creek runs up against and cuts through the glacial till of Yankee Ridge moraine, a low-lying ridge that bisects Clay County in a west by southeast direction. Containing several sloughs, the area was known as early as the 1830s as a breeding ground of the much feared ague and miasma. Consequently, it was avoided by early homesteaders.

Only with the reclamation programs of the 1890s was Potter Addition's niche sufficiently drained and rehabilitated to make it safe for human habitation. But even this monumental effort could not overcome the five generations of cultural prejudice that had by then attached itself to this benighted area. Besides, by the 1870s Grand Prairie had expanded to the south and the west toward the open prairies and away from the forested marshes upon which Potter Addition would later be built. Already a degraded niche in Grand Prairie's social ecology, the tract was further devalued when industrial enterprises began to move in during the 1890s. First a tile and brick factory was built some one eighth of a mile from what would later be Potter Addition's southwestern edge. Located on the opposite bank of Salt Creek, the factory stripped off the marginally productive top soil from the surrounding land and mined the glacial clay that lay beneath Yankee Ridge. When the demand for drainage tile and paving bricks subsided in the first decade of this century, the brickyard was converted into Grand Prairie's garbage dump. The dump remained there until the early 1930s when it was moved to a rural location east of Grand Prairie. It was also in the early 1890s that the Big Four railroad repair shops were built on the niche's southern border. This was followed within a decade by the construction of Grand Prairie's sewage treatment plant. Built on the same side of Salt Creek as the dump itself, some three quarters of a mile to the east, and situated only a few hundred yards from what is now the southeastern corner of Potter Addition, the new sewage plant made the area residentially attractive to only the most hard-pressed people. More than half a century of ecological marginality and historical drift had given the area north of Grand Prairie a pariah status. By 1910 the area had taken on an even more marginal character. By then, the county poor farm had been built on the southeasternmost corner of the niche, while the county orphanage was constructed on its far western edge. The location of these institutions consolidated the area's reputation as a natural dumping ground for the functionally superfluous humans and waste materials that were regularly spun off by Grand Prairie's physical and institutional metabolisms.

Potter Addition's first residents arrived in 1927, and from the beginning, the pace of the community's social life, like that of its niche, has been tied to the economic and ecological rhythms of Grand Prairie. Sitting on a rectangular piece of land some eighty acres in area, it is immediately flanked on its eastern and western sides by fallow fields of dubious agricultural value. To the north it is bounded by Spooner Road and on the south by Salt Creek. Once a beautiful, meandering stream, Salt Creek was deepened, straightened, and incorporated into the local drainage district as part of the aforementioned reclamation efforts. By the 1930s, however, Salt Creek had been reduced to little more than an open sewer.

Bordered on the south and west by city, and on the north and east by farmland, Potter Addition's immediate locale now forms a natural area in Grand Prairie's larger ecological system. It is culturally and socially a rural-urban zone of transition.[2] Because it is ecologically situated on the edge of a large urban area, Potter Addition possesses neither a clear-cut urban nor rural identity. As with most zones of transition located on the rural-urban fringe, the sixteen-square-mile niche that houses Potter Addition and its immediate environs is given over to mixed agricultural and residential use. In the last sixty years the niche has become home to a typical rural-urban fringe population.[3]

Most who first settled on the edge of Grand Prairie found their way there by one of two paths: The first was taken by those who worked in town but preferred a rural life-style. Living on the unincorporated fringe, they could keep one step ahead of the city's crowding and outward expansion, and still enjoy the ambience of rural living in their leisure hours. The second path was traveled by those who had been forcibly uprooted from the land. Resisting urban assimilation, they gravitated to the rural-urban fringe in order to retain the last semblance of a rural way of life.[4] The fact that Potter Addition was located at the confluence of these two migratory streams and that its residents moved to the city's edge in order to preserve a set of threatened social values had a profound impact on the type of poverty that developed there.

III. SURPLUS POPULATIONS

Almost a hundred years ago, a decade after the Civil War ended, an unprecedented series of economic and social calamities began to beset Middle America. Beginning with the panic of 1873, heartland farming was wracked by a string of economic depressions that would continue until the end of the century. The panic of 1873 signaled the end of Clay

County's pioneer society—one that had been loosely constructed on an egalitarian democracy of autonomous, petty producers and small property owners. This simple society had shown strains as early as the 1850s, when railroad interests and East Coast financial powers first began to transform Clay County's social structure. By the end of the Civil War the transformation was almost complete. Grand Prairie's little democracy was in its last throes, and was being replaced by a class system composed increasingly of closed agricultural classes and a city-based financial and political elite.

By the 1880s, Clay County's economy had been integrated into the rapidly expanding international grain market. Suddenly it was swept up in the catastrophic rhythms of scarcity and glut that devastated the world's grain-growing areas for two decades. Moreover, the *concentration* and *centralization* of agrarian capital was revolutionizing Clay County's mode of petty agricultural production. The concentration of agrarian capital came to Clay County in the form of an increased use of farm machinery. While making farm work easier, this mechanization revolutionized the productivity of farm labor to such an extent that large portions of the existing agricultural labor pool became progressively superfluous.

In addition to creating a reserve army of agricultural laborers, mechanization also introduced new economies of scale into the area's farming. These economies dictated that the new agrarian technologies could most profitably be employed if individual farmers increased the size of their landholdings. In a frontier setting, where there is no shortage of new land, these expansive economies of scale would have had few destructive effects. But in Clay County, where there was no free land, and few wetlands or waste areas left to be reclaimed, the new concentrations of capital radically altered the structure of rural society. These new economies of scale accelerated the centralization of capital—the process by which larger shares of land and productive facilities were owned by fewer and fewer producers. Like agrarian capital's concentration, its centralization created its own type of surplus population, this time composed of *dispossessed farm owners*. The logic of capitalist development slowly winnowed each new generation of agricultural producers. Sometimes farmers were replaced by aspiring newcomers who themselves did not last a decade. At other times the failure of the many allowed the surviving few to prosper at the expense of their neighbors. In either case, each new cohort of aspiring farmers contributed to the process of capital's progressive concentration and centralization.

The effects of this double transformation of agrarian production are evident in the statistics on farm size and farm ownership in Clay County. In 1900 Clay County could boast of no less than 4,316 farms; by

1940, the first decade in which gasoline-powered machinery fully dominated the county's agricultural production, the figure had shrunk to 3,122—a loss of 28 percent. By 1959, this figure had dropped to 2,620, or about 61 percent of the number of farmers working the land in 1900. During this same period, the average size of farms in Clay County increased. In 1900 the average farm in Clay County was 145 acres in size, almost one third larger than the average farm size in 1870. Following the trend into the present century, the average acreage per farm in 1940 had risen to 191 acres, and by 1959 had grown to 229 acres. By 1900, with most of Clay County's land already under cultivation, the growth in average farm size could only be achieved in one way: by one group of farmers surviving and feeding off the failure and misery of their neighbors.

The social costs levied during this era of consolidation were equally profound. The American dream of agrarian mobility based on cheap land was fast coming to an end. The agrarian ideal, so cherished during America's Progressive Era, was a vision of a large mass of petty producers moving step by measured step up the rungs of an agricultural ladder, rising from farm laborer, to landless tenant, and finally to unencumbered farm owner. That dream, all but dead in Clay County by 1900, was snuffed out by the decade-long depression of agricultural prices in the 1920s. The days were gone when a family could move to Clay County, armed with nothing but their collective labor and ambition, and in one lifetime become unencumbered proprietors of the land they worked.

The new economic order was marked by a growing separation of the farmer from a key element of the agrarian means of production. In place of the Progressive's movement's ideal of the agricultural ladder, a system of land tenure evolved that permanently barred the majority of farmers from ever owning the land they worked.[5] The rural Midwest would henceforth be stratified by a set of relatively fixed statuses, and with each passing year the social structure of the agrarian hinterland would increasingly resemble a caste system. Again statistics give startling confirmation of Clay County's narrowing agricultural opportunity structure: Completing a trend that had begun in the early 1890s, by 1920 fully 60.6 percent of the farms operating in Clay County were being worked by tenants. In 1930, the figure had changed little at 60.2 percent, and only fell below 50 percent in 1950. Even more indicative of the emergent agricultural caste system is the fact that between the decades of the 1920s and the 1950s, some 75 percent of Clay County's productive acreage was absentee owned.

The demographics of absentee ownership in Clay County tell us something of the cultural context in which agrarian property institutions evolved during this time, for roughly 90 percent of the absentee owners lived in the county or in areas adjacent to it. In Clay County there was no distant, faceless Shawnee Land and Cattle Company as in John Steinbeck's *The Grapes of Wrath*, knocking down farmhouses and vacating the land. Title to Clay County's land was held by county residents who were for the most part well-known locally and fully integrated into the local class and status systems. The social availability of these local landowning elites was conducive to the development of a loose system of paternalistic indulgences. This paternalism was, in turn, embedded in the aforementioned oligarchy of courthouse politicians, railroad lawyers, and local bankers.

By the late 1920s the agricultural opportunity structure had petrified not just in Clay County, but throughout America's heartland. If proof of the watershed nature of these changes is needed, one has merely to thumb through any of a dozen *Agricultural Experiment Station Bulletins* of the day. They document fully an agrarian opportunity structure in crisis throughout America's Corn Belt. Scholars knew full well they were at a crossroads and that they could do little to prevent this unfolding tragedy. They were witnessing the demographic collapse of the last vestiges of the Jeffersonian dream. As the land was emptied of producing families, scholars sensed they were in the twilight of "American exceptionalism"—that consummate myth of the Progressive era that gloried in the claim that America had somehow survived the Cassandra-like pronouncements of populists and Marxists alike.

Families were now being ejected from the land in record numbers as a new cycle of agrarian concentration and centralization cut down another generation of hopefuls. The story of those driven from the land followed a typical pattern. Those who lost their farms might leave the land immediately, or hold on to their rural heritage by becoming tenant farmers. Similarly, tenants under the same economic duress could either migrate or buy a few more years on the land by becoming agricultural proletarians and selling their labor to those who had survived the latest market shakedown. Finally, the rural proletarians, their luck having run out, usually had little choice but to leave the land. Stumbling stunned into the large cities, they settled in the slums and joined the latest battalions of America's industrial reserve army. Some, still yearning for the land and a return to it, never adjusted; others, glad finally to be rid of the pain and uncertainty of rural penury, left and never looked back.

There was, however, a heartland variant of this stock set of scenarios. For a few there was a way of temporarily escaping this one-way road to urban alienation. They drifted first into small nearby hamlets seeking work and settling in for a few years until the need for regular work pushed them into midsized cities such as Grand Prairie. Others making the trek accumulated a large enough stake after a few years to buy cheap land on the cities' fringe. Whichever path was taken, the story was much the same: Destitute and having skills of little value in a town setting, the proximity of the countryside offered a way out. From town or hamlet a man (and if not him, his sons) could find part-time employment on a nearby farm. Sporadic farm work, when woven into the patchwork of those short-term jobs available to a town's newcomers, made up a minimalist strategy for economic survival. In many instances the move to a place such as Grand Prairie was followed by a retrograde series of short returns to the land or to one of the small hamlets that dotted the hinterland. But such moves were followed by a move back to town, as the reluctant emigré's options progressively narrowed. Finally, with compromise seen as being inevitable, a man might move his family to the city's edge and settle there permanently.

That is how the people came to Potter Addition. With the exception of the laboring poor of Grand Prairie who sought their own "place in the country," Potter Addition was founded by persons who were, at most, no more than two generations removed from the land. The founding families of Potter Addition already had deep, multigenerational roots in Clay County and its culture. While being in the lower ranks of Clay County's and Grand Prairie's class system, they nonetheless claimed cultural and social prerogatives that outlanders could not. They also had strong sentimental ties to the land, so that their gravitation to the rural-urban fringe of Grand Prairie signified an unbroken commitment to a rural way of life.

Potter Addition's founders thus set about to reconstruct the life of the small hamlets and isolated farms they had known in their youth. With nostalgia as a conscious guide, and working under the material constraints imposed by dire need, the founding families of Potter Addition forged in those early years a community that saw itself as an egalitarian collection of small freeholders. Only their poverty and the occasional moral fall of a family member or neighbor through drink, infidelity, or a run-in with the law challenged its aspirations.

Two more migratory waves would follow. A group of depression-driven refugees flooded out of the Appalachians in the prewar years, bringing with them a rich folk culture, but one that often seemed too exotic for the stolid inhabitants of the heartland. The second wave came after the war. Predominantly residents of the counties in the southern half of Potter Addition's home state, this postwar cohort consisted of technologically displaced, rural proletarians. With each cohort's arrival, Potter Addition inherited a new set of problems: alcoholism, broken families, child neglect, and an alien, often demoralized poverty that shocked the founders. In time, Potter Addition's original image was transformed. Grand Prairie had originally seen Potter Addition as being populated by people who were hardworking and moral, but poor. That conception, so assiduously cultivated by the community's founders, increasingly gave way to the opinion that Potter Addition was an alien coven of criminals and outcasts.

In the process of solving problems and managing these soiled identities, Potter Addition gained an evolving, if fragile, sense of its collective self. Driven at times as much by internecine struggle as by a sense of collective defense and destiny, Potter Additionites constructed a community that honored their small-town and rural origins. Living on the rural-urban fringe, family heads held jobs in town and in their off-hours fostered rural life-styles and identities. In Potter Addition gardens could be tended and livestock raised. Fields adjacent to a man's home could be hunted, or a trap could be set on the banks of Salt Creek. During the Great Depression, these leisure-time activities would take on a more serious tone as they became ways of putting food on the table. But even during the hardest of times, life on the edge of Grand Prairie was much more: Huddled on the fringe with others like themselves, families could practice the revered "old timey ways" of their parents, and their parents' parents before them. In Potter Addition the stranger could yet find cheap land, build upon it, and maintain the cherished, rural values of a fading past. And sweetest of all, the dispossessed might finesse a small victory from the very system that had so recently overwhelmed them. This was the promise of Potter Addition and all the other unnamed Potter Additions that blossomed on the edge of mid-America's cities in that era of rural tragedy.

IV. THE MATERIAL INFRASTRUCTURE OF COMMUNITY

Potter Addition was originally parceled into sixty-four lots. The four southernmost lots south of Banks Avenue originally measured five acres apiece, while the remaining sixty were one acre in area. Over time, the process of subdivision created the present total of 102 parcels (see Figure 3.1). The smallest parcels are now one eighth of an acre in size, while the largest is three acres—the undivided holdings of an absentee landlady. The majority of the lots are one-half acre in size. This is enough land to build a house on, have a small garden, a fenced area in which to raise small livestock, or room left to build a second dwelling.

Potter Addition itself sits on the rim of a natural bowl, resting half in and half out of it. Actually a shallow land depression, the rim of the bowl is formed by the leading edge of the Yankee Ridge moraine. Some

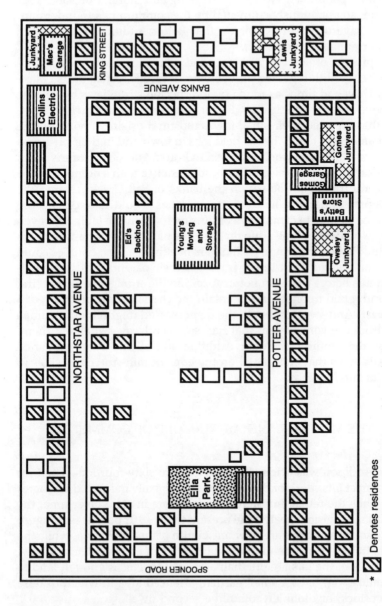

Figure 3.1. A street plan for Potter Addition showing the locations of major businesses, social centers, and residential structures in 1968*.

* Denotes residences

forty feet deep, the depression reaches its lowest point at Salt Creek, the southern boundary of Potter Addition. The Grand Prairie sewage plant is located in the bowl on the other side of the creek. During periods of equipment failure at the sewage plant, the bowl becomes a catchment basin for noxious fumes as the community is blanketed with phosgenes, sulfur compounds, and the smell of rotting garbage. Because the bowl concentrates the fumes hourly, in ever greater intensity, residents often have little choice but to curtail outdoor activity. While such breakdowns occur only once or twice a year, they are more than noisome intrusions, especially for families with asthmatic children.

Some wags joke that Potter Addition has the best-kept roads in the county, since the county road commissioner, the owner of a thriving moving van company, lives in Potter Addition and stores much of the county's equipment on his and a neighbor's adjoining acreage. Potter Addition has no paved sidewalks and no public street lighting, but the area is nonetheless well lit. Typical of the community's individualistic spirit and its abhorrence of any form of taxation, several attempts to raise money for street lights have failed. Instead, as if to show the folly of "collectivism," many have installed their own night-lights. Maintained by the power company for a nominal monthly fee, the garish blue lights allow a person to protect his or her property for pennies a day. At times, unintended "public virtue" does emerge from such individualistic pursuits of "private vice." As one resident boasted, "I get my lighting free, now that both of my neighbors have installed night-lights."

As for the other utilities, city water and gas came to the community in 1963, and most homes were hooked into the water system by 1966. Several residents, seeking to amortize recent investments in wells, were not yet in the system in 1968. Sanitary sewers were installed in 1977, while storm drains were available to half of the community at the time of my fieldwork and were accessible to all by 1980. The sanitation sewers became a flash point in early 1967, when residents learned that they had been paying a sewer tax since 1929 for services not rendered. After the smoke cleared, the sewer district agreed to allow free hook-ups when sewers were finally laid. Residents grudgingly assented to this compromise, but only after pointing out the incident as yet another example of the "screwing over" Potter Addition periodically receives from Grand Prairie.

There was no sorer point of contention in the 1960s between residents and Grand Prairie's political leadership than the issue of housing. Always a source of finger-pointing, the labeling of Potter Addition as a slum by those outside the community has always provoked outrage among residents. In early 1966, for example, shortly before I took up residence in the area, a notorious document, the Vinton Report, spotlighted the poor housing conditions and makeshift sanitary facilities of many homes. While it was difficult to deny many of the report's assertions, angry residents nonetheless maintained that the report painted the community with too broad and too biased a brush, ignoring the decades of hard work that had made the area "much better than it used to be."

This was still an issue in 1978 when a HUD-financed report discussed Potter Addition's housing. The deficiencies listed in that report paralleled those recorded in my field notes a decade earlier. The HUD report was itself part of a three-year, community development block grant designed to improve housing in Potter Addition and two other unincorporated areas. In Potter Addition, fourteen structures were rehabilitated using federal funds, while five were privately renovated with low-interest private loans. In contrast to the Vinton Report, Potter Addition had gained significant concessions from local authorities concerning the community's reputation. The introduction to a HUD brochure entitled *Clay County Community Development: Potter Addition Improvement Project, 1980,* respectfully describes the community:

> Located directly northeast of Grand Prairie's city limits, Potter Addition is one of the early settlements of the . . . area. Since this neighborhood is neither within the Grand Prairie city limits nor incorporated as a municipality, it has not had the usual municipal services provided by local property taxes.
>
> Compounding the community's efforts to cope with unpaved streets and standing water has been the challenge of buffering homes from two adjacent salvage yards, an automotive repair garage, and a moving van company.
>
> Potter Addition residents have long been actively involved in working toward improving their community. Many of these residents, who are descendants of early 1900 settlers, still live in their original homesteads, on which time has taken its toll. This neighborhood of about 500 persons has remained a close-knit, independent community, reminiscent of their southern heritage and the closeness that once characterized many American communities.
>
> It is this spirit that has motivated a strongly determined, energetic and tenacious group of Potter Addition citizens to work for the changes resulting in the Potter Addition Improvement Project.
>
> With its rolling terrain and deep shady lots, the small historic settlement of Potter Addition is beginning to blossom. The Clay County Board and Potter Addition residents can be truly proud of the improvements that their cooperative efforts are bringing to this community.

The change in tone between this document and the earlier Vinton Report is a study in contrasts. In less than two decades Potter Addition's protracted ideological struggle had wrung significant verbal concessions from Grand Prairie as to what kind of community it was and what kind of people lived there. The "southern white trash" of the 1940s had suddenly become "descendants of early settlers" with a "southern heritage." This small triumph of symbolic politics, wrung from the "powers that be" by a once pariah population, should alert us to the fact that there is a special elan in Potter Addition, one that frees its people and its culture of poverty from the stereotypical demoralization that is supposedly a cultural correlate of poverty.

V. THE MATERIAL CULTURE OF POTTER ADDITION

A community's appearance can communicate more than the ecological and economic processes that determine its physical layout. Properly interpreted, its physical configurations can yield fruitful insights into the cultural premises that undergird a community. Walter Firey (1947) was one of the first to show us how to interrogate the ecology of a community in order to extract from it the value premises that organized it. In his study of land utilization in Central Boston he showed that land use, zoning ordinances, and the struggle over the symbolic meanings of space can be used as indices of the social logic and value commitments of those who are actively engaged in constructing the everyday life of a local community.

Building codes and zoning ordinances reflect this collective effort to order space and its material contents socially according to an indigenous cultural paradigm. Both specify the types of physical structures, social activities, and persons that a given social logic can permit to coexist in the same space. In the case of fringe communities such as Potter Addition, however, it is not codified, urban constraint, but freedom from codes that holds the key to the social meanings embedded in Potter Addition's material culture. The very absence of regulations has, in fact, always been a cultural feature of the fringe that has made it an attractive place to settle. Because of this, we must interrogate the regulatory silences, so to speak, for it is the very absence of city zoning ordinances and building codes that makes possible the nonstandard uses of fringe social space and material culture.

When "symptomatically read," Potter Addition's housing reveals three things. First, the collage of ramshackle dwellings speaks of poverty and hard times. Second, the use of exotic or borderline means to achieve the culturally approved desire of owning one's home reveals the presence of Mertonian "innovation" (Merton 1968). Finally, when people talk about their community, they personalize its material infrastructure. It is as if each building over the years has acquired an identity that gives it a biographical relevance. Such talk indicates that the physical presence of the community is involved in an objectification of personal, as well as collective, biographies. A fusion of things and self has occurred so that sentiment, individual identities, and a certain sense of collective self become embedded in the material layerings of community.

As to the first point, the large proportion of trailers and jerry-built houses suggests a population with meager resources that secures housing as best it can. Houses without city water or indoor sanitary facilities were not unknown in the community in the 1950s, and as late as 1968 there were still houses that lacked one or the other. Structures with dangerously substandard electrical wiring were still an often-stated worry of those living in the area. In many homes, cockroaches and mice were so entrenched that their elimination was all but impossible.[6] Extermination was periodically attempted, but with few lasting results. Outsiders usually attributed the persistence of vermin to slovenly housekeeping, but such explanations ignored the age of Potter Addition's housing and the perpetual flow of renters in and out of the area. The junkyards and the nearness of open fields were, furthermore, a constant, renewable source of mice. Thus, some women established a détente with the mice and stored their food in covered coffee cans, even as they went about resetting their baited traps.

As to the second point, that of Mertonian innovation, the American passion for home ownership is an obsession in Potter Addition. This obsession is anchored in the rural axiom that those not owning property risk slipping into the demiworld of drifters, urban slum dwellers, migrant workers, and other rootless wanderers. This hunger for land and home ownership is, hence, fertile ground for generating anomic conduct. The average resident can seldom secure housing through normal channels, e.g., by hiring a contractor to build a house or qualifying for normal bank financing. Instead, many houses either are bought "on contract," thus circumventing the usual financial tests imposed by banks, are built by residents in their spare time, or have rooms added on as the need arises.

Mertonian innovation occurs when the lower-class individual secures housing by using means that respect the letter, if not always the spirit of the law; such means allow the person to acquire a valued cultural goal that society has placed outside the reach of his or her class. The recognition that one is beating the system at its own game is revealed in that rare "sin of pride" when a man or woman describes how a house was built using unorthodox materials or ingenious construction techniques.

The visually most obvious forms of this kind of innovation are to be found in structures that once served radically different functions. The already discussed railroad boxcars joined to form a single residence, six chicken coops combined to form a single dwelling unit (abandoned by the time of my arrival), two converted pig houses, a converted garage, and a dirt-floored barn rented out as housing in the 1940s (torn down by the early 1960s) are examples of this kind of structure. All attest to the innovative processes that often produce Potter Addition's jerry-built housing.

Putting these most obvious examples to one side, we can differentiate between varying degrees of innovation. Beginning with the least exotic, there are those houses which were built in Grand Prairie and later moved to Potter Addition. They have remained unaltered except for being set on new foundations. They represent some of the soundest housing in the area, and with a little money and work could be restored to their former bourgeois glory. Further up the scale of innovation is housing which combines two or more structures, some of which were put to nonresidential use prior to their becoming houses. Here we have, to borrow Levi-Strauss's (1963, pp. 1–34) term, the work of *bricoleurs*. Unlike housing that has been regulated from its very inception by the inner development of some architectural notion, *bricoleur* housing does not exhibit the physical unfolding of a coherent, regulating ideal. Instead, *bricoleur* dwellings are pieced together with *a concrete logic* that involves a haphazard accretion of parts and remnants of other structures.

The *bricoleur* builder honors the pragmatics of the moment, employing a worldview that takes no particular offense at esthetic loose ends but, quite to the contrary, delights in this one-of-a-kind functional recombination of disparate parts. Often, the former history of the structure and its materials, even as they are given a new function, are preserved and communicated to the public. Two houses in Potter Addition exemplify this: The first, on Potter Avenue, began as two houses located in Lower Potter Addition. They were originally among ten such structures built south of Banks Avenue by an absentee landlord in the early 1950s. When they became run-down and proved to be marginally profitable, they were sold off one by one, with none leaving the community. The two we are interested in were placed flush to one another, a doorway was knocked through their adjoining walls, and the two houses were combined to form a single dwelling. The place where the gabled roofs met was perfunctorily joined and covered with tar paper to prevent leakage. The house was left crowned with its curious double-eaved roof and rented out. Its M-shaped roof served as an historical inscription telling what it had once been and displaying the process by which it was assembled. A second form of bricolage construction consisted of an elongated, rectangular structure, with a shallow-pitched, hyperbolic roof, that resembled the short-order railroad diners so much in vogue a few decades ago. One such "diner" was bought by a neighbor and added onto the back of his house; a door had been cut in the common wall, and the "diner car" was serving as a bedroom for his youngest son. Again, no attempt had been made to hide or harmonize the larger square living structure with the later addition.

Finally, bordering on the boxcar and chicken coop forms of innovation, unorthodox building materials were constantly being used in housing construction and repair. Stories of landlords sinking fifty-gallon oil drums into the ground and using them as septic tanks are a thing of the past. Also gone is the practice of one quite notorious family that allowed sanitary waste from inside the house to empty into the crawl space between the floor and the ground. In some instances, long since past, substandard construction went hand in hand with theft as some residents improved the quality of their housing at a neighbor's expense. Such midnight requisitions inevitably become part of the community's tongue-in-cheek folklore. Thus, as one of my most trusted resource persons once told me:

> A tale went around that any time someone built out here, John Gorman would add a room onto his house too. He would slip out at night and steal the lumber. Carl Seivers moved a lot of lumber down here on his lot from a house he was tearing down in Grand Prairie. He claimed that old Gorman was taking the lumber and nailing it onto his own house. Gorman was also the one who went to the dump, got cardboard boxes, and lined the inside of his house with cardboard boxes instead of wallboard. He put wallpaper over the cardboard and had a pretty nice looking house. The next people who moved into the house thought at first that they were nailing things into wallboard.

In another instance, foam rubber was used as a substitute for wallboard and papered over. This made for a string of hilarious tales about subsequent renters and owners trying unsuccessfully to hang pictures on walls of foam rubber. In such cases as these, a cut-rate alternative to expensive materials helped someone achieve their goal of owning a "good house," and while dubious on several counts, the substitutions were not illegal in this unincorporated community. Midnight requisitions are, of course, another thing. Though relatively rare, they are part of the illegitimate opportunity structure that seems to thrive on the unregulated fringe. Take, for example, tapping into storm sewers to get rid of sanitary waste:

> A lot of your sewage out here is going into an open pipe down here by the creek. A lot of homes are hooking into the storm sewers, which is

illegal. It's polluting the streams. I've threatened more than once to go down and plug that pipe up and see just how many toilets start overflowing out here.

On the edge of urban regulation and rationality, the people of Potter Addition have carved out a niche in which "poor people can have more than the law allows." Often walking the thin line between culturally disapproved practices and outright illegality, Potter Addition's housing is a finely polished mirror that reflects the social and economic situation of its residents.

Housing appearance also attests to what I will call a serial mode of construction. Here a family begins, say, with a two-room house; then, as it grows, or as the ownership of the house changes hands, another room is added, and then another, and yet another. Rather than being built all at once, the house, like an organism, sprouts appendages. The following passage describes the process by which this occurs:

> I don't remember who built this place to start with, but it was originally a one-room house. The people who owned it would sell it off to somebody, and the new owner would build another room onto it. About everybody who got ahold of it built another room or two onto it, until it got to be a pretty good-sized house.
>
> Lots of these houses started out that way and then got added onto. Tom, next door here, built as his family growed. He started out with just a couple of sheds put together that they moved in from the highway. They bought a third shed later to keep their garden stuff in, and when his boy got married, they fixed it up a little bit and the boy and his wife lived there for a while. Later on, they added to that shed, and his mother-in-law, who's old and feeble now, lives there.

An unintended consequence of this form of housing construction is that housing loses much of its abstract, commodity character. That is, Potter Addition's housing is not a commodity in the usual sense of the word. It is seldom built to be sold to an anonymous buyer on an open market. For those with roots in Clay County for two generations or more, Potter Addition's housing takes on both an historical and biographical relevance. Thus, during my fieldwork, I might be driving down a street with a friend or a neighbor and he would suddenly point to a house and say, "That used to be my Aunt Mildred's house that sat over in the Negro district until old Bergman moved it out here sometime in the forties. He sold it to Terry North, who built onto it in the late fifties."

Structures in Potter Addition thus acquire a "humanity," as personal biography and the history of the structure merge to form part of a

common stock of cultural knowledge. This anecdotal folk knowledge—
where a house originally sat, how many times it had been moved, when
and how it came to Potter Addition, and its construction history since
the move—gives Potter Additionites a sense of place and material root-
edness they might otherwise lack. At times, a home can take on an
almost mythic reality, having a long history before the person bought it
and being invested with biographical relevance as it is built onto. One
such residential prehistory is recounted with impressive detail:

> This little house I got out back was my original home when my Mom
> and Dad first moved here. It was up by the Sinclair Oil Station at Four
> Corners, where the town is now. The station was made of this real shiny,
> glazed green and white brick. Next to that station in the 1920s there were
> a half-dozen little cabins. They weren't very successful in those days, and
> you could probably rent them for a dollar a night. They weren't nothin'
> like motel-type cabins; they were just little bitty houses, one or two room
> affairs. This little house I'm rentin' out may be one of those cabins that
> used to sit up by the gas station. But, anyway, I remember they moved it
> over to the north edge of the field where Grand Prairie High School is.
> Then Shorty McCall moved it over to Clear Lake Drive, there by the A-1
> Tire and Battery. This little house has been moved several times. It's
> traveled around quite a bit.

At other times, housing is a physical and temporal marker that serves
as a benchmark of one's growing up, or of long friendships that are still
flourishing. This is shown in the following anecdote in which the person
glides in memory from one structure to another and, in doing so, concomitantly maps the course of a long and valued friendship:

> Bert Hiller moved a lot of houses out here in the 1940s and put them up
> over on North Star—just south of Banks Avenue there. One of the houses
> was my grandmother's before she died. Marshall Perrin's house was what
> you would call an old three-room shack. Me and Marshall is like brothers.
> I help him out, and he helps me. I helped him put the upstairs on that
> three-room shack of his, and I helped him build on the kid's room, and
> then the living room. Later on, we moved in that little shack that his mom
> and dad lived in before they died. It came over from where the junkyard
> is now. His youngest daughter lives there now.

From this and earlier anecdotes we can see that housing is a crucial
vehicle for an externalization of biography. The historical strata of physical artifacts are thus fused so that person, thing, and residential place
form a set of self-referencing and reinforcing elements.[7]

VI. THE JUNKYARDS

Potter Addition's unincorporated status makes it a magnet for those seeking to escape city taxes, zoning laws, and restrictions upon free-wheeling life-styles and pariah businesses. In 1967, there are no less than ten small businesses located in this community of one hundred or so households. They span a wide spectrum of commercial possibilities: a well-drilling outfit, a backhoe service and trucking company, a construction trucking outfit, a furniture moving and warehouse facility, a small one-room grocery store, an electrical supply warehouse located in a structure that was once a residence, and three garage-junkyards. In all cases but one, the businesses are run by residents of Potter Addition. In three instances—the backhoe service, the well-drilling outfit, and one junkyard—the businesses are secondary occupations. That is, the owners run them from their front rooms, but earn their livelihood at some other work. None of these men, however, are getting rich from their businesses. Such enterprises are often pleasant diversions that provide a few extra dollars income.

Most businesses are run in a low-key manner and do little to alter the pace of residential life in Potter Addition. The junkyards are the exception, for they are often blamed for giving the community a black eye. Many residents of Grand Prairie who know of Potter Addition (and in 1967 there were many who did not) claim that the yards, along with the autos parked on residential acreage, make Potter Addition look like a "wall-to-wall junkyard." As unfair as this outsider's impression may be, it is nonetheless a reality with which residents must cope. Unfortunately, the price of such bias goes far beyond bruised feelings. It is often levied in monetary terms:

> The junkyards and the area's background, what people have heard about the type of people they think are living out here, is really unfair. One of my neighbors has to sell their place, and they can't do it because of the locality. If it had been in a different locality, it would have been snapped up in nothing flat. That's what they told me. They couldn't sell it. They wanted $10,000 for it. A half-acre of ground and a beautiful home on the inside, all combination aluminum windows, and a patio with a screened-in back porch—all that with a full basement! It would have been snapped up like nobody's business with its half-acre of ground, but not out here.

Despite such resentful anecdotes, the community is not of a single mind when it comes to the junkyards. On the one hand, there is the depression of property values, the vermin that inevitably inhabit the yards, and the visual ugliness. On the other hand, the ethic of radical negative freedom that is so often bandied about by Potter Addition's defenders places limits of conscience on how far one can go in impinging upon the rights of these pariah enterprises. Commitments to decent living demand the removal of these businesses, while the advocacy of abstract principle forces tolerance upon residents and a moderation of their demands.

While usually tolerant, many Potter Additionites resent this democratic premise gone haywire. One junkyard in particular is a sore point. This is Bull Gomes's garage and junkyard—the northernmost yard and, by far, the busiest in the community. The personality of the owner and the yard's location in Upper Potter Addition make it a perpetual point of controversy. Gomes is an intelligent, aggressive, quick-tongued, and consummately foul-mouthed individual. Graced with a sharp intellect, a wicked sense of humor, and a creative streak when it comes to inventing new four-lettered phraseology, Bull is straightforward and honest in his dealings with others. His wonderfully clothed, obscenity-laced directness severely tests the radical laissez-faire values of the community and the much-valued, taciturn demeanor of its males. Beneath this brassy exterior, however, lurks a sensitivity to the complaints leveled against him and his business. There are genuine moments of accommodation in which a conscience-stricken Bull, bowing to pressure, but never admitting to his sins (that would be *just too much* for Bull), cleans up his business and "tries to be a good neighbor." These seizures of civic responsibility quickly pass, however, as Bull reverts to his old ways. Then once again, after a period of mounting protest, he will "take the pledge" literally to "clean up his act." If Bull and his junkyard were located in Lower Potter Addition, along with the rest of the junkyards, his establishment might be less notorious. But set in the center of the community and run by this mercurial individual, Bull's business is a constant source of scandal and controversy.

VII. BETTY'S MARKET

One establishment, Betty's Market, is at the very heart of Potter Addition and is a focal point of community integration. It is housed in a two-storied structure. The store and a back kitchen take up the first floor, while the residence of Betty Stans and her husband, LaRue, are on the second. From seven in the morning, until six in the evening, six days a week, members of the community mingle at the store, chat with one another, and in so doing provide Potter Addition with an outward sense of community. The spatial and temporal rhythms of Potter Addition's everyday life have been set by Betty's market for almost a decade now.

Her establishment is the nerve center of the community, a place where people gather to talk and visit. It serves as the Potter Addition Volunteer Fire District's dispatch center and houses the fire department's siren. Over the years the Market's reputation as Potter Addition's communication center has spread beyond the boundaries of the community and is well-known in Grand Prairie itself. When outsiders need directions, are trying to find a particular house, or are inquiring as to a certain person's whereabouts, they are told to go to Betty's. School administrators, social workers, and other social control agencies use the market as a point of entry when dealing with the community. Betty's Market is perceived as a safe haven in an otherwise shadowy terra incognita. Information runs in the other direction as well. If residents want to know, say, when a power outage is expected to end or when a community meeting is scheduled at the firehouse, they phone Betty's. If a rumor is about in the community, it can best be confirmed or discarded by "calling down to Betty's."

The market is also a locus of various ritual activities that sustain Potter Addition's community consciousness. During the slower daytime hours housewives come to Betty's to shop and gossip. Escaping the loneliness of the household, the maddening company of preschool children, or the irritation of an interfering, retired husband, they come to the small twenty-by-thirty-foot one-room store to visit. At the north end of the store sits a meat case, a counter, and an old-fashioned glass-fronted candy case heaped with various sorts of penny and nickel candy. On the other side of this intentionally formed barrier is a three-foot-wide aisle, a wall of shelving that holds personal hygiene items, a meat scale, and two stools, one for Betty and the second for invited others.

From behind the counter Betty holds court and orchestrates the interaction that flows around her. She is in her seventies, has pure white hair, is small in stature, and is slightly hunched in posture. She is usually clad in a man's plaid shirt, women's jeans, white socks, and loafers. Kind to a fault and soft-spoken, she is a person whom it would be difficult to cross, but God help you if you did. On those rare occasions when she does allow a flare of temper to disrupt her accommodating maternalism, it becomes clear *who* rules the Stans's roost and why.

Shopping and visiting are ritualistically intertwined at Betty's. If a woman wants only food, she will usually send a child with a note and money, or instructions to "put it on the bill." Otherwise, shopping is a thinly disguised pretext for socializing, as she leisurely wanders the aisles, talking to Betty or other visitors, removing cans or jars from the shelves, and carrying them to the counter. Making several such swings through the store, she returns to the counter each time and puts her groceries in a slowly growing pile. The stream of conversation rises and falls as new customers or salesmen come in and those who have finished their business leave. At times, the conversation may shift to gossip concerning the person who has just left or to a subject that might have proven embarrassing to the customer. On occasion, a mother shows up to display her newborn son or daughter. To monitor the infant's physical progress, Betty may remove a large sheet of butcher paper from a roll, place it on the meat scale, and weigh the infant. The result is always a spur to further praise and advice.

Betty's Market is, in short, female turf. Men may come to the store and pass the time of day as they pick up whatever it was they came for, but then they go about their business. There is no written rule that says they cannot stay and talk, just as there is no written code that keeps women from joining the men around the open hood of a car, but they seldom tarry. The claque is more often interrupted by children. Preteens, clutching pennies and nickels, stampede into the store to purchase Betty's penny candy. Some bring empty pop bottles whose deposit value is used to buy the candy.[8] Occasionally, teenagers come in, but if they have kin shopping there, it is best they keep going; otherwise they may be driven blushing from the place by well-intended teasing or innuendo about their current love life. From time to time, a hapless man gets caught in this "ganging up" juggernaut, though here the sensitive subject of sex is never broached.

The market serves the community in other ways. It is a school bus stop and a morning madhouse on winter days when it is too cold for the children to wait outside. For this reason, women usually put off shopping until the bus leaves. Occasionally, a fight breaks out between two waiting children. Betty can usually separate them, but when they are too big, she sends for LaRue or some other nearby male. On rare occasions, Betty baby-sits the children of families whose parents must be at work early and who would otherwise have to leave their children unattended. Certain families even make arrangements for Betty to give their children lunch money and charge it to their grocery bill. Betty gives credit to many households and frankly admits that it is crucial to keeping the market's doors open. She has carried many families during the long winters of part-time employment, and if it were not for this, many larders would have gone empty over the years. For others, Betty is a source of small, interest-free, cash loans, a practice in which she has been stung more than once.

Finally, Betty's Market is designed to look like and be an old-fashioned country store. It was intentionally made so by Betty and LaRue, and is kept that way by those who shop there. It has been sentimentally fashioned after a store that Betty knew as a child in Ohio. The store and its ambience are thus a fabric woven from complex strands of nostalgia, tradition, personalist indulgences, occasional intrigues, and no-nonsense economic arrangements. There is no easy way to separate Betty's rational self-interest as a businesswoman from the familylike overlays of personal caring that determine who receives her services. Both Betty and her customers admit that many of her items, such as meat, are exorbitantly priced. Both also acknowledge that most shopping is done in Grand Prairie's supermarkets. This latter admission does not cause rancor on Betty's part nor self-reproach on the part of her loyal customers for not patronizing exclusively the establishment of a good friend. Some see the higher prices and Betty's extending credit as a fair trade-off, while others defend her prices as just, given that Betty is a "little guy" trying to make it in a world of economic giants. These commercial considerations are minor, however, in determining how people view Betty and her establishment. The market is a crucial node of collective self-consciousness, one that helps residents define "what it means to be Potter Addition." It is in Betty's Market that the material and ideological dimensions of Potter Addition's vibrant subculture merge, intertwine, and come alive.

VIII. THE QUESTION OF CLASS

Betty's Market is too vital an institution to fit the drab and condescending stereotype that many critics of the culture of poverty concept insist must be a part of the inner life of the poor.[9] The vitality of the culture is further revealed in Potter Addition's aggressive response to the Vinton Report and other such criticisms. Add to this the radically different imagery that the HUD document adopted in describing Potter Addition and its people in the 1970s, and we have some idea of the ideological triumphs of which Potter Addition is capable. Such victories in the domain of symbolic politics certainly do not fit the morose picture that social scientists so often paint of poor people.

There are, in fact, many concrete cultures of poverty in America, each reflecting in its internal coloration the historical circumstances from which it is synthesized. Variations in relative well-being and the personal morale of its incumbents give each culture of poverty its own special sense and way of doing things. Poverty's picture is further complicated by the fact that the economic and cultural lines separating the near-poor and the poor are not fast and set. In the 1980s we learned that many of our poor are the working poor, and that being poor, with its attendant social uncertainty, is not the sole province of those living on welfare. Even more instructive is Michael Harrington's (1984) recent voicing of America's best kept "dirty little secret"—that many members of America's working class barely manage to skirt material poverty on a day-to-day basis, and that it would take (and has taken) very little to push many families over the poverty line. In reality, those working class families that are technically on the respectable side of that line, are no more certain or secure than those caught below it.

What is true of the idea of poverty is also true of our conceptions of class when it comes to understanding the everyday life of the poor. When one follows any of Potter Addition's families through its life cycles, it becomes apparent that conventional conceptions of class based on income, occupation, and socioeconomic status are not wholly adequate for grasping the lived realities of lower-class life. If we are to understand poverty as it occurs in places like Potter Addition, we need a more flexible way of talking about class. Such a remapping of class and its meaning has been advanced in E. P. Thompson's writing of history "from the bottom up." He has warned scholars not to reify class and its correlates, but to attend instead to the historical and biographical particulars through which class expresses itself:

> [I]n discussing class, one finds oneself too frequently commencing sentences with "it," it is time to place oneself under some historical control, or one is in danger of becoming the slave of one's own categories. Sociologists who have stopped the time-machine and, with a good deal of conceptual huffing and puffing, have gone down to the engine room to look, tell us that nowhere at all have they been able to locate and classify a class. They can only find a multitude of people with different occupations, incomes, status-hierarchies, and the rest. Of course, they are right, since class is not this or that part of the machine, but *the way the machine works* once it is set into motion—not this interest and that interest, but the *friction* of interests—the movement itself, the heat, the thundering noise. Class is a social and cultural formation (often finding institutional expression) which cannot be defined abstractly, or in isolation, but only in terms of relationships with other classes; and, ultimately, the definition can only be made in the medium of time—that is, action and reaction, change and conflict. When we speak of *a* class we are thinking of a very loosely defined body of people who share the same categories of interests, social experiences, traditions and value system, who have a *disposition to behave* as a class, to define themselves in their actions and in their consciousness in relation to other groups of people in class ways. But class itself is not a thing, it is a happening. (1966, p. 295)

In this passage Thompson addresses many of the problems I have encountered in reconciling the historical particularism of Potter Addition's culture of poverty with sociology's universalizing thrust. I have tried to understand "the machine" as it is has been experienced by those who live in its lower recesses. I am more interested in the dynamic fluctuations of class and poverty in their everyday "frictions" than in the formal sociological paradigms under which life in Potter Addition might otherwise be conceptually subsumed. I have hewn as closely as possible to a peripatetic sense of social class, poverty, and the subculture of poverty while staying within a sociological framework, per se. Thus, when I refer to the people of Potter Addition as a whole, I will use the term *lower class*, or alternatively, *the poor*, knowing full well that neither rubric can adequately capture the dynamics of class and community as they have evolved in Potter Addition.[10] There are, for example, too many families in Potter Addition who in the 1960s would be classified in strictly static terms as being "stable working class," but who only a decade before were impoverished. These latter still have fearful memories of those earlier, harsher times, and their everyday conduct still shows traces of past scars. Many other residents still live hand-to-mouth existences, experiencing a rapid succession of good times and bad so that they are neither stable working class nor lumpen proletariat.

Complicating the overall picture of class and poverty in Potter Addition, is the "contradictory" class situation of the founding families and their offspring. Their ancestors were some of the first settlers in the county, and by Clay County's reckoning this gives them prerogatives that newcomers and "aliens" can never claim. Clay County's dominant system of xenophobic discriminations puts these people closer in status to the institutional leaders and moral entrepreneurs of Grand Prairie than to their neighbors in Lower Potter Addition. At the same time, Potter Addition's leaders are still, in terms of economic class, "the hardworking, moral poor" and occupy the lower rungs of the economic ladder. Again no single analytic scheme can do justice to or capture the tensions and contradictions that permeate the class situation of these people.

Finally, in considering the actual class location of Potter Addition's culture of poverty, we must take into account the social-psychological implications that living a large portion of one's life in poverty entails. There is a set of subjective factors that have profound consequences for the reality of class and poverty in Potter Addition. The everyday experience of poverty and the memories of past deprivations become intertwined with the present-day, objective determinations of class. Subjectively, poverty as a way of life does not immediately vanish once material need is eliminated. There is a "cultural lag" of trauma and pain, which leaves a hardened residue of chronic self-doubt and anxiety about the future. Such fears are seldom extinguished by a few "fat" years. Having once been poor, Potter Additionites know the grim truth of capitalist society: A sudden, unexpected return to poverty is always an imminent possibility.

The World of Work

During my first months of fieldwork, I left Potter Addition during the daytime and went to work like others in the community. As they went to their jobs, I went to the Clay County Courthouse and the university library and spent hours poring over some thirty years of Potter Addition tax rolls and Grand Prairie city directories. After gleaning the names of those who owned or had owned property in Potter Addition, I constructed occupational profiles and residential histories. As I settled into the community, the names of renters, past and present, and former residents would come up in stories and conversations with friends and neighbors. I would then add their names to the list of people to be researched. During this initial research, I discovered what historians who study the lower class have long known: The documentary traces left by the poor are so episodic that much of their history is lost forever.

Despite the gaps in the official record, the pages of the Grand Prairie city directories yielded enough information that I was able to construct occupational time series for many of the community's residents and absentee landowners. The documents showed job histories of utter chaos. That is, the occupational lives of Potter Addition's poor diverged dramatically from the orderly career trajectories of middle-class men and women. Potter Addition's work histories seldom exhibited logically ordered patterns in which one job served as a substantive prelude to the next. Instead of a chain of occupations arrayed in a hierarchical unfolding, I discovered jumbled job histories in which a man might begin his occupational life as a gas station attendant, graduate to being a roofer, take a job as a janitor, and then five or ten years later return to being a gas station attendant.

As my research moved from the library into the community, the disorderly work lives of Potter Addition's males loomed ever larger as an explanation for much of what I was recording daily in my field notes.

Achievement patterns, family power arrangements, the formation of gender-specific peer groups, and the kinship-based xenophobia of Potter Addition were traceable in many instances to the uncertainty of its residents' occupational careers. Moreover, in talking with people about their work, I began to realize that disorderly careers were not in and of themselves anomic paths to failure. They were often rational responses to an unpredictable occupational environment. In the majority of cases, Potter Addition's disorderly careers displayed as much rationality relative to poverty's variable economic environment as did the orderly, ascending careers of those who occupied stable class niches. Instead of the contents of lower-class work life being a "cultural deprivation" or an inferior template of life at the top, Potter Addition's occupational culture displayed its own class-based logic.

I. DISORDERLY CAREERS IN POTTER ADDITION

Potter Addition has a four-tiered occupational structure. The lowest tier is the most numerous of the four and consists of unskilled occupations: laundry workers, roofers, waitresses, meat cutters, cafeteria workers, janitors, short-haul truckers, and unskilled construction laborers. These occupations are usually low paying, nonunion, and marked by cyclical fluctuations in employment. The second tier is composed of skilled craftsmen in the construction trades: electricians, pipe fitters, carpenters, millwrights, teamsters, and the like. These workers usually make higher hourly wages and have better job protection than those in the first tier. Despite this increment of security, however, this type of work is subject to seasonal variations in employment, so that by year's end this second group is largely indistinguishable from the first.

The third tier cuts across the first two and is distinguished not by what the worker does, but by where he or she works. This stratum consists of men and women who work at the university in such capacities as janitors, plumbers, truck drivers, electricians, and food workers.[1] Though at the bottom of the university hierarchy, their jobs share many of the stable characteristics of labor's primary sector. These jobs provide the worker and his or her family with a sense of security and predictability that is relatively unknown among most other blue-collar employees and service workers in Clay County. This is due in part to the fact that the university is a union shop, which requires that all its employees join a union. Even more important, though, is the fact that the university provides its employees with a bureaucratically stabilized work environment. This occupational group, while numbering only fifteen households, has formed a stable core of community leadership throughout Potter Addition's history. Numbered among them are many of the community's founding cohort and their children.

Finally, a handful of small businessmen and salespersons occupy the fourth tier. Since I discussed this group in Chapter 3, I will not list them again, except to add to it three persons who run businesses located *outside* the community: a husband and wife who operate a small restaurant in Grand Prairie that caters to lower-blue-collar clientele, and a car salesman who works for the Grand Prairie Pontiac dealership.

Contingencies related to the age and sex of heads of households cut across and complicate this four-tiered occupational structure. In the early years of marriage, a young couple in Potter Addition is often plagued by the young man's inability to earn an adequate living for his family. In other households—those headed by working grandmothers, young divorcees, or women who have been deserted by their husbands—the situation is desperate for different reasons. Here the feminization of poverty, like the problems linked to the early stages of the lower-class family's development cycle, intensify the purely economic problems that lower-class households confront. For this reason, I will defer consideration of these complicating factors until later and concentrate for the moment on intact households and the variable occupational environments with which working males must daily deal.

Four aspects of lower-class work life establish the foundation of variable environments in Potter Addition: (1) the abnormally long period of trial and search that precedes a man's settling into a lifetime job, (2) the seasonal nature of construction work, (3) the lack of specialized skills that might otherwise give an individual some market leverage in selling his labor, and (4) the relative inability of unions in Clay County to stabilize the economic lives of their rank and file politically.

The first of these sources, the extended period of job search and trial, makes every new household vulnerable to economic crises. As studies of lower-working-class entrants into the job market have shown, the first decade of work is taken up with a more or less continual casting about for jobs. While most young workers experience such a period, its untoward extension among lower-class entrants is crucial in shaping the domestic relations of Potter Addition's fledgling households. Typically, the young man drops out of school somewhere in his sophomore year. Having few certifiable skills, the only work available is usually back-breaking and psychologically unrewarding. The odious nature of the work, combined with the young man's personal sensitivity and often surly demeanor, ensures that he will pass through a rapid succession of jobs in the first three or four years after leaving school. If he is still living at home, he can use his adolescent status as a hedge against the harsh discipline of the labor market. Short bursts of employment are inter-spersed with extended periods of "laying around the house." Despite dire warnings from his parents that leaving school means finding full-time work immediately (a ploy that often forestalls his quitting for a few months), they usually relent and "carry the kid."

If the young man gets married after dropping out of school—and it is not at all uncommon for one event to coincide with the other—the social definition of his idleness radically shifts. It is one thing to be single, unemployed, and living at home. In such circumstances the young man is half-jokingly referred to as a "lazy kid" by his parents and is good naturedly carried by them. Sporadic employment ceases to be a joking matter, however, when the boy marries. Once he must earn a living for his family, his former occupational default, treated so lightly before, now threatens both his sense of manhood and the autonomy of his household. With the birth of his first child his situation noticeably wors-ens. Financially dependent upon his parents or, more likely, upon his wife's parents, the young man who is unable to find steady work is slowly deprived of those masculine prerogatives he might otherwise claim as the family's uncontested breadwinner. Furthermore, by the time he graduates from the trial and search phase of his career history, he and his wife are generally near the end of their childbearing years. The coincidence of the long job trial period, its attendant economic uncertainty, and the money burdens that most young couples experi-ence create a household struggling to maintain its autonomy.

The second condition generating economic uncertainty in the life of many of Potter Addition's households—even its mature ones—is the seasonal nature of work. Many of the community's skilled workers are employed in the construction industry. Although well-paid, this "aris-tocratic" stratum of workers is vulnerable to fluctuating income and seasonal layoffs. I can best communicate how the seasonal nature of construction work creates a variable economic setting for construction workers' households by drawing from my own biography, for what I experienced in my youth was common in Potter Addition.

I first became aware of variable environments while growing up in Wood River, Illinois, as the son of a journeyman pipe fitter and welder. Of course, I did not know variable class niches by this name, but by my early teens I knew that not all pipe fitters were alike. There were those who worked on construction and those who worked at the Standard Oil of Indiana refinery in Wood River. It would have been difficult to miss the difference between the two, since my father periodically voiced his contempt for the timid "thirty-year men" who chose security, sobriety, and domesticated certainty over the heroic building professions. Even though like my father, many of these thirty-year men were craftsmen, construction men invariably looked down upon the latter as being less adventurous and less manly. Part of the reason for this contempt, of course, was that Standard Oil at that time had a company union, for which organized labor had nothing but contempt.

Even as a child, though, I saw other differences that my father seldom discussed. I was struck, for instance, by the paradox that even though refinery pipe fitters earned hourly wages that were lower than my father's, they owned their own homes, appeared not to know the desperate, dark winters that construction families knew, and led secure lives of blue-collar boredom. The Harvey household, on the other hand, existed in a world of "excitement," punctuated by moments of sheer economic terror. My father had long been addicted to the nomadic life of construction work, replete with its Byzantine camaraderie, its work-related jealousies, and its two-fisted drinking rituals. In construction work the hourly pay was excellent, but employment was spotty. Slack periods often lasted long enough that we had "to pull up stakes" and move to a new town. There was also the omnipresent fact of seasonal fluctuations in employment. Winters were harrowing and invariably lean, while summers were wonderfully fat—euphoric periods of potlatch extravagance and carefree leisure.

Life in the Harvey household was that veritable economic roller coaster to which I have already alluded. There were occasional years when a stint of inside work during the winter leveled out this seasonal cycle of boom and bust, but these were the exceptions that proved the rule. More often than not, slack periods could total as much as two months of idleness in a bad year. During those cold, dark seasons, life's unpredictability was most keenly felt as the threat of my father having to "sit the winter and draw rocking chair" loomed ever larger with each passing week. Winters were periods of depleted savings and living "on the cuff" at Sid Goldfarb's IGA. In the spring, as work picked up, the family stopped avoiding creditors and started paying bills again. Summers were frenzies of "living high off the hog." Work was now steady and overtime abundant enough that the family was "knocking a hole in its bills." By late summer or early fall we had actually caught up. From then until early December, any surplus was used to make new capital purchases or was saved to tide us through the bad times looming ahead.

The irony of our lives was that we were never poor. Yet in winter we knew a genteel, working-class poverty, that form of marginal deprivation that George Orwell (1958, pp. 121–30) tells us breeds among the young a snobbish and painful sensitivity about even minute social differences. There was always the terror of not having money, of not paying bills, and there were brief moments of insight when both parents cursed the vagaries of "this damned life on construction." Living in

Potter Addition forced me to recall my own painfully uncertain past as
I began to recognize in the lives of others the fears and preoccupations
I had known while growing up in Wood River. Thus, I gave an all-
too-knowing nod to the reply I received one day when I asked a man,
"Would you advise a young person to get on at the University, or get a
job on construction?"

> Would I advise a young guy to go to work over at the university? Well,
> I'd have to know what his job was going to be at the university. If he is
> going to be a flunky and is young, and is most likely not married, and
> wouldn't need much income to start off with, I would tell him to try to get
> into construction and learn yourself a trade. On the other hand, if he was
> going into the university as an apprentice on a trade, then he would
> actually be better off going over to the university than going into construc-
> tion. He won't have a big income, but he'll have an income that is steady
> year around, where on construction he won't be able to work if it is bad
> weather. Of course, sometimes you do get inside work, but for a lot of the
> time during the winter a lot of people are laid off.
>   At the university, he's going to be, as soon as he's worked himself up as
> a journeyman, making as much as he would out there. Of course, it's
> going to take him four or five years to do it. It's just like the guy that's
> studying to be a doctor. He's taking a hell of a beating for a lot of years to
> get up to where he's going to make himself some money; this is something
> you got to look for, too. Learning your trade by working at the university,
> means you have to take a beating too; but I would actually advise the guy,
> if he's going to work up into a trade, to go to work at the university, work
> for less, and get a steady income year around. On construction, you'll
> work all summer long and then maybe they won't have enough work for
> you in the winter—and then you're gone, just like that.

The third factor that generates economic variability is the low political
and market leverage of low-skilled jobs. If a person has a scarce skill, he
can use it to stabilize his economic life chances. That is, a craftsman
carries his unemployment insurance with him wherever he goes in the
form of his skill—or so it was once thought. He can bargain with a boss,
and failing to strike a suitable deal, can "take himself and his craft down
the road to the next guy." This type of leverage not only stabilizes
occupational life chances, but also breeds a self-confidence that one
seldom finds among the unskilled. In Potter Addition, however, the
craftsman is usually employed in the construction trades. While there is
this requisite pride in one's craft, seasonal fluctuations in weekly income
often offset any market advantage that might otherwise be gained.

Finally, the alternative to skill-based market leverage—collective job
protection—is not really a possibility in Potter Addition. Unions have

never been especially strong in Clay County, and while they can enforce the rule of a union shop in certain sectors of the local economy, such as the university, their bargaining power has been limited. Although they can negotiate a contract, they are not always able to enforce its day-to-day provisions. More than once I talked to men who told of conspiring with their employers to circumvent various provisions of a union-negotiated contract. Such evasions were not the product of perversity, but a realistic response to the politics of the workplace. All knew of grievance procedures that had backfired or had seen business agents muscle a man to drop a legitimate grievance in order to bolster the union's position in some upcoming negotiation. Hence, many paid their dues as a condition of employment, and then cut their own under-the-table agreements with the boss.

One union man sat one night and told me of his plight. He is not untypical of many in the construction trades. A fifty-two-year-old cement finisher who occasionally "sidelines" as a long- and short-haul driver, he has worked for the same contractor for five years and has established a secure relationship with him. He sees himself as an aging worker with declining prospects and is so far into the collaborationist game that he fears exposure as much as he dreads being dismissed by his employer-patron. Because of his age and attendant fears, he allows himself to be worked overtime, often without extra pay. He fears going to the union over such treatment because he might be exposed as a scab for his under-the-table dealings. And even if he were to win a grievance, he would be exposed as a stool pigeon. This breach of personal honor, combined with his fear of exposure and dismissal, makes him a compliant worker. This intelligent but unschooled person feels he can do better if he and the boss negotiate their own under-the-table agreement. Rather than submit to a Kafkaesque grievance machinery, he stabilizes his world by playing to his boss's paternalistic instincts. On those occasions when he drives, for example, in return for working as many extra hours as possible at regular union scale, this aging man concedes the following:

1. no special compensation for overnight truck hauls;
2. no per diem on such trips;
3. working overtime for no, or drastically reduced, overtime pay rates;
4. no added compensation for loading or unloading his truck.

In each case, the employer promises to "see what he can do" and in reality does little. The man is *grateful* to get the extra hours of pay at union scale, even if they are not at overtime rates. Extra pay at union scale, after all, is better than no pay at all when one lives the uncertain life of a construction worker.

It would be an exaggeration to call this person beaten, but at fifty-two—already an old man in the construction industry—he knows that his options have diminished to the vanishing point. At his age manly pride gives way to putting food on the table, keeping a roof over his family, and having few illusions. His scabbing and the uneasiness he feels over it shows that he understands far too well the algebra of what Bertholt Brecht called "the basic food position."

II. THE JACK-OF-ALL-TRADES

Variable environments give work roles a texture and content that they do not have in a bureaucratic setting. The early job sacrifices usually associated with white-collar work, for example, have meaning only in the context of an organic career, and only if it is assumed that later payoffs will somehow compensate for earlier, self-imposed deprivations. These patterns of deferred gratification ultimately presuppose the existence of a stable, social universe—one that displays more or less lawlike regularities, temporal continuity, and long-term predictability. Furthermore, as Tumin (1953) has noted, careers often assume the existence of a sinking fund that can be drawn upon during the early phase of education and training, when deferral levels are supposedly at their greatest. Either parental wealth or some institutional subsidy must exist that can sustain the young person during his or her training and early employment. This fund of "domestic capital" and a validated sense of future certainty form the infrastructure of careerism and inspire its requisite optimism and personal morale.

Because it is perpetually in rupture, the occupational world of the lower-class worker exhibits few of these traits. Chronic uncertainty decimates the sense of optimism and psychological certainty so necessary for unimpeded career planning. Instead of being an assemblage of permissive supports, the lower-class microenvironment is a constant source of threat against which protective measures must be taken. By the time a lower-class male reaches his midtwenties, he and his family have learned that occupational disasters have a bewildering array of sources and can seldom be preempted. In fact, the least adaptive strategy imaginable would be one that subordinates immediate success in the job hunt to future possibilities. With the wolf at the door and having few resources upon which to draw, a strategy is needed that maximizes immediate success in the job search and minimizes long periods of unpaid idleness. If the lower-working-class household is to survive, the man must develop talents that enable him to qualify for as many jobs as possible, as quickly as possible. In a world of chronic economic need, almost any job that quickly brings in desperately needed cash, no matter how short-lived or how low paying, is preferable to no job at all. Waiting for the "right job to come along" when you are a member of an industrial reserve army is suicidal. A job that will open up opportunities in two or three years is all but useless when one is two months behind in the rent and bill collectors are banging on the door.

If the person had savings or capital to fall back upon, or a life history in which such withholding had actually paid off, then things might be different. But, then, if the person had sufficient domestic capital to fall back on, or more occupational leverage, he would most likely not be among the superfluous. The immediate need to put food on the table and get out from under the press of unpaid bills allows little breathing room, and no escape from the need to have a job *now*. And once having obtained a job—usually one that is unattractive and just this side of peonage—the man is trapped. He will work at an unattractive job as long as he can since he needs the money. But, ultimately, the time comes when he can no longer tolerate either the work or the boss. He then quits and goes back on the job market. Unemployed once more, he quickly eats up his savings, and the cycle of need, economic panic, groveling to get and keep a job, and the subsequent onset of alienation begins again.

Given these unrelenting pressures, what strategy could best offset this chaos? In Potter Addition, the typical solution is to be what residents call a jack-of-all-trades. In this strategy one accrues a wide range of shallowly developed skills and learns to do a little bit of everything. If this means running the gamut of available unskilled and semiskilled occupations, and passing up specialized training in a field that might later eventuate in a bureaucratic career, then so be it. To specialize means limiting one's occupational options, while the jack-of-all-trades strategy spreads the risk of unemployment across as many jobs as possible.

This jack-of-all-trades orientation carries with it, however, an unanticipated irony. While such a strategy often checks the staggered occupational tempos that threaten to inundate the worker and his family, at the same time it reproduces the occupational foundations of the variable class niche that he and his family occupy. Thus, even as the gambit of a wide-ranging job search succeeds in solving the family's immediate plight, it fails to eliminate the objective foundations of economic bondage. Adaptation, in this case, precludes liberation from the contradictions of the lower-class predicament. Few people in Potter Addition see the darker side of this jack-of-all-trades orientation. One reason for this is that the strategy is rooted in the agrarian ideology that links many Potter Additionites to their premigration past. A great many of the older residents learned their jack-of-all-trades approach to work while on the farm. There farmer and handyman alike had to perform a variety of tasks quickly, and with a minimum of expense (i.e., with "bailing wire or whatever else was lying around"). Even a superficial mastery of a wide range of craft skills often might decide who would and would not stay on the land for another year. This jack-of-all-trades orientation survived the move to town, where the ability of a man to do many things in a passable fashion could mean getting and perhaps keeping a job. In this way, the jack-of-all-trades orientation was doubly validated in Potter Addition: The aura of tradition combined with a newfound adaptive efficacy created a solid countercultural commitment to the jack-of-all-trades worldview.

III. LOWER-CLASS WORK VALUES

Passed on from one generation to the next, the jack-of-all-trades orientation and its values have become the occupational grounding for Potter Addition's culture of poverty. Just as stable occupational niches tend to validate the wisdom of specialization and professionalization in bureaucratic settings, so Potter Addition's variable economic environment authenticates the wisdom of the jack-of-all-trades gambit. As such, it is part of the community's occupational lore and is passed on matter of factly.

The general process has been outlined by Kohn (1969). He notes that working-class fathers judge the performance of their male children in terms of the implications their behavior has for future occupational success. The father, naturally enough, uses standards that he finds useful in attaining success in his own line of work. Such is the case in Potter Addition. As good parents, lower-class fathers prepare their children for success in the only kind of work they know. They pass on their experience to their children and in the process reproduce themselves and the jack-of-all-trades outlook for another generation.

In socializing their children to cope with the life they know best, parents communicate norms and perceptions that are often the inverse of career-oriented values. This means rewarding broad-ranging mechanical skills, physical agility and strength, and a dogged persistence to continue a task despite its estrangement. These are the generalizable personal resources that can be used to meet the challenges of variable life chances. If parents abstractly verbalize professional aspirations for their sons (and they do so constantly), they nonetheless reward them for their physical abilities and mechanical adeptness. Thus, in Potter Addition a passionate commitment to "man's work" lies at the very center of the cultural preferences that make up the lower-class work ethic. In contrast to the routinized performance of professionals, Potter Additionites view day-to-day work and its performance in purely personal and charismatic terms.[2] Job performance for them involves a volatile expenditure of bodily energy and intellectual cunning. It is not defined, as in the case of bureaucratic workers, as a series of measured expert responses applied to administratively limited and standardized problems. The good worker is one who makes do with resources that are immediately at hand, and does so at a moment's notice. He can operate on his own without having to rely on the expertise or cooperation of strangers.

Honest work in Potter Addition is usually defined in terms of manual and physical labor. It is only seldom intellectual. The occupational hero is not the person who excels in manipulating persons, the other-directed leader of a team or a team player, and certainly not a director or a planner. Rather, virtuosity resides in physical strength and the manipulation of objects. The "real man" is capable of epic feats of physical strength and the subtle mechanical dexterity that evolves from a lifelong acquaintance with a job. Occupational heros among the lower class are regarded with awe and are the subject of legendary tales. The folk hero John Henry is prototypical: muscle and heart, endurance and sweat, a quiet self-deprecating master of practical skills.

The only intellectual respected is the engineer, and then only because he represents the convergence of sophisticated mechanical problem-solving *and* its application. White-collar work is the province of women, i.e., secretaries. Men employed in such pursuits are usually regarded as frauds and effetes. University professors are seen as the worst of the lot—hypocritical, arrogant, lacking in common sense and compassion, and either ignorant or insensitive to the needs of common laboring people. The class tension between the two is summed up by a university worker as he discusses his boss—a man with a Ph.D.:

> That's the kind of guy he is. This is one of the types you run into. You should see the swell house he's got and everything. I can tell you of all kinds of types that you work for over there. They want you to work for nothing. He looks at me and thinks: "You're poor, you don't deserve nothing. I'm rich, I earn my money." He'll put in the hours I do, but he won't put out the physical exertion I put out. I don't even think he puts in that much mental strain, come to think of it. He thinks that he is earning his, but that I'm not earning mine.

A third aspect of the jack-of-all-trades counterculture involves the stance that the lower-class worker adopts toward abstract knowledge. Whereas the professional values abstract knowledge for its ability to subsume a broad spectrum of empirical cases under a single principle, the jack-of-all-trades eschews all highfalutin pretense. Instead of building a general system of knowledge from which a family of practical solutions can be analytically deduced, the worker in Potter Addition assumes a *concrete*, materialistic approach to ideas. Generalized knowledge is not half as important as the sudden insight that directly sparks the solution to a pressing problem. The concrete art of a craft, with its cumulative knowledge gleaned from long years of experience, is preferred to the contemplative workings of the intellectual. Each problem is approached on a one-of-a-kind basis. When asked to generalize from a given success to a formal class of explanations, the Potter Additionite feigns ignorance of principles. He parries a request to generalize from the particular event by saying, "I don't know what made that damned thing stop working, and I'm not sure what I did to get it going again, but whatever I did sure as hell worked!" This concrete mapping of knowledge reflects a different mentality than that which operates among the planners and administrators of official public culture. It embodies a radical pragmatism that glories in the particular and the substantive, and refuses to sacrifice the individual event to arid formalisms. It is a materialist logic more at home at the inventor's workbench and on the isolated farm than in the corporate planner's office.

In sum, as far as work is concerned, the Potter Addition man wants a fair wage. The job should involve a task at which he can excel, while the best jobs are those which are self-managed and free from the interference of a boss or foreman. The effervescent, charismatic tenor of work life, the rejection of systematic knowledge as its foundation, the downgrading of occupational specialization, the emphasis on physical prowess, and the valuing of pragmatic effect over rational planning put the work culture of the lower class at eternal odds with the bureaucratic ethos. For these reasons, paths of upward mobility usually preclude movement toward white-collar work, for even if the subject could qualify educationally—which he usually cannot—the lower-class work culture into which he has been socialized would make any long-term assimilation difficult.

If there is a path out of the lower-class world of work, it is through entrepreneurship. Chinoy (1955) and others have documented the blue-collar dream of owning one's own business. The dream of being your own boss, of "doing as you please," and of being independent are at the heart of the factory worker wanting to be a small businessman. There is a deep cultural affinity between the lower-blue-collar world of work and petit bourgeois entrepreneurship.[3] In the world of small business, with its "anarchist," individualist, and highly personalist atmosphere, the lower working class encounters a life-style that is compatible with its jack-of-all-trades orientation. In such cases, social mobility can occur without drastic cultural dislocation, for it is little more than a short *intracultural* movement from one marginal way of life to another. This cultural affinity is illustrated in a story that one resident tells about a small delivery business he started shortly after World War II:

> I always liked working for myself, like in that little delivery business I started after the war. In fact, in the job I work at now I'm practically working for myself, because I don't really have a boss. The guy over me tells me what he wants me to do every morning, and at noon he tells me what he wants me to do in the afternoon, but there's nobody looking over me. As long as I do what he tells me, I can do it however I want to. I don't have no chatter from nobody. It's really a nice job.
>
> But that delivery business was the job I really liked, even though it gave me a lot of trouble. I know when I first started, I didn't make nothing, but after a while it gradually worked up to where more and more people found out about it. See, the stores didn't advertise that we had a delivery business. If people asked, "Do you have anybody that delivers for you," they would say "Yes." They wouldn't come out and say that they had this delivery service, so it took a long time working up the business. It was a prime opportunity, too. There wasn't any delivery business amounting to anything up in town. Most everybody was packing it to their cars or taking it home in a taxi. Business was fine through the week for one man, but come Saturday, I would be delivering to way past midnight. Some people weren't too happy about me coming, knocking at their door come midnight. Of course, they were still waiting for their groceries.
>
> Then the damned old truck would break down on you. At that time, where the Commercial Bank is now, there was a locker business located there. It had cold storage and such. The fellow that operated that little place was Joe Teasdale. I went to him about making deliveries for him, and he said that was fine. He had a truck and did some of it himself. He said he would be better off to have me do it. So we made a deal and I delivered meat for him. There were several times when that old truck of mine broke down and I had to borrow his truck. That darn old clunker of mine was on its last legs. I'd go by and say, "Can I use your truck? Mine broke down." "Sure, there it is, go get it, use it." He never charged me a penny for using it. On top of that, every Saturday evening I had my choice of a cut of meat, whatever I wanted—a little bonus. He was one swell guy, and most all the guys at the stores were pretty darn good. I delivered for Clark's (at that time they were Piggly-Wiggly). I charged twenty-five cents a delivery and they would take a quarter from a customer and put it in a little sack and lay it on top of the groceries. They would write down the name and address so I would know where to take the groceries.

Those Saturdays got me down, though. I didn't have enough help on Saturdays to get stuff delivered on time. But what hurt me most was bad equipment. You couldn't buy a new truck. This was right after the war and you couldn't buy a new truck. You had to buy an old junk and try to keep it running. Through the week you had time to throw away, but come Friday, and especially Saturday, then you had more than one guy could take care of. Then on top of that I got into some trouble with the government. They wanted transportation of property taxes. I had never even heard of it. It's not too much, one percent, but over time it amounted to quite a little bit. By the time I borrowed money and paid the taxes off I was in trouble. I almost always was in debt to some crazy finance company, trying to keep the truck running and such as that, but the back taxes were the last straw. That's when I said, "Well, it's time to get out of this deal." From then on, I drove trucks on construction. I hauled concrete, sand, gravel, cement, plaster, and all kinds of building materials. I finally got on at the university in 1951, and I've worked there ever since.

The path to entrepreneurship often reflects a lingering commitment to a rural way of life. In that the autonomy of the small farmer remains the cultural ideal for many in Potter Addition, entrepreneurship is a compromise path by which one recoups that independence and autonomy. The mythical life of the self-employed seems as close as most will get to the idealized freedom of that now-vanished world.

CHAPTER

5

Labor, Leisure, and Ideology

The people of Potter Addition are committed to giving a fair day's work for a fair day's wage. This is not to say that everyone in all phases of his or her work life is wholeheartedly committed to work. We have seen how young men move from job to job early in their occupational lives as they are socialized into the realities of living on the edge. In time, however, all but a few will reconcile themselves to a life of labor and find jobs that give some small measure of satisfaction. Nor is this to say that over the years the community has not had its fair share of adult slackers. Such persons are usually seen as objects of humor or held in the same contempt that the community reserves for "welfare cheaters."

While these attitudes are common among those who live in Potter Addition, the *meaning* of work is radically different for men and women. For men, work is imbued with issues of self-validation and social esteem. Women, in contrast, have far less invested in their jobs. There are, of course, many working women in Potter Addition: Some wives work to supplement their husband's income; older divorced women are primary breadwinners in their households; and a handful of aging grandmothers work to support themselves, a disabled husband, or a dependent adult daughter and her young children. These women often work grueling hours at physically demanding, low-paying jobs. Despite their pivotal economic role, however, Potter Addition's working women seldom regard their jobs as measures of self-worth. Work for most women is a matter of material survival. If it were not for the money, most would probably not work. There would be little loss of self-esteem, for traditional nurturant identities would more than compensate for any crisis of self-confidence.

The situation is different for men. The credo of giving a fair day's work for a fair day's wage is a point of pride. In Potter Addition, a man's sense of masculinity is irrevocably grounded in the fact that he is a

73

steady worker and the family's breadwinner. It is a poignant fact of lower-class life, however, that the jobs that these men hold seldom command sufficient social esteem. Most men resent this, but can do little to change public culture's evaluation of them and their work. Given this resentment, how does the lower-class male handle the fact that he works at a job that is considered menial by "the better people" of Clay County? How does he neutralize the charge that since he works at a job that is boring, undemanding, and dirty, he himself is lazy, dirty, and devoid of talent? How does he distance himself from the stigma attached to his job?

The answer to these questions is found in Potter Addition's ideological life. In an attempt to counter the stigma attached to them and their jobs, the poor construct subterranean ideologies that can symbolically neutralize the stigma meted out by "their betters." In some instances they create countercultural definitions that defend *both* their jobs and themselves.[1] In other instances, they concede that their jobs are dirty, boring, and unsatisfying, but dissociate themselves personally from the demeaning nature of the dirty work they are forced to do. Here they demand that people differentiate between who one *really* is and what *one has to do for a living*.

The plausibility of these claims and their ability to maintain morale are maximized when the stigmatized have at their disposal a cloistered staging area in which they can act out their counterideologies free from fear of detection and hostile rebuttal. In such sheltered enclaves, protected from the censuring gaze of institutional elites, a complex of well-rehearsed rituals and beliefs can be constructed and acted out that refute the demeaning claims of public culture. Actualized before a sympathetic audience, these subversive definitions form the active basis of a counterculture of poverty. They are often fabricated in the protean work cultures that spring up in modern industrial settings, or in out of the way places where public functionaries seldom intrude.

Potter Addition provides the latter type of setting. It is an ecologically and socially isolated cul de sac that is perfect for acting out subterranean rebuttals to publicly assigned stigma. Its isolation on the fringe provides a safe haven in which to construct scenarios that negate the demeaning judgments that public culture levies against the men of Potter Addition and their community. Moreover, since these debunking rituals and identities are seldom meant for the ears of unsympathetic outsiders, they seldom have an overt political character. Instead, they are designed to play to audiences that have a vested interest in debunking the wisdom of public culture. Thus, their ideological message usually remains sub-rosa and *retreatist* in content.

In this chapter we will explore two such ideological complexes. Both involve social rituals in which Potter Addition's men "play at work" during their leisure hours. In this free play of labor, they display skills and perform tasks before appreciative audiences that give substance to counteridentities and claims of self-worth.

I. LEISURE TIME FARMING

Gardening and animal husbandry are ubiquitous in Potter Addition. When you ask people why they tend a garden or raise animals, they invariably give an economic reason, and, in truth, during hard times, gardening and husbandry put food on the table at relatively cheap prices. Despite such real economic motives, the passion for gardening and livestock raising has symbolic meaning as well. These agrarian pursuits help to form a key aspect of the community's identity: what it means to be Potter Addition. They are used to underscore rural loyalties and identity claims—of proclaiming who they *really* are and where they come from.

An ironic contradiction between local class structure and culture, moreover, gives Potter Addition's agrarian claims an unusual set of ideological possibilities. The first leg of this discontinuity is grounded in the fact that Clay County's rural heritage is revered by farmer and townsperson, rich and poor alike. Even Grand Prairie's urban-bred, economic elites, though seldom having farmed and, indeed, having profited from the serial destruction of the land's producing classes, are caught up in the mystique of Clay County's *agrarian ethos*. This commitment of all classes to a common value complex is complemented by a second anomaly, one embedded in Clay County's system of social stratification. Since most of Potter Addition's residents are descended from families with demonstrable ties to the land, they can, despite their lowly class placement, lay legitimate claim to this agrarian ethos more easily than can Grand Prairie's ruling elites.

When combined, these two realities, one cultural and the other class-based, create a contradiction in the everyday life of Clay County, for access to agrarianism's cultural mystique is inversely distributed throughout the class structure. Because these valued identities cut across class lines, the rural dispossessed and the wealthy farmers of Clay County share a common attribute from which the city's upper classes are excluded. This contradiction forms a rich ideological lode, which Potter Additionites exploit in their unending struggle with Grand Prairie's respectable classes.

Thus, the people of Potter Addition romanticize their rural past and value anything that is "old timey." This can range from the canning of fruits and vegetables and the reading of monthly farm journals, to being up in time to listen to Joe Davis and his "Country Squire Show"—a mixture of country music, "down-home talk," and farm reports from the livestock and grain exchanges in East St. Louis, Chicago, and Kansas City. At the core of this complex is gardening. Available to even the poorest of households, it can be used to express antimodernist discontent and reaffirm the inherited knowledge and traditions of rural America. In the course of discussing gardening, the old-timey practices of the southern hill folk are invariably resurrected. Long dissertations on the superior flavor of sassafras ham, details on sugar curing techniques, the stringing and storing of "shuckey beans," or the preserving of apples and cabbages by burying them are but a few of the subjects that may be brought up in an evening's casual conversation. If the person is old enough, he or she may even speak from firsthand knowledge, having witnessed such things as a youngster. The old-timey ways and the mountaineers who still practice these arcane arts "back in the hollows" are made larger than life in these conversations. Their traditions are treated as folk wisdom that is all the more valid because it is fast disappearing. On occasion head-shaking anger is directed at the modernity that is eradicating the old ways. These rare shows of bitterness decry the disruption of the folk-learning that many had begun "back home," just before they were forced to leave. In each monologue there is a scripted ideological assertion: Potter Additionites are "just down-home folk" honoring a traditional past—not the demoralized dross that public culture claims. These protective claims are little more than empty posturing, however, if one does not own land, for without land and the solidity that comes with being a landowner, even the smallest denial will come to naught. Let us see why this is so.

Above all else, owning even the smallest patch of ground in Potter Addition gives a family the wherewithal to be a member of Potter Addition's ritual community of landowners. This group informally regulates the life of the community. When backed up by decades of residence—the longer one lives in Potter Addition the more one can lay claim to "being Potter Addition"—one can declare rightful citizenship in this local *gemeinschaft of property owners*. Belonging to this *gemeinschaft* (one that excludes transients and all but the longest term of Potter Addition's renters) allows landowning neighbors to relate to one another with a stylized etiquette that regulates community relations.

The link between owning land and being granted the rights of legitimate personage is clearly seen in the mythical camaraderie that is established between landowning neighbors. People in the community often boasted that as late as the 1950s neighbors still walked off boundaries together and established property lines with a handshake. To own land in Potter Addition meant entering an honorable community of social equals in which a few inches or a foot of land one way or the other was not half as important as the trust and goodwill that neighbors ritually enacted on these occasions. These cavalier practices conspicuously displayed to the world that Potter Addition was a rural folk community—not a den of niggling, social outcasts.

This claim, however, had begun to show strains by the 1960s. By the time of my arrival, there had been incidents in which feuding neighbors had resorted to the extreme and costly measure of hiring a surveyor to come out and fix property lines. On these occasions, relations had soured to such an extent that the ruling norm of "speak no evil in public" had often given way to the bitterest of backbiting. Hiring a surveyor, however, was seldom motivated by a concern over a few square feet of land. It was either an act of spite or, more likely, an attempt to restore social recognition of one's civic rights. Whoever called in an outsider to settle an internal issue was almost always seen as being in the wrong and the act was generally regarded as an affront to the entire community. The roots of disapproval resided, no doubt, in the fear that if the community were ever systematically surveyed and realigned, many would suffer serious property loss. But, as with so much else in Potter Addition, more than economics was involved, for displeasure with the party calling in a surveyor also had at its center a vital moral dimension.

This is illustrated in a humorous anecdote concerning two men who had for years shared a common driveway that straddled their adjoining properties. The driveway, some sixty feet long and twelve or so feet wide, permitted each of them vehicular access to the back of his lot. A feud over access to the driveway had been simmering for years, since one man's car or truck parked in the driveway blocked the other's access to the back of his lot. Despite provocations on both sides, each had shown amazing forbearance and had suffered in relative silence. Neither, however, had been that anxious to establish the true boundary line. It had been walked off before either had come to Potter Addition, and both knew its true location was not where it was assumed to be. For fear of finding out, and not wanting to be "chickenshit," each had ruled out surveying. The matter remained dormant until one of them accidentally backed his flatbed truck into the house of the other, badly cracking its concrete block foundation and, according to the house's owner, shifting the frame on its foundation.

This was the last straw. The houses's owner retaliated by hiring a surveyor. Much to his chagrin, the results showed that the property line ran eighteen inches from the south foundation of his house, while the other ten or so feet of driveway belonged to the truck-wielding neigh-bor! The injured party's threat of many years' standing—to build a fence down the *very middle* of the driveway (an act that would have hurt him as much as it would have spited his neighbor)—was now moot. The driver of the truck, on the other hand, let the matter drop, even though he could have—thanks to the neighbor's survey—built his own fence with impunity and had a private driveway to boot!

I believe that there are two reasons why the truck's driver did not build the fence. First, had he done so, he would have violated the system of norms that had already put his neighbor in hot water with the community. Second, he might have very well been shot. If this seems extreme, consider this: His neighbor not only had to repair his damaged house, but short of a lawsuit, had no recourse but to pay for the repairs out of his own pocket. On top of that, he, and not his freewheeling neighbor, was the object of opprobrium for having called in a surveyor. Finally, not only was he out the surveyor's fee, but *because of his own action* he could now lose a driveway to boot. This last ignominy, doubly painful because it was self-inflicted and further compounded by the actual loss of appreciable footage from the "good side" of his property, might well have moved him to violence.

This story was told to me on three different occasions, each time by a different person. The only variation in the narrative was the degree of baroque detail with which the tale was spun, and the differing shades of malicious glee with which it was told. The butt of the tale was always the homeowner who had brought in the surveyor, though obviously a pow-erful brief could have been presented against his neighbor. Of the two, the aggrieved homeowner was seen as being more in the wrong. What made the tale such a juicy piece of gossip, however, was the poetic justice contained in the episode.

Having established the role that land tenure plays in Potter Addition's indigenous status system, let us now turn to the role that land owner-ship plays in Potter Addition's ideological struggles with outsiders. As we have said, if a man owns land he can do more than "just talk a good show" when claiming a nonstigmatic counteridentity—he has the wherewithal to demonstrate his prowess in being, say, a good farmer or stockman. The very act of tending a large and impressive garden, or raising horses or cattle, keeps alive in a nonwork context a symbolic claim that can effectively debunk public culture's stigmatic assessment. While the number of families raising large livestock for their food value had diminished by the 1960s, animals still abounded in the community. A few families still raise an occasional sheep or a couple of head of cattle, but the actual butchering of animals has all but ceased. Horses and ponies are the most common form of livestock and are kept largely for recreational purposes.

Potter Addition's rural heritage is also expressed in other ways. Two or three families, for example, kept hunting dogs. My next-door neighbor, a heavy-equipment operator, owned and proudly displayed a matched pair of purebred Blue Tick hounds. He purchased them for the then extravagant sum of $250. He also kept (well out of sight) two golden ferrets, which he used for rabbit hunting. This form of sport had long been outlawed, yet my neighbor ignored the law, claiming that ferret hunting was part of his Appalachian heritage and that he would keep and use the ferrets as he saw fit.

At times the sacrifices and toil needed to keep livestock year round seemed irrational—even to those who did:

> People keep a cow. They invest more money in that damned cow than they could ever spend buying milk from the dairy, but they'll still keep that cow, and I don't know why. They'll go out there and work and feed it, and by the time they get everything fixed up, they could have got their milk cheaper at the store. Maybe they figure they're gettin' a better type of milk, I don't know. You get that type of people out here. Another type is like Sutton, for example, with his cows, or Ken Smith with those horses that he rents out for rides at the Fair, or Ed Johnson, the beekeeper out here. At one time he had twenty hives of bees. He went through all those other stages of raising cows and pigs and goats, and now he's doing beekeeping—but not so much for profit. If it was me, I would try to raise somethin' and see if I could do it profitably. If I raised bees, for example, and things changed so that I couldn't raise bees profitably anymore, I'd get rid of them and try somethin' else. I'm always lookin' for a certain addition to my income; but everyone ain't that way.

If viewed from a purely dollars-and-cents perspective, raising livestock on only an acre of ground is, indeed, irrational. When seen as a symbolic act, however, as a way of displaying one's commitment to a particular life-style, the investment of time and money in leisure-time gardening and animal husbandry becomes quite rational. They are acts of *conspicuous consumption* designed to legitimate claims to otherwise protean identities.

These ideological functions are especially apparent in the area of livestock trading. Several men in Potter Addition take great pride in being good judges of horseflesh. They regard themselves as even better traders and spend no small part of their discretionary incomes and leisure time pursuing horse trading as an avocation. But as one might imagine, such play has a deadly serious side, for fragile egos are constantly at risk. This ego involvement, not to mention the morally marginal atmosphere that permeates livestock trading, was long ago noted by James West (1945) in his study of Plainville:

There also live in and about Plainville a number of part-time "traders," and several full-time "traders." "Trading" serves in this community three very important functions: (1) It is an important form of barter through which people exchange livestock and other possessions outside the regular commercial system except for cash "boot." (2) It is a sociable male pastime. (3) It provides the most approved channel for male aggression against other males ("nobody ever heard of a woman trader"). (4) It provides for some males a full release, and for nearly all males an occasional release, from the community's sanctions for hard work—the approved "making it the hard way." Many merchants and farmers "trade on the side."

The point of trading is of course "profit," but it is also to "get the best of" or to "outwit" one's trading partner (opponent). The ritual of trading is both long and complicated. Most trades involve lengthy verbal sparring and bantering; disparagement of the partner's goods, and "brags" regarding one's own goods; numerous offers, refusals, and counteroffers; and (often) recountings of "famous" local trades. A man is admired for trading victories, and even for deception of his trading partner, if he has only concealed or evaded reference to flaws in articles offered. Deception must follow rigid rules. To lie directly is to "cheat." (pp. 20–21)

As in Plainville, the intensity of feeling that surrounds trading and the role it plays in affirming one's character is repeatedly played out in Potter Addition. This can be seen most clearly in the horse-trading tales that circulate in the community and the uneven smile that often plays across a man's face as he tells of some legendary trade. As in West's description, the more dubious the exchange or outrageous the ploy used to clinch a deal, the better it serves as a demonstration of the storyteller's prowess.

One such incident actually occurred during my stay in Potter Addition. The storyteller, Linus Collier, had been employed as a carpenter at the university for fifteen years—a job that paid well, but one he hated. He had come from a long line of stockmen and had relatives who still farmed. Even after coming to Potter Addition he had rented acreage and tried his hand at raising grain, hoping someday to return to full-time farming. Occasionally on weekends, he still traveled with his son-in-law to DeSoto, some one hundred and fifty miles to the east, to attend the regional horse auction. Sometimes he would go to buy, at others to sell. On this particular occasion, he had sold a quarter horse and her foal for $255. The mare, to hear him tell it, was so mean that he and only he was horseman enough to ride her. The truth of his boast was soon confirmed by the buyer in a particularly humiliating and painful set of encounters. A week or so after the purchase, the man called and demanded that Linus return the money and take the two horses back. After some heavy bickering and bartering, Linus bought both animals back for $200. Linus, of course, took immense joy in this. The story validated his identity as not only an expert horseman, but as a shrewd trader to boot. His sin of pride was further exacerbated by the fact that he had made $55 off the deal—a killing if there ever was one.

The incident confirmed Linus's sense of worth in a way that his job at the university never could, for all the lines of force in his story pointed to an unspoken affirmation of an essential and unjustly interrupted occupational identity. It does not require too much reading between the lines to see the point of Linus's parable: He is really a stock raiser, and not a carpenter. With a little capital and a couple of breaks, justice may yet triumph; before he dies Linus may yet make it back to being a full-time stockman instead of a well-paid "flunky" serving snobbish professors and snot-nosed kids.

II. THE CAR CULT

Even more than agrarian leisure, the activities of the car cult are a way of acting out alternative occupational identities. As with the agrarian mystique, the car cult expresses a common core of masculine passions that cuts across class lines. Its activities offer Potter Addition's males the kind of social recognition that is at the very heart of Potter Addition's subjective class struggle. The community abounds with shade-tree mechanics: Many men are excellent auto repairmen and there is hardly a man in the community who cannot perform an impressive range of auto repair and maintenance activities. The fascination that many older residents show for automobiles, trucks, and things mechanical started on the land where knowledge of the workings and operating of farm machinery were occupational staples. This love affair with the automobile began at an historically propitious moment, for these people came of age in those decades when gasoline-powered farm machinery was rapidly replacing the horse as a source of power in the rural Midwest. While an interest in things mechanical had always been an integral part of that rural tradition, in the Midwest the inventions that transformed agriculture in the nineteenth century had come spilling out of inventors' workshops and converted barns at such a rapid rate that in great measure the mechanical revolution of the heartland's petty mode of agricultural production was a self-contained process.

Prior to World War II, as the latest wave of mechanization spread like a prairie fire throughout mid-America, Clay County's romance with the automobile and all things mechanical became even more frenzied. Thus arose the fascination with the automobile as a mechanism. The auto was something to be torn down and put back together, and for the young, a means of testing their fledgling manhood. The rural roots of the car cult were noted in passing one afternoon by Carol Thomas, a woman who from time to time half-laughingly—and half-resentfully—sees herself as being abandoned by her husband for a Ford truck of obscure vintage:

> Kevin has always worked on some kind of farm machinery or cars ever since I've known him. I can remember when we used to have an old twenty-eight Chevy. When we got married, we got it, and he'd constantly tinker with that thing. He sold it to Andrew Ridgeman, who owned the store down here. That was the *oddest* looking little car. [laughter] But, he's tinkered with cars ever since. He'd always go over to his brother's, where they would be taking motors out of cars, putting them in, or doing something else to them. . . .
>
> Kevin's got to have something to do, to tinker with, to play around with. Just like Sunday. It was rainy and everything, but he was out working on his truck—putting a new hinge on the door and messing with the motor in the blue Chevy—just anything so he could mess with the truck. I think he spent most of Sunday out there in the garage working on it. Sometimes I think he would put different radios in it, seeing which one was going to play the best. [laughter] Anything he can rig up—that's Kevin!
>
> I think if Kevin thought he was smart enough, he would go into mechanics. I really think so, because he likes to do that kind of work. But there are so many garages now, Dave. If you go in and ask to be a mechanic, you have to know just about everything. You've got to have special training in it. I know my cousin, Norm, gets the car, and if he doesn't know what's wrong, he comes and gets Kevin. Kevin will go up and help him fix it. He knows how to do it, but a lot of places won't hire you now unless you've got some kind of training in it.

Grand Prairie's occupational structure also reinforces the biographical tendencies that people like Kevin Thomas, Sr., have for remaining part of the car cult. Despite the presence of the university (or perhaps because of it), Grand Prairie's division of labor is a curious mix of urban and rural components. Its uneven development is evidenced by a relative lack of industrial and assembly line technologies. Those industrial occupations that might otherwise absorb large numbers of displaced rural proletarians are underrepresented in Grand Prairie. At the same time, much of Grand Prairie's nonuniversity, lower-working-class job slots are located in auto-related, transportation sectors. Thus, there is a disproportionately large number of jobs for drivers in construction and short-distance hauling than might be expected for a town of Grand Prairie's size.

We may gain some sense of how the job market sustains the car cult by looking at the occupational histories of those who have owned land in Potter Addition since its inception. In surveying 172 male job histories for which sufficient time series were available, 64 of 124 property owners (52 percent) were found at one time or another to be gainfully employed in an auto-related activity. By contrast, 37 percent of the 48 absentee owners were so engaged. Of the 64 residents employed in auto-related occupations, 40 (63 percent) were truck drivers; the remainder were garage mechanics and service station attendants (15.6 percent), sanitary haulers (one), operating engineers (two), chauffeurs (two), and automobile salesmen of various stripes (three). Six heads of households worked at more than one of these occupations in their lifetime.

Fully 43 percent of those who drove for a living (truck drivers, chauffeurs, and heavy-equipment operators) did so for more than half of their occupational lives. Furthermore, in examining the actual career phase in which driving for a living occurred, the data show that 32 percent did so during the last half of their gainfully employed years. An additional 35 percent drove for a living intermittently throughout the entire course of their work life. Driving was thus not simply a matter of adolescent wish fulfillment. It was not a fantasy job taken early in life for the fun of it, only to be abandoned in favor of a "more serious" job when family responsibilities increased. For many it was a steady means of livelihood. Caution must, of course, be exercised in interpreting such fragmentary data. Yet, even within the data's limits, this much is clear: Auto-related activities have historically been a major source of gainful employment for Potter Addition households; and, for most, this was a long-standing commitment.

Autos are not consumer status symbols in Potter Addition in the same way they are elsewhere in America. While the new car is coveted by all, and its purchase would be a major event in the life of any household, it is seldom the focus of cult interest in the same way that an old clunker is. The car cult defines the automobile as a mechanism to be renovated, repaired, or cannibalized. A clunker serves as a mirror for reflecting a man's mechanical abilities and trading prowess. It is a material medium through which he can display latent skills that are only seldom elicited at work. This may explain the inordinate passion for wrecks and clunkers. Of course, the prohibitive cost of a new car undoubtedly looms large in shaping the value preferences of car cult members. We should not, however, make too much of this, for the fact remains that the clunker—by absorbing a man's skill and labor—becomes a value-added phenomenon in a way that a new car never can. Rarely a week passes that a clunker does not require some new attention or improvement. With such instrumental rationales ready to justify more work in the driveway, the used truck or automobile is a permanent source of masculine expression, mechanical challenge, and, we might add, momentary, knuckle-busting frustration.

Car repair combines the pragmatics of work with esthetic sensibilities so that what is otherwise hard, physical labor takes on various aspects of play. In a more humorous vein, tinkering with autos and repairing them is also one of the few inviolable refuges a man has from female carping. When bested by his wife in a verbal dispute, in trying to avoid some domestic chore, or in order to escape a noisome visit with in-laws, the man can retreat, unchallenged, under the car hood. Because excuses for such retreats are often framed in a jargon that the wife seldom fathoms, the car cult's web of activities offers men a safe, foolproof haven. Faced with such a gambit, the wife will typically relent, but not without the suspicion that she has been snookered. Because auto mechanics seems to be a purposely mystified domain, the car cult with its exclusively male context is often an object of mild irritation and some good-humored teasing. Much of this doubting and the mocking acceptance of her husband's slick fait accompli is evident in Carol Thomas's description of the car cult's place in her household, and how it turns women into auto-repair widows:

Dave:	I've noticed most of the men out here like to tinker with automobiles. Have you ever noticed that?
Carol:	Yep, [laughter] and don't ask me why, Dave. I don't know. [laughter] Ever since I've known Kevin, in fact before I knew him, he has worked on cars.
Dave:	Where did he pick up the skill?
Carol:	I don't know that either, but I think if he bought a brand-new car, he'd tear it apart. [laughter] At one time I thought I married a car. [laughter] I don't know. He has always tinkered with cars, ever since I can remember, even when we first dated. It's the same way with my brothers; since they have been big enough, they've tinkered with cars. Why? I don't know. Now, just lately, my brother's oldest is starting to tinker with them. Kevin and my younger boy, they are getting so they like to tinker with cars. Why? Again, I don't know. I look at Henry Baker, next door down here; he loves to work on cars. He's constantly tinkering with cars. A lot of times I've asked why. Kevin just says, "I don't know. I just like it." [laughter] But he's always been that way. Look at all the junkers young Kevin brought home— the one he bought yesterday. He was out there at six-thirty this morning working on it, and it still won't start.
Dave:	Do you think it's got something to do with getting a good deal out of something?
Carol:	I don't know, Dave, whether it really is or not. I really don't. I guess they just have to have something to tinker with, so they

go out and tinker with them. That's the only thing I can figure. When it's nice, Kevin's constantly out there tinkering with the cars. He's never in the house. Somebody will come and say, "I need help, will you come and help me?" and there he goes. My oldest brother, a lot of times, will get cars and things. Of course, with him having the garage it's different—it's a business. But Kevin goes up there and tinkers with cars. He used to go to his cousin's, the one who owned the Sinclair Station, and tinker with cars up there.

Kevin used to have people he had never seen or met ask him to fix their cars. Other people would tell them how good Kevin was to work on cars, and they would come and want something done. Sometimes if it was just a minor job, he'd go ahead and do it, but I mean if it was to change a motor or something like that, he would refuse. Because, really, back then, we didn't have a place to do it; our garage wasn't big enough to do that. On the other hand, he did help one guy change a motor out there. They had a *party* changing that car, laughin' and gigglin' and goin' on. It was something "real special," I guess, to go out there and change a motor of a car. I used to get so . . . oh, I'd get so mad! After two or three years, though, it just grew on me. It doesn't even bother me now—*much!* [laughter]

Rivaling auto repair and renovation, a second ritual involves the swapping, buying, and selling of automobiles. Sometimes trading and renovation are combined, as when a man comes by two cars, neither of which runs well. He then cannibalizes them to create a single operating vehicle. For example, a neighbor once boasted that he had got a 1960 Chevrolet for only forty-five dollars. The car came cheap because its transmission was busted. Since he had a car up on blocks with a working transmission that would fit, he bought the car and after a week of work had assembled a "just like new" car. He showed the same hubris my neighbor had shown in his unconscionable horse trade. He had made a deal that was shrewd to the point of thievery. Such coups are the occasion for a well-rehearsed smugness designed to impress the listener, or perhaps to get his goat if the listener is the former owner of a certain 1960 Chevy.

The general rules for trading horses and trading cars are about the same. The same spirit of play and ego enhancement animates both to the extent that the generalization from the horse to the auto, which West noted in Plainville, is equally applicable to Potter Addition:

The "old time trader" was primarily a "horse trader." A trader in land and crops (either harvested or still in the field) was usually called a "speculator." Traders now trade anything—pigs, calves, crops, tools, cars, car parts, and odds and ends accumulated at farm auctions. One trader, speaking of cars, said, "If the gub'ment just didn't make you license them things to run 'em, there'd be more car-traders now than there ever was horse-traders." I asked a country preacher if he "traded much." He said, "Oh, yes. If I hadn't be'n called to preach, I'd 'a' be'n a trader." Trading is included in many a "commercial" transaction. The Plainville Ford dealer said, "I never just sell a car. I have to take in another car, and generally a cow or some pigs or chickens or corn or something. They want to trade." (West 1945, p. 21)

Auto racing is a third complex of car cult activities. Grand Prairie is on the local stock car and "modified" circuit. Beginning in late spring, the county fairground's racetrack, located within easy walking distance of Potter Addition, hosts a variety of races and demolition derbies. The nearness and social accessibility of the track and its culture provide a continuing set of reinforcements for the car cult, and gives it a "good 'ole boy" tone that has come to be identified in popular culture with both the South and the lower Midwest. Races are also held in four other communities within a sixty-mile radius of Grand Prairie. So it is not uncommon for residents to drive north to Farmer City or east to Edwardsville and attend races on nights when the Grand Prairie track is dark.

Equally important in this context is the fact that Potter Addition and its junkyards are a magnet for local racing drivers just breaking into the circuit. Bull Gomes, especially, is sought out for his legendary expertise in matters of repair and rebuilding, and the wealth of spare parts available at his junkyard. Consequently, when some minor cinder track luminary shows up to talk, get a part, or have Bull do specialty work, the area's youngsters gather to see, close up, the man who the weekend before performed so heroically.

A handful of the community's residents have actually raced in their youth and enjoy no small reputation because of it. Upon marriage, however, their wives have usually laid down the law and the danger of racing is traded for a measure of domestic calm. One former race car driver and now a small businessman, has hit on the compromise of sponsoring a stock car. For a modest sum, the retired racer keeps in touch, gets cheap advertising for his business, and gains access to the pit area during the race. The latter carries with it substantial prestige, and may even enable the sponsor to have input into that night's strategy.

Racing is not, however, universally admired in Potter Addition. It is seen by most as a young man's sport, one that requires a little daring and bravery, and a tad bit of craziness to boot. It is, at best, a phase that one goes through but eventually outgrows. An adult might sit in the stands for an evening's entertainment, but any man over thirty who still devotes a serious part of his life to this sport is looked upon somewhat askance. This ambivalence is captured in the following monologue, in which Bull is seen as less of a serious professional, because of his catering to the racing crowd:

> You take some of these guys, they're damn good mechanics, but there they are, fooling around with these junkyards. Why don't they get them a little schooling and get them a job in a good shop? They could really put their knowledge to work. Why don't they? Take Bull down here, he's a damn good mechanic. That's all he does all his life, and that's all he knows. But where does he end up working? In the junkyard. He likes to be in the junkyard—working in the junkyard. That's his nature. If it was me, I'd have myself up here at one of these here places along the highway. I'd own my own building. I'd have my own men working under me. I don't know if he drinks or not; I don't know that much about the man. All I know is that he's a good mechanic and that if he was up on the highway he could really be taking in the money. If he's that good a mechanic, he could get a good job!
>
> I wouldn't be satisfied working down there in the junkyard tearing out those parts. I'd want to work on the very, very best. He doesn't have that ambition. I don't know why he acts this way. I don't know why he don't quit foolin' around with junk. A colored man came into Betty's one day and said, "I used to be in the junk, but I got out of it. I can't make a cent." He said Bull is a good enough mechanic that he could make a lot more than this here nickel and dime stuff. He said, "You can't make nothin' off of some kid driving up and wanting a spark plug. You'll run there in the back and get it and charge him a quarter for it—or something like that. He's losing money—what he's gonna get off that part ain't gonna pay him for his time." Nickel and dime and quarter stuff! Why don't he just stay in the mechanic business? That's what he advertised when he came into the community. He advertised he was gonna be a garage mechanic, and as good a man as he is at that work, I believe he could do better if he would concentrate on that. But he's one of these type of people that loves to surround himself with junk for one reason or another.

Despite occasional adult ambivalences, the children of Potter Addition are entranced by the racing mystique. Even before a boy is recruited by his father to help in repairing and rebuilding autos, his peer group oversees his initiation into the car cult. Not only do children hang out at the junkyards to watch for and on occasion see a celebrity, they also integrate the racing world of stock cars into their play life. A play group will, for example, disappear from the streets for the better part of a summer day, only to emerge with a "racer" they have just built. Such race carts are usually built from cast-off two-by-fours, with wheels garnered from defunct wagons, baby carriages, or an occasional bicycle. The racers are usually propelled by a second child pushing the cart with a long two-by-four, a discarded rake or hoe handle, or an old broom. The carts ape in their construction the stock cars they are meant to represent: Front axles are longer than the back ones, and the front wheels are often swiveled and splay outward.

Once built, the carts are raced on lower Potter Avenue since it sits on the steepest slope in the community. The races are a mixture of preteen fantasy and documentary reality. On occasion, "crash helmets" are worn and racing flags manufactured. One boy went so far as to make a set of green, yellow, and checkered flags with which to act out the role of starter. Replete with a stand for holding the flags, he ran the race, working the flags with the same mechanical movements and stiff, stylized postures he had seen used by the starter at the fairgrounds.

Real life is further imitated when a child assumes the identity of a driver who is currently burning up the local tracks. Paralleling the adult reality they see and reproduce, the personal conflicts that often occur are sometimes settled with grudge races. And, as in that other world of racing, the race's outcome may not fully resolve the issue in question. On those rare occasions, a bloodied nose or bloused eye is needed to restore one's damaged honor. Since it is not unknown for ten or fifteen children to witness and take their turns in these races, such fights, ringed by a tight knot of onlookers, are not difficult to spot, and invariably draw the attention of an adult some twenty seconds or so after the decisive blow is landed.

A final source of commitment to the car cult originates in the fact that the repair work of the shade tree mechanic comes close to epitomizing the lower-class occupational ideal. Leisure-time auto repair places a premium on both strength and manual dexterity. Working under the hood entails a craftlike, personalized relation between oneself and the object being repaired. It often allows for a charismatic display of mechanical virtuosity. Thus, the remark "Nobody knows Fords like Robbie Taylor" is not an uncommon assessment in Potter Addition. Robbie's gift is easily tested and seldom open to extended debate. Either the car that no one else could fix runs after he labors over it, or it doesn't. No amount of verbal fog can ever change that fact.

Shade tree diagnostics also rewards those who can make do with what is at hand. When someone says, "That thing is being held together with spit and bailing wire," several implicit judgments are being made. There is the feigned disbelief and joking disapproval of the Rube Goldberg improvisations themselves. Along with the feigned disapproval and head shaking, there is also a grudging admiration for the radical pragmatism that has assembled a bizarre combination of parts and materials to create a more or less functioning whole.

The particularistic approach to knowledge employed in the lower-class occupational ideal is equally at home in the car cult. The fact that two different makes of car are seldom comparable and that no two cars, even of the same year and make, run exactly the same is constantly underscored by persons involved in car talk. These differences are often mythologized with a claim that every car has its own personality, and that when it comes to auto repair, no amount of educated theorizing or abstract speculation can substitute for the kind of practical knowledge that comes only from "the school of hard knocks." There is a refusal, moreover, to generalize one's knowledge; instead, particular elements of folk wisdom coalesce to form a growing body of nongeneralizable knowledge.

Such is the structure of discourse that regulates the car cult's activities: It consists of a multitude of piecemeal facts linked in a series of particularistic chains. Each link is an exception to what "the manual says." Like the secrets of a guild, transmitted in actual practice as the occasion requires, this knowledge of particulars, integrated by a materialist logic, is an offense to the abstract, formal bent of the scientific mind. Yet it is knowledge that works, whereas (as I was told repeatedly) "going by the book" meant having a car that was little more than a permanent driveway adornment. Not going by the manual and outdoing the "smart guys with college degrees" was in itself a shadowy triumph over institutionally endorsed knowledge.

Finally, the freedom from supervisory authority and the camaraderie of work that is so much a lower-class requirement gains its apotheosis in shade tree diagnostics. Under the hood you are your own boss—free from anyone telling you what to do. You do your work when you please, how you please, and at a pace you set yourself. Friends and neighbors are free to come and watch as long as they stay out of the way or do not break your concentration.

III. THE SUBJECTIVE REPRODUCTION OF MALE MORALE

The car cult and agrarian leisure rituals allow Potter Additionites to construct from the cultural materials at hand alternative, ego-enhancing images of self and work. These dissenting images can neutralize the ideological stigmata that public culture appends to poor people and their dirty jobs. Designed for other members of the lower-class peer group, this debunking imagery is seldom meant to be heard outside Potter Addition. Because these images are not openly confrontational, they cannot qualify as fully developed forms of class consciousness.[2] Instead, they are the largely defensive identities of a politically weak and mar-

ginal class. Such debunking is best used to finesse those powerful institutional forces that daily try to cast the poor in the role of degenerate
lumpen proletarians.

The implicit counterclaims lodged in the activities of the car cult and
leisure-time farming are, therefore, instruments for maintaining a fragile
morale. Since they are half real and half fantasy constructions, they are
not the stuff from which aggressive class-based demands are to be
made. In fact, the construction of alternative identities is not unlike
other processes that we have thus far witnessed. We have seen a similar
parrying of public standards in the construction of *bricoleur* housing and
in the formation of occupational ideologies. We will encounter throughout this volume similar subterranean gambits. They are protests designed to elude the spirit of hegemonic conventions, while avoiding the
wrath of the local powers that be. In each case we will witness a pow-
erless class contesting local customs *without directly challenging* public
culture's gatekeepers. Similar to the "murmuring" of the peasantry or
the sub rosa rebellion of the "dangerous classes," Potter Addition's
protean subculture is filled with muted dissent. Such dissents are the
nascent protests of a proud population caught on the edge between
rebellion and conformity. On the one hand, the people of Potter Addition want to be accepted by the parent community. Perhaps having
always been on the edge of respectability, even when they were living
on the land or in rural hamlets, Potter Additionites appropriate the
revered symbols of heartland culture and use them to legitimate their
dissenting identities and counterclaims. In creating these shadowy
ploys, they work the interstices of local culture, mine the discontinuities
and social contradictions that structure the parent culture itself, defend
themselves as best they can, and seek public acceptance whenever it is
offered.

On the other hand, because they are excluded from full and legitimate
access to institutional participation by "their betters," Potter Additionites are potential recruits for political insurgency. The subterranean subculture of parallel, debunking definitions and meanings may in the right
circumstances become the seedbed of class-conscious social action. The
people of Potter Addition often seem to be waiting for a chance to
translate their own parochial rebuttals into a more universal language of
militant class awareness. There were in fact brief moments in the 1960s
when the radicalism of that period seemed to strike a resonant chord
with Potter Addition's slumbering populism. But neither an unfettered
acceptance of public culture nor overt political insurgency has carried
the day. Instead, the counterdefinitions of self and community can only
deflect the immediate, negative consequences of stigma. The car cult
and leisure farming have effectively forestalled individual demoraliza-

tion and allowed Potter Addition's poor to cope with the imposed regimen to which Clay County subjects its poor. At the same time, the very success of subterranean resistance has become an essential elements of the bitter reproductive dialectic by which local capital periodically renews itself.

6

Saving and Spending

The people of Potter Addition live lives of radical uncertainty due to their economic superfluity and cultural marginality. This uncertainty is most obvious in the everyday world of consumption and the means people use to survive. When it comes to making a living, Potter Additionites have two alternatives: They can either compete as if they were on an equal footing with members of other classes, play the standard commodity game, and risk going under; or they can forge alternative economic forms that deviate from the accepted market principles. Faced with this double bind, they end up playing both sides of the street. Whenever possible, they enter local commodity and labor markets and compete as best they can. But when the market fails to provide life's necessities, they turn to traditional cultural indulgences or find other ways to survive.

This chapter will describe how Potter Addition secures its everyday material existence. It begins with a discussion of the general consumption strategies that Potter Addition's poor employ in their material struggles. It will show that while these strategies enable the lower class to survive on a daily basis, they also play an unintended role in the region's political economy. Within the domain of lower-class life they help reproduce the market system of Clay County and Grand Prairie. The chapter closes with a discussion of some of the everyday strategies that Potter Additionites use to stabilize their chaotic class niche.

I. VARIABLE ENVIRONMENTS AND THE ECONOMIC CONSERVATISM OF THE POOR

If it were not for variable economic environments, the most rational consumption strategy would follow a worst case scenario. One would

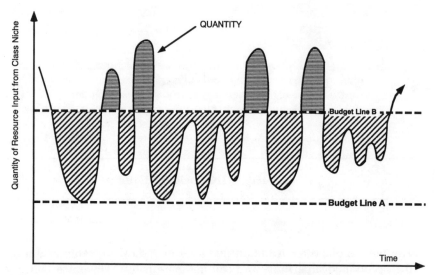

Figure 6.1. Consumption schematic for lower-class households.

make a conservative estimate concerning the rate and amount of resources that his or her niche would make available at any given point in time, and no matter how much cash or other resources were made available, a person would only engage, *ideally at least*, in subsistence expenditures. No greater future input would be planned for than the minimum amount dictated by past experience. In plotting this austere economic course, the person would take into account not just available cash, but also potential credit and the social welfare wages at his or her disposal. Because future resource input would be perceived as being uncertain, every dollar spent would be treated as if it were the last dollar the person had in his or her possession. The person would refrain from making any expenditure that was not deemed absolutely necessary, for any higher propensity to consume would invite disaster.

This hypothetical level of household expenditure, as well as one that posits expenditures above that minimum, is illustrated in Figure 6.1. The lower horizontal line (A) represents a conservative, subsistence budget, while the upper line (B) depicts a higher, nonadaptive level of household expenditures.[1] The aperiodic curve with its irregular peaks and valleys depicts the hypothetical levels of resource input that characterize the lower-class niche. The hatched areas below expenditure line B represent periods of crisis in which spending exceeds available resources. The shaded areas above the line represent "surpluses" in the household budget.

We can see from the illustration that Budget Line B exposes the household to a series of inevitable crises. These crises cannot be predicted because of the aperiodic fluctuations of resources. Nor can they be dealt with within the constraints of the second budget line, for Line B represents a *maximum* level of available assets and an exhausted credit line. Unless extra-market resources can be tapped, any time the curve dips below the line, economic crisis is imminent. By contrast, budget line A represents a Spartan existence that few in a society that doles out status and esteem on the basis of consumption would be prepared to accept. As such, it is far more a typification of the Malthusian ideal than a description of actual conduct.

This combination of scarce resources and future economic uncertainty often breeds timidity among many Potter Additionites. Having little faith in the future, since the past has been little more than a running string of disasters, there is a fixation upon preserving the hard-won fruits of past accumulations. The following is the account of a man who has spent much of his life in the direst of poverty and who has only recently seen things take a turn for the better. His account of an economic plunger's aggressive conduct and his pejorative portrayal of his own, more sane economic philosophy underscores how chronic uncertainty often breeds an obsessive caution among its victims:

A lot of people out here live in shacks, but they're paid for. A man in town lives on a higher scale of life and he's in debt "up to here." He don't know where he's going to get his next payment. Some of them guys turn out rich, and some of them fall on their face. This Norton that run Norton Electric down in Grand Prairie, he's dead now, but he lived through World War I and he told me this story. He said that he owed so much money at one time that he didn't even know where he was going to get the money to pay the *interest* on what he owed. He didn't worry about paying friends off. All he worried about was paying interest. He died a wealthy man! Me, I can't do this. I can't risk the little bit I've got against making myself a fortune. When World War I came, before the prices raised, he studied this in his mind. He's not a real highly educated man, but he went down and started buying property at prewar prices. He saw this war coming on. He saw this at the beginning when Germany started raising hell. He figured, "If I lose it all, I ain't losing nothing because I ain't got nothing to start with." He went down and he borrowed and borrowed, and once in a while he'd pay on the principal—if he had it. Sometimes he even wondered how he was going to make interest payments. Here is what he was doing: If he bought this property, he rented it out; then he took this rent money and instead of paying on the property that he bought, he would buy another piece of property. He had so much God-damned debt! But he said, "I could sleep at night. I could go to bed and sleep at night. I didn't worry about it." But me, I couldn't—I'd be up all night! "My God, how am I going to make these payments?" I can't do this, but he did.

I don't want to risk this house to get five more houses. I'll keep this one free and clear. I won't mortgage it to go and get another house, but a lot of people will. They'd have their house free and clear, mortgage it, and take the money and go and buy another place. They'd get rent off of that to pay this mortgage. But I can't do this. I want something I can call my own. This is it! This little patch of ground! It's important! I ain't going to go down there and put my neck in a noose, and let some businessman pull it shut on me and lose everything. This house here don't have no mortgage on it. I don't owe anything on it. It was built by my own hands. I feel freer than if I lived over in Bellefountain Acres and knew I was going to die of old age before I got it paid off. That would be a burden on me and mine.

Now one fellow I know actually lives over in Bellefountain. He's got the same income I've got. He's indebted for the rest of his life. He's in his fifties. He never expects to live to pay that house off. That doesn't worry him. He treats the payments just like rent. He puts himself on contract and he lives a little better. He's got a little better house—no, a much better house! But yet, what has he got? He's got payments for the rest of his life. Now this fella, it doesn't bother him. He thinks, "Well, I've got a house and I'll live in this house until I die and I don't care what happens to it."

Me, I'm different. I don't want to live in this house and have these payments over me. I think about what if a depression hit? What if I should die first and my wife couldn't make these payments, where'd she be? I got this way of looking at things. See, there's different psychologies; different people look at different things in different ways. I think, "Well, my wife couldn't work and make as much money as I do. She can't pay this house off. She'd have to go back to living poorly—and this happens." I talked to an insurance man. You'd be surprised how much this happens. A man will buy this house, but his wife will know no more about his business than his neighbor will. The man's driving a nice car, a late model car, and making payments on it. He's living in a nice house and making payments on that. What he *actually owns* and what he can say is *actually his* is very damned little. He's wearing business suits and he's making payments on them. His wife is living in a modern kitchen that's got all the latest gadgets. Yet he's doing all this through debt. If you look at him and you look at me, you see two different personalities. He's doing it all in debt. His wife would probably look down on my wife and me. She'd say, "Well, look where they live. They live in Potter Addition. They don't have such a fine house. We've got more room. We've got bigger rooms. We've got better furniture, and ours was carpenter built; it ain't self-styled." But what happens? The guy falls over dead of a heart attack. He's working extra hard to keep all these payments up. Then what does his wife have? They tie up the car—it's not paid for—and they tie up the house. They tie up everything! Where do you find her at? She has to move into a small apartment and do her own cooking and go out and get herself a job. She ain't got nothing. She's worse off then than my wife. But when he was alive, you would have sworn to God that he was making five times more than I'm making. He's not thinking of the future. He's not thinking of his wife's security. If this woman would meet my wife on the street, she'd snub her. She'd say, "Well, that's Potter Addition." Me, I got to pay so much out in insurance every month. What am I getting for it? Actually, nothing. It's something for the future, in case I die. I was the same way with my mother. I carried an insurance policy as well as putting money in the bank. Because if I should die, my mother would have been in bad shape. I transferred this all in my wife's name now. I'm thinking if something happens to me it would give her a new start.

Concern with the future and its dangers belies the claims conservative social scientists make about the poor's supposed lack of future orientation and their inability to defer gratification.[2] Lack of discipline, an inability to plan for the future, and the improvident conduct that flows from character defects, we are told, are at the core of every culture of poverty. As the above monologue suggests, however, these explanations are quite wide of the mark. Potter Addition's poor, in point of fact, do practice self-restraint. They save, and are, as with this man, very much future oriented. They attend to the future as much as anyone—they just do not count on it. The lower-class person learns from his or her experience and plans for a future that will deal its worst blow when least expected.

In truth, most families in Potter Addition try to save. It is usually to no avail, however, for variable environments make the act of saving a Sisyphean task. During my fieldwork I heard the same lament over and over again. A woman would be saving money for a down payment on a house, a car, or some major appliance when a capricious move from "out there" would swallow up her small nest egg. Attributing her loss to a powerful animus, she would often feel a sense of bewilderment at being overwhelmed by forces beyond her control, not unlike that experienced by the victims of natural disasters. There would also be a deep anger at having worked so long and hard for something, only to be deprived of it at the last moment by a doctor, hospital, grasping landlord, or some other "perverse force."

On occasion, saving for the future is seen as an act of hubris which eventually invites "punishment." This kind of feeling was often voiced in Potter Addition. Speaking of their loss as a "retaliation," people often used the half-joking manner that sometimes masks an unapproved or embarrassing mystical belief. At those moments, saving was seen as the *cause* of "nature's striking back." The sudden unexpected loss was viewed as an act of poetic retribution, brought on by the arrogance of the victim for wanting to be something he or she was never meant to be.

Sociologists often take such fatalistic accounts as signs of social anomie (Merton 1968, pp. 201–204). The use of such accounts to explain misfortune indicates that the person employing them lacks a *structural interpretation* with which to understand the misfortune. Such interpretations are thus little more than self-inflicted degradations that absolve the system at the expense of the victim. Such "superstitious accounts" should not be written off as defective mental sets; nor should they seduce us into blaming the victim. It is far too easy to talk of "animistic thinking," treat it as a sign of backwardness, and then interpret the symptom as if it were the cause of the misery itself. Such inverted folk explanations should be taken for what they are—limited ideologies that shroud the social origins of one's own powerlessness in individualistic accounts. They are reified explanations that for all their darkness and despair give the victim a measure of perverse comfort.

Looking past the self-accusatory accounts of the poor, we can better understand the fate of household savings in Potter Addition if we treat their loss as but one more consequence of living in a chaotic class niche. The conservative premise alleging lack of impulse control is particularly misplaced. Jan Newton (1977) is closer to the truth when she asserts that the poor are as rational and self-disciplined within their class context as is any professional or white-collar drudge. What separates savers from nonsavers is not a relative capacity to defer gratification, but the power to control the moves that emanate from their class niche.

Some people in Potter Addition are actually aware of how their uncertain niche and its pandemic crises create an overly cautious and fearful attitude. In the following monologue, the man who earlier discussed securing the here and now weighs the wisdom of using his hard-earned money as investment capital:

> Who's secure? You can go to a doctor now and he can take your whole life savings on one little thing—cutting out one little part of your body. You know there ain't that much damned work to that. If he spends all day cutting out one piece, he's only done a day's work, but he can charge you thousands of dollars. You can be poor, you can think of yourself as being safe, but when you get older they can take it all away from you. Take this guy who just died, the one I was telling you about, the guy who owned all of those apartments in Grand Prairie. He left a hell of a lot of money to his heirs. Just think of having enough money to pay forty thousand dollars for a piece of property and having to go into debt to put a big apartment building on it. I can't conceive it in my mind. I can conceive that there's somebody in this world that's got that much money, but if I had forty thousand dollars, I'd throw it in the bank. He evidently has got more than forty thousand dollars, because once he buys the place, he's got all this construction cost. A man with that much money should just throw it in the bank and take the interest and live off of it, not be fooling around and worrying about putting up a big apartment building. Why worry about stuff like mortgages and building costs?

Given the recognition that one cannot stabilize one's life world, economic rationality lies in protecting what one already has, not in risking hard-won surpluses. In the above quote, we hear voiced the poor man's eternal fantasy of throwing a large sum of money in the bank, kicking back, and living off the interest. But even in this fantasy, there is less commitment to capital accumulation than a desire to have a safe hedge against material fears and uncertainty.

II. VARIABLE ENVIRONMENTS AND "NIGGER-RICH" LIFE-STYLES

A second strategy for coping with economic uncertainty inverts the logic of this Malthusian gambit. This strategy advocates something akin to an inflationary psychology, instead of frugally accumulating and perpetually protecting what little one has from a capricious environment. Since one has no certain knowledge or faith as to what the future holds, this strategy advises "spending it while you've got it." It is preferable to spend what little you have now, than to save and be forced to surrender your hard-won "capital" to another later on. Any money you spend now, you benefit from; any money you save, you are saving so that someone else can confiscate it. In terms of self-interest, spending as much money as you have as quickly as you can is one of the few ways of dealing with an insane economic environment over which you have little control. It is, of course, true that when bad times come again there will be no savings to fall back on. It is equally true, however, that you have seen hard times before—seen them and somehow survived. Given these contingencies, the most reasonable tactic is to treat all available income as though it were that fabled last marginal dollar—as if it were, no matter how large the sum, a subsistence amount. The poor know that in their niche future uncertainty is the rule, and that they must respond to the here and now. In a life space wracked by continuous shock and rupture, deferred gratification and saving is preferred only by those who revel in their own victimization.

When faced with general inflation, the so-called hidden thief, middle-class persons engage in similar "spendthrift" behavior. In both cases the rational response to an uncertain future is the same. Social scientists and economists reluctantly judge them to be correct in this low-saving, spend now conduct. Such conduct is sympathetically interpreted as a rational-but-regrettable action that will benefit the individual, even as it worsens the overall economy. While they technically demur it, social scientists concede the wisdom of the bourgeoisie's nonsaving and may even admire the egoistic ruthlessness entailed in this act of enlightened self-interest.

The same conduct, however, is sneered at when practiced by the poor. It is labeled "immediate gratification" and seen as a mark of improvidence, if not outright moral degeneracy. The seamy underside of American folk culture has even coined a term for such conduct. When a poor person engages in such spendthrift conduct, he or she is acting "nigger rich." To spend all you have, to live for the moment and ignore the future, to live beyond your class-allotted means (the real crime for which the poor must ultimately be held to account), only to sink back into poverty at the next instance, that is the essence of *undisciplined self-indulgence*—of being nigger rich. But it is *only* nigger rich conduct if it is engaged in by the lower classes. When was the last time we heard a respectable bourgeois reacting to double-digit inflation so labeled?

We should not be surprised or shocked by the term *nigger rich*. This is simply another case in which the self-satisfied classes have hegemonically transformed their sacred in-group virtue into a poor person's system-threatening out-group vice.[3] In a society long accustomed to viewing class through racist lenses or ethnic stereotypes, the term *nigger rich* appalls us with its visceral frankness, even as it reveals the self-delusions of the speaker. Its contradictory semiotics instruct us, even as they obscure a reality that must not be confronted if the delicate taste and conscience of "good" people are to be preserved.

The term has the genius of obscuring the uncomfortable commonalities in conduct and logic between those at the top and bottom of society when both are confronted with economic uncertainty. It deprecates alternative values and class-based rationalities and obscures from view the incipient class struggle that perpetually threatens to engulf us. If social order is to be maintained, at no time can class-based explanations be honored in the popular consciousness, nor can they be used to account for the disparities between rich and poor. Such differences are best explained in terms of individual, racial, or ethnic differences.

Nigger-rich conduct, then, is the rational conduct not of blacks, but of the poor generally—those who know that in their particular, terror-filled niche there is no sure tomorrow. In a social universe ruled by chaos, rupture, and shock, nigger-rich expenditures and their cautious counterparts are equally sound solutions. Paradoxically, future uncertainty elicits diametrically opposed strategies: one is timid and defensive in tone and verges on a hoarding mentality; the other, outwardly profligate and freewheeling, springs from an equally well founded distrust of what the future holds. Both posit living on the edge, but never beyond it.

III. MINING THE INTERSTICES

In a life chronically short of cash, any activity that allows a person to evade the cash nexus is a valuable asset. This is especially the case in

Potter Addition, where growing and canning one's own food is a common practice. The community's fringe location and large lots make it a natural space for such money-saving activities. Thus, a great many families plant vegetable gardens on a regular basis, and, in the past, several raised and butchered their own meat. The gardens in the community vary in size from small forty-by-forty-foot plots to areas a quarter of an acre in size. My landlord, for example, planted one of the largest gardens in the area. He grew potatoes, corn, radishes, tomatoes, lettuce, cabbage, pole beans, squash, cucumbers, and melons. He did, however, take his gardening more seriously than most. He had even invested in a gas-driven tiller. Most families used forks or spades to break the ground in the spring. On occasion, a friend with a small tractor and plow might save a family a day's work by breaking the ground for them.

The planting and tending of a garden are largely solitary activities, something best done alone, at one's leisure. Harvesting, however, is another story, for in Potter Addition, as elsewhere, it is a pretext for getting together with friends and kin. Early fall sets off a round of visits in which brown grocery sacks brimming with ready-to-eat fruit and vegetables are exchanged and people settle in for an evening of coffee and conversation. Canning is another seasonal pretext for mothers and daughters to visit, and, at times, entire sibling groups gather to can food for the winter. During such gatherings, family recipes and the folklore of food preservation pass from one generation to the next.

As important as the ritual aspects. of gardening and canning are, most people see gardening as a hedge against hard winters and the stop-and-start cash flows that accompany them. Hence, as one woman told me:

> A lot of people gripe at me because I can. They think it's old-fashioned. It might be old-fashioned, but by God, many times I'm thankful that I can. Because that's what me and the kids live off of. But me, I like to can, so I guess that makes a difference too. My family loves to eat my canning; last night I opened up some peaches—the first thing I've opened since I canned this year. Oh! Two quarts didn't even make a smell. They were gone, just like that! My husband thought, by God, he had died and was in heaven. I always have canned, ever since I've been married. First year I was married I canned. A lot of people think it's terrible and that it's a waste of time, but really and truly it isn't. It gives me something to do, and later I can sit back and eat when everybody else starves. [laughter]

In this passage we get a feel for the ego-enhancing role that gardening and canning play in affirming the woman's traditional sense of self and family. We hear the pleasure she takes in her family's polishing off two jars of peaches, as well as the echo of past poverties. The tongue-in-cheek comfort she takes in knowing that she may yet have the last laugh when it comes to her gardening and canning is her way of dispelling the pain of past bouts with hard times, as well as a fear of their sudden return.

Potter Addition's fringe location has other economic advantages as well. For example, as late as the mid-1960s its land values and property taxes are low enough that even the poor can afford a piece of the American dream. Scraping up the cash to pay one more year's property taxes on even this little-valued land, however, requires year-long sacrifices and finagling. At the same time, buying land at low prices would be seen as self-defeating if its value were to be assessed at ever higher annual rates. There is thus a veritable obsession in Potter Addition with resisting general tax hikes and communitywide "improvements." Any move toward village incorporation is similarly scotched for fear that a village board, once elected, will get "power crazy" and start voting in "frills" and other dubious "improvements" that residents cannot afford.

Underscoring this latter anxiety, rumors periodically sweep the area that dark forces in Grand Prairie are plotting to incorporate Potter Addition into the city. Such stories invariably stir up a hornet's nest of fear as people feel the American dream shifting beneath their feet. Sometimes these fears evoke curious inversions of conventional thinking. Thus, a woman patiently explained to me one evening why the clutter and eyesore of Bull Gomes's junkyard was not all bad. If, she argued, the junkyards were cleaned up, the area would become attractive; if the community started looking nice, a better class of people would start moving in and begin "improving the area," thus bidding up property values; if this happened, the poor people of Potter Addition could no longer afford to pay their property taxes; this would cause a diaspora as Potter Additionites moved to other low-income areas, hence breaking up her community. Furthermore, those promoting development were "not really Potter Addition." They were not interested in staying and building up the community to make it better. They were, instead, traitors who merely wanted to raise land values so they could make a real estate killing and go live in suburbia.

If this logic seems a bit strange, many residents nonetheless endorsed it as a practical guide for everyday conduct. For example, one man living on North Star Avenue explained why he never painted or fixed the outside of his house. He reasoned, in the best tradition of the poor-mouthing farmer who never paints his barn, that improving the looks of one's property would only result in catching the county assessor's eye. Using the most pristine of neoclassical calculations, he had long ago concluded that surface esthetics were a poor trade-off for higher taxes. It was thus far more reasonable to live in a sound house, let it *appear* to be a dump, and take the difference between the taxes that he paid and those he might have to pay on improved property and spend it on his wife.

Another man ran his business in the same way this person kept his house, and for the same reasons. He had originally opened a junkyard with his son. The son had managed the yard full-time, while the father worked at his usual job and helped the son on weekends. When the son died in an auto crash, the father shut down the yard. The office was now dark and the sign was taken down, but on weekends he still cut up autos for junk and cannibalized cars for their parts. In this way, however, the business licenses, renewal fees, taxes, etc. were avoided. He continued to do a word-of-mouth business in which customers sought him out at his home. He estimated an annual savings of nine hundred dollars through this under-the-table arrangement. Again, the conscious projection of a worst possible image was used to avoid what was considered a senseless and confiscatory set of taxes.[4]

A third working of institutional interstices involves the eternal search for deals. Women especially show amazing resourcefulness when it comes to ferreting out bargains. They are denizens of cut-rate retail outlets, dime store sales, secondhand shops, the Salvation Army, the Catholic thrift store, garage sales, and rummage events. There is a spirited competition in all this, if not a certain teeth-grinding tautness, as women search for a "just-like-new" blouse, toaster, television set, or used piece of furniture. Bargain hunting is a major female recreation, and, as with so many other economic activities, its ritualistic aspects validate the woman's economic prowess. Sometimes, the ritual moment of getting a deal overshadows the actual exchange value of the object. Periodically, the competition to see who can get the best deal at a rummage sale becomes so intense that egos are bruised and minor, short-term rifts between friends are precipitated.

The material result of this spirited recreation is that much, *but by no means all*, of Potter Addition's material culture seems secondhand. As with the exteriors of their homes, and so with many of their interiors, the community's material culture is to some degree a collection of used clothes, used cars, used appliances, and used furniture. In their mining of Grand Prairie's physical tailings, lower-class families ground much of their material life in the cast-off remnants of other classes. Like those niches in the biotic web that reduce dead organic matter to inorganic substances, Potter Addition is the last stage in Clay County's "commodity metabolism." It stands between the ongoing material culture of Grand Prairie and the refuse heap. Once having said this, we must not get too carried away, for the women of Potter Addition do not tote home junk. They are too proud and too wily to be ragpickers. What they bring back is by any measure "good stuff." The bargains they get are in truth "real deals." Their families live better because of their efforts and in the process they surrender relatively small amounts of scarce cash to get comparatively new items.

Finally, there is what is now called "the underground economy." Once again the jack-of-all-trades complex enters the picture, for the same broad-ranging skills that maximize employment chances also give the average male the ability to perform a wide range of do-it-yourself activities, such as auto repairs, housing and appliance repairs, and home building projects. In each instance, these do-it-yourself projects conserve scarce cash. Moreover, if one cannot perform some task, a relative or friend can be asked for advice or help. As one informant proudly told me:

> We can do just about anything out here in Potter Addition. We're a jack-of-all-trades and the master of none. If you can't do it, you can ask one of your neighbors, and he's going to tell you how to do it.

In this way the community serves its residents as a collective pool of diverse knowledge and skills from which each family draws, and to which each contributes.

While labor bartering and do-it-yourself activities decrease reliance upon the cash nexus, they also have a second, unanticipated consequence. The exchange of labor services and skills, as well as the borrowing of tools and other paraphernalia, creates intricate webs of reciprocity between various kinsmen, sex-specific sodalities, and peer groups. A typical set of complementarities and the solidary set of social relations they engender is revealed as a long-time resident talks about labor exchanges within his peer group:

> Just like me and Eddie. Anything I need help with, I can go to him and ask him, and he's willing to help. It's the same way with me. If Eddie comes and asks me to do wiring work, I do it. Just like he was down there helping me put up trim today. All I have to say is that I need some help, and he's right there to help me. The same way with him if he needs help. All he has to say is "Woody, I need help," and I'm right there to help him. Just like yesterday when I went to put up that sign. I said, "Eddie, our sign is shot and I've got to put up a new one on Saturday." He said, "I'll be down to help you." We just hang together and always have. Just like if I wanted Roy Brewster to help me, old Roy would be right there.
>
> Here's another example of what I mean. Most of us out here have all built our own homes. I've built three of them myself. Eddie built that one of his and then Ken, his brother-in-law, built the house on the west side of Eddie's. We all helped Ken build that one. We all worked together.

Eddie knew carpenter work, and I did electrical work up at the university. Ken worked up in the lumberyard for ten years and got to be a pretty good mill hand. Heck, we all go together and can just about do anything we want to do. That's the reason why we all hang together, and if one guy needs something they all chip in and help. That's the same way we built that fire station. There wasn't a doggone one of us that knowed how to lay out a concrete block. [laughter] Eddie, he could lay up a corner. He would go over there and start laying up the corners, and the other guys would run the lines, and they laid up that there fire station in no time flat. I think they did a doggone good job when you consider what they knew when they started out. By the time they got done, they all knew how to lay block. But that's the way they do. It's like I say, they're not afraid to tackle anything; they just jump into it! If one guy knowed how to do something, the rest of them would pay attention to him. If they'd ask him how he'd done this, or how he'd done that, they'd pay attention to what he said. They wouldn't say "No, that ain't the way to do it, I think this way is better." They wouldn't do that. They would just take his advice.

At times, these systems of labor exchange form a conscious constellation of patterned evasions of the market. These avoidances are recognized as being actions that cheat the spirit of the market. There are even those, such as Charlie Barker, who ideologically justify this as a class-based subterfuge, seeing it as sidestepping a system that discriminates against its lower orders:

Dave: Do you think it's better for a guy to learn one thing, say, as far as work—learn one thing only and follow it straight through, or to learn a lot of things?

Charlie: I would say a lot of things, but the thing that he likes to do best, he should follow that one the most.

Dave: Well, why do you think he should learn a lot of things?

Charlie: Well, take right now, like me for instance. If I want to have a new house, at my wage I can't afford to pay your average electrician to do the wiring. So, if I know enough that I can do my own wiring, I am saving quite a bit of money. I can't afford to pay out that kind of money. I got to work twice as much to pay him his electrician's wage. I got to put in two hours' time to pay one hour of an electrician's. Of course, if you're making pretty good money, twelve thousand or twenty thousand dollars a year, then you're making the wage that the electrician is making. *Then you can afford to pay his hour with your hour,* but when you're making less, you can't do it. [emphasis added]

Dave: So what you're saying is that what you learn on the job doesn't stop at five o'clock. You learn a lot of things that you can use around the house. Something like that?

Charlie: Of course. Right now, the little leak that I told you that I got—it

would probably cost me twenty-five or thirty dollars to have a
man come out here and fix it. Well, I could fix it myself probably
for a couple of dollars out of my pocket. Of course, I'm going to
spend my time doing it, but my actual expenditure will cost me
maybe a couple of hours. I imagine it's probably a nail that has
come out. All I got to do is to go buy me a little can of putty. In
fact, I've got some of that, so I don't even have to buy anything.

Dave: What are the types of skills a person should pick up?

Charlie: I would say a little bit of everything in the line of construction
work. Everybody wants to be a homeowner at some time, and
if you can learn a little bit about anything that you do around
your house, I would say this is going to save you quite a bit of
money over a period of years. There's just lots and lots of people that gets their toilet stool plugged up. A lot of people don't
even know how to use these plungers. Maybe that's all you
need to clean it out; anybody with any sense at all can work one
of them.

Dave: But you say a guy that makes twelve thousand dollars a year
doesn't have to do this.

Charlie: Well, I would say now that he would have to be making more
than that, but of course, not really either, because twelve thousand dollars a year is pretty darn good wages. That's a thousand dollars a month—that's good wages! You wouldn't necessarily have to do repair work yourself. You could afford to hire
someone to come in and do it.

Charlie has constructed a superb rationale for an informal system of
labor exchange built upon a jack-of-all-trades ideology.[5] Whereas many
sociologists believe that a detailed technical division of labor integrates
various occupational segments of society into a web of organic dependency, he sees only exclusion and class-specific advantage resulting
from this complex division of labor. Charlie views social integration
from the bottom, looking up, and sees a different social order than do
most sociologists, who stand near the top, looking down. Salaried
equals, and only salaried equals, can take full advantage of these soli-
darity-producing interdependencies. If in a class society, some people
must work two or three hours to secure one hour of a professional or
tradesman's services, then such ratios bar the full social participation of
the lower classes. It forces them to retreat into the past and resurrect
historical modes of cooperation, and use these alternative economies to
survive.

IV. ALTERNATIVE ECONOMIES

Potter Addition's economic world consists of two mutually antagonistic structures that run parallel to one another: The first is composed of

normal market transactions. The second consists of a shadow economy of deviant opportunity structures located in family, kinship, and patron-client relations. The antagonisms between them are due to the conflicting norms that ground each. The market system is, ideally at least, a rational arrangement that rewards only those performances, skills, and output levels for which buyer and seller have freely contracted. Judgments and rewards are made and distributed in an emotionally neutral and rationally calculating manner. Material life chances are determined by the convergence of two impersonal factors: the perceived value of the particular skill being sold, and the relative scarcity of that skill. Whether one works, and feeds and houses one's family, is determined by untrammeled self-interest and the impersonal action of supply and demand. Using Parsons's (1951, pp. 45–67) scheme of pattern variables, we can typify action orientation in capitalist markets as follows: (1) A person is evaluated and rewarded solely on the basis of *performance*; (2) only those *specific* activities contracted for are judged; (3) all evaluations are made in an atmosphere of disinterested *affective neutrality*; and (4) the individual is objectively evaluated according to *universal standards* of conduct, that is, the person's task performance is ranked as being either better or worse than any other performance in the same category.

Potter Addition's alternative opportunity structures, by contrast, employ norms and values that are the opposite of those used in commodity markets. Their normative content is grounded in what scholars today call a moral economy.[6] That is, individual behavior is judged on the basis of who one is, not on what one actually achieves. Rewards are distributed on the basis of affect, so that the emotional tenor of a relationship determines how and why resources are distributed. Finally, group welfare takes precedence over egoistic advancement, so that the subordination of individual advantage to the good of the whole is the norm. Returning to the pattern variable paradigm, we can say that Potter Addition's moral economy judges the worth of the person not by universalistic criteria, but by *particularistic* norms. The instrumental tenor of the market is now inverted; persons relate to one another as if they were ends in themselves; aid and largess are given (or withheld) on the basis of interpersonal *affectivity*. The fact that a person can be related to in a holistic fashion in family, kinship, and clientship circles means that his or her needs are evaluated and met according to what Parsons calls a *diffuse* mode. This holism is opposed to the aforementioned market-based specificity. Performance criteria are now tempered with status considerations. What you achieve and how you perform are no longer the sole criteria by which you are evaluated. The moral economy of family, kinship, and patronage relations makes room for a variety of indulgences and situational exceptions so that the individual is judged by *ascriptive criteria*, not just performance.

These two evaluative systems are antagonistic to one another in capitalism's specific context. The norms that govern family and kinship organization, for example, would be disastrous if used as guides for judging economic performance in a fully rationalized capitalist economy. Not only would the efficiency of capitalist enterprises suffer, there would be such a terrible misallocation of talent and accountability that society's material foundations would be threatened. The opposite is also true. A nuclear family stripped of its intimate interior and run according to strict canons of capitalist rationality would be impaired in its ability to socialize the young and perform its various psychosexual functions (Parsons, Bales, et al. 1955, pp. 3–34).

The conceptual opposition between market norms and the premises of the moral economy is fundamental to both structural-functional and critical paradigms. Thus, Polanyi (1944) has maintained that in the early nineteenth century England's economy tried to accommodate *both* value complexes. During this crucial period of transition, nascent capitalism and its emergent market structure was forced to share the economic stage with the last vestiges of aristocratic paternalism. Polanyi believes that this evaluative ambivalence was destroying the economic and moral basis of society. The crisis passed only when the Poor Laws were reformed and free market capitalism was allowed to gain a political monopoly in the decades following 1834. But once the free market took hold and was able to commoditize the very substance of human needs, England was plunged into a second, even more destructive crisis. The market, allowed to allocate human necessities through its own mechanism of supply and demand rather than on the basis of actual need, began to destroy an entire generation of workers. If it had not been for the rise of ameliorative reforms and legislation, Polanyi believes that capital would have eventually reduced English civilization to an industrial barbarism. The historical outcome, however, was quite the opposite. Due to the impact of the reform movement, the legislative struggle to balance the needs of capital accumulation and the needs of society began.[7]

In terms of abstract sociological analysis it is true that when the two value complexes are distilled into ideal-typical clusters, they form mutually exclusive and antagonistic formations. It is also true that if a social system is to be *organically integrated* in the way that conservative social science demands, concrete role expectations must be unambiguously structured to express *either* affectivity *or* affective neutrality, but not both; *either* performance *or* ascription, but not both, etc. Once, however, the twin premises of self-equilibrating systems and value consensus are disallowed, the pattern variables can be used to construct an alternative conception of social structure.

As Bendix and Berger (1959) have proposed, social structures can be seen as a *balanced tension* of contradictory values and norms. That is, social structures are compromise constructions created by "tragic actors" whose limited possibilities for social action do not enable them to resolve effectively the irreconcilable social demands placed upon them. Unable to resolve these paradoxes, these actors synthesize a fragile set of practices and roles. These ambiguity-ridden, ad hoc compromises, in turn, eventually evolve to the point where they become the established protocols of organizational life. So conceived, social structures cease to be grounded in internally coherent value systems and become instead open, synthetic systems composed of structured ambiguities and ambivalences.

When seen from this more open perspective, economic roles *in the concrete* are an explosive mixture of affectivity *and* affective neutrality, of universalism *and* particularism, of specificity *and* diffuseness, etc. Role requirements can be honored as they stand, partially evaded or obeyed as the situation warrants, or renegotiated without loss of their overall integrity. In his discussion of kinship, clientship and friendship, Eric Wolf (1966) has, in fact, noted just such an uneasy amalgam of coexisting historical forms and modes of production in the structure of modern social formations:

> The anthropologist's study of complex societies receives its major justification from the fact that such societies are not as well organized and tightly knit as their spokesmen would on occasion like to make people believe. If we analyze their economic systems, we shall find in any one such society resources which are strategic to the system—and organizations set up to utilize these strategic resources—but we shall also find resources and organizations which are at best supplementary or wholly peripheral. If we drew these relations on a map, some areas would show strong concentrations of strategic resources and the accompanying core organizations; other areas would appear in grey or white, economic *terra incognita* from the point of view of the larger system. The same point may be made with regard to political control. There are political resources which are essential to the operation of the system, and the system will try to remain in control of these. But there are also resources and organizations which it would be either too costly or too difficult to bring under direct control, and in these cases the system yields its sovereignty to competitive groups that are allowed to function in its entrails. . . . Sometimes such informal groupings cling to the formal structure like barnacles to a rusty ship. At other times, informal social relations are responsible for the metabolic processes required to keep the formal institution operating, as in the case of armies locked in combat. In still other cases, we discover that the formal table of organization is elegant indeed, but fails to work,

unless informal mechanisms are found for its direct contravention, as in
the network of *blat* relationships among Soviet industrial managers. (pp.
1–2)

Turning to Potter Addition, we can see that its dual economy, far from
being a barnacle on a rusting hull, is an integral part of the normal
metabolic processes that make up Clay County's economic life. A layered composite, the shadow economy of kinship, family, and patron-
client relations, while outwardly operating by rules that contravene the
neoclassical spirit of market relations, actually augments market processes. The subterranean economy is an alternative source of goods,
monies, and services that surplus populations can draw upon during
periods of extended unemployment. Since there will be a future need for
this reserve army, it cannot be allowed to perish; but at the same time
the market cannot sustain this marginal labor force. Consequently, an
extramarket mechanism must evolve that maintains the superfluous until they are needed again.

Employing rules and sentiments insulated from the logic of capitalist
markets, the protean economies of family, kinship, and clientship *dialectically complement* the normal processes of market allocation. They "fill
in the gaps" of market functioning, even as the culture of the market
brands them as paternalistic regressions. Rather than being external
structures that threaten the operations of local markets, the moral economies of the poor are historical survivals—vestiges of a not-too-distant
past that have been *sublated* and made part of the market's everyday
operation. The shadow economies of lower-class life are thus only formally deviant; substantively, they are essential elements of capital's reproduction.

Every household in Potter Addition operates with one foot in Clay
County's market economy and the other in its class-based moral economy. When a person cannot obtain the necessities of life through the
one, he or she turns to the other. When hard pressed, residents seek
help from "their own." As might be expected, family and kin form the
most visible part of Potter Addition's expressive economy. The relative
gradations that determine which kin are sought out is schematized in
Figure 6.2. With ego's household at the center, we find concentric circles
representing parental households, the households of uncles and aunts,
their siblings and peer group members, and finally distant kin. The
relative position of each circle represents the probability with which aid
is sought from each. The shaded, sectoral division roughly depicts the
relative accessibility of the husband's as opposed to the wife's kin. Thus,
parental households—usually the wife's parents—are the first place to
which young people turn in times of need. Aid usually flows through

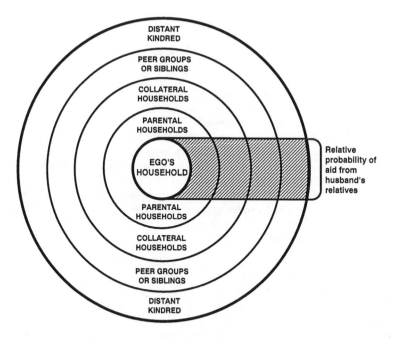

Figure 6.2. Sources of aid to households in Potter Addition's alternative
economy.

the mother-daughter conduit. Parental preoccupation with their adult
children's finances usually begin with the children's marriage. In many
cases the parental homestead temporarily becomes a joint household as
the newlywed daughter and her husband are taken in. Witness, for
example, the discussion of one person recounting his early residential
patterns during the depression:

Dave: If it's not too personal, I take it that a great many people out
here have seen rough financial times. During the rougher times
when you were out of work or work was partial, how did you
usually make it through?

Nelson: Oh, about fair I would say.

Dave: No. I mean, where did you get money from?

Nelson: Well, I never did borrow money to live on. I always managed to
pick up a little money here, there, and the next place—enough
to eat on and such as that; and, of course, by the time I was
married I was working at Vander's Warehouse. It was steady at
that time; I got twenty dollars a week. There was a few times
when I would run a little short; then I would go ask Dad for a
few dollars. If something happened to come up—if I needed a
few dollars—I would go borrow twenty from Dad and pay him

back. But this was in later years. When I was first married, my wife and I lived with her folks. Of course, at that time they were happy to get five dollars a week for us to stay with them. That's what we paid them—five dollars a week. In fact, I still had money to pay the loan company on my automobile. [laughter] It wasn't much of an automobile [laughter]

Dave: Why did you decide to move in with your wife's parents, as opposed to your parents?

Nelson: Well, mostly because I stayed with them just before we were married. Like I say, this is back in hard times. The two boys, her brothers, and I would take the old car and go out to the country junk piles. We would pick up iron and metal, go sell it, and make a little money to buy some bread—something like that. We ate a lot of water gravy in those days. We had to! We'd take that bread and dunk it in the water gravy and that would be supper a lot of times.

As in this case, many parental households are only marginally better off, yet the children are still taken in. One young woman told me of her and her husband living for some months as newlyweds in the front room of her parents' home. Two years later, the woman's brother and his new wife also took up residence in the same front room and lived there until they got on their feet. Another couple began marriage when the girl was barely sixteen and the boy seventeen. They moved into a small house owned by her parents, and lived there rent free. The daughter continued to eat breakfast and lunch at the parents' home next door, just as she had done before marriage, while her husband took his meals at his place of employment, Grand Prairie's first Hamburger Emporium. Since they lived rent free and only had to pay for their evening meals, they could have saved most of their money. As the woman laughingly remembers, however, "We blew it all, like any kids our age would have done."

In some cases, children are given a small parcel of land upon which to build, or land with a house or trailer already in place. While such gifts are often minor in terms of their total cash value and usually come from the wife's family, such a "dowry" often ensures that the daughter will remain in Potter Addition, near her mother and father. If a divorce ensues, the young woman can then remain in the community and draw on the nearby resources of her parents' household. When parents are not in a position to give aid, as is often the case in the poorer households, other kin are sought out. The rule is to seek first the aid of a favorite aunt or uncle, and failing that, older married siblings. The frequency with which an older sibling is sought out is usually diminished by two factors: First, because aid is needed during the hard-pressed, child-bearing years, the older sibling is usually no better off financially than his or her sibling. Second, there is the problem of adult sibling rivalry. At any point in time the two may be in the middle of a spat, or in the process of recovering from one. After exhausting this circle, one seeks out more distant kin. Appealing to this outer circle of kin is a direct function of (1) the severity of the family's need, and (2) the financial status of the relative. It seems that in every kin group there is at least one relative in this outer circle who has made it. These relatives are seldom contacted for minor loans or help, but are saved, so to speak, for larger favors, such as getting a child a job, obtaining large cash loans, or cosigning a note.

When a Potter Additionite moves beyond the boundaries of immediate family and kin to work the interstices of public culture, the norms regulating the informal opportunity structures of kin and peer group also guide the forging of alliances with outsiders. Personal deals are struck and claims are made on the basis of special, one-of-a-kind relationships that a Potter Additionite establishes with a specific business person or institutional representative. Paralleling the formal institutional structures of Grand Prairie is a vast network of personalist arrangements of which the poor avail themselves. This domain of informal indulgences softens the otherwise forbidding rules that technically govern relations between classes.

During the two summers of my stay, for example, I helped run the Potter Addition Youth Club's movies. The projector, drop cords, and most of the paraphernalia needed to show the movies were the property of the university. A member of Potter Addition Youth was employed as a university electrician and, being on good terms with the stockroom attendant, had "checked out" the materials that were needed to show the movies. I never screwed up the courage to ask the man if this was aboveboard, and given the tight-lipped manner in which he offered information as to how he came by the materials, I never pushed the issue. The same was true of the green, slat park benches we sat on during the movies. I was told that the head of the Grand Prairie Parks Department was a "good friend" of Potter Addition Youth and a "good guy" to boot. He had put the benches on "permanent loan" to the community. Since Potter Addition was an unincorporated area and not part of Grand Prairie and its parks system, I could not understand how this had been carried off. When I asked how we had come by the benches, I was told that the Parks Department head always "looked out for people out here in Potter Addition." This was hardly to the point, but since the reply was filled with a guarded ambiguity, I assumed my question had been understood and that this was the best answer I would get. Again, for fear of stepping into a sensitive area, I backed off and perhaps unjustly assumed the worst. A final example of indulgences occurred during the Detroit riots and those following Martin Luther King's assassination. As racial tensions soared in Grand Prairie, both Grand Prairie policemen and sheriff's deputies went out of their way to contact friends and relatives in Potter Addition personally, alerting them to possible troubles and urging them to get their relatives out of the black North End until racial passions on both sides had cooled.

At times it seemed that for each formal rule someone in Potter Addition had cultivated a relationship that could circumvent it. As in the case of economic relations, people played both the informal and formal sides of public culture to their best advantage. There were few in the community who were not able to turn such indulgences to their personal ends or to the community's advantage when the need arose. With a humorous myopia that at times verged on the scandalous, each household would defend its own personalist network of indulgences, while denouncing the deals struck by others. In fact, the latter were invariably offered up as evidence of the corruption of the cliques who ran Grand Prairie.

Similarly, whether or not one is granted desperately needed commercial credit is seen as depending on how one relates to the person doling out the largess. The credit arrangements at Betty's Market are typical. Betty is always the first to admit that without extending credit to selected customers she could not keep her doors open. Who obtains credit depends on how reliable the person is seen to be and whether or not Betty likes them. This latter judgment, however, seldom works alone to bar the extension of credit. Betty is, after all, too good a businesswoman for that. The decision to extend credit is, nevertheless, a complex business:

> Take the Judsons—they are renters. They have been in and out of here for ten years, I would guess. They don't have good credit down at Betty's. She carries them down there at the store and will tell you, "I carry them by the week. When they don't pay me this week, they don't get no groceries next week."
>
> I ain't braggin' or boastin' or nothin', but if I go down to Betty's, she carries my family by the month. If I go down and say "Betty, I ain't got enough money to pay you this month," she says, "Oh, that's all right." Or if we want something, like this summer my husband wanted a little hand truck for this business he runs on the side—it cost $30—he said, "I don't have the money to buy this hand truck with, but I want to look at your wholesale catalog." This is an item she don't handle in the store, so all he would have to pay, if he bought it, was the wholesale price. He told her, "Someday, Betty, I'm gonna get me one of them." She offered to order it right then and there. He told her, "I can't pay for it," but Betty said "Well, don't worry about it, just whenever you want to pay me for it. When you get the money, you pay me for it." You think she'd do the Judsons this

way? No! The Judsons would get it and never pay her for it. Within two months it was paid off. She knew she was gonna get her money. Anything I want like that she'll do, 'cause she knows me. She knows I'll pay. There's been a few times I haven't been able to pay my grocery bill—somethin' come up and I'd be a little short—but I always catch up. She trusts me completely. But, the Judsons—gettin' back to the Judsons—she don't dare go two weeks' behind on them. She won't get her money. She knows this. So she tells Henrietta Judson, "You pay me every week. The first week you don't have all of it, you don't get no groceries." You know why? 'Cause Henrietta's a drunk! If she starts gettin' behind, she can't ever catch up. It's easier to keep up than catch up.

Hence, the personalist interpretations of Gans's (1962, pp. 163–70) urban villagers is an equally potent ideological orientation in Potter Addition. Far from being a "sour grapes" reaction to "being on the bottom," it expresses the lived reality of the economic and political indulgences that Potter Additionites daily exploit and see being used by others. Never a right that can be legally adjudicated when they are not honored, these indulgences are nonetheless a crucial collection of shadow assets that can be drawn upon when needed.

Among this collection of assets there is what I will call a family's ace in the hole—that one extramarket resource that the person knows he or she can always summon during hard times. Of course, the command of such hole cards is not the sole province of the poor. Pilcher (1972, pp. 86–95), for example, has documented a similar phenomenon in his study of the Portland longshoremen community. The week-to-week uncertainty of work on the docks is like that faced by many construction families. Longshoremen have found ways, however, of evening out the seasonal variations in income. They use the salary surpluses earned on the docks during good months to buy real estate, become partners in small businesses, or engage in marginal agricultural activities such as "stump ranching," the part-time farming of marginal or recently reclaimed land.

Yet for all the similarities between the occupational variability of the longshoreman's life and that of Potter Addition's, there are significant differences. Unlike Potter Addition's situation, the International Longshoremen's and Warehousemen's Union (ILWU), through its militant left leadership and the struggles of the last five decades, has politically stabilized the longshoremen's occupational niche. This is true for few other working- and lower-working-class groups. The structure and level of wages are such that most longshoremen are able to muster sufficient savings to secure their lives against the seasonal vagaries of the docks. There is also the legendary support culture of the longshoremen, one that is adjusted to the rhythms of fluctuating employment and that forestalls the fatalism, anomie, or personal isolation a variable environment might otherwise generate.

The three conditions which undergird the security and solidarity of the longshoremen's culture are seldom known in Potter Addition households. Two or three families in Potter Addition, however, resemble Pilcher's longshoremen in that they are "silent partners" in a business. We have already met the junkyard owner who, with his son, went into business junking cars and selling them for scrap. The junkyard was his ace in the hole. When things were slow in his regular line of work, he could go to the yard, spend a leisurely day cutting up cars with an acetylene torch, and make a few dollars that way. The junkyard, however, gave him a *second* hole card, the possibility of making a windfall profit. He had come by this wonderful something for nothing because of a long-time friendship with the owner of Grand Prairie Chevrolet. For years his friend has sent him all of his junk autos, as many as eight to ten at a time. The junkyard owner was proud of the fact that he has never been charged for the junk autos—not even the cost of towing them to Potter Addition. When cut up or cannibalized and their parts sold, these junkers are "pure profit."

Aces in the hole are not always circumventions of the market. On many occasions they can be a second skill that is ever at the ready. Several men in Potter Addition, for example, served in the armed forces as cooks. They told me that there is always a demand for short-order cooks, and that if they were ever laid off, they would have short-order cooking to fall back on. While many voiced a preference for cooking as an occupation, its low wages made it at best a stop-gap job—an ace in the hole when all else failed. A family man could not for long make a decent living doing short-order cooking, but it was always there, ready to see him and his family through hard times.

In several cases, aces in the hole take the form of classic, patron-client relationships. Such relations are usually rooted in rural biographies and are often understandings that were originally negotiated by the person's parents or grandparents when they were still on the land. More often than not, such patronage is part of a family's "inheritance"—an unbroken set of rights and obligations between two families that are honored and renewed in every generation. One such relationship is discussed by Carol Thomas and concerns her son, Kevin, Jr. He has just begun to follow in his grandfather's and father's footsteps by establishing a third generation of patron-client obligations between the Phelpses, the family who owns a local farm, and his family, the Thomases.

> My boy really enjoys those jobs, Dave. Since he's gone out to Harold Phelps and worked on his farm out there, there's a lot of difference in him. You can really tell. He's really anxious to go out there in the morning, and

when he does come home he ends up going right back out. He just seems so much happier out there.

Now, we've known the Phelps ever since we've been married, and Grandma Phelps helped us. Kevin worked for her when we were first married, and she helped him. Martin and Roseanne, Grandma's kids, helped us when we were first married. In fact, they all helped when we first got married. Even three years after we were married, why Kevin would go out there and help them and they'd raise cain if the kids and me didn't come out with him. I guess Kevin, Jr., was out at Grandma's here a while back, and she complained that we hadn't been coming out to visit—that's when he started to work there. I don't know, they seem more like a family to us, really, than even our own relations sometimes. But I know everybody notices the difference in Junior since he's been working out there. He really loves it. Now, Harold Phelps owns and runs what used to be Grandma's farm. He can't afford to have somebody help him all the time.

But when Junior has worked for him, he has really enjoyed it. He loves to drive tractors and trucks, or anything like that, and Harold says he's not afraid of work. He comes early and stays late, and he couldn't ask for a better worker. Junior tries to do just about everything that Harold teaches him how to do. I know many mornings last month there, when they were shelling corn and taking it down to let it dry and store it, why on those mornings, he'd leave here about four o'clock and it would be nine or ten o'clock at night before he would get back.

The other day when they didn't work, Harold went ahead and figured up his time and give him his money. Junior worked about three weeks—it wasn't quite three weeks—but he had drawn better than three hundred and some dollars for that. And you know, that's darn good money for farm work. But Harold told Kevin, he said, "By God, your boy is worth every penny I give him." He asked Kevin what he should pay Junior, and Kevin said "That's up to you, because you're the one that hired him." Kevin, Jr. said that he sat and figured about $17.50, or pretty close to $19.00 a day is what they gave him. It is the same way with Kevin; he can go out anytime he wants, and Harold will give him work before he hires anyone else. He knows Kevin will give him a good day's work. In the winter when construction is slow and no money's coming in, Kevin can always get two or three days' work on the farm.

Junior gets his meals out there, too, just like Kevin did when he worked for them full-time. When I lived out south there, on the farm, a lot of times I'd go help and fix dinner. My God, you've never seen so much food in all your life. I bet over half of it wouldn't be eaten. But they always fixed so much. Even if you would just go out and visit Grandma for awhile, she'd ask, "You want something to eat? You want this? You want that?" She's always got stuff there. She bakes a lot—or she used to. I reckon she still does, but she's so crippled and bent over now that she don't get out too much. But she loves her cooking. Oh, I just wish sometimes we were back out there, Dave.

The Thomases are not unique in having this type of patronage as their ace in the hole. At the same time, Potter Addition's demographic situation has matured over the years. Such paternalistic hole cards, grounded as they are in traditional obligations, become an ever more diminishing possibility with each passing year. As that rural heritage fades, and as Grand Prairie itself evolves, the nature of the region's moral economy will itself change. New urban-based aces in the hole will replace the alternative economies that now sustain Potter Addition and reproduce the political economy of Clay County and Grand Prairie.

7

The Uxoricentric Family

There are three types of family in Potter Addition. The first is organized along traditional lines of *patrilateral domination*. It is found among the stable working-class families who founded Potter Addition and among the blue-collar entrepreneurs who settled in the community in the late 1940s. In their structure and everyday operation they resemble the families of Grand Prairie's petit bourgeois elites. The second type is what I will call the *uxoricentric family*. In many ways it is an inversion of the first in that its power and authority rest not with its males, but with its women.

While the uxoricentric family is Potter Addition's modal family type, it is not ideal typical of lower-class family life. That is, the structure of uxoricentric family life is not the fullest expression of lower-class life, nor is it the family form that is most congruent with poverty's variable class niche. That designation goes to Potter Addition's third constellation, the sibling-based family. The sibling-based family emerges in situations where both parents have defaulted and where the children are forced at an early age to fend for themselves. Huddled together in horizontally organized, protective groupings and integrated by little more than ties of sibling solidarity, this third family type and its kinship groups faithfully reflect the "minimalist" organizational premises that poverty's uncertain niche allows.

This third family type will be discussed in later chapters. The structure and dynamics of uxoricentric family life will be the primary concern of this chapter and the next. Before beginning, however, a caveat is in order. The analysis that follows will, of necessity, be tentative. Using an approach that Paul Sweezy (1943, pp. 11–19) has aptly labeled "the method of successive approximations," I will restrict my analysis to the domestic interior of uxoricentric family life and for the moment ignore the larger set of kinship relations in which uxoricentric households are set. In later chapters our findings concerning uxoricentrism's domestic interior will have to be placed within the larger context of lower-class kinship and reassessed. While the actual scope of those revisions will be limited, they will add significantly to our overall understanding of life in uxoricentric households. With this proviso in mind, then, let us turn to an examination of uxoricentric domestic life.

I. THE PARSONSIAN MODEL

The nuclear family is defined as a two-generation household of sexually cohabiting adults and their unmarried children. It has been argued in several quarters that this configuration is firmly grounded in a set of invariant natural facts. Because the family is composed of a mutually reinforcing set of biological tendencies and integrative roles, it performs a set of sociological functions that are indispensable for society's continued existence. For this reason, many family sociologists argue that the nuclear family of husband, wife, and unmarried children is a universal structure, i.e., that occurs naturally in all societies.

The functions performed by the nuclear family vary according to the sociologist consulted. At a minimum, however, the family is thought: to form the primordial basis for a natural economic division of labor in that the household is an elementary unit of social production and consumption; to socialize and educate the young during their formative years; to be the locus of legitimate biological reproduction; to bestow social legitimacy upon children; and, finally, in those modern societies devoid of elaborate kinship structures, to be a key form of emotional integration and socially sanctioned displays of eroticism and mutual affection.

The most thorough analysis of the structural interior of the modal American family is that developed by Talcott Parsons in *Family: Socialization and Interaction Process* (Parsons, Bales, et al. 1955). Treating the nuclear family as a small work group assembled to perform certain tasks, Parsons views its role structure in terms similar to those depicted in Figure 7.1. According to this schema, the two-generation nuclear family is stratified along two orthogonal axes. The horizontal axis organizes family life along the biological parameters of age and generation, while the vertical axis discriminates between the sexes and their biological differences.

These two natural axes also organize the family sociologically. Differentiation along the horizontal axis is the basis for an asymmetrical allocation of power and authority within the family. Legitimate authority is ascribed to the parental generation, while dependent, unmarried chil-

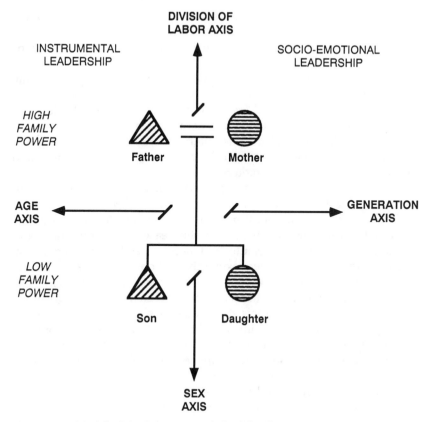

Figure 7.1. Model of the Parsonsian nuclear family.

dren occupy roles with little power or authority. The vertical axis is socially mapped to become the basis for a division of labor in parental leadership. Ideally, the father provides instrumental leadership for the family, while the mother manages the family's socioemotional domain. Structured like a work group, the Parsonsian nuclear family needs coordination of its activities, a sense of direction, a critique of individual role performance, and the establishment of group goals. These needs are met by the family's instrumental leader. In modern societies, the husband's occupational role has *traditionally* made him the family's instrumental leader. His breadwinning role of necessity carries him into the larger community, where he becomes a natural conduit through which the values and performance standards of the community enter the everyday life of the family. He is thus well suited to critique the extent to which the family and its conduct conform to the larger cultural patterns of the community. *In his role as father*, the man evaluates the family's socialization efforts and its cultural reproduction activities. When necessary, he criticizes and levies sanctions against deviations from the societal norm.

The wife, by contrast, bears and rears the children while managing the household. Given her everyday domestic duties, she is well suited to be the family's *socioemotional leader*. As the socioemotional leader, it is her job to soothe ruffled feelings and defuse the hostilities and tensions caused by the father's instrumental interventions, admonishments, and criticisms. She mediates between the authoritarian "boss/father" and the subordinate "children/workers."

Both forms of leadership are necessary in maintaining a coherent family organization, and both are dialectically linked. If instrumental leadership is to be effective, it must of necessity create tensions as the family adapts to new situations. For this reason, the very success of instrumental leadership calls into existence the need for socioemotional intervention. Once, however, expressive solidarity has been reestablished under the other's leadership, the family is ill prepared to meet its next adaptive challenge. Thus, when the next challenge does arise, the family's expressive solidarity is shattered by a series of new instrumental demands. It is at this point that the dialectical cycle that animates family life moves into its next phase. The husband/father steps in and begins once again to direct and discipline the family in its task-oriented activities.

It is possible for these leadership roles to be reversed, or for husbands and wives to share leadership in both spheres. It is also possible for *one person* to carry out *both* leadership roles in a serial fashion. This is, in fact, one of the findings of Bales's (Parsons, Bales, et al. 1955, pp. 259–306) small-group experiments on task group leadership, which Parsons used in developing his model of the nuclear family. Parsons and his colleagues, however, give several reasons why leadership operates better in a differentiated role setting.

There are, of course, numerous objections to this model. Any student of contemporary American society will see that this model is archaic. In the forty years since its unveiling, it has been superseded by more democratic versions. As monopoly capitalism and its administered patterns of mass consumption have matured, the themes of personal discipline and sexual restraint so crucial to the Parsonsian model have all but vanished in many sectors of American life. Bernard Farber's (1964) "permanent availability" model, to mention but one, penned as it was in the early 1960s at a crucial moment in the evolution of America's consumer culture, better describes family life among today's professional classes. While not developing the model of permanent availability from the Freudian framework that Christopher Lasch (1978) employed, Farber has nonetheless anticipated the family form that would be required to sustain the culture of narcissism. His permanent availability model of family life is one in which the parents are more committed to their own development and self-realization than they are to the orderly replacement of family culture across generations. The historical shift from the "child-oriented family," with its conservative goal of transmitting a family's culture from one generation to the next, to the new "parent-oriented family," with its emphasis on meeting the personal and mobility needs of the parents, connotes in the very terms themselves the dramatic change that family life has undergone since Parsons penned his work.

In this work, however, we are not interested in the cutting edge of family life; instead we want to understand the bypassed forms of family life that capital's uneven development has left intact throughout the American heartland.[1] In this region the family that Parsons described still enunciates the *ethos* that dominates much of mid-America. Proof of this can be found in the fact that as America sinks further into reaction in the 1980s and 1990s (and rejects many of the last five decades' hard-won progressive freedoms), it has done so largely because neoconservatives have captured the social issues. Denouncing alternative lifestyles and cloaking themselves in the mantle of prolife and profamily values, they have rallied support for their regressive economic and political programs. The family form they celebrate and "protect" is the traditional family we have described here.

There are other reasons, though, why this stodgy Parsonsian model should serve as the starting point of my analysis. As with so much of his sociology, Parsonsian family theory was as much a retrospective summing up as it was a description of "the way it was" in the mid-1950s. Sensing the cultural anomie of monopoly capitalism and anticipating its crisis of societal integration, he sought to read into monopoly capitalism a moral content drawn from an earlier age. The capitalism of the nineteenth century, grounded in the culture of petty producers, was his implicit model. It is thus no accident that his theoretical vision cast the family as a productive unit, geared to a disciplined production of commodities by morally bound, self-censoring producers. Nor is it an accident that Bales's synthetic work groups, formed in the small group laboratory, served as the empirical grist for his theoretical ruminations. In Bales's laboratory findings, Parsons discovered not so much empirical support for his vision, as he did a set of "projective tests" that fit his preconceptions of how and why the family could be a dynamic, morally integrated social system. In truth, Parsons depicted neither a universal configuration, as Zelditch claimed (Parsons, Bales, et al. 1955, pp. 307–

52), nor a newly emerging family form ready to meet the challenges of modernity. His model was, in fact, a paean to a lost domestic ideal. In de-emphasizing the historicity of the family and the uneven development of American society, Parsons failed to see that the outmoded culture that housed his family was dying in consumer-oriented, urban America. Only in America's encapsulated hinterlands would this family of producers remain viable.

One of the clearest expressions of the ideal-typical Parsonsian family is found among Grand Prairie's petite bourgeoisie, the conservative, commercial elites who daily manage the affairs of Grand Prairie proper. A close variant of this traditional family type is also found among Clay County's conservative farmers, many of whom are of Frisian ancestry and who adhere strictly to the piety of an unreconstructed Lutheranism. These latter diverge from the Parsonsian model only in the emphasis they give to the intergenerational transmission and expansion of their agricultural landholdings. Economically similar, yet culturally distinct, these two groups lead family lives that are the living embodiment of the Parsonsian model. Their control of Clay County's political and cultural life, moreover, empowers them with the kind of cultural direction that Antonio Gramsci (1971) referred to when he talked about the hegemonic powers of a dominant class.

Held in the hegemonic grip of local culture, the people of Potter Addition tend to judge the success of their families in terms of these archaic petit bourgeois standards. Ironically, however, the class situation of Potter Additionites requires them to seek practical solutions to family life that often invert the moral prescriptions of local culture. Nowhere in Potter Addition is the distance greater between what people say and what they do than in the area of family life. This is especially true of the uxoricentric family, which is itself a normative *composite* of practical lower-class adaptations and petit bourgeois aspirations.

II. THE JURAL DEFAULT OF THE HUSBAND

The occupational and economic primacy of the male is at the core of what I will call the petit bourgeois family (Parsons 1949, p. 261–68). Eliminate that primacy, and the entire set of age- and sex-graded roles collapses. The failure of the young husband to be an adequate breadwinner is, in fact, at the core of uxoricentric family organization, for what begins as an economic failure is soon translated into a refusal to honor the husband's claim to instrumental leadership.[2]

In that so much of uxoricentric family life flows from this default, it can be seen as a cascading series of accommodations designed to offset the impact of the husband's economic failure. From the beginning, the young husband is under the gun—and little wonder. He usually marries at age sixteen or seventeen, and if he has not yet left school, he usually does so shortly thereafter in order to support his new family. His job prospects are limited by his lack of formal education. This is usually compounded by the fact that he lacks a craft or skill that might secure for him a well-paying job. His bride is generally about his age, if not a year or so younger. In many cases she is pregnant when they marry. An abortion might ease their growing economic plight, but in the 1960s, abortions are illegal and not easy to come by, especially if one is poor. Even if they were legal, abortion would seldom be an option. In this child-oriented subculture, children are so valued, especially as grand-children, that such an act is close to unthinkable.[3] Putting the infant up for adoption is also a closed option. While it is not unknown for some-one to give up one's flesh and blood to strangers, it is seen as being morally odious. Everyone in the community seems to know of cases in which a woman after putting her baby up for adoption, "went crazy with grief." For example:

> If I lived to be a hundred and had a thousand kids, I don't think I would have ever given one of them away. I knew a woman out in the country here who gave away her first child. I think it started preying on her mind, because when she finally married, got pregnant, and miscarried, she went out of her mind crying and screaming for that first baby. I knew her husband real well; he was really a swell guy. One time he told me, "Edith, I don't know what I'm gonna do. We've gone to the doctor and talked to him, and he says he doesn't know what to do about Maggie's carryin' on." But I think what caused all that was giving away her child—it began to prey on her.
>
> That's why I think a young girl who gets "that way" should keep the kid. It's best just to keep the kid. I don't think they should give them away unless they are going to be mean and brutal to that baby.

At times, such sentiments are poorly masked rationalizations. Al-though it is true that having abortions and putting one's own up for adoption is seen as immoral, it is also true that some Potter Additionites possess a streak of puritanical meanness that says, "If you play, you pay." The child is often viewed as retribution for the sin of fornication. As one resource person noted (and since the tape recorder was turned off, this is not strictly verbatim), "Out in that community the feeling seems to be that having a baby out of wedlock is a sin and that a young girl pays for her sin by going ahead and having the baby and raising it." This is, perhaps, too harsh a picture of Potter Addition and its morality.

Actual judgments are usually more muted and the motives behind them more complex than this cold assessment of an outsider would suggest. As in so many other aspects of small-town life, not just the life of this class, moral perceptions are relative to the situation and to the person being evaluated. It makes a difference *who* is pregnant. If it is someone else's daughter, or the daughter of an enemy, then premarital pregnancy is indicative of a deep moral flaw. In such instances the sin of illegitimacy becomes an endless subject of gossip, sniggering, and innuendo—always carried on, of course, outside the earshot of the girl and her relatives. If a year later this same critic's daughter or the daughter of a relative or close friend becomes pregnant, then the same moral infraction is excused as "something that happens," or shrugged off rather matter-of-factly with, "She's done no worse than any other kid out here."

There is more than a grain of truth in this last account. Rates of illegitimacy have been appallingly high for the last two cohorts of young women. There are, however, several reasons, other than "social disorganization," that can account for these high rates of premarital pregnancies. First, there is often the failure of mothers, either out of embarrassment or puritanical shame, to instruct their daughters in even the rudiments of sex. Second, the ubiquity of pregnancy prior to marriage tends in some ways to diminish the stigma of illegitimacy. Such "tragedies" are generally discussed for a month or two, and then dropped. To dwell on the subject for too long is sooner or later to invite comment about *your* past, or the transgressions of *your kin*. Finally, there is the paramount fact that children are wanted. It is true that as the child grows he or she is less the center of attention and is ultimately handed over to the youngster's peer group. But as objects of affection babies are sought and valued by both sexes, most especially by the maternal grandmother. In fact, it may be more to the point to say that a baby is valued not so much as a child, but as a grandchild.

If the daughter has been locked in a protracted, rebellious struggle, with her mother, the infant may become both a prize proffered to the mother and a weapon with which to fight back. On the one hand, illegitimacy is a striking out, one of the few ways a daughter can set her mother back on her heels. At the same time, the child is a gift—an attempt to appease the one person whom the girl loves and needs, but also fears and hates. As for the young man, the sexual double standard means that he is less blameless, but no less responsible. He is usually encouraged by his family "to be a man" and urged to "do what is right by the girl," even though she may be unfairly depicted by her future in-laws as a seductress. Manly honor and responsibility are usually met with varying degrees of shock, though there is the usual fear of "catching hell" from one's parents for "knocking up" the girl. Marriage and fatherhood, on the other hand, are faced with surprisingly little *visible* trepidation. Many young men exhibit the kind of fatalism that we find in the following exchange between Rose Harrington and her brother, Sonny. Rose is about to blindside her brother in a raucous, playful exchange. This jousting, however, masks a bitterness and personal resentment that Rose discusses after Sonny leaves:

Rose:	What's this I hear—you got to get married.
Sonny:	Who said?
Rose:	Don't lie to your sister, Sonny.
Sonny:	Who said?
Rose:	Don't worry about it. I guess everybody makes mistakes, but a daddy at sixteen? [laughter] That's nothing, I was a mommy even younger. [more laughter]
Sonny:	Don't lip off.
Rose:	I'm not lipping off, Sonny. I just want to know if it's true. I just want to prepare myself.
Sonny:	For what?
Rose:	I don't know . . . (long pause, as if thinking up a reason) I'm afraid you might ask me to baby-sit.
Sonny:	Shit!
Rose:	What are you going to do for a job? I'm not getting on you, now; I'm just asking.
Sonny:	I got a job.
Rose:	Whereabouts? [Sonny does not answer her query]
Sonny:	I got to go to work at three o'clock, that's why I wanted Jim to take me over to the other side of town.
Rose:	Well, son, why don't you ride him over there right quick then. [Sonny leaves with Rose's son, Jim; Rose turns to interviewer and continues]
Rose:	Well, Dave, there's going to be a little hell to pay on this one. He is going to need someone to stand up for him. I know Mom a little too well. Mom's going to be pretty harsh. I'm just so afraid what's going to happen is that she's going to rave and cuss and everything else. I'm just so afraid! Although Mom really shouldn't say anything, because he's not the only one. [laughter] Because my other brother and his wife, Cher, had to get married. Really, I blame Mom a lot for it. Maybe I'm wrong. I'm not saying my kids are angels, because I can just imagine about what they have done. They have probably done the same thing; but I have warned my kids about it and tried to explain to them, which Mom never did that much to any of us kids.

I don't know what was the matter with Mom, but I told Wanda about that when she was ten years old. Then I got a call from her Scout leader, who asked if they could have permission to see this special film on a young girl turning into a woman, and I told her yes. I thought it was one of the greatest things a child could see, and Wanda went to it. That's the same way with boys when they had sex education classes at school. They tried to teach them what's good and what's wrong, and I think that's good. A lot of people gripe because they teach it, but I think they do darn good by teaching this in school. That's one thing I will give them credit for.

The young couple's attempt to establish an autonomous household is threatened, if not doomed, from the start. The requisite economic and emotional security needed to establish a new conjugal unit, free from the dependencies of premarital life, is seldom granted. The girl's love/hate relationship with her mother is suddenly intensified with the onset of pregnancy. The mother, seldom more than a stone's throw away, shows a new interest in the young girl now that she is carrying her grandchild. In some few cases, this interest may be the first attention the mother has given the girl in years. In either circumstance, the girl's dependency and the mother's domination tend to intensify.

The young husband's fate is quite different. He has one task to perform: to provide for his wife and child. Wedding gifts and small cash loans can help the couple set up their new home, but obviously they are not a substitute for a steady income. Unschooled and untrained, launched into an unduly extended search and trial phase of his work life, the young man is ill equipped to meet the financial challenge of being a steady provider. We can gain a sense of the dimensions of the crisis the new couple faces from Rose Harrington's discussion of Sonny's immediate prospects:

Sonny and them are supposed to get the marriage license tonight and they'll get married, he said, either this evening or tomorrow. Her mom paid five hundred dollars down on a trailer for them, so I guess they're going to be living in a trailer. They bought it over here in Jefferson's Trailer Court. I don't know whether they are going to go ahead and let it set there or not. I think they have to pay twenty-five dollars a month. I don't think that's bad, I really don't, but I'm just wondering if they're going to be able to afford it. I told Sonny, "You're going to have to stop to think!" You're going to have your trailer payment, plus you're going to have to lay money aside for this baby that's due." He only gets paid every two weeks, and there is a lot that's coming out of that check already. He's got trailer payments, the new baby, and I think he told me he will have to pay Jefferson thirty-seven dollars a month for rent and water; that doesn't include his electricity. He's getting paid ninety dollars every two weeks. I told him, "You're going to have to stop and think, now."

Sonny is clearly on the edge. Not only is he barely solvent, he has already taken his first loan from his wife's mother. While technically this was a wedding gift, he has begun his marriage in *social debt*. This will most assuredly be thrown up to him by his wife or mother-in-law in a future dispute. By being a stable provider, Sonny could have taken the first step in asserting his manhood. He could have closed off the new conjugal unit from interference and predation, and established himself as the uncontested instrumental leader in his household. Failing to close off the family circle, however, means that in all likelihood Sonny's wife will be little more than her mother's daughter in years to come, and that Sonny himself will be little more than an appendage to their matrilateral alliance.

When the young husband fails to provide, it is usually the wife's mother who picks up the slack. Although the grandmother is generally in her midthirties by the time her daughter marries, her household has economically stabilized to the point that she can help. Thus, when requested, aid comes readily, but not without strings. In return for financial aid, many grandmothers demand a say in the actual rearing of the child and in the running of the young couple's household. Such concessions are usually granted at the expense of the husband's self-respect and instrumental authority. Since it is his failure that has made the request for aid necessary, it is only natural that aid be bartered in return for the husband ceding some portion of his authority to the new provider. The displacement of the husband by the maternal grandmother is discussed quite matter-of-factly by Sue Martin, who, at the age of twenty-seven, is the daughter of Mary Stoner, wife of Al Martin, and mother of Kay—the oldest of four children:

> Mary will let me go further as soon as she thinks I can afford it. You see, money means a lot to my mother; if you don't have any, you're not nothing. As I see it, Mother will hang on to little Kay until I have become wealthy, which will never happen. Until then, I'll have to put up with this. I can't give Kay the things that Mother can, so Mama is going to hang on. I guess that doesn't make any sense, but that's the way it is. What makes it so damned hard is that since the day Al and I were married, it has been one financial crisis after another. It's been, "Mom, we've got to borrow money to buy the clothes to send Kay to school," "Mom, Kay needs a new pair of shoes and we just don't have the money," or "Mom, we've run out of money and don't have any bread or milk in the house." No matter how successful Al could become, he could still never come up with what Mother gives our daughter. Mother will give her things that I think are too damned silly to buy for her, and I come to resent this. It's only human nature to resent it, but what are you going to do about it? She's her grandparent; and Dad's just as bad—he goes out and buys all four kids

horses, toy tractors, and bicycles, and crap they don't need. He goes out and buys it for them, so he's just as bad as Mother in the long run. You ask me if this has undercut my authority with my kids? Ha! I told Al when I married him the way I felt about my mother. He knew how I felt. He knew how Mother felt about me. So, he has just learned to live with it. He accepted it when we got married, and he's lived with it. He hasn't liked it all the time, but you ask him and he'll admit that Mary Stoner is one of the greatest people that ever walked on the face of the earth, because she's helped us when nobody else would. I won't say that he takes it lying down; he sits there and grits his teeth and clenches his fist and bites his tongue to keep from saying anything, and I love him very much for it, because it would make it so difficult for us if he acted any other way. Then it would be strictly, "All right, it's going to be me or your mother." This is a decision that would be very difficult for me to make. Sure, Al loves me and Al has done everything a husband can do, but Mother has done things that most mothers wouldn't do. This is the distinction between me and the rest of the girls out here. My mother has done things for me that are not expected of a mother. Most mothers would have gotten so damned sick of their daughter running out and doing what I did, time after time, that they would have said, "The hell with it, just get out. I don't ever want to see your face again." My father told me that more than once, and my mother politely told him to go to hell. "That's my daughter," she said, "and she'll live with us as long as she wants to!" Sure, Al hates it and I hate to feel this way, 'cause I know it hurts Al, but what can you do? She's my mother.

The strength of the mother-daughter bond and its permanence is underscored by the hard-edged nature of Sue Martin's admission that choosing between her mother and husband would *not* automatically be a choice that would preserve her marriage. We can also see that the cohesion of the mother-daughter sodality and the husband's problematic relation to his own household are but two sides of the same coin. This paired set of family characteristics, as we shall see, forms the structural core of lower-class family life.

III. THE HUSBAND AS AFFINE

The young man's predicament can be epitomized by saying that he is a husband, but only marginally a father. In order to explain this statement, I must use a distinction that is often employed in kinship analysis. The concrete family group lies at the intersection of two domains of kinship: the *domestic domain* and the *politicojural domain*. The domestic domain embraces the material foundations of kinship and includes the material resources available to the family group, and the sentiments and commitments that regulate the household's ecological adaptation to its physical and social environment. The politicojural domain, by contrast, is symbolic and normative in its content. It consists of a set of cultural discriminations that are formed around the parameters of descent, inheritance, and marriage. When these discriminations are applied to the everyday challenges of group life they produce households, families, and descent groups—a collection of kinsmen who are morally committed to the collective welfare of one another. Thus, the jural domain morally orders the interaction of kinsmen and their families and regulates relations between different kinship groupings.

The two domains can be seen as relating to one another in the same way that the Marxist economic base relates to its cultural superstructure. That is, the material and ecological settings of group life (the domestic domain) delimit, but do not directly determine the politicojural norms that regulate kinship structures. Thus, the domestic domain of lower-class life, conditioned as it is by its variable class niche, delimits the possible patterns that can emerge to integrate lower-class family and kinship formations.

When I say that the male is a husband, but only marginally a father, I mean that his family activity is largely confined to the domestic domain—the household's everyday material transactions and emotional dealings. He is a sexual mate and companion to this wife, and is perceived by his children as a loving but sometimes ineffectual bumbler. This latter perception flows from his impotence in the family's jural domain. He is not fully a father in the jural sense, for to be a "genuine" father he would have to exercise instrumental leadership legitimately, be the internal court of last resort within the family, be respected by his in-laws, and serve as the family's representative to the larger community. Once stripped of these traditional prerogatives, if he stays in the family, he has little choice but to retreat into the domestic domain. In that restricted space, he can reestablish an already shaky family status.

In Potter Addition, with some significant exceptions, the father is a loving, if at times inconstant mate to his wife, and a doting, affectionate "daddy" to his daughters. To his sons, he is too often a shadowy figure—an uncertain source of discipline and often an openly negative role model used by the mother to chastise the son. For all this, however, the man is never a fool, and by no means a fop. He is, in fact, often the swaggering stereotype of a male, and a consummate model of masculinity. If he were any less brave or physically masculine, any less mercurial in temperament, or any less prone to physical violence when honor required it, he would be seen as less of a husband by his wife and viewed with even less admiration by his children. Before marriage his drinking, brawling, wild honky-tonking ways, and sexual prowess, while technically demurred, make him extremely attractive to the young woman who will become his wife. After marriage, these traits are dampened, but seldom lost. His machismo, though double-edged and capable at times of making marriage a living hell for the wife, is also the demeanor that she once loved and respected, and even now still ambivalently desires in him.

As the children grow up in a domestic world largely structured by women, this masculinity, when combined with the perception that the man lacks effective authority in family councils, makes him a favorite with his daughters. To outsiders, he may appear to be the household autocrat—stern, taciturn, still physically virile in his early fifties, and still capable of measured, violent outbursts—yet his children know that this front is a sham when it comes to them. His studied, hard exterior has a soft underbelly that any daughter worth her salt can shamelessly exploit. This is evident in Sue Martin's loving characterization of her father, Harold Stoner:

Dad is a kind of a kid at heart, you see. He would blow every cent he had if it was up to him. Everything he's got, he's got because my mother had the brains to get it for him. He doesn't care as much as Mary does; I think this is the whole thing. You can't get around him any easier *if he knows* what you're doing. He just doesn't care as much as Mother does. I mean, Mother has and always will be tough. But Dad, he's kind of "Well, if you don't get it done this week, you'll do it the next week," or he'll do a favor for somebody. Everybody likes him because of this. He's got no *particular* friends out here; *everybody's a friend!* He's always got a nice word for everybody. I don't know of anybody that really dislikes my father out here. Nobody likes my mother, but nobody dislikes my father. He just kind of sits back and beats around the bush; he'll hum-haw around; he'll discuss first one thing and then another, and pretty soon you get the idea of what he's trying to get to. It takes him such a long time to get there because he doesn't want to hurt anybody's feelings or step on their toes. I guess my family is like some others out here that way. For example, when there are any big financial decisions to be made, Dad doesn't decide—Mother decides. For example, when they decided to go into farming after the war, down by DeSoto, even though he was going to do all the work, it wasn't my dad that made the decision; it was my mom. Even today, Mom puts so much money into Dad's checking account, and if he blows it, well, that's it until the next payday. Mother pays the bills; Mother makes the financial decisions; Mother tells him when he will and when he won't buy a new car.

My dad's no softie, though. He's a boy who was born in Tennessee and raised by a hillbilly. He'll help you every bit he can, but don't cross him! If you get him mad at you, you're in big trouble. I mean, he can be just as nasty as any man I've ever seen, but everyone likes him. He's easygoing and it's almost impossible to get him angry. You really have to just about get down and stomp on him to get him mad at you. He'll take most anything from anybody, and people out here walk on him a lot, but there comes a time, and then watch out.

The one-dimensional, surface machismo described by Sue paves the way for the rise of a family "gynecocracy"—an arrangement in which women assume the responsibilities for leadership, the internal domestic critique of family life, and, on rare occasions, a limited, representation of the family to the larger community. This female-dominated family is what I refer to as the uxoricentric family. By definition, the uxoricentric family is composed of two conjugal households, each of which is an ecologically independent entity. In reality, they are two halves of a single, fused social structure. Like the jerry-built houses of the community, the uxoricentric constellation is an unseemly adaptation and fusion of two otherwise independent structures. The wife and mother run their respective households, even as the gynecocratic power structure allows the older woman to dominate both. United by the mother-daughter umbilical, there is a constant flow of personnel and resources between the two households. Leadership in the uxoricentric household still partitions itself along the generational axis of family life. But instead of the dividing line being drawn internally to a single household, as it would be in the Parsonsian nuclear family, *it runs between the two households*. The ecological line that once spatially separated the two now marks the boundary between jural superordination and subordination.

The second distinguishing trait of the uxoricentric family is the cross-generational reproduction of male superfluity. Male default is as much a requirement of uxoricentric family life as male domination is a necessary component of its petit bourgeois opposite. The uxoricentric family is either surrounded by a penumbra of jurally dispossessed males, or is devoid of men altogether. Where divorce or desertion has not occurred, the male's jural superfluity becomes a necessary precondition for the formation of gynecocratic domination.

The status of the husband as a mere affine to the uxoricentric configuration is often acknowledged in the way that the community refers to certain women in everyday conversation. It seems that no matter how long a woman has been married, if she has grown up in the community long-term residents refer to her by her maiden name, and only occasionally by her married name. Sue Martin, for example, is still referred to as Sue Stoner in everyday conversation. She becomes Sue Martin if a stranger cannot link the "Stoner girl" with "Al's wife." This convention is in part a product of habit. Having grown up in the community, she has always been a Stoner and unextinguished verbal usage preserves her as a Stoner even now. There is more, however, to this terminological rigidity than unextinguished habit. It communicates a deeper truth about the husband's status in uxoricentric families: his social marginality. By retaining the woman's maiden name as a term of reference, the community implicitly affirms the permanence of the gynecocratic core and its crucial role in family life. The terminology also betrays the fact that even though married, the young wife's community status still flows as much, if not more, from being a daughter in her parents' household than from being the head of her own family. Periodically, a man may show mild irritation at this and other petty slights that render him socially invisible. There are even times when he breaks his silence, as happened one day when I asked a man which sex dominated Potter Addition's family affairs:

> I don't really know. I think the area is mostly female-dominated myself, if you want my personal opinion of it. That's just an opinion—I don't really know. But, what would you call Helen Gilbert, for example? Her man and her never got along and she run him off—that's female domination. Of course, I don't know the inner workings of it. He used to hide out in the back shed all the time, working on his hobbies. He was a nut on those hobbies! Helen used to say that he hid out there all the time because he looked so damn bad that nobody could stand and look at him in the face or talk to him. They was always fighting, always in an argument.
>
> Of course, when he tried to make the kids behave, they called him an old son-of-a-bitch and did what they wanted to. They finally just drove the man off. What do you call that if it ain't female dominance?
>
> I know several families around here where I think the female is the stronger of the two. I can think of several cases where the woman is the stronger type; you know, has things pretty much her own way. I think Thelma Evans was the stronger of the two. I don't know if you consider my wife stronger than me or not. As far as our family is concerned. I try to take the lead on a lot of things, and we get into fights, but that's only natural.

In a community composed largely of uxoricentric households and kinship groupings, the jural rights traditionally assigned to men become *contested, achieved statuses*. Once instrumental leadership is ceded by the male in those early years of marriage, he is usually not allowed to reclaim it without a struggle. It matters little that a decade later he may be capable of assuming his full financial and jural responsibilities. By then, he must contend with two women and a ten-year history of their working things out on their own. If he tries to reclaim his full jural citizenship, he will have to wrest it from them.

IV. PROTRACTED INTIMACIES: MOTHERS AND DAUGHTERS

The young husband's jural dispossession and the wife's mother's usurpation of instrumental leadership gives renewed impetus to the dependency relationship that already exists between mother and daughter. In the Parsonsian family model, the daughter's dependency is the crucial block to her achieving full autonomy as a person and to her maturing as a responsive mate. If she is to mature socially, it can only be by achieving parity with her mother. Such dependency struggles are the feminine analog to the Oedipal situation, and are not easily navigated by the lower-class woman. Always a perilous point of transition in the petit bourgeois family, this dependency often becomes a permanent feature of lower-class families. Being the integrative force that holds uxoricentric households together, the relation so distorts the modal pattern of petit bourgeois family life that the course of the family cycle is itself altered.

To begin with, the early age of marriage finds the young wife ill prepared to establish an egalitarian relation with her mother. The economically open household, created by the economic default of the husband, forms the foundation for an even more intense dependency. These bonds take on an added emotional weight if the daughter was a rebellious adolescent and is now in the midst of a crumbling marriage or a precipitous motherhood. She is forced to "grow up" overnight and, as in Sue Stoner Martin's case, guilt and remorse over years of treating her mother badly are intensified by the mother's unstinting aid and seemingly unconditional love. Marriage is frequently not a declaration of independence from the mother, but a dramatic ritual that celebrates the return of the prodigal—often bearing the child as a gift.

The nature and state of the mother-daughter dyad is given a new structural inflection with the emergence of the gynecocratic core as the main reproductive unit of uxoricentric culture. The mother-daughter relationship and its integration is the structural linchpin of the orderly replacement of the family's culture from one generation to the next. In some ways, the mother-daughter dyad resembles the "mum relation" documented by Young and Willmott (1957) in their classic study of British working-class family and kinship in East London. Potter Addition's family structure differs from the British case, however, in that there is an ambivalence and tension interlarded with love and dependency that the British researchers seldom emphasize.

Variations in the female dyad's emotional rapport and its degree of autocratic organization produce profound differences in the composition and integration of the female core. The variations in the mother-daughter relationship and the impact of that variation on the daughter's autonomy will be illustrated in three brief sketches. The first concerns

Sue Martin and Mary Stoner, two women whom we have already met. Their relationship is prototypical of what happens when a female autocrat takes over the running of her daughter's household, and in so doing founds a classic uxoricentric family culture. The second sketch involves Nancy Norris and her mother, Freida Walsh. As in the Martin-Stoner case, the father's instrumental role in guiding the orderly replacement of family culture has collapsed, and with it the patrilateral focus of family life. Unlike the Martin-Stoner example, however, this default has not produced a uxoricentric counterform. Instead, Nancy Norris's life is filled with conflict and retrospective bitterness. Freida's husband has long since departed, but before he left he tried to reassert his jural rights and failed. This resulted in a decade of domestic turmoil that had two lasting results: It scarred Nancy Norris and turned Freida into an even stronger, if more shrewish, woman. The family structure emerging in the Walsh and Norris households is not, as in the Stoner-Martin case, one of a matricentric culture securely organized around a two-generation female cadre that is now socializing a third in order to perpetuate the gynecocratic core. Instead, two women are locked in an unending series of recriminations and self-feeding circles of guilt.

The last sketch is the most extreme and by far the least representative of life in Potter Addition. In the story of Lee Vestman and Laura Case we encounter a mother-daughter bond so intense and involuted that it allegedly destroyed the daughter's marriage even before the jural default of the male could take place. Here the mother did not take over the daughter's household, for the household was never given time to form.

A. Sue Stoner Martin

We have seen Mary Stoner force Al Martin to the periphery of family life. Her autocratic domination, however, while it may someday drive Al away, is not dysfunctional to the gynecocratic core's social reproduction. While Mary's autocracy has kept Sue and her husband in a form of emotional peonage and debt bondage, it has nevertheless effectively ordered the world of this three-generation core. Mary's personal domination is the ordering principle that integrates the two households into a single unit. Autocratic, yet in her own hard way a very loving woman, she has ordered the life of those around her for almost two decades now. Sue will in all likelihood be left with just enough ego strength that upon Mary's death she will assume the same autocratic posture vis-à-vis her daughter that Mary has assumed toward her. Mary's two grandsons will probably be socialized to follow in their father's and grandfather's footsteps. If both possibilities are realized, then the orderly replacement of uxoricentric family culture will be assured for another generation. In the following passage Sue Martin tells us of the emotional debt bondage that lies at the very heart of the gynecocratic core:

See, where my old lady is concerned, I'm chicken, Dave. I guess you got to stop and look at it this way. First of all, this is Mary Stoner we're talking about, and I tell you she doesn't care whose toes she steps on when it comes to her granddaughter. Kay was her *first* granddaughter, and that counts for something, too. I guess you might have expected me to stand up to her, but you just don't understand. You see, your wife *did not* have a child out of wedlock that her mother raised for fifteen months. Mom came to think of Kay as her own daughter. With that in my background, I can't just tell her to go to hell. That's kind of like saying, "Sure, today if I were to get pregnant and had a baby and my mother pulled the crap that she did then, I would do different." But that's not how it happened. I can't say to her, "This is my child. Flake off!" My mother would walk all over me if I said that. You see, it just goes back to what I'm saying—I'm horrified at my mother. She kind of scares me.

I can see that you still don't understand. Let me explain it this way. I owe my life to my mother. I owe the very fact that I even have a child now to my mother. When I was fifteen and I got pregnant, there was nobody but Mother. She stood right there and told the whole country to go to hell. "This is my daughter. She made a mistake. It doesn't have a God-damned thing to do with you, so just flake off, friend." When Kay was born, I didn't have any money. Mama came through with a vaporizer. New clothes? Even today when Al and I can't afford to buy Kay something that Kay really wants, who comes through? Mama!

Let's go back a minute. I said I fear Mary, but that's not just so. For example, let's take Dad. Really, I think it was as much him paying the bills when Kay was born as it was Mom, but he didn't stand there beside you holding your hand during labor like Mother did when nobody else in the world seemed to care. So, really, it's not fear, it's just that she's done so damned much for me. How can I just say, "Go to hell, Mary. Just forget you're my mother." I just can't because, you see, she *is* my mother, and when I was putting her through hell, she stood there and took it, which is more than a lot of mothers out here did for their daughters. There have been other girls that have gotten pregnant, and their families have forced them to marry before the child was born. They knew it would make the girl miserable and the children miserable, and as a result of this everybody *was* miserable. But my mom didn't do this—she was patient and let Al and me work things out.

It seems likely that the emotional bonds that tie Sue to Mary Stoner are secure enough to assure family continuity. It is also clear that in Mary Stoner's eyes Al will never earn enough to be a good provider and, hence, will never again be a potent instrumental leader. For these reasons, the orderly replacement of gynecocratic family culture has little to do with Al. His coming or going is largely superfluous to future family functioning. Mary's death is another matter, for only then will we discover if Mary's autocracy has stripped Sue of the will and emotional strength to step into her mother's shoes and begin reproducing with Kay the same gynecocratic forms. Sue, with her brightness and swaggering verbal style, seems to be thriving now. Though assimilated into her mother's world at the moment, the crucial question remains: Can she shift overnight from being a submissive satellite to being an autocrat like her mother? Will she have the strength to dominate her daughter, and, in doing so, complete another cycle of uxoricentrism's reproductive process?

B. Nancy Walsh Norris

We will probably not have to wait for Freida Walsh's death to decide Nancy Norris's case. What is still a pending question in Sue Martin's life seems resolved in Nancy's case. In her twenty-five or so years, she has never obtained a secure, aggressive sense of self, and probably never will. As Nancy tells us, she has always been in the middle of fights—first between her mother and father, and then between her husband and mother. Her marriage, initially seen as an avenue of escape, has become a trap. What appeared to be an exit from the pain and turmoil of her childhood has become just another way of "being caught in the middle again."

Nancy, in fact, was never her own person. The hapless figure she cuts in her own narrative is one of a totally objectified being with little or no autonomy. We listen to her and are reminded of the heroine of Elizabethan and Appalachian ballads; victimized equally in her parental home and now in marriage, her biography is a continuous series of claustrophobic encounters and defeats. She was probably never strong. Just as assertive and aggressive fathers often emasculate their sons, so Freida's monolithic presence has bred an uncertain daughter.

Nancy constitutes with Freida and her seven-year-old daughter a much different triad than that found in the Stoner-Martin family. Her husband, Tuck, has divorced her and moved to Indianapolis, where he has remarried. He has visitation rights to his children, but has not exercised them since 1965. Driven out by Freida and her contempt for him, much as she drove out her own husband, Tuck has reproduced the pattern begun by Nancy's father, Ben. This double expulsion has destroyed any possibility of a male-oriented family culture, and at the same time it seems unlikely that a gynecocratic core will form. As one listens to Nancy's narrative, there is a growing realization that precious little exists between Nancy and Freida that would allow for cultural continuity built on feminine solidarity.

Thus, neither a patrilateral public culture nor a matrilateral counterform will take shape in the Walsh-Norris households. Instead, self-weaning pity, mixed with feelings of love and hate for one another, produces a family culture riddled with anomie. Nancy knows this, just as she knows that her string has run out. For her, Potter Addition is a suffocating place. The community has cast her as the centerpiece of a cruel morality play. She talks of leaving Potter Addition, as do so many of her generation, but like them, she stays. Potter Addition is all she has ever known, and the safety of this particular, predictable hell is preferable to the freedom and social void that await her elsewhere. At one time she was a beautiful woman, but a hard life is slowly changing that. At one time she openly aspired to be better than her neighbors, let them know as much, and failed—a triple crime in Potter Addition. It is the crimes of hubris and failure, as much as anything else, for which she now pays. With a family to raise, abandoned by her husband, and having few employable skills, she lives partly on welfare, and partly on her mother's largess—a gift for which she pays dearly.

Like Sue Martin, she feels cheated and knows she deserves better, but she has not survived as well as Sue. Sue's hard-bitten shell is all front and she knows it; but it serves her well as long as she is not pressed too hard. Nancy Norris does not have even that ersatz shell in which to hide. Instead, she presents an image of exhaustion, playing her role with a passivity that masks her occasional capacity for a defensive and protective cruelty. Knowing these facts should alert us to a certain sadness in her voice, which the written narrative cannot convey. The sadness is there as she relates how her life as a perpetual pawn and outsider began.

> I don't know. This is hard to explain. I mean, when we were kids my Dad and I were always together, while Mom and Joey were closer. After he and Mom split up, there was always Mom and Joey, but I was kind of left out. Maybe it's just pettiness on my part, you know, to feel that way, but then I had people tell me this, so it's not *all* imagination. Mom and Joey always acted sort of superior to me. It was like she thought more of him than she did of me.
>
> Even before Dad left, things weren't what I would call real good. Dad was always highly jealous. I don't know why, because Mom never did say anything that made me think he should be, but the problem was their ages. Dad was something like ten years younger than my Mom. I don't know whether that made him feel insecure—whether he thought she'd find someone else her own age, or what. But they would argue about almost anything. He would say that she had someone visiting her or

something like that. Like I say, he was highly jealous and it would have been different if he had a reason, but I never did see that he had a reason. He'd come in late at night and yell and holler that he saw a car go around the road and he thought it had been here. If someone would come in and have coffee, my sisters or someone, he'd check the dishes to see how many dishes were dirty. Then the next day Mom would start in because of what he had said the night before. It was just one constant argument after another about something, and I don't know why. To this day, I can't figure out why.

Now, who was the more dominant? Was that the question? I would have to say Mom. Dad tried to stand up to her, but I don't think *anyone* can get their rights with Mom. That will just never be! But I remember he would try to stand up to her, and that would make her awful mad. I have seen her hit him, and he never would hit her back. This kind of made me mad at him, because I wanted him to slug her back. I'm like that. I think if you hit, you deserve to be hit back.

What made it all so unnecessary is that they fought most of the time over silly things. For example, Dad is a stickler for having things done the way he wants it done, and if they're not, then he raises Cain. Mom and him would stand up and argue until he was blue in the face about it. I mean, if he wanted something cooked a certain way, he wanted it cooked that way, and if it wasn't, he'd have a fit about it. As far as she was concerned, if he didn't like it, that was tough, you know? I've always heard that it was all Dad's fault, but if you lived there you knew it wasn't. It was fifty-fifty in my book. In any marriage, even in my own marriage, it wasn't all Tuck's fault, and it wasn't all mine.

Because of their fighting and bickering, there was always this constant tension. Your stomach would knot up in a ball when they would come together. It didn't seem to bother my brother Joey. Maybe it did and he just didn't show it; but me, I know when they would argue I would cry and beg them to stop, or I'd lay there in bed with the pillow over my head. He would come home about one o'clock or two o'clock at night from where he worked as a janitor and they would start in. I had times as a kid that I would sit down for no reason and just burst out crying when nothing was wrong. There was no reason for it. I think it was nervous tension from being in constant turmoil, afraid there would be an argument when he came home.

They broke up several times before they got divorced in 1959. I remember because I got physically sick. I thought they were going to involve me in the divorce, trying to make me say that one was more at fault than the other, afraid Mom would have me say that Dad was the one who started all the arguments. I was sick in bed for two days because of my worrying about having to take sides. Thank God, though, they didn't involve me, because I was in the middle.

If we are to accept Nancy's account, her problems with Freida began long before her father left home. They are grounded in the polarization of a crumbling marriage, one in which Nancy and her father somehow became allies. She now sees those early years as ones of progressive estrangement from Freida and her brother. The pain of those years, the sense of always being dragged into the middle of parental disputes, and finally the terror of having to take sides in an open court battle are all recounted with a pathos that suggests that these original alienations and their subsequent ressentiment are still unresolved. Being in the middle of the turmoil, treated as the surrogate of a parent who is already disengaging himself from a hellish marriage, and wanting a way out, she seeks escape as so many other young women of her generation and class have done—through marriage:

This is the way it was when Tuck and I got married. I think I wanted out of conflict. I wanted out of hearing how Dad was no good, and so on and so forth. Because, let's face it, I worship Dad. I know he's got his bad points, but I still worship him—even today. I haven't seen him in ages, and the last time I saw him, we got into an argument, but I still worship him.

Anyway, I married Tuck when I was just four months short of being seventeen. I'd known Tuck all my life, since I was two weeks old. He held me on his lap then, when he was six or seven years old. I got married and the hell of it was that I didn't have to get married. I had a church wedding. Tuck couldn't afford it, since he had a job at a gas station. Mom borrowed a hundred dollars and signed for it so we could get married at the Nazarene church up on Spooner Road. I don't know why Mom ever consented. Dad was so indignant he wouldn't even come to the wedding. Instead of standing up to Mom and saying, "No! She's not getting married," he just skipped over the whole damn thing. This is one of the things that kind of makes me look down on him a little bit. He could have stood up to her that one time. I think she consented because she wanted me out from her hair.

What did I want out of marriage? Freedom more than anything else—I think! [laughter] I wasn't conscious so much of having a home and a family and all that. I remember I didn't want to have a family right away. I wanted to wait, but Tuck said he wanted children and that this is what he got married for. That's why Tommy came so soon. It was his idea, because I didn't know anything. I was pretty dumb. I remember asking him stupid questions like "What's a lesbian?" I know it sounds weird that anyone that age didn't know all that. I remember before how terrified I was when Mom explained the menstrual period to me and how you're not supposed to let a man touch you. I remember asking her how to prevent this. But when it came to having our children, Tuck was kind of the boss.

But see, I got married to get away. Maybe it was because Mom hemmed me in so much, but when I got married, it wasn't freedom. I went from one trap to another. We were married and he started working nights, and we were only together during the day. He came home and slept and I was up and out. Then he started coming home later and later, and usually he had been drinking. When I was dating him, I was glamorized by his drinking and smoking. I didn't realize he was going to make it a way of life, but pretty soon I was alone, and him out drinking. I went from one trap to another. And Mom was always there. "Do this! do that! or do something else!" She was more or less letting me go on my own, but was always in checking, making sure things were done "just so."

Mom always treated me like I was inferior, even after I married Tuck. When Tommy was born she bought quite a few clothes and things, more or less to show us we couldn't. It was like she was saying, "Look what I got—big me and little you." This was always the impression I got with her. By now you can guess I've got a "thing" going with her. It sounds like I'm on a kick against her, and maybe I am. Maybe I resent her because Dad left and isn't around, and I blame her for his leaving. I've got lots of resentment; I know that, and I try to control it.

Sometimes I just don't understand how her mind works. She bought lots of things for Tommy, but didn't seem to care about little Craig. Even now, when I ask her to watch the kids, she doesn't want to be bothered with Craig. She says, "Well, I can't handle him," or gives some other excuse. It's always been this way. "You can take Craig with you." It was like that even when he was tiny and wasn't any trouble.

Beginning with when I was pregnant, all I would hear was, "Why did you get pregnant?" Like it was a crime to begin with. I think she didn't want me to have any kids. I don't know why, but I mean this is the impression I got. When Tuck came along she thought he was great to a certain extent, but she turned sour on the idea of me having kids. Maybe she thought that Tuck couldn't provide for me or something. I really don't know; I just kind of got this impression. I know when I was pregnant with Tommy, and Tuck was going straight from work to the tavern every night and not coming in at all, that she would say, "Why did you get pregnant?"

I was married for, let's see, four, five, six years, and had Tommy, Craig, and Elizabeth during that time. After I had Tommy, we moved to the trailer down on Banks Avenue here. When he was a baby he was always getting a sore throat or a cold. He had pneumonia one time, and the doctor thought it was the oil heat in the trailer. That's when we moved uptown. When we lived down on Banks, Mom was down there constantly. When we got the apartment in Grand Prairie, it was still the same; Mom was there about every day. She stopped by on her way home from work.

Tuck's and my marriage actually got better in some ways when we moved to the apartment; but then Tuck took up his drinking again—just about the time I thought things were improving. I think he had personal conflicts of his own that he was worrying about, you know, other than just our marriage. This thing about his mom and dad giving him up to strangers bothered him, and things that I found out later had happened preyed on him. I hear he still drinks quite a bit. I tried to be helpful and understand, but he seemed to regard me as a kid—someone who couldn't tell him what to do, even though this might have helped our marriage. He thought, "Who the hell are you?" But despite this attitude and his drinking, I was fairly happy there in the Ohio Street apartment. He was still

drinking enough that he couldn't pay the bills when he should, so we had
to move out of the apartment because he owed them rent.

Then we moved down on Elm Street. It was a nice house and we paid
seventy-five dollars a month, but this was too high for our income bracket.
We weren't making that much, so we ended up coming back out here to
Potter Addition and lived four houses up from Mom. That's where Tuck
and Mom really got into it. Before, when we lived down on Banks, she
was trying to stick her nose into our business, but Tuck never said too
much. Now Mom was down at the house all the time trying to run us. I
wanted to pick up and leave, but Tuck didn't have the guts to do it.
Moving would mean having to go out and find some place to live, and that
would have been too big a struggle for him.

In Nancy's eyes, Freida seems more determined than ever to run the
show, and after the birth of Tommy, Freida's domination seems to intensify. In truth, Nancy's situation is more desperate than before. Her
father has left town, and with him Nancy's last ally. Despite her retrospective denunciation of Tuck, it is obvious that he honestly tried to
resist. There is, in fact, that fleeting moment, when they move to Grand
Prairie and seem about to break free of Freida. This dash for autonomy
ends, however, when economic and personal problems drive the young
couple back to Potter Addition and renewed dependency. Nowhere in
the interim has Nancy come to grips with the love that binds her to her
mother, nor the hostility that deepens with each passing year. Furthermore, the options that were open prior to her marriage have been exhausted and Nancy's situation has worsened. How much so, she now
discovers upon returning to Potter Addition.

Then, all of a sudden, things changed. Everything all of a sudden was
sweet as pie between the two of them. Both of them were trying to tie me
up or something. They were keeping me here—not letting me get out and
away from things. He could have said, "Come on, let's leave; we're
moving," and I would have been willing, but he never had the guts to
stand up to Mom. Just like Dad! This is one thing that spoiled the whole
marriage. *All of a sudden they were together.* If they got in a fight, one of them
would come to me and jump on me about the other. For example, Tuck
wouldn't go to Mom and holler at her; he would come to me and tell
me—throw it up to me like it was all my fault. If she had something to say
about him, she would come to *me!* There I was, right in the middle again,
just like Mom and Dad. I think they planned it! [laughter] It was a conspiracy between Mom and Tuck! She's always tried to dominate me, like
she wanted to breathe for me or something. I'm, you know, kind of buggy
or something, but she wants to dominate me. But then, at the next moment I feel that she doesn't love me, so why bother. You know? I was
someone she could tell what to do, where she couldn't do the same to
someone else. Now we lived right down the street, only now we had her

grandchildren to boot. More bossing now. "You do such and such this way for the baby." Tuck was drinking just as bad as ever, and I was hearing about how he drank and "You'll never have nothing!" The whole bit. In fact, our marriage could have broken up sooner if it hadn't been for my persistence to show her. I would have been better off if it had broken up then, because it wasn't going to work anyway. She was always telling me to leave him and get out on my own, but I was determined to be defiant. She would try to boss us, and I would dig in.

I remember one time in particular that I felt kind of sorry for Tuck, and there was a whole big incident about it. I had been doing a neighbor's ironing, and Tuck was out. In fact, he was supposed to be home in the morning, and he came in loaded about one o'clock in the afternoon. We had been arguing and he said that it was my fault, that I let Mom push us too much, and this was why he was drinking *this particular day*. I agreed with him and apologized, and I was crying. He was holding me in his arms, and Mom came in and started butting in, wanted to know what he had done to me—if he had hit me, or what. I said, "No, he hadn't," but she didn't believe me. She started cussing him and everything, and he naturally started out the door—back to the bar. Just as he was about to leave, I remember he told her, "You old son of a bitch, you go home and mind your own business." She picked up a pan to hit him and he grabbed her arm and slapped the hell out of her, and this is what she needed. There I was, though, right in the middle of the conflict again, trying to break up another fight. I was right back with Mom and Dad. This was the whole thing all over again, and he was, you know, fighting back, and it kind of did me good to see him hit her. She called the police on him, and he was picked up.

Freida's suffocating love produces chaos in her daughter's life. Tied financially to Freida, having hoped that Tuck would be the instrument of her liberation, Nancy bitterly recounts her husband's rout. Had Tuck submitted, made his peace with Freida's autocratic ways, and retreated into the shadows, then perhaps some modicum of domestic order might have been salvaged, though frankly it is difficult to see how this would have come about. As it is, the refusal of two husbands to cooperate in their jural degradation has created familial bedlam. Nancy, not having Freida's strength, has seen her life become a Balkanized middle ground, so much so that life in Potter Addition has become little more than a form of house arrest.

C. *Larry Vestman and Laura Case*

The final example of a young woman being caught in the grip of maternal domination is so extreme that lesbianism is invoked as a possible explanation for the unseemly strong mother-daughter bond. Such a tabooed subject is almost never broached in this highly puritanical community, even under the most severe circumstances. This anecdote comes from one of my most trusted resource persons, yet we must be cautious in accepting every detail of his story. It is obvious that Larry's older brother—the person who is telling the story—is coming to his defense, and that the family has closed ranks in support of one of their own:

Well, you know, really I think the only reason they got married was because she thought she was pregnant. When she found out she wasn't, then she went back home to mama. Then they went back together a second time, and they separated again. The third time she was just about two or three months pregnant when she went to live with her mom. Larry couldn't even go out to see her hardly. Her mom was such an old biddy anyway. She moved on account of her mom in the first place.

I've never seen a mother act the way that woman does. I mean, it's shocking. Some people are saying that Larry must have done something, but I know better. It isn't Larry, it's Laura's mom. She listens to her mom. Laura's really a mama's girl. She just upped and went home to mama. When they first got married, they was getting along real good, until her mom kept butting in on them—"Laura, go here! Laura, go there!"—so Laura went back to mama. Larry decided that he would give her another chance. He came out here and talked with Harriet and me. I told him, "Well, Larry, maybe Laura just hasn't grown up yet. Why don't you just get a place of your own and try it again?" I think Laura was sixteen years old when they first got married; I'm not too sure. Anyway, Larry took her back and got them an apartment. I loaned him the money to pay the rent on it and told him we would help him clean it up, because the people told us that it really needed to be cleaned, since these other people had been really dirty. I told him that we had extra paint and would come in and help paint it. He said, "Okay, as long as the old lady stays away, it'll be all right." I asked, "Why?" He said, "You just won't believe it." Of course I thought he was kidding on how Laura's mom acts, but actually I think she's a queer. Because when I took the paint and went down there and her mom was there, when I walked into that basement apartment, there stood Laura and her mother in the front room. Her mom was kissing her and everything else. I just put the paint down and walked out. Larry came out front and said, "Now you see what I mean? Laura just won't get away from it."

I think they lived in that apartment for about a month, and then Laura went back to mama. Then, after Peggy was born, she got a divorce from Larry. Larry worked day and night then, but he always tried to go out and see the baby because, boy, that baby just thinks the world of her dad. To this day, she still does, and it makes Laura's mom mad that that little girl thinks so much of her dad.

Then they decided, well, to give it another try. They went together just like they did before, and Laura said that she wanted to get married again. She'd leave her mom and have nothing to do with her. They got married again and rented Wayne Zimmer's trailer that my other brother and his wife used to own and that Wayne bought from them. They moved out in it, and Larry got her new furniture and everything. I think they lived out there a good two months and was getting along just fine. Then one morning he went to work, and when he come home, she was gone. So he called to see if she was up to her mom's, and she said, "Yes, I didn't feel good, so I went up to Mom's." So she stayed out there for quite a while, and Larry said, "I'm going to ask you one more time to come back and act like a wife. I can't have this no more." He was working day and night trying to make a go of it and get her what she wanted. She said she wanted a colored TV, so Larry said, "If you come back, I'll get it." He goes up and gets her a colored TV, and she comes back for about a month or so—long enough to get pregnant again. Now she's gone home to her mom and is living there.

These three sketches have explored the emotional integration that binds mother and daughter to one another in Potter Addition. Though the female dyad's social integration and the relative autonomy of the daughters vary widely among the three, uxoricentrism's prototypical expression was found in the Stoner-Martin households. The other two cases showed us the mother-daughter dyad operating in situations in which neither uxoricentrism nor patrilateral domination could emerge. What is now required is an examination of the actual social dynamic which reproduces uxoricentrism from one day to the next. That will be the focus of the next chapter.

8

The Antinomies of Family Life

I. GENERATIONAL COMPRESSION

The ambiguities of family structure in Potter Addition are sometimes reflected in its terminology. The term *mother*, for example, is employed in the usual manner to refer to a genitrix. On occasion, however, *mother* may be used by a grandchild when addressing his or her grandmother. In these cases, usually where a marriage has failed and the children are being raised by the grandparents, the terms *mama* and *grandma* are often used interchangeably. Sometimes, the grandmother reciprocates, referring to the child as "my boy" or "my girl," and encouraging the child to call her "Mom" or "Mama." As we can see from the following passage, residents view such practices uneasily:

> Those people have drunk and fought for years and have trouble staying together. Their little girl has lived with her grandmother, Mrs. Markey, for two years now. I know you've seen her, Dave, she comes here to the store a lot to buy pop and candy—that's Mrs. Markey's granddaughter. The Markeys have raised her so long that she just calls them Mom and Dad. I don't know if the little girl actually knows the difference, just to be honest about it. You would think she knows the difference, wouldn't you? She's got about three or four brothers and sisters living elsewhere, but she should know.

A second terminological practice suggests yet another way in which generational lines are blurred. A mother sometimes refers to her children, herself, and even her husband as *us kids,* and in one or two families a mother will address and refer to her daughter as *sister*. These sibling terms of address are used interchangeably with the children's first names and invariably express affection. Terms such as "us kids" or "sister" suggest an egalitarian relationship between parents and their children that is at odds with the Parsonsian model. The authority structure of these families diverges from that of the traditional petit bourgeois ideal. Instead of having two generations demarcated by sharp lines of authority, the parents and children are bound by close ties of pseudosiblingship.

The first terminological usage makes the mother and grandmother functionally interchangeable in the eyes of certain grandchildren. This is reinforced and extended by the second convention, in which parents and children regard one another as quasi-siblings. The two practices can be subsumed under a single principle: *the compression of generations*. One woman summed up this compression in an offhand comment:

> When I raised my sons and daughters, I more or less grew up with them and could not appreciate being a mother and raising children. I can hardly wait for Wilma to get married and have children so I can raise kids and appreciate doing it.

Pregnant at sixteen, married at eighteen, and expecting to be a grandmother at thirty-seven, she tells us what is obvious. At sixteen, although biologically a mother herself, she was not yet an adult. Still bound to her own protective mother, she raised her children as though they were her mother's children. She grew with her children and was more a sister to them than a mother. Technically she was the primary socializer of her children; in point of fact, her mother made the decisions when it came to raising them. Now on the verge of being a grandmother herself, she is looking forward to the joys of motherhood for the first time. Her daughter Wilma will not simply present her with grandchildren; Wilma will provide her with a new batch of children to raise. Since Wilma is just turning seventeen, she will be, like her mother, a child bride, a child mother, and a quasi-sibling to her own children.

The compression of generations is at the core of the cultural reproduction of the uxoricentric family. In the usual sense in which we use the terms, there are few mothers, daughters, grandparents, husbands, or wives in much of Potter Addition. In place of the Parsonsian two-generation, neolocal, nuclear family, there is a three-generation uxoricentric arrangement. Thus, for example, while the young mother is technically the person who raises the children, it is more accurate to say that she merely *tends* her children, while the jural authority that actually controls socialization resides elsewhere. Instead of being a mother and wife, her key family status is determined by the alliance she forges with her mother. With marriage and the birth of her first child, she has become a *daughter/mother-sibling*.

The birth of her first grandchild constitutes a more radical biographical break in the life of the woman than does the birth of her first child. The grandchild's birth represents the final step into full-fledged adulthood. Until now, the woman has been a sibling to her own children, taking refuge in her mother's support and expertise. As a result, her own household is a relatively egalitarian affair in which generational differences are invoked only when it is absolutely necessary to fend off chaos. Otherwise parents and children act as if they are part of a single cohort. Since authority lines are drawn as much between households as within them, generational power differences separate the grandparental cohort and the two generations immediately below it.

Starting with the grandchildren's preteen years, there is a tendency, as Nancy Norris's previous testimony has revealed, for the wife's mother to shift more of the day-to-day child-rearing duties to the daughter/mother-sibling. With the advent of a fourth generation, the jural autonomy of the daughter/mother-sibling is finally realized. At the age of thirty-six or so, echoing the career cycles of the sons of Irish farmers, the mature woman finally assumes full adult status. The daughter/mother-sibling becomes a *mother/grandmother*. In her new status, she assumes full jural responsibility for rearing her grandchildren as one gynecocratic structure dissolves and a new one takes its place.

This is, of course, the ideal scenario. The actual evolution of the gynecocratic core is often riddled with everyday exceptions. Having four parents in two households, for example, intensifies the problem of communicating a consistent set of parental norms to the children. This problem worsens each year as the child grows, becomes "con wise," learns to mine the anomalies of authority that run between the parental and grandparental households, and plays one set of adults off against the other. Thus Sue Martin explains:

You see, things are kind of equally split between me and Mary. This creates problems, to say the least. I don't know exactly how to explain it. Kay knows that she can live with me, and that I want her to live with me. She knows that I love her and I would do anything on the face of this earth for her. She also knows that any time she wants to, she could move in with her grandma. It makes things difficult, but you learn to live with it. You can't have *everything* your way, you see.

When Kay and I were living with Mother and Dad—this is when she was first born—Mother and Dad got to feeling like Kay was their own daughter. So, Mother and Dad got to treating her like a daughter. I would say, "Kay, you will not take that toothpaste and spread it on the bathroom floor." Mother and Dad would come right behind me and say, "Kay, honey, you can do whatever you Goddamned well want to do!" Even today, I say, "You *will* learn to write your papers neatly." Dad will come right behind me and say, "Well, it's not that important. After all, she is trying." Al will spank her for something she's done wrong. She'll run to Grandma and tell Grandma and, in turn, Grandma comes over and crawls all over us. We're beating her precious little thing! It's happened a number of times!

My husband takes this with a grain of salt now. He doesn't like it at all, but like I say, Al realizes that I am so indebted to my mother, not financially, but Lord knows I am, but more. My mom has helped us a lot these last years. You see, she has other granddaughters, but none of them are as important to her as little Kay. It's the fact that she helped raise Kay for so long. It has been Mama who helped us when we got low on money. It was Mama who bought the school clothes for Kay to go to kindergarten in. Therefore, Mother feels, "Look, this kid is as much mine as it is yours." It was Mother and Dad who stayed up nights taking swing shifts with me when Kay was sick because she couldn't drink milk. I remember at that time she was practically starving to death before we found something she could drink. I know you can say biologically I am the mother and should have my say, but big deal. My mother figures that she helps buy that kid clothes, and she's got as much right to tell her what's right and what's wrong as I do. That's the way she figures it. I figure that she's not going to tell Kay anything that will hurt her.

As you might guess, sometimes Mother gets in the way, but Mother never interferes with minor authority. She always steps in during a major crisis. The grades that my daughter made in school this last quarter to my husband and I were horrible, and we felt it shouldn't have happened. To Mother, she was a little girl. You know, "She's getting interested in other things now. Sure, things like this happen." We didn't see it this way and we had a squabble about it. Any little thing we do, like disciplining, she usually stays out of. It's the major things that we differ on—that we have what you might call "comments on." What I'm talking about here are such things as sex education, grades, etc. Kay, for example, went through a period where she was taking things that didn't belong to her, and she still does. On top of that, she lies like a trooper. Mom says it's just a part of her being insecure. She's not happy, and all this kind of crap. And Al—Mom sees Al as being too strict with her. But we never really differ on the minor things, on the little everyday things.

At times generational compression goes so far as to collapse the structure of family authority itself. This is a special danger in those families in which there has been a *double parental default,* i.e., when the young husband's jural default is followed by the wife's mother's inability to order the life of her daughter's household. Under such circumstances, generational compression transmutes the possible construction of a gynecocratic core into the collapse of the family's authority structure. This situation is epitomized in Sarah Lane's account of how she once neutralized her mother's jural right to criticize her conduct:

Wayne and I decided not to tell anyone I was pregnant. Things started to get confused, though, when Wayne left town in March. He was going out of town to get construction work so he could get money for us to get married. We kept all this secret. He would send money orders every week, and I put them in a savings account. After July, the checks stopped and we never saw or heard from him again. By then I was showing, and when Mom realized I was pregnant, she got real mad.

Granddad, who had been like a father to me since Daddy died, never said too much about me being pregnant. In one way, I think he was even glad I was going to have a child. When I went to the hospital, Mom went with me. She sat there all night and cried and from time to time stopped long enough to tell me, "You got no business getting yourself this-a-way." Then she would begin crying again! Finally, the nurses told her she would have to leave—she was getting me too nervous.

After I had Mike, I came back home and lived with Mom. I worked in the day, and Mom worked at night. That way she could baby-sit for Mike while I worked. Life was okay there, but she kept harping at me about getting pregnant and not being married. I didn't say much back. Then one day she called me a whore. I can remember that so plain. It wasn't too long after that I found out she was pregnant, too. It was then that I told Mom, "Remember that name you called me last month? Well, I think that name you called me kind of fits you, too." She said, "What's that?" I said, "I understand you're pregnant, too." Mom said, "Whoever told you that was a damn liar." I said, "Mom, I suspected it for a long while, so don't *you* lie."

It wasn't long after that she had Kit. After Kit, Mom couldn't say a lot to me about having Mike, because it was plain that Kit was illegitimate, too. After that, the only time we came to what you would call blows was when she told me I was an unfit mother. She was obviously drunk, but she made me so mad—it was untrue—that I hit her. I'm a good mother, and if there's anything I hate, it's for someone to say I don't take care of my kids. Mom slapped me and I slapped her. That was the only time we really came to blows.

In the Lane household, the mother's moral authority has collapsed to the extent that the generational axis that ostensibly orders petit bourgeois family life has given way to generational compression. With her out-of-wedlock pregnancy, the mother's right to be the family's instrumental critic has been so compromised that even the uxoricentric alternative is not a viable possibility.

As we saw in the last chapter, the uxoricentric family is premised not only on generational compression, but presupposes the transformation of traditional male authority as well. The husband's jural disenfranchisement does not begin with, but rather culminates in his economic default. The foundation for usurpation was actually laid a decade earlier, beginning with the sins of the father. Because the male child is strongly identified with the father, he often becomes a surrogate for the father. This propensity to establish cross-generational, same-sex identities tends to divide the conjugal dyad vertically and has a profound effect on the socialization of both sexes. As the father is progressively pushed to the family's jural periphery by his wife and mother-in-law, his own son begins to replace him in the eyes of the women. The boy becomes an object of cathexis and a foil for establishing the solidarity of the gynecocratic core. In effect, he becomes the "other" in the full Sartrean sense of the term.[1] Whatever identity he accrues will be mediated by the project that the gynecocratic core lays out and pursues. Concomitantly, the boy's own sense of self will be heavily influenced by the interpretations of a group of jurally assertive females and an instrumentally weak or nonexistent father figure.

With each passing year, as the father reveals himself more and more to be a failure, the women will increasingly strive to counter his default by raising his son to be a "success." The son will become the women's project: He will atone for the father's sins by becoming everything the father never was. Not only does this create tensions and ambivalences within the son, it often places the father and son in competition with each other. In such competitive instances, the father becomes increasingly jealous of the relationship that the boy has with the women of the core. As the father is moved to the jural periphery and the son is shaped to be his mirror image, the son is caught in an ever-widening series of double binds.

This process of emotional displacement and substitution eventually manifests itself in a series of dialectical ironies. The female core, which is now striving to socialize the boy will ultimately fail in its project of creating a male free of the father's flaws. Instead of raising the child to be the opposite of their betrayer, through their efforts they produce conduct and outlooks that increasingly resemble the long-banished father. This outcome takes place whether the father is present or not. In fact, the irony of uxoricentric socialization is most instructive and more cruelly realized when the father is absent. In order to understand this irony, let us reconstruct the early years of the boy's upbringing.

The boy's father is in deep trouble by the time the child is three or four years old. Repeated failures to make good at various jobs and periodic budgetary crises, combined in many cases with a headlong rush into the machismo of the local bar culture, have made the father's relationship to his family tenuous. On the part of the wife, shock after shock has turned romance into cynicism and despair (Nancy Norris's narrative in the last chapter is illustrative of this process). The husband comes to be seen as useless, or worse, as a drain on scarce family resources—a constant consumer and an inconstant provider. By the fourth year or so of the marriage, the romantic rationalization that every family's early years are plagued with hardship has given way to the reality that the past is also the future. Seen as inept, and often finding comfort among friends in the bar culture, the young husband rapidly cools himself out of the family. The increasingly embittered wife, egged on and abetted by a supportive mother who is probably guarding her own status in the gynecocracy, begins to reorder her emotional and domestic priorities. She is ready to raise her family with or without the man. As cynical as it may sound, the male has completed his family responsibilities; having impregnated his wife several times, he has given her children—and her mother grandchildren. He is now free to follow his own path. Whether he leaves or stays is moot; his wife and her mother can make do on their own. In terms of the reproduction of uxoricentric cultural patterns, it may even be better if he deserts the family altogether. Since he is a nonpresence, it will be easier for the women to reconstruct ideologically from the whole cloth of uxoricentric interests a more coherent negative model for use in the boy's socialization.

From this point on, the boy's upbringing is redolent with Freudian overtones. The women now emotionally appropriate the child, each in her own way, and each for her own purpose. In the case of the young wife, the boy replaces the father as an object of affection. Her love for the son, however, genuine as it may be, is cursed with all of the unre-solved conflicts of her relationship with the father. The mother/ grandmother, by contrast, has her first male child. The boy is hers to spoil and dote upon as she pleases. This stereotypical spoiling has a darker side, however, for spoil him as she may, with each new year she sees more and more of her son-in-law in him—and perhaps even echoes of the man she herself married. In each case, the child is subjected to a contradictory alter-casting by the two persons most important to his socialization and self-formation. He is spoiled and socialized into tough-ness and masculinity by the women and later by his juvenile peer group. Though he may have a grandfather or some adult neighbor after whom to model himself—a living model of what a *real* man is supposed to be—these masculine images are ultimately sculpted to meet the needs of the gynecocratic core.

If the boy has a sister, he may notice by ten or eleven years of age that he and she have taken different paths in their socialization. He is en-couraged to be the cock-of-the-walk. As the "little tough," he is allowed to range a bit farther and be a bit more unsupervised than his sister. He is, after all, learning to be a man in the traditional sense of being mas-culine: becoming autonomous (perhaps even a loner), being able to take care of himself in a fight, and learning how to be popular with his male peer group. He is, in short, honing his talents to be a mate and husband.

His sister, by all counts—especially her own—is more oppressed. She is kept closer to home, where she helps clean house, does domestic chores, baby-sits for her younger siblings, and becomes a maid to her mother. Dragooned into this domestic toil, the girl sees her brother as having more fun than she, and, indeed, he probably does. What neither realizes is that both are learning skills that are conducive to reproducing uxoricentrism. She is learning domestic responsibility, while he is being raised to be jurally superfluous.

It is true that the daughter may enter a "latency period" in her socialization toward responsibility. During this period she may become a rebel, a hell-raiser, and even behave in a sexually scandalous manner as she declares her independence from a life of care. This short springtime of self-assertion ends, however, with her first full-term pregnancy. At that point, her mother arrives to take her and her child in tow and to get on with the business of reproducing the gynecocratic core.

By then her brother will have traveled a different path. It is only a matter of time before his grandmother notices that "he's growing up to be just like his no-good father." The panicky mother may also vent her spleen along similar lines and tell the teenager, "You're treating me just like your father did." In most instances, the women seem unaware of the contradiction: The man has been gone for a decade and yet, with them as the primary socializers and with the male peer culture of Potter Addition as their back-up, the absent father has still had a powerful influence on his son's upbringing. How can they account for this ironic outcome?

There would seem to be two possible explanations: The child has either been raised that way, or heredity has won out. The nurture explanation would suggest that both women, in using the husband as a negative role model or referent, have unwittingly provided the son/ grandson with a detailed blueprint for rebellion. In her own confusion, the young wife, first as a mere child-bride, then as a despairing and often bitter woman, has inadvertently raised the child so that she reproduces her ex-husband *as she remembers him*. While she may have found other males in the family or community to serve as ego-ideals and regularly urged the child to emulate them, she has also trotted out the father on a regular basis for purposes of admonishment. Now that adolescent rebellion has come, when the boy "turns rotten" as many do— drinking, cussing, brawling, and whoring—the mother seeks solace in the claim that she is not wholly responsible: "He is doin' just like his daddy did." The unfortunate woman and her mother look on in shock, but not surprise. Viewing the wreckage of their dreams, they see the contemptible father reborn.

Unwilling to accept the fact that their own nurturant efforts created this irony of socialization, the women may seek an explanation in biology: The boy has turned out to be like his father because of an unalterable genetic foundation, which no program of socialization could possibly change. Reifying the bitter outcome of their efforts, they seek comfort in accounts of defeasibility (Scott and Lyman 1968). Not wanting to admit that what they hated in the father they also grudgingly cherished, both women absolutize the father's evil by grounding it in the very nature of masculinity itself. Out of their own mixed feelings concerning the boy's father, nursing emotions still left hanging, and with no proper way by which finally to put them to rest, the women have created a self-fulfilling prophecy.

Seeking to deny this fact, they have little recourse but to trace machismo to nature itself. In adopting this reified account, they assert, as would most conservative ideologues, that the will to violence, philandering, and familial irresponsibility are inherent parts of the male constitution. The economic and jural default of the male is seen as a natural fact waiting to flower. The daughter/mother-sibling, now turned mother/grandmother to her own daughter's son, has discovered an ideological charter to explain why the son has become what he has. Like her father, and her husband, and her daughter's husband, her grandson now begins to tread the path of jural failure. Set in the bedrock of male biology, such behavior is expected and even greeted with half-relief when it finally begins to emerge in the grandson's conduct. The emergence of the feared traits is welcomed with that strange mixture of despair and comfort that comes when one's worst fears are finally realized. For her grandson not to exhibit these traits by a certain age is as much a cause for alarm as is their scheduled arrival. The failure of such traits to materialize may be signs that he is "queer." Once the banished father's traits do appear, the plausibility structures of lower-class life are fatalistically reaffirmed.

Until now I have focused upon the structures that compose uxoricentric family life: the ideal patterns of male and female socialization, the various patterns of gynecocratic solidarity that lie at the heart of uxoricentrism, and the familial processes that produce male superfluity. The schematic in Figure 8.1 sums up those various analyses. As a structural schematic, it depicts an ideal-typical model of a three-generation uxoricentric family, replete with its gynecocratic core and its halo of jurally superfluous males. The model, as with ideal types generally, is purely formal and static in nature. It does not claim to describe empirical reality as such. At no time have I argued, for example, that all families in Potter Addition exhibit the full array of features I have ascribed to uxoricentrism. There is, it is true, hardly a family in Potter Addition that does not exhibit one or more of the characteristics I have attributed to uxoricentric

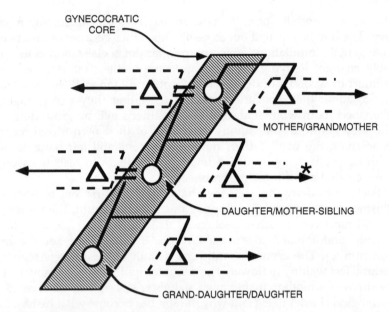

Figure 8.1. Schematic of uxoricentric household.
    Note: The arrow and dotted boxes denote the jural exit of the male from the decision-making processes of the uxoricentric household via socialization or the actual instrumental default of the family's males.

family life. More significantly, no one family possesses the full range of uxoricentric traits discussed here. With the above schematic in hand, let us turn to the dynamics of uxoricentric life and examine the process by which the structures of uxoricentrism are themselves reproduced in everyday life.

II. THE DIALECTICS OF UXORICENTRIC FAMILY LIFE

In the analysis of the uxoricentric family structure, lower-class family life as it is actually lived has appeared more austere and stressful than it is. There is, to be sure, no shortage of pain in lower-class households, but it is offset by ample measures of love and warmth as well. This intertwining of love and pain is an integral part of the roles that make up lower-class family life and, as in most families, it forms an emotional nexus that gives rise to turbulent relations and mixed loyalties. We have already witnessed this ambivalent doubling of emotions in the case studies of feminine solidarity within the gynecocratic core, in the analysis of the young husband's loss of leadership, and in the ironies of male socialization. We must now turn to a more systematic examination of the contradictory content of uxoricentric family roles, for in these contradictions and the emotional turmoil that often surrounds them we will find the driving energy of uxoricentrism's dialectical reproduction.

The fundamental contradiction of uxoricentric family life springs from the fact that Potter Addition and its subculture of poverty never operate in isolation from the value premises of Clay County's other classes. Being part of heartland culture itself, Potter Addition's culture of poverty contains important elements that originate outside its class niche. While this is true to some degree of all of the family cultures that Potter Additionites construct, it becomes especially problematic for uxoricentric families and their way of life.

The uxoricentric family is a composite structure—an uneasy amalgam of contradictory class-based norms and beliefs. Rather than destroying its internal coherence and integration, however, uxoricentrism's contradictory normative composition forms the foundation for its dialectical reproduction. We have already encountered the idea that institutionalized social forms can be a composite of contradictory normative prescriptions. In Chapter 6 it was shown that Potter Addition's everyday consumption activities were based on a combination of market-based and moral economy normative orientations. These two antagonistic systems were synthesized by the people of Potter Addition into a dialectical unity of opposites that enabled them to survive economically. The same thinking can help us grasp the nature of uxoricentric family life.[2]

In Potter Addition's case the idea that a stable form of family life could be an amalgam of contradictory value orientations is by no means far-fetched, for the petit bourgeois and uxoricentric family forms are far more than mere theoretical constructions. They are consciously recognized antinomies of everyday life and form part of the common stock of knowledge that makes up Potter Addition's culture of poverty. On the one hand, the hegemonic conception of family life that rules Clay County is embodied in the Parsonsian, petit bourgeois cultural ideal. As the hegemonic ideal, it constitutes the taken-for-granted, background assumptions for all classes as to what marriage and family life *ought* to be. On the other hand, the uxoricentric family is the product of the class-specific praxis of a fraction of Potter Addition's lower class. It emerges as a "natural" response to their niche and endures not because its legitimacy can be defended in the higher courts of heartland culture but because it secures real-life survival, whereas petit bourgeois orthodoxy cannot.

Potter Addition's people are socialized into both systems. The one is transmitted through standard channels of public culture (schools, churches, local mass media, etc.); the other is constructed by them as they meet the challenges of lower-class life. As a result, uxoricentric family organization is formed from an alternating mix of class-based "innovations" and aperiodic affirmations of the abstract, petit bourgeois ideal. Consequently, many Potter Additionites are caught between pragmatic constructions that work but cannot be legitimated, and hegemonically sanctioned family forms that are legitimate but cannot be sustained in the lower-class niche. Unable to resolve this contradiction, uxoricentric family life flows back and forth between antinomic possibilities.

These antagonistic presuppositions are managed through a mechanism I will call "provincialization." Drawn from Suttles's (1964, pp. 4–8) concept of "provincial morality," provincialization refers to the process by which a class subculture comes to grips with hegemonic norms that countermand its natural class standpoint. The provincialization of ruling norms occurs with the misappropriation of the real substance and intent of public culture for purposes other than the faithful replication of the larger system. Provincialization is the openly ideological use of an alien system of moral prescriptions to protect and reproduce a "deviant subculture." Suttles describes provincialization in his study of the Addam's area in Chicago's Near North Side as follows:

> In examining slum neighborhoods it is customary to accept compliance with public morality as a kind of high-water mark of organization from which departures must be "explained." It is possible, however, to look upon communities as a confederation of groups and organizations which support public morality primarily as a means of protecting themselves against one another. In this sense public morality is not so much the heart-felt sentiments of people as a set of defensive guarantees demanded by various minority members. Within the privacy of their own local groups, people may fall back on quite a different set of standards and practices. The morality practiced in a family need not be that which they would like their neighbors to observe. Those who share a neighborhood, in turn, may feel free to relax from the stringent code they support from the remainder of the community. (pp. 4–5)

The ideological appropriation of public culture, when used to control one's adversaries socially, requires that public culture be defined at its most rigorous and pristine. This permits the harshest judgment possible and isolates the adversary from respectable company. Indeed, the coercive power of public culture lies in the claimant's ability to maximize the cultural distance between the sanctioning source that enforces the ideal, and the parochial position of the adversary.

When applying Suttles's concept to the uxoricentric family, however, we must remember that provincialization in this case is not being used to legitimate the claims of a territorially distinct group, but is an intra-familial movement through which the abstract ideals of petit bourgeois family life are perversely used to prop up a set of uxoricentric power relations. We can best grasp how provincialization operates in the uxoricentric context by drawing a metaphorical parallel between its workings and that of Hegelian dialectics. The petit bourgeois family is the moral norm toward which Potter Addition's lower class aspires. It is a powerful spiritual magnet for the majority in Potter Addition, al-though most people are continually frustrated in its actual attainment. Like Hegel's self-positing *Geist*, however, the very ideality of that cul-tural truth, given the material reality of lower-class opportunity struc-tures, makes it useless as a firm guide for everyday conduct. With peo-ple's lives mired in the material and social limitations of their class niche, actual family conduct is for the most part the very antithesis of the hegemonic norm. Most heads of household know there is a gap between the public ideal and the everyday reality of family practice. This is the source of the lower class's *unhappy consciousness.* They know what is "right" in terms of what family life ought to be, but this ideal remains abstract and unobtainable.[3]

With this unhappy consciousness also comes an *unhappy conscience,* for one cannot view the relative ease with which others appear to achieve the hegemonic norm without attributing to one's own self a sense of personal failure for not having done the same. Except on those rare occasions when ressentiment can be rallied to claim that family tranquility among the petite bourgeoisie is itself a duplicitous sham, the enunciation of the ideal always carries with it an implicit critique of lower-class life. In the light of this unhappy consciousness and its stig-matizing potential, the two value systems stand side by side in uxori-centric family life, relating to each other in a continuous oscillating movement. When the provincializing shift in family norms occurs, it is more often than not instigated by the female autocrat and directed to-ward a subordinate member of the uxoricentric household. Such a shift inevitably brings in its wake the trauma of negative self-evaluation. In order for such a shift to occur, the protective silence by which petit bourgeois prescriptions are ignored almost from the beginning is bro-ken, and the implicit "deviance" of uxoricentric roles (as defined by the canons of the petite bourgeoisie) is openly addressed. At this point, petit bourgeois culture, which is little more than a distant, external standard, is exhumed from its resting place and used by the matriarch to evaluate actual performance.

The mother/grandmother's autocracy then entails, among other priv-ileges, her right cavalierly to relinquish and repossess domestic authority as she sees fit. Consequently, at a moment's notice the older woman, tiring of the arduous demands of the mother/grandmother role, can "pull rank" and "get technical" by saying, "Take care of *your* child. After all, *you're the mother, not me!*" This breaking of the consenting silence can signal either a momentary shift in which the mother/grandmother tries to meet a more pressing need, or a more permanent realignment of domestic responsibilities. In either case, the legitimacy of this shift appeals to the standards of the larger culture and the validity of its family norms.

The role of matriarch suddenly becomes that of a culturally sanctioned grandmother, while the daughter/mother-sibling is expected at a moment's notice to become a "normal" wife and mother. Even the husband's role (if he is still around) transmutes as the opportunity of domestic closure once again seems within reach. With such a shift, the politics of family life takes a new turn. Ostensibly the provincializing of family roles enables the older woman to flee her responsibilities legitimately by appealing to the ideal role prescriptions of the petit bourgeois family. Under the prior arrangement, her household and that of her daughter were fused structures because the unity of the gynecocratic core overrode the ideal of nuclear families being autonomous, isolated, and conjugally closed entities. Now, invoking the power of the autocrat that once united the two households, the mother/grandmother capriciously calls on that same hegemonic ideal as she rallies abstract right to her side, and in so doing alters the rules of the family game.

Though appearing to liberate her daughter and son-in-law, any such liberation is usually temporary. The history of the daughter's emotional dependency and her continuing economic plight form chronic fault lines that cannot be eradicated overnight. The reality of uxoricentric family life allows the older woman to reclaim her familial prerogative with relative ease. When the time to return to the uxoricentric status quo is at hand, provincialization allows the same dissembling silences to be reinstated. And once that happens, fused households and uxoricentric family norms resume unabated.

Provincialization, then, is a system of social control that can be used both to expand and to constrict the latitude of autocratic discretion. But how does provincialization itself actually reinforce the control structure of the uxoricentric household? The actual act of control comes with the first breach of the agreed-upon silence that lies at the very heart of uxoricentric family life. The call to "take care of *your* child" is a coded degradation ceremony. Compressed within it is the implicit charge that while the activities of the daughter/mother-sibling have been tolerated as a patterned evasion of accepted family norms, they were never viewed as legitimate. The call for the daughter/mother-sibling to "take care of *your* child" carries with it a latent charge of parental neglect. It is a willful exhuming of the soiled history that created the uxoricentric arrangement in the first place.

With this quixotic pronouncement, the daughter is called to account. It is her and her husband's original role failures and their subsequent inability to rehabilitate themselves vis-à-vis petit bourgeois culture that have always been the crux of the family's woes. Never mind that it is a situation from which the older woman has profited emotionally. It is still a mess by the dominant culture's reckoning, and this fact is forced to the surface by the command to "take care of *your* child." Like an astringent that removes oxidized layers from a dulled metallic surface, the call exposes all of the tacit, protean evasions that have thus far grounded uxoricentrism's everyday functioning.

Just as the mother/grandmother's exit is a degradation ceremony, so is her return. The older woman generally reclaims her autocratic position when the daughter's household is confronted with yet another crisis. With the mother/grandmother's return, the daughter and her husband are forced tacitly to admit that they have once again failed to live up to the demands of petit bourgeois family life. The degradation implicit in the older woman's return was bitterly summed up by Nancy Norris in the previous chapter. Every gift from Freida, she declared, bore the message "Look what I got! . . . big me . . . little you." Nancy's utterance is but one of many examples of the personal degradation that lies at the heart of provincialism's dialectic. It speaks eloquently of the social control possibilities implicit in the provincializing autocritique of lower-class family roles. Hence, the oscillation from the abstract cultural ideal, back to a class-necessitated reality, and then back to the petit bourgeois family norm is achieved through a set of emotion-laden shocks. Each shift is either a celebration of public culture or its dissembling suspension. Whether voiced or not, as when Sarah Lane is accused of being an unfit mother, or communicated nonverbally with another in a long line of bailouts, as in the Martin or Norris families, the young men and women are required periodically to say *mea culpa* and begin again. In each cycle, unverbalized "lies" alternate with bad faith breaches of silence that enunciate an abstract "truth" that is no closer to reality than the conventional conspiracy of silence upon which uxoricentrism itself rests.

The provincial evaluation of the husband's role is both easier and at times more devastating.[4] He has been socialized to believe that a man should run his own household and provide for it. When he fails in this and the mother/grandmother usurps his instrumental role, unlike his wife he does not have the patterned evasion of uxoricentric roles to fall back on as an alternative source of self-validation. He is, instead, akin to Georg Simmel's (1950, pp. 402–8) "stranger": He is *in the family*, but *seldom of it.* With his instrumental leadership impaired or entirely usurped, he becomes a peripheral fellow traveler.

In certain circumstances he may share with his wife the same quasi-sibling status she has established with their children. Between them, they may even administer to the socioemotional needs of their family— that is, when the mother/grandmother does not choose to play that role also. But in later years, if and when his occupational vulnerability diminishes, he will seldom be allowed to reassume instrumental leadership. By then, gynecocratic control will have taken on a life of its own. The women, having paid dearly in the past for their ascendancy to leadership, and now reaping some of its advantages, are not about to hand over power to this most ephemeral of family members. No matter what alleged changes may have occurred occupationally, his continued cooling out will be accomplished by a periodic rereading of the original bill of particulars.

Such dramaturgical presentations follow a set pattern. Periodically, the petit bourgeois ideal of the autonomous husband/father is held up to the male, while a litany of his past failures is read out. The litany, once completed, serves as corroborating evidence as to why he should *still* be defined as jurally suspect. Such comparisons of what he was and what he ought to have been are dredged up with unremitting rancor. Usually carried out by the wife to his face in a domestic tiff, or by his mother-in-law (more often than not behind his back), this implicit assault on his manhood normally goes unanswered. The question "Why can't you be like other men?" is only rarely voiced, for it is usually a potent part of the silence that encases uxoricentric roles.

The questions go unspoken because they are in most cases moot. The male knows that for many years he has been and may yet again become an inconstant provider. If, even in his own eyes—especially in his own eyes—he had been a "real man," he would have been a better provider. If he had been a "real man," as Nancy Norris has told us, her husband Tuck would have found a way to block the mother's interference in their household. But Tuck did *not* provide, and Freida *did* take over. While the man knows that it is not all his fault, there is enough truth in these one-sided indictments that any rebuttal would be merely an invitation to break the already strained, protective silence. With no foolproof rejoinder, he can only retreat to the margin.

There is a second aspect of the provincialization of the husband's role that, unlike the wife's, is an ever-present feature of the husband's uxoricentric role expectations. If the provincialization of female roles tends to occur in dramatic bursts and disjunctions of family life, as when the uxoricentric household expands and contracts, the contradictions defining the husband's role are part of the everyday structure of uxoricentrism. As we have suggested, the uxoricentric configuration relegates the male to the de facto role of being a socioemotional leader in his own household. As an expressive leader, his family role performance actually reinforces the power and authority of the gynecocratic core. At the same time, because he is the man of the household, he is expected to discipline his children physically. Such a punitive role, however, would conflict with the de facto expressive niche that the uxoricentric family has carved out for him. While he is expected to be a de facto *daddy*, he is also expected to be a stern disciplining *father* de jure. Any demand that he act as the latter—and here is where provincialization enters in—is based not upon an appeal to his actual family status, but is predicated instead upon the traditional petit bourgeois ideal of how a jurally assertive, male head-of-household should act.

Such contradictory content is a setting for yet another preordained failure and default. To be both permissive and punitive, marginal and jurally authoritative, is all but impossible. Stripped of his jural authority for all practical purposes, his punitive role is regarded by both his children and himself as painful and confusing. Unable to integrate the affective and punitive roles allotted to him, required to punish on demand without having the legitimating halo of instrumental authority to back it up, the father is usually a half-hearted and resentful "executioner." It is not surprising that he shows neither élan nor conviction in this role. Nor is it surprising that his failing to perform adequately is taken as additional confirmation that he is not yet jurally mature.

The male's quiet interactional style is a further impediment to his being a firm disciplinarian. Sue Martin, in discussing her father's unassuming manner and his reluctance to draw lines until really pushed, recites these traits with *loving approval*. This same style, so loved by his daughter, is at the same time a constant irritant to his wife and mother-in-law. More often than not the wife explodes in anger, saying that the husband, along with all his other failures, cannot even do something as simple as keep the children in line. This criticism is directed at the man by a wife, or is voiced in his absence before a group of assenting women who know her story all too well. Thus, men are dismissed constantly as not caring if the children "run wild," and of not making them mind.

When a woman is forced to do her husband's job as family disciplinarian, she seldom lets him forget it. The incident will be tucked away to be used at a future date. On some future occasion he will be reminded of that lapse and adjured to change, usually with the full knowledge that he probably will not. The point of such pleading is not, of course, to alter the man's behavior, but to use the husband's guilt against him. As an aside, if we seem too partisan on the husband's behalf, we are not; the wife's mother by keeping her daughter dependent provides ample ammunition to the husband so that he can counter with a few well-placed fusillades himself. Such pain, inflicted as a defense against hurt, does not eradicate the original injury nor ease the situation for either husband or wife. Such hurt is usually a ploy to reestablish a consensual silence. By the time the silence comes, however, provincialization has once again secured the husband's jural superfluity.

Uxoricentrism's provincializing dialectic suppresses dissent in the family's lower ranks, while strengthening its autocratic structures at the top. I believe that provincialization's basic function is to reproduce the political status quo of family life. Because of this assumption, I have played down those few instances in which provincialization is instigated by a status inferior and projected "upward" toward the parent. We know, for example, that Nancy Norris and Sue Martin judge their fathers both in terms of what they are and what they should be. If they ever do this to his face, I do not know, though I doubt it. We saw in the Sarah Lane excerpt that her mother's illegitimate pregnancy provided Sarah the pretext for actually castigating her mother. This would seem to be a classic case of upward-directed provincialization. It would, however, be difficult to argue that any determinate family power relation was either changed or reinforced. Sarah, it will be recalled, raised the norms of public culture not so much to call her mother to account as to exonerate her own conduct with a well-placed *tu quoque*, no more, no less. Based on what I saw in Potter Addition, I would assume that provincialization is more often than not initiated by a status superior and stabilizes the existing uxoricentric hierarchy. In this way public culture plays an unwitting role in reproducing a "deviant" family form.

9

The Dialectics of Lower-Class Kinship

Potter Addition's way of life is notorious on several counts. One source of disrepute is Potter Addition's kinship system. During the best of times, the people of Grand Prairie regard it somewhat curiously and humorously as a social fossil from another era. In darker moments, Potter Addition's "hillbilly clans" are looked upon as but one more sign of the backwardness of the "southern low-life" who live on the edge of Grand Prairie. To have so many kin so nearby, to be so tightly bound to one another and so xenophobic, to nurse decade-long grudges against kin without apparent provocation or reason seems unnatural to these staid bourgeois.

These impressions, once shorn of their mystification and virulent class prejudice, however, reveal something important about Potter Addition and its people. Indeed, its kinship structure is often Byzantine. A complex layering of kinship relations has been generated over the years by multiple marriages, adoptions of orphaned kin, and divorces followed by remarriages. Thus, it is not uncommon for two persons to be related to each other in two or more ways. Even the residents of Potter Addition sometimes become confused about the structural intricacies of its kinship system. On more than one occasion I saw someone become exasperated at his or her inability to get straight how a thrice-removed or more distant collateral was related to them.

Indeed, Potter Addition's kinship system seems more typical of the inbred hollow cultures of Appalachia than a product of America's stolid prairie interior. True to the stereotype, relations between kin often show an astonishing volatility. Warmth and total emotional involvement can suddenly and inexplicably be transformed into bitter antagonism. Such intense, almost feudlike shifts generate a perpetual array of bewildering kin group realignments.

To dismiss these shifting relations merely as "Southern," is to miss the crucial role that class and poverty play in shaping Potter Addition's kinship system. This chapter examines the material infrastructure of that kinship system and the role it plays in the actual maintenance of lower-class households. We will see how cycles of commitment and estrangement, as well as the shifting composition of kin groups themselves, are often reflections of the economic mapping of kinship roles. Finally, we will see how this type of kinship is itself a source of social uncertainty in Potter Addition. To use Meyer Fortes's (1958, 1969) terminology, in this chapter I will analyze the *domestic domain of kinship* or, as it is sometimes called, the *external system of kinship*. In this context the term *external system* denotes the material foundations of kinship, i.e., the ways in which households in a single kin group cooperatively secure their economic, ecological, and social adaptations to the world about them.[1]

I. THE STRUCTURE OF THE PERSONAL KINDRED

Kinship systems are usually organized around one of two descent rules: *unilineal* or *bilateral*. In contemporary American society bilateral descent systems predominate. In many traditional societies, however, unilineal descent, or some variant of it, is often the rule. In unilineal systems, kinship reckoning, social identity, material inheritance, and community standing pass through either the mother's line (matrilineal kinship) or the father's line (patrilineal kinship), but not both. In so-called bilateral systems, kinship reckoning is not limited to a single parental line. The fact that a person can trace descent through either the mother or the father, or through both at once, depending on the system in question, structurally separates most forms of bilateral descent from their unilineal counterparts.

Bilateral and unilineal systems also differ in how they actually organize kinsmen into concrete groupings. Since an individual's identity is limited in unilineal descent systems to a single line at birth, the boundaries of his or her descent group are sharp and clear-cut. The "corporate" nature of such descent groups gives unilineal kinship rights and obligations a relatively unambiguous character. In bilateral kinship systems (referred to by some as "cognatic kinship systems"), descent group membership is more ambiguous. Persons are seldom provided at birth with a sharply defined group of kinsmen to whom they are irrevocably tied for life. Instead, who is and who is not kin is often a function of individual choice and the mutual consent of the parties concerned. Moreover, the rights and obligations that regulate relations between kin are not established through preset formulas as is usually the case in unilineal systems.[2] Instead, rights and obligations are subject to constant bargaining and periodic renegotiation.

This negotiated dimension of kinship is at the heart of the relatively open and structurally "loose" nature of bilateral kinship roles. Potter Addition's kinship relations, as we shall see, often exhibit just such a fluid and open composition. Its kin groups are often characterized by flux, changing social composition, social ambivalence, and turmoil. But what part of this flux and openness belongs to the structure of bilaterality proper, what part to the nature of lower-class life and its niche, and what part to social anomie, per se? Before we can answer this question and assess the impact that Potter Addition's variable environment has upon kinship structure, we must first understand the indeterminacy of status and role that is characteristic of bilateral kinship generally. Let us therefore begin by examining the structure of bilateral kinship roles themselves.

Roger Peranio's "Descent, Descent Line, and Descent Group in Cognatic Social Systems" (1961) is a landmark attempt to clarify the key concepts that lie at the heart of bilateral kinship theory. Working from Davenport's (1959) earlier theoretical efforts, he differentiates between the abstract, categorical elements of cognatic kinship and the actual groups that are created when these categories are used to order kin relations. Beginning with the issue of genealogy, we know that in a bilateral system the individual can trace his or her ancestral origins through several possible descent lines. Starting with one's parents as "points of attachment," the individual can identify four possible descent lines that radiate *outward and upward* from him- or herself. These descent lines pass through his or her parents and terminate in his or her maternal and paternal grandparents. Similarly, eight descent lines can be traced through great-grandparents, sixteen through great-great-grandparents, etc. By using each of these lines the person can trace in a treelike fashion all of the possible consanguineal relations (or blood relationships) which he or she can *technically* claim.

Once this tracing is done, and standing at the apex of a genealogical branch, so to speak, the person (or "Ego") can reverse this upward direction of counting kin and move *downward* and *outward* from any given lineal ancestor. By counting downward and outward from a given ancestor, Ego can identify collateral relatives (granduncles, grandaunts, uncles, aunts, cousins of varying degree and distance, nephews, nieces, etc.). These downward-radiating lines of collaterality shaped in the pattern of an inverted V, link Ego first to an "apical" ancestor and then from that ancestor to collateral kin. The resulting collection of relatives is called a *stock* and is analogous to the lineages found in unilineal descent systems. Similarly, when Ego goes from one apical kinsman to another, and counts all the stocks that radiate from all possible apical ancestors, he or she assembles a list of all those persons he or she can legitimately claim as kin. The resulting family tree is called a *cognatic web of kin*, and the pool of relatives thus formed a *bilateral kindred*.

Though we can fruitfully compare many of the characteristics of unilineal lineages and bilateral stocks, they are not the same in all aspects. One major difference is that bilateral stocks, as we have just seen, are reckoned from the viewpoint of the individual—they are Ego-centered. An important consequence of this Ego-centeredness is that the composition of the bilateral kindred varies from one set of siblings to the next. Unlike unilineal systems, in which all the members of a descent group recognize one another as belonging equally to the same clearly bounded body of kinsmen, in bilateral systems *only siblings possess identical kindred*. Because of this Ego-centered determination, a cognatic kinship system consists of an overlapping collection of many individually reckoned kindred.

This overlapping structure gives cognatic descent systems their seemingly diffuse and arbitrary character. There are no sharp, a priori mechanisms, as in the case of unilineal systems, which clearly demarcate boundaries between kin and non-kin. There is, instead, an indeterminate genealogical halo that separates one kin group from another. The way in which one counts collateral relatives also contributes to the seemingly arbitrary nature of kinship boundaries. Since the collateral lines that radiate downward and outward from apical ancestors can extend indefinitely, some conventionally recognized limitation is needed to restrict collateral recognition. Societies that practice bilateral kinship delimit collateral relatedness by drawing an arbitrary line between kin and nonkin. This line specifies the genealogical distance and degree of collaterality that society recognizes as being sufficiently close to allow two persons to define one another as kin.[3] Thus, in some societies collateral recognition may be limited, for example, to "third cousins," while others may recognize more distant degrees of cousinship.

A bilateral kindred, then, is a diffusely bounded pool of relatives that has Ego at its genealogical center. It is not a real, sociologically integrated descent group. Instead, it is an abstract *category* of all the possible relatives that a person can claim as kin. From this abstract set of potential kinsmen, the person is permitted to choose those kin with whom he or she will actually "affiliate" (the actual degree of latitude of choice, of course, varies from society to society). Depending on the society, the subject may "activate" certain descent lines and affiliate with either the father's side (patrilateral affiliation), the mother's side (matrilateral affiliation), or both sides (bilateral affiliation). Which rule is followed, as well as the degrees of collaterality which one recognizes, is determined by social convention.[4]

The mapping of this categorical group by any of the above rules of affiliation generates a subset of the bilateral kindred called the *personal kindred*. From this personal kindred, Ego selects a subset of kinsmen with whom he actually casts his lot. This concrete group constitutes Ego's *bilateral descent group* or, alternatively, his *cognatic descent group*. Through a process that Raymond Firth (1963) calls "operationalization," kin are selected with the expectation that they will be able to provide emotional support, status, mutual aid, and protection in times of danger. I will call this collection of "operational kin"—persons who are kin in fact as well as in genealogical determination—an *effective personal kindred*, or *effective kin*. In using the word *effective*, I wish to denote the intentional and instrumental nature of the process by which Ego constructs his or her everyday descent group.

The optative nature of the effective kindred makes its assemblage an arena for bilateral bargaining. As Firth has pointed out, one's choice of kinsmen is never unilateral. Not only does Ego choose who will be his or her effective kin, but he or she is equally chosen by them. Moreover, the actual honoring of kinship obligations is neither automatic nor a foregone conclusion. The rights and obligations linking Ego to a concrete descent group are a function of *ongoing* negotiations so that one must periodically renew the actual terms of group membership.

These indeterminate tendencies give the inner structure of cognatic descent groups a highly charged political character. In the particular "multi-lineal system" (Parsons 1949) that characterizes American kinship, affiliation is bilateral and effective kin group membership can be shifted several times in the course of one's life. Americans, for example, can abandon certain segments of their effective kindred with relative ease and form other alliances from within the existing pool of kin. Added flexibility in constructing one's effective kin group comes from the fact that Americans are seldom required to activate an entire descent line when forming their effective kin groups. In practice, we often recruit effective kin on a narrow, individual basis. For example, when we ally ourselves with a favorite cousin, we do not have to extend the same terms of commitment and deference to his or her parents, i.e., our uncles and aunts.

Bilateral kinship, then, has built into its very structure a certain fluidity and variability. Moreover, the voluntaristic and negotiated nature of these roles is not due to the dynamic vagaries of industrial societies and their alleged downgrading of kinship. Such vulgar materialism has, of course, often been used to explain the "shallowness" and "looseness" of modern kinship obligations. Such interpretations usually ignore the fact, however, that pre-industrial societies with bilateral systems also negotiate obligations and construct equally loose kinship arrangements [see Firth's (1963) work on the Maori, Freeman's (1955) analysis of Iban kinship, and Pehrson's (1954) study of the Arctic Lapp].

The optative process by which cognatic descent groups are formed in everyday life gives kinship relations an unmatched flexibility. In modern social settings this flexibility is often expressed in terms of bilaterality's ability to foster a diverse set of kinship configurations within a single society. At times bilaterality's optative nature, its variability over time, and its ability to generate several kinship configurations at once can be mistaken for social anomie. But the selection and maintenance of kinship obligations are as rule determined and morally binding as are the more precisely defined commitments of unilineal systems. When anomie occurs in bilateral systems, it does so for the same reasons that it does in unilineal systems: either normative contradictions have matured to the point that incompatible role prescriptions can no longer be segregated or ignored; or an externally induced disruption has temporarily prevented the orderly reproduction of kinship's domain.

II. KINSHIP AS IDEOLOGY

The multiform and often contradictory functions that bilateral kinship plays in contemporary American society have led Bernard Farber in his *Conceptions of Kinship* (1981) to approach American kinship and its indigenous conceptions as though they were "ideologies." He suggests that different social classes, ethnic groups, and regional subcultures use the same broad bilateral principles to construct a diverse set of configurations, which promote a wide range of vested interests. Moreover, individuals, in making certain assumptions about what kinship is and how it operates in everyday life, socially construct their kinship universes. In doing so they are both guided and constrained by the objective social situation in which they find themselves. Kinship relations are thus the joint product of individual intentionality and formal constraint. As intentional acts, kinship rights and obligations reflect the social placement of the person and the immediate needs that such a placement engenders. As a formally constrained and rule-governed act, bilaterality limits the extent to which kinship commitments can be altered to meet the immediate needs of the moment. While people can select from a range of permissible kinship models and still remain within the formal limits that define what kinship is and what it is not, they are not completely free to slough off old obligations and construct radically new kinship commitments. The available models of kinship possess an autonomous, historically independent reality, and a social inertia that resists unabated opportunism.

The fact that kinship conceptions cannot be easily abandoned and reassembled underscores the fact that kinship's ideological constitution refers to the objective affinity that exists between conceptions of kinship and the class or status characteristics of the specific situation in which Ego finds him- or herself. To be sure, there can be no ideological dimension of kinship without the personal appropriation of one conception of kinship over others; but given this necessary synthetic moment, kinship's ideological character resides ultimately in the capacity of social structures, and the objective interests that accrue to social positions, to direct the individual's choice.

In a study conducted in Phoenix, Arizona, Farber (1981) investigated the actual ideological alternatives that people use in their everyday kinship reckoning. He found no less than five different ideological conceptions of kinship. Based on historical research, he labeled these five forms: (1) the parentela orders; (2) the standard American; (3) the civil law; (4) the canon law; and (5) the genetic model of kinship. All except the standard American model operated in a prior phase of Western history. Each, moreover, represented a modal solution to the structural contradictions that had shaped the particular historical formation that originally gave it birth. No longer serving the societywide functions they once had, each nonetheless had persisted. Operating in the modern context, they presumably fulfill an equally vital set of segmental interests.

The ways in which the specific conceptions of kinship differ among themselves is not of immediate concern. Another of Farber's findings, however, is crucial to our work. He found that the five "models of collaterality," could be grouped into two overarching sets. Three (the parentela orders, standard American, and civil law models) sharply stratify kin groups by distinguishing between collateral and lineal relatives, while the remaining two (the canon law and genetic models) put lineal and collateral relatives on a relatively equal footing. Using spatial metaphors, Farber effectively contrasts these two modes of kinship stratification. The first constructs a highly differentiated and segregated kinship space. This space is partitioned into a series of clearly distinguished regions, which segregate those kin who have powerful claims on one's resources and time from those peripheral relatives whose claims are far less binding. This same segregating propensity governs the interactions between kinship groups as well. The second kinship space generates a relatively homogeneous space by organizing kinship roles along the lines of a so-called *gradient principle*. This latter principle minimally differentiates between kin at the center of that space and those located on its periphery. In such a homogeneous space, the either/ or logic of exclusion that strictly orders the first kinship space is replaced by a logic of homogeneity and inclusion. Whereas the former compartmentalizes various categories of kin and isolates them from one another and from the larger society, the latter tends to maximize the number of personal alliances that Ego can forge with kin, as well as nonkin.

The sociological significance of these two types of kinship ideologies resides both in their propensity to create either segregated or homogeneous domains of kinship, and in the way that these spaces effect the social interaction and integration of persons and groups in society. For example, members of a class or an ethnic group that is perpetually surrounded by enemies and imbued with a sense of social superiority, or a unique cultural or religious mission, would have reason to keep the cultural boundaries between themselves and outlanders distinct and sharply ordered. Not only would such a group practice endogamy, it would in all likelihood differentiate itself into a set of exclusive descent groups. There would thus be a tripartite affinity between this particular group's position in the larger social order, its sectarian interests, and a highly structured and tightly bounded kinship space. Such a stratified kindred would, as Farber (1975) has shown elsewhere, operate to preserve existing monopolies of power, wealth, and social privilege. Conversely, in a socially homogeneous population there would be minimal stratification, and little awareness of a discrete "them" confronting a clearly demarcated "us." In such a social setting there would be no need for a rigid system of discrimination. With minimal resources to conserve, little prestige to protect, power to exercise, or privilege to defend, a highly stratified kinship space would be superfluous. Instead, a kinship space with a shallow gradient structure would be more fitting.

Farber maintains that these two spatial metaphors can be used to describe either the dominant kinship patterns of an entire society or the kinship systems of specific classes and ethnic groups within a single society. The latter possibility is of special interest to us, for the above metaphors can be used to typify class subcultures in late capitalist society. For example, the need for highly segregated kinship spaces would typify the ideological predispositions of the upper classes, while homogeneous, gradient-structured kinship spaces would be more compatible with lower-class needs and interests. By the same logic, the gradient model describes the lower-class world of kinship that operated in Potter Addition in the mid-1960s, while the segregated model better reflects the social position and interests of the petit bourgeois elites who dominate Clay County and Grand Prairie.[5]

III. CENTRIPETAL AND CENTRIFUGAL KINSHIP SYSTEMS

We can now identify two sources of social uncertainty in the everyday life of the lower classes. The first is rooted in the material premises of the capitalist mode of production. It expresses itself in the lower-class context as a variable class niche with which lower-class households must daily cope. The second source of uncertainty is located in the relatively open structure of bilateral kinship—in the "cultural superstructure" of lower-class life—and is reflected in the variable nature of relations between kinsmen. When taken together, this convergence of forces originating in both the material base and the ideological superstructure can be shown to be responsible for much of the social uncertainty that haunts the everyday lives of Potter Addition's poor.

We now need a way of mapping this convergence onto the concrete relations that make up the domestic domain of kinship. Farber's (1971, 1975) concept of "family estates" provides us with just such a tool, for it treats a household's material wealth and its status honor in the community as if each were part of a domestic capital. This domestic capital is of two types: *material and symbolic*. Irrespective of a family's actual class position in late capitalism's social formation, many aspects of family life have been transformed into an accumulated domestic capital. Both forms of family capital promote the welfare and consumption careers of family members and secure the household's existence as an autonomous domestic unit. A family's *material estate* consists of the combined energies and time commitments of its members, their emotional commitment to one another, and the material assets that they have at their disposal. A family's *symbolic estate* consist of its community status, the reputations of the notables and celebrities that it can claim genealogically, and the scarce symbolic resources that fall under their exclusive control (Farber 1964, pp. 285–332).

Farber argues that in any given society a family's culture and its kinship nexus can either preserve its capital by drawing its members inward into compact exclusive nuclei, thereby maximizing its accumulationist tendencies, or disperse its estate and propel its members outward into the larger society. Drawing upon the language of classical mechanics, he describes the former as a *centripetal* and the latter as a *centrifugal* kinship system. Replacing the former spatial metaphors with their dynamic counterparts, he speculates as to how each actively reproduces its respective class system:

> Definitions and assumptions applied in the development of the centripetal-centrifugal kinship typology are . . . derived from an economic per-

spective. Persons are viewed, for example, as the property of kinship units, and physical property is regarded as an extension of its owners. With members considered as assets (or in some instances deficits), the typology refers to tendencies in kinship systems to accumulate property or to disperse it. Assuming that "saving" or accumulation of property is a hedge against status loss, kinship systems can be analyzed in terms of their orientation toward saving. A kinship unit oriented toward ensuring the security of its members should be organized in ways which would generate the development of conduct appropriate to status maintenance. Such kinship systems, aimed as they are toward the accumulation of property, stimulate the stratification of society and support the development of factional regimes. On the other hand, those kinship systems which are oriented toward the dispersal of property throughout the society (as a matter of common interest to all kinship units) stimulate the homogenization of society and bolster the development of communal regimes. Kinship systems which tend to emphasize saving (*i.e.*, centripetal systems), because of their orientation toward status maintenance in an indefinite future, involve long-range perspectives, establishment of mechanisms for stabilizing obligations, and a redundancy of family roles. However, systems which stress distribution of property throughout the society (*i.e.*, centrifugal systems), because of their orientation toward immediate psychological and physical comfort of the mass of the population, involve short-range perspectives, use of mechanisms for maximizing cross-pressures, and a minimum of kinship obligations. (pp. 875–76)

Given Potter Addition's class situation, centrifugal norms should predominate but not monopolize its external system of kinship. This centrifugal tendency would have three consequences for the structure of the lower-class domestic domain: First, centrifugal norms would organize lower-class kinship space along the aforementioned gradient principle. The gradient would minimize the social distance between close and distant kin, so that an effective kindred at any given moment would be as all-encompassing as possible. Second, this homogeneous space would also make the household boundaries highly permeable and facilitate the free flow of persons and resources within a given descent group. Finally, centrifugal kinship would weaken the boundaries separating kin and nonkin, facilitating the process by which friends could become "fictive kin" and enter the innermost circle of intimate kin.

This centrifugal structuring of kinship space, when developed in the extreme, poses a fundamental predicament of *domestic closure* for lower-class households. The issue of domestic closure involves the household's ability to defend its social autonomy and material interests from the claims of other families in the descent group. We can best grasp the nature of this predicament if we first examine how closure operates. A closed household is one that accumulates domestic capital in an orderly manner. It expends its capital judiciously in order to assure its members a stable set of personal identities and community-based careers. A family can only practice closure, however, if it can protect assets from the external predation of friends and kin, while at the same time honoring the redistributive claims that kin and close friends periodically make. An *open household*, by contrast, cannot balance its own needs with the claims that kin and friends put on its domestic capital. To the extent that its boundaries cannot be closed, its domestic capital is at constant risk. While such predicaments on occasion plague us all, in poverty's variable niche this balancing often produces integrative crises in lower-class descent groups.

Thus, a family must find a way of protecting its meager assets, while simultaneously honoring the redistributive claims its kin can legitimately make on its estates. It must remain in good standing with its kindred, since these kin may well be needed to see the family through some future crisis. The balancing of family self-interest and descent group responsibility is all but impossible to manage in situations where the domestic capital of a household is part of an alternative economy. Thus, the variable class niche and the centrifugal tendencies that characterize Potter Addition's kin organization prevent many households from working out adequate, long-term solutions to the predicament of closure. These centrifugal tendencies do not operate unchecked, however, for centrifugal pressures, in turn, set in motion a set of centripetal countermovements. The desire of a family to hold on to what little it has limits the extent to which centrifugal kinship norms can impinge upon the everyday operation of the household. There are, to be sure, times when the family honors centrifugal norms and enters the cognatic web of mutual need. During these times its domestic capital is in constant jeopardy. At other moments it conforms to centripetal dictates, preserving its domestic capital and risking the alienation of its kinsmen. When combined in a nonanomic manner, the two tendencies give rise to a dialectical alternation of centrifugal and centripetal norms, which regulates the process by which family estates are cyclically augmented and dissipated. Under the shaping force of such a dialectic, life in a lower-class household becomes a series of advances and retreats from kinship entanglements.

IV. CENTRIPETAL AND CENTRIFUGAL KINSHIP IN CLAY COUNTY

The normative dialectic of Potter Addition's domestic domain does not take place in social isolation. As in the case of the uxoricentric family's provincializing dialectic, the dialectic of kinship's domestic domain often draws its content as much from the premises of local, heartland culture as it does from the culture of poverty. This is readily apparent when we examine the various ways in which specific racial and ethnic groups in Clay County organize their domestic domains, for within Clay County's cultural horizon extreme centripetal and centrifugal forms of kinship can both be found.

At kinship's centripetal pole there are those farmers of Frisian descent whose ancestors settled the swampy northeast quadrant of Clay County late in the last century. Using their knowledge of how to reclaim and farm the county's fertile wetlands, these farmers prospered over the years where others failed. In the 1960s, their flourishing descendants embodied the centripetal ideal in Clay County. While to my knowledge there are few studies of these farmers in the present literature, Sonya Salamon and her colleagues (Salamon 1980; Salamon and Markan 1984; Salamon and O'Reilly 1979) have recently investigated a group of midwestern farm families whose cultural traits, ethnic origins, and family and kinship practices are practically identical to the Frisians living in Clay County's hinterland. Like Salamon's families, these traditional households organize agricultural production along strictly family lines. The most successful families are able to preserve and expand their agricultural capital and landholdings in each generation, and pass on their agrarian way of life to their children. Land is usually inherited by both sons and daughters equally. In the son's case, inheritance may be preceded by a decade of tutelage in which the father and son work the land together. For the daughter who marries, land and inheritance become a dowry, while rental income from the land serves as a parallel form of social insurance for spinsters. The family life of these farmers and the prosperity they have achieved is the standard by which all who embrace the agrarian ideal and its centripetal ethos can judge the progress of their own lives.

The families of Potter Addition, of course, cannot claim the same degree of centripetal closure as the conservative farmers of Clay County. They do not, however, occupy the opposite pole of kinship organization. The black lumpen proletarian families of Grand Prairie's North End better approximate that centrifugal extreme. Among the lower strata of the ghetto, the integrity and autonomy of the nuclear household are so compromised by pecuniary need, social crises, and a running series of consensual unions that households and their impoverished domestic estates are often fused together to ensure their collective survival. A fluid concatenation of friends, family, and near kin enters into collective living arrangements so that a single adaptive network emerges—one whose meager resources, when pooled, meet the immediate needs of all who join it. The material estate of a household is thus absorbed into the network and made available to all. The pressing needs of the moment, not the preservation of an autonomous estate, determine the allocation of the collective resources of this lumpen assemblage. It is, in fact, almost as if entire households in the North End had been swallowed up and absorbed into a homogeneous network of unending need, becoming mere nodes of monetary and material transfer within the fluid collectivities of which they are a part. This extreme of centrifugality in Clay County resembles in practice the organization of kin and friends that Carol Stack (1974) has so painstakingly and compassionately documented in her superb ethnography, *All Our Kin*. Her study could just as easily have been done in Grand Prairie, so similar is her depiction to that which Michael Lewis (1978) encountered in his study of Grand Prairie's North End.

When seen against the background of the black lumpen families of Grand Prairie's North End and the Frisian farmers of Clay County, Potter Addition appears to occupy a structural middle ground. Within the historical and cultural horizon of Clay County, the Frisian farmers establish the limits of centripetal organization as it is lived in this heartland setting. At the same time, Grand Prairie's poor blacks may be said to embody the opposite, centrifugal limit. Potter Addition's domestic domain can be seen as a synthetic combination of the two polar forms. Consensual unions, for example, while tolerated by the black community's lower class, are puritanically frowned upon in Potter Addition. At the same time, Potter Addition's households are more stable. The ownership of land (with all that that implies culturally in the heartland) places limits on the degree to which long-term collective structures and centrifugal norms can become the rule in Potter Addition. Concomitantly, Potter Addition's variable niche limits its ability to construct centripetal structures which would equal those of Clay County's successful farm families.

The formal dialectics of Potter Addition's domestic domain are therefore more than abstract, theoretical possibilities. They are lived alternatives that bracket everyday conduct. The inchoate existence of the black lumpen proletariat on Grand Prairie's North End is well known, deplored, and even feared by Potter Additionites. Most know personally of cases in which a friend, neighbor, or ex-resident of the community has gravitated toward that pole of family life. Concomitantly, the Frisian model with its strong core of father and son working the land is known and admired, and serves as an ideal for many, enunciating what they and their parents once were and staking out what they still hope to become.

In sum, Potter Addition's domestic domain occupies a structural middle ground in Clay County, walking a tightrope between two very real extremes. On the one hand, there is the normative prescription for the nuclear family to "take care of its own before all else." If this were the sole norm for ordering relations between a descent group's various households, this centripetal rule would soon fragment the lower-class kindred, and reduce it to a series of relatively isolated, self-interested, autonomous households. Potter Addition's system of kinship would then resemble the Frisian, family-based enterprises discussed above. On the other hand, the centrifugal principle of support for one's kin dictates that no kinsman be treated as a stranger and that he or she be aided at all costs. Under such a norm, kin and even close friends would gain full access to a family's material resources. If implemented in the extreme, beyond the horizontal or vertical mergings of uxoricentric households, a fusion of households and families resembling the collective security arrangements reported by Stack (1974) would become the rule. But when both tendencies are given equal weight, simultaneously sanctioned, and balanced in everyday interaction, as is presently the case in many of Potter Addition's households, a dialectical constitution of the domestic domain becomes the rule.

V. OPEN AND CLOSED HOUSEHOLDS IN POTTER ADDITION

Household openness in Potter Addition is indexed in several ways. The most obvious is the ease with which friends are assimilated into the family and its intimate circle of kin. The willingness of people to manufacture honorary uncles, aunts, grandpas, and grandmas from circles of close friends is one of the most striking aspects of Potter Addition's family life. There is also the frequent, short-term "adoption" of children by nonkin. In such instances a family takes a child under its wing. This usually happens when the child is from a single-parent household or from a family in which parental neglect is obvious. During such adoptions, adults (men with boys, women with girls, and grandmothers with the very young of both sexes) assume limited parental and protective responsibilities. Under this ephemeral system, children are constantly running between households, "sleeping at home, but living elsewhere." Such adoptions are usually not threatening to the child's biological parents, except in those cases in which the adoption is taken as an implicit criticism of the parent's character or child-raising ability. Such adoptions are always short-lived. They are usually terminated by the adopting adult when frustration with the child erodes the original joys of surrogacy.

There are occasions, however, in which the incorporation of strangers into the family endangers its autonomy. On such occasions a move toward centripetal closure is set in motion. These countermoves are most clearly and dramatically seen in families in which double parental default has already created chronic openness. In the absence of structural buffers such as patrilateral or uxoricentric organizing principles, such families are periodically forced to fend off the emotional encroachment of strangers. Given the prior demoralization of the parents, this task usually falls to an older child, in most cases the oldest female child. Both as "the little trooper" of her youth who has suffered hardships gladly and assumed responsibilities beyond her years, and now in later life as the family's social guardian, she spends a good portion of her time protecting the emotional capital of the entire sibling group. Because the family boundaries of the sibling group are so intertwined and permeable, protecting the emotional and material estate of her family entails defending the inherited kinship capital of her siblings as well. Take, for example, the situation confronting Mary Graham, born Mary Morris. Her family was part of the third migratory wave that settled in Potter Addition shortly after World War II. When her family moved from the land, her parents' marriage collapsed and Mary became the "family guardian," a role she has played for almost twenty years. At present, Mary is preoccupied with her mother's growing vulnerability to a young man's friendship:

Mary: Henry Curry's the one who's really broke our family up. He was a friend of my brother's. Marvin kind of felt sorry for the kid, because Henry's wife left him. Of course, he's got a little boy and has been having quite a problem with him because the little boy won't live with Henry—he won't live with his mom, either. He lives with Henry's folks. He seemed like a pretty nice guy when we first met him, but when Mom took sick, he stepped in. He didn't want us kids to go to the hospital, he didn't want us to have anything to do with Mom.

Dave: It sounds like he's almost part of the family.

Mary: He *isn't* one of the family, and he'll *never* be one of the family. [said with great anger]

Dave: Why do you say that?

Mary: Because none of us like him. If we go to Mom's and he happens to be coming over, he'll call her and ask her, "Well what are you doing tonight?" and Mom will say, "Talking to the kids." Then he'll say, "Well get rid of them, I'm coming over." It makes us kids kind of feel "left out," because we have always been a close-knit family until just here lately. We used to go to Mom's after supper every Sunday. We've done that for two years now.

Dave: What happened to change it?
Mary: Henry don't want us around. He'll go out and get Mom and take off with her before any of us even has a chance to get there.
Dave: If she doesn't like him, why does she put up with him?
Mary: Because he hangs there all the time. As far as Mom going with the guy, I can't see why he should have anything to do with Mom, and Mom is stupid to put up with it because Mom is fifty years old and he is thirty-five. I mean he does take Mom to town and take her bowling and all like that. That's alright, but when it comes to interfering with the family, then forget it—that's wrong. Just like now when we was going to have the dinner for my brother, it was his fault that we didn't have it. He told Mom if we was having the dinner, we was going to have to invite him and his friends.
Dave: I don't understand. Is he a friend or a boyfriend?
Mary: Well, he's supposed to be really a friend, but I don't know, Dave. [laughter]
Dave: No, I don't mean having sexual relations or anything like that, but is it friendship or is there affection there?
Mary: I don't think really there is either one, actually. Mom just hasn't got the nerve to tell him to go away and stay away. She does his ironing and his cleaning. He pays her for it, and this does help Mom out. But he don't like us kids because, us kids, we laugh and joke. When we get together we're one, big happy family, and he doesn't like this because we don't include him in everything.
Dave: Well, what did you say to him about this?
Mary: Well, we've asked him, "Why don't you just stay out of our lives?" As far as coming and visiting Mom, we don't mind it. We don't mind if he wants to come and take her to town. That's all right, because lots of times we don't have a chance to or don't know when she's going. But I told him off one time over there, when me and him kind of got into it. We was at Mom's and he got to kind of popping off. I said, "Henry, listen. You might run over other people, but I think Mary Graham is just about as big as you are, and you don't run over her! It's my Mom and I'll come and see my Mom any time I get ready to, whether you like it or not." So, he don't hardly speak to me now. He could step on me and he still wouldn't see me. He's just that way. But lately, we sure miss going to Mom's.

Henry threatens the sibling group's access to a valued piece of family capital—the mother's affection. If Henry is successful, he will drive a wedge between the mother and her children. Mary's confrontation with Henry is obviously meant to restore the fragile unity of an already decimated family by reasserting the rights that kin have over nonkin in everyday family life. Strangers like Henry, however, seldom disrupt family routines the way kin do. Antagonisms between affines can be especially disruptive to the unity of the household. One of the most severe forms of affinal conflict occurs when orphaned brothers or sisters are taken in and raised by an older sibling and his or her spouse. Such situations are a natural laboratory for studying the dialectical alternation of centrifugal openings and centripetal closings between family and kin. When a sibling group allows one of its members to take up residence in an adult sibling's home, as in the case that follows, but refuses to relinquish effective control over the orphan's upbringing, a mundane problem of household demography is soon translated into a crisis of domestic decision-making.

In the following narrative we have a case in which Mary Graham actually accepts her husband Grant's youngest brother into their household and tries to raise him as one of her own (itself an attempt at domestic closure). Her husband's siblings will have none of this. Because of their refusal, Mary is made to feel that she is little more than an interloper in her own family:

> We was married in March and got Danny in May. We was glad to have Grant's little brother—he was an orphan and he was kin. Tony, Grant's brother, and Linda, his wife, asked us to take him, and we did. They done me dirty, even on that. When I took Danny, he never had a sign of clothes. He could put two or three pants on and his hind end would still show. After we bought all new clothes and took him to the doctor and got him all cured—he had a bladder problem—then they wanted him back. I would try to raise Danny like he was one of us, one of my family, and they would undercut me. They would criticize me for being too strict. They started saying to Danny—and he was just a young kid, so he didn't know any better—"You don't have to mind her, she ain't your real mom. They ain't your real mom and dad." Then Danny would come home and mouth off and repeat what they had said when I told him to do something. When it looked like I might have to have surgery, and with all the problems that Tony was creating between me and Danny, it became too much. I told Grant we'd have to send Danny to live with Tony and Linda, and he agreed.
>
> Danny came back and lived with us twice more. The second time, he had ended up moving in with Grant's brother, Hinton, and his wife, Carmen. They really made him toe the line—washing his own clothes, pitching in on household chores, things like that. I couldn't see him doing all that, so when he asked to come back, I told Grant, "Well, we'll go ahead and try it one more time." So we took him back. He moved out to near Madrid with us. Things went real nice until he was about fourteen, really closer to fifteen; then Tony and them started on Danny again. I would tell Danny to do something and he would start cussing at me and

say, "I don't have to mind you. Why should I? I don't have a mom," or "Tony says you're too mean to me." So I told Grant, "Well, it's either him or me, I don't want that type of thing going on around my kids!" That's when Oralee and Judd Howe, Grant's cousins, took him. After that, Danny begged to come back, but I just wouldn't have it. Finally, a year later, we took him back again. By then he had gone from Judd's back to Hinton's and Carmen's. He moved back in, and for about two months everything was nice. Then it started all over again. You see, Tony and Linda usually let him do as he pleased. When he wanted a drink, he drank; and that's something I never did approve of. That's what was at the bottom of a lot of the trouble. Danny would go to Tony's and he'd come home after they'd been drinking and carousing. I got to hollering about it.

So Danny decided he'd be happier away from me so he could do as he pleased. I think he stayed with Tony and Linda for awhile and then went back to Hinton and Carmen. When he went back to Tony's they let him quit school. He only made it to the eighth grade, and they let him quit—he didn't even make it to high school! After he got into it with Carmen, he went into the service because, really, none of them would take him.

Just as the male in the uxoricentric family is little more than an "in-marrying affine," so Mary feels she is being cast in the role of an outsider by her own husband. The dilemma of closure is threefold: Mary must raise her young brother-in-law as one of her own, honor her affinal obligations and do both without compromising the integrity of her own household. Beginning ostensibly as an issue of household demography, of who is and is not "family," the crisis of the Grahams' domestic domain soon becomes an issue of contested jural power. The protracted struggle over who will control Danny's socialization goes on for years. For the moment, though, closure seems to have been achieved, but not without its price.

VI. THE MERGING OF HOUSEHOLDS

In my analysis of uxoricentrism, I have already documented the vertical merging of households and the requisite restructuring of nuclear family roles that it entails. A less permanent form of merging occurs with the horizontal joining of sibling or collateral households during hard times. Unlike uxoricentrism, horizontal merging leaves the roles of the involved nuclear families relatively unaltered. In such instances, only the material bases of domestic life are amalgamated, and consequently the organization of the constituent families drifts toward, but stops short of, an actual structural fusion. The two families never take the final step of redefining and reconstituting nuclear family roles.

The emotional tension that surfaces in the course of these joint living arrangements places limits on the extent to which full domestic fusion can be achieved. The incipient emergence of centripetal tendencies can be seen in the following narrative. In it, Mary Graham gives us a feel for why merging occurs in the first place, and how strains in joint residency sets off a countermovement toward closure:

> About three months after we were married, that would be . . . ah . . . November of 1947, Mark and June Graham, Grant's brother and his wife, came upstairs to talk to us because they were having trouble making it. Mark wasn't working then, so in the next months we started chipping in on buying groceries. I wasn't too happy about us buying groceries; we were pretty stretched ourselves, and for a time there all Mark would do was lay around the house and drink beer. About this time, June had Austin, and I was two months pregnant with my second. We was bringing in about fifty dollars a week—Grant's salary from his two jobs, and my little sum from baby-sitting. We were feeding four mouths—six if you count the babies and their needs. A month later, right in the dead of winter, Bobby Graham and Harriet Lorton, Grant's brother and his girl-friend, came to stay with us. By then, Mark and June had moved into town and we had moved downstairs where they had lived, so we had an extra room to put them in. The kids didn't have any money, so we fed and housed them. Bobby was eighteen, and she couldn't have been even that. I guess they would still be living with us if we hadn't got that letter from Harriet's mom. It said that if she wasn't home in a week, they was going to have the law after her. So they went out and got married. They stayed with us a while longer and then got a place of their own.
>
> We lived by ourselves for, I think, a year, and then my brother, Vernon, stayed with us, but he helped us. He'd give me so much a week for groceries, plus ten dollars a week to do his washing and ironing and clean his room. Then he left and we took in my brother, George. He had just got married and we had him and Alice living there with her little boy from her first marriage, Conrad. My son, Jerry, was two by then and Conrad would run and jump on Jerry's back. I was always saying, "Conrad, don't do that." Alice got mad at me for trying to make him mind. Finally one day Conrad jumped on Jerry right after Jerry had got over one of his sick spells and Grant went in and whipped Jerry because he had hit Conrad back. I told Grant, "That's it! We ain't fighting no more about it, this just can't go on." They moved out and right away I took in some of Grant's relations, but I can't remember who stayed there with us for awhile. After they moved out, Bobby and Harriet were having hard times and they came to live with us a second time. By then, we were moved into Tim Painter's house up the street here, and they lived with us there for about three weeks.

Conflicts between the two couples' children and the issue of their being disciplined eventually caused her brother George and his wife to leave. But note that even before that the two families took special efforts to remain relatively autonomous of each other. Both maintained their respective cultures and identities, and "defended their own," even as they shared their daily bread. Each did its best to be tolerant of the other's idiosyncrasies and family practices, but sooner or later, the strain of accommodation became too much, and George moved his family out.

The social strains that result from joint living arrangements take another form in the next anecdote. Here, reciprocities that might otherwise structurally integrate two households cannot compensate for radically different life-styles. Again we hear Mary talk:

> Edna really wasn't the *big* problem, Floyd was the problem. They would fight in front of us and the kids somethin' awful. And, too, there was his drinking. He didn't drink all that much and, even if he did, I wouldn't have cared. But he was causing problems between us and the owners of the place. The owners didn't care if we drank. The only thing they didn't like was if a bunch of cars was pulled up in front of the house with people sitting and drinking in the cars. Whenever Floyd would invite a bunch of his friends out, that's what they would do, sit in the car and throw beer cans all over. Of course, him and Grant got into it over Floyd's language. He told Floyd that as long as they lived there he didn't want him coming in the house using filthy language around the kids. He didn't care how much he drank, but this sitting in the car and drinking and cussin' in front of the kids had to stop. He said that it wouldn't look too good if a bunch of people drives by and sees a bunch of drunks. They might go and tell our landlord and get us thrown out. Finally, I told Grant that I just couldn't take it no more. They was going to have to get out. They left and moved to the place where they live now.
>
> After Floyd and Edna left, I told Grant we was never going to let nobody else live with us, but then when Danny, his youngest brother, got out of the army and got married, they come out and wanted to stay for awhile. We really got along good. After all the trouble Grant and me had when we were raising him—all that guff from Grant's brothers—we never had no trouble when him and his wife came to live with us. After about five months, Danny said that he thought it was about time they moved out. They got a home of their own. But, see, when they were with us they helped, they went half on groceries. Maybe Danny would work one full week, and he'd have more money than Grant—that week he'd buy groceries. Then the next week we would. Most generally, however, we went together and bought groceries. It worked out pretty good that way. They helped me on the light bill; one month they would pay it and the next we would pay. The only reason they stayed so long was that being newly-weds, they really couldn't afford the price of rent at that time. Danny said he'd rather come out home and live with us. They had two rooms upstairs. They ate downstairs and everything, but they slept upstairs. He said if we'd let him stay there at least a couple of months, he could get a pretty

good start. I think they lived with us about five months. Then they moved out. After them, it was nothing but just "company." What I mean is, no one came to live with us for long stretches of time.

Mary's ventures in joint living provide us with a sense of how the dialectic of the domestic domain unfolds in the everyday lives of the poor and where the roots of that dialectic reside. What is unique in Mary and Grant's case is the inordinate number of times they are sought out for aid. Much of the reason for this lies in the fact that both come from families that no longer have parents to whom the children can turn in times of need (Grant's parents were both dead, and Mary's family had undergone double parental default). Equally instructive is the fact that although the strain of sharing material resources creates tension, a much greater source of divisiveness lies in the conflicting cultures of the families involved. This latter source of antagonism contributes no mean measure to the breakup of the joint family and facilitates a return to the centripetal norms that support the autonomy of the nuclear family.

VII. THE IRON CAGE OF RECIPROCITY

The opposition that exists between a family asserting its material autonomy and the honoring of a kinsman's call for aid does not in and of itself generate the dialectic of the domestic domain. A family could in theory cut this particular Gordian knot by either abandoning its kinship commitments or by allowing its domestic estate to be absorbed by the never-ending demands of kin. If either alternative is embraced to the permanent exclusion of the other, the dialectic of centripetal and centrifugal norms in kinship's external system ceases to operate. It is only when a family tries to honor both centrifugal and centripetal norms *simultaneously* that the dialectic of kinship's domestic domain occurs. The synthesizing power of this dialectic has both a substantive and formal moment. On the substantive side of this equation there is the *normative moment* of kinship. Kin by definition are *different* and must be treated as such. The fact that a kinsman is making the request gives it a sense of moral coercion and urgency that it would not have if a stranger or friend were making it. The former is imbued with an emotional power that places a household, regardless of its class, at the center of a set of conflicting emotions. On the formal side of this equation, *the norm of reciprocity* forges centripetal and centrifugal norms into a potent unity of opposites. A history of mutual gift giving between kin makes every new request for aid a pretext for remembering unpaid, past reciprocities.

Receiving a gift from a relative places the person in a perpetual, open-ended debtor status. Because one has benefited materially from a past transaction, one is indebted to the donor until accounts can be settled at some future date. The general nature of this obligation is summed up by Gouldner in his discussion of "the generalized norm of reciprocity":

> There are certain duties that people owe one another, not as human beings, or as fellow members of a group, or even as occupants of social statuses within the group but, rather, because of their prior actions. We owe others certain things because of what they have previously done for us, because of the history of previous interaction we have had with them. It is this kind of obligation which is entailed by the generalized norm of reciprocity. (1960, pp. 170–71)

The norm of reciprocity is usually seen by social scientists as a source of social integration and institutional stabilization. A history of mutual gift giving supposedly builds strong bonds of affect between those involved in the exchange. Working from the consensual bias of structuralism or structural-functionalism, however, social scientists have for the most part underestimated the material moments of social exchange and how chronic need can erode the integrative powers of generalized reciprocity. Reciprocating when one cannot afford to do so often reveals a darker side of this generalized obligation. It can often create its fair share of resentment and personal schism.

Why, though, would someone bridle at the repayment of a favor, especially when a close relative is involved? The best way to answer this question is to examine a hypothetical case of reciprocity as it might occur in Potter Addition. Imagine if you will a young couple struggling to stabilize their life chances. After several years of marriage they have finally begun to accumulate a small domestic stake. Suddenly they discover that their newly accumulated estate seems to be attracting one needy relative after another. Since most of these kin were generous in the past, helping the couple through difficult times, they now feel morally bound to comply with the request. Yet, even as they honor the commandment of reciprocity and technically acknowledge their past indebtedness, they harbor feelings of being put upon.

Ironically, this grudging attitude is often most marked when the request is the culmination of years of reciprocal gift giving. Sometimes the person feels guilt at his or her own pettiness and these feelings overlay the feelings of resentment. But, such guilt notwithstanding, these reciprocities eventually fall victim to selective memory. Personal reciprocity histories are privately reconstructed by each party so that sooner or later each recalls "those few times when we requested a little help," and the "hundreds of times we helped them without receiving so much as a thank you." Such distorted recall is a constant correlate of kinship reciprocity among those who cannot easily repay what was once so desperately sought. These "cycles of reciprocity" [to borrow Claude Levi-Strauss's (1969, pp. 438–59) succinct phrase] thus create not only periodic renewals of solidarity; they can also engender spiraling feelings of disaffection. Mary Graham shows us this more somber side of reciprocity, as she suddenly displays an uncharacteristic bitterness concerning "unpaid reciprocities":

> That fall, in October of 1951, or some such, we moved out by Piedmont. Those were our best years. Sometimes you would get lonely during those hard winters, but in the summertime I didn't mind it, because I was always out in the garden or out in the yard doing something. Until I got my driver's license it was lonely, but once I could get out and around, it wasn't too bad. I'd give anything in the world to go back out there and live. See, we raised chickens, we raised ducks and all different kinds of animals. We had one old goose that loved to chase me. Of course, we didn't have no bathroom then, so we had to go outside. That old goose would just delight in getting me out to that outhouse and then he'd sit at the door and wouldn't let me out, and I'd have to scream, "Grant! Grant! You come help! You hear?" I was scared of that old bird. He was a monster!!
>
> A month after we moved to the farm, Grant got laid off from work and we were back to living on twenty-seven dollars a week for a good part of the winter. A group that did our freezer in that next spring was my cousin, Shirley, and her husband, Denton Hayes: They stayed with us for two months, starting in March. Grant was just then starting to get some time in on construction after an awful long spell of no work at all. I can't remember just why they come out. I think Denton was trying to get a farm job out here. He had to wait a month before it would start, and he was barely working, part-time, here and there. They lived with us until they got a house, three miles from where we lived.
>
> I always liked Shirley, but Denton always struck me as a . . . well, as a . . . just let it go. Considering some that we had come stay with us, they wasn't so bad. The only thing that aggravated us with them was that we had just filled our freezer. Shirley would take two pounds of hamburger from the freezer every day and use it to fix his lunch. Imagine, two pounds! I mean, that's really too much. At the same time, if Shirley and them had the money, why they helped. At the time, too, Dad was in the hospital again, and she was real good about helping with the kids and taking care of them for me while I went and stayed with him. While I was at the hospital with Daddy, she made sure the kids was fed and clean and everything. Shirley is still that way. She's about like I am. *She helps people and gets dirt back in her face.*
>
> Daddy got over his sickness and out of the hospital just in time for me

to go in. I was pregnant with my third child and was awful sick a lot, *awful sick!* I was in bed more than I was out. . . . Floyd and Edna, Grant's brother and wife, came to live with us. They came out and took care of me and helped around the house. We furnished all the groceries and everything because, well, we felt like we really should. But, actually, it was more work after a time for me by her being there. She didn't make her three kids mind, and they tore up more than you could clean up. There was the usual fights between her kids and mine, and we had some words a couple of times over that.

That winter, and it seems most every winter after, we had a whole string of relatives come and stay with us. Out there, we raised our own chickens, hogs, and had bought half a beef. I canned all my fruit and vegetables and had my own potatoes in the cellar. We furnished food for them all. Now, when Jack and Liza, my brother and his wife, came to live with us, they did give us either fifteen or twenty dollars a week on groceries. But then they got so they wouldn't even help with groceries. That's when the arguing started and that's when they left. I don't want to seem cheap, because there was times when they helped me over some rough spots, but you have to remember, when they came out Grant was unemployed. The only cash he was bringing in to feed us all was his compensation check, and what food we had gotten together had to carry us through a pretty long winter.

This passage opens with a nostalgic recall of her short and happy respite on the farm and of her desire to be back on the land. There is also a brief allusion to how rural life eases the harshness of poverty by allowing people to grow and preserve their own food. Nonetheless, there is still the financial strain of two families living in one household and having to get by on resources that would barely support one. The reciprocities that hold these families together in this instance go beyond mere material support and include emotional and other forms as well. Yet, even here, the wide range of reciprocities that would otherwise broaden and deepen the interpersonal commitments between kin are seen by Mary as barely balancing out the irritations that accompany the accommodations required by joint residential arrangement.

Throughout Mary's narratives we have seen a subterranean weighing of the complementarities offered by kin in partial payment for her and Grant's aid.[6] We are not, however, privy to those earlier instances in which she and Grant received aid from those moving in with them. This rational weighing of the favors exchanged, the very fact that it is being done at all, suggests that kinship reciprocity produces unanticipated instrumental orientations that counteract the morally integrative aspects of kinship reciprocity. The failure to give tit for tat is an enduring source of discomfort for this otherwise generous woman. This weighing of values is, furthermore, not just a quantitative reckoning of dollar equivalents being exchanged; there are also qualitative judgments being made about the comparability of things exchanged. Mary's mental balancing of accounts is constantly updated and refurbished. She usually keeps such calculations to herself. Rather than "having it out," she swallows any anger over her felt exploitation, which adds to an unvoiced but ever-growing list of resentments.[7] In the privacy of her immediate family, she can get some mileage out of playing the martyr, as when she empathizes with cousin Shirley, saying "she's about like I am. She helps people and gets dirt back in her face."

Occasionally, though, even martyrdom cannot choke back anger. It is then that she breaks her silence and explodes over what has to be tolerated where kin are concerned. Such was the case when she told of the time that her Uncle Stan and Aunt Opal came for a short visit and stayed the better part of the winter:

It was even worse when Aunt Opal and Uncle Stan came out and lived with us. What happened was that Aunt Opal and Uncle Stan and their five kids came and stayed three months. They had bought them a place out here at Rodgers' Heights and then rented it out and moved to a farmhouse just north of Farmer City. They lived up north for some time, but then the farmer wanted the place—he wanted it right then. I don't know exactly what happened, but they had to get out, pronto. That's when they stored their furniture and brought their chickens and pigs and everything else out to our house. They stayed with us until they could get the renters out of their house, clean it up, and move in. A good part of the time they weren't even there; they were at work or over fixing the Rodgers' Heights place. What I ended up being was a baby-sitter for their five kids, that's what it boils down to.

There was another dirty deal—they had a freezer full of meat. Instead of Stan bringing the freezer out, he took it over to a cousin's of mine, a niece to him, and left his meat there. He stored better than six hundred pounds of potatoes in my basement and brought thirty chickens out, but in order for me to kill one of his chickens, I had to kill all of my chickens first. The whole blessed time they lived with us he bought, I imagine, three gallons of milk and maybe a loaf of bread a week. I think they really took advantage of us, they truly did! I remember I used up all my potatoes. I said, "Uncle Stan, how about giving me ten pounds of potatoes before you leave?" He said, "Oh, I can't do that." "Well, Stan, I've used all the potatoes that I've grown while you've been here. I've used practically all my meat. You've drank up all my milk and everything. You could at least give me ten pounds of potatoes." Well, he finally give me ten pounds, but—wow!—he hated to part with every one of them. He's so stingy!

To this day, I can't figure out why I didn't throw him out. I guess I'm just softhearted. I guess one of the reasons they came to us instead of some others in our family was because we was stupid enough to go to their house a lot of times. We used to visit them really more than any of our kin when they lived over in Farmer City. Grant and Uncle Stan always got along, and me and Aunt Opal always enjoyed each other. After that happened, we never did, what you would say, go around them too awful much. But as far as really hard feelings, there wasn't no hard feelings . . . not really . . . .

It is a credit to Mary's self-critical honesty that what starts out as a tale of unilateral exploitation becomes clouded in mid-course as Uncle Stan and Aunt Opal's past generosity slips unexpectedly into her story. The long history of reciprocal exchanges between the two households suddenly softens as her point strays. She recalls with a sudden twinge of sadness that there was once something very special between the Grahams and Uncle Stan and Aunt Opal and that now it is gone. One can, of course, speculate as to how Stan and Opal might reconstruct *their* own account of that same history of reciprocities. Would Stan and Opal recall the countless times they opened their house to their niece and her family? Would they remember honoring the norms of hospitality, feeding "God knows how many meals to the entire family," or keeping them overnight as guests? Would they be able to recall free baby-sitting, and even dredge up a couple of outstanding loans that got the Grahams through a bad period or two? And, finally, in that mental ledger kept so meticulously by those who so freely mete out what they cannot really afford to, would they claim that a decade or more of kindness and distant generosities on their behalf had more than balanced out the "minor inconveniences" of a "few months" stay with the Grahams? The answer is most assuredly yes—if for no other reason than that *so many different kinds* of goods and services have been exchanged that the empirical record can be made to support any number of self-serving reconstructions.

At some point the generalized norm of reciprocity among the poor, requiring as it does aiding relatives when one seldom has enough to support one's own family, comes to be seen as an "iron cage" of unending, unilateral exploitation. Among the poor, chronic economic need strips reciprocity of much of its playlike character and diminishes its ability to integrate lower-class descent groups ritually. It would, of course, be foolish to deny that reciprocity strengthens social relationships. It would be equally foolish to overlook, as many consensus theorists have, the second, more somber side of reciprocity in which material conditions limit its integrative possibilities.

The schematic in Figure 9.1 summarizes the dialectic of reciprocity and the contextual forces which ostensibly set it in motion. It specifies the material conditions which create the centripetal/centrifugal dialectic

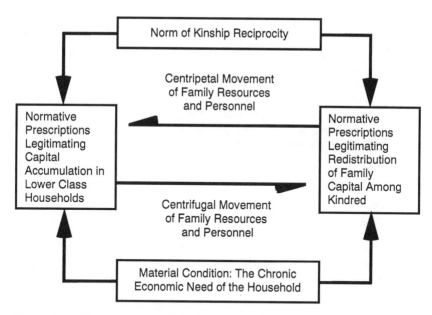

Figure 9.1. The normative dialectic of the external system of lower-class
kinship.

of the domestic domain, and schematically depicts the crucial mediating
role which both chronic need and reciprocity play in joining these two
antagonistic commandments.

Before concluding our analysis of the dialectics of the domestic domain of kinship and the crucial role which the norm of reciprocity plays
in shaping that dialectic, one final observation seems in order. Mary's
narratives have revealed an unexpected finding regarding the social
psychological mechanisms by which reciprocity maintains social integration. In addition to the ostensible solidarity which builds with each
new reciprocity, her tale of Uncle Stan's and Aunt Opal's stay reveals a
second way in which a reciprocity history binds kin to one another. The
norm of reciprocity can *negatively integrate* a kindred by forestalling a
final break. This "backhanded" integration keeps kin together, not by
increasing emotional closeness, but by preventing a final breach of an
already strained relationship. Hence, the countertides of personal amity
and enmity are suspended and replaced by a moral and emotional ambivalence.

Reciprocity thus sustains relations between kin even where it can no
longer increase levels of solidarity and personal commitment. In this
latter instance, the metaphor of the iron cage seems especially apropos.

The guilt and ambivalence that often sustain the shell of a formerly vital relationship frequently amplify the growing sense of kinship being a prison to which one must permanently reconcile oneself. Such ambivalences and the conditions that generate them not only explain much of the "hillbilly" conduct and Byzantine structure that shape Potter Addition's kinship universe, they also form a prologue for the consideration of the sources of moral integration of lower-class descent groups as they interact with other similarly constituted kin groups. That is the subject of the following chapter.

10

The Moral Foundations of Lower-Class Kinship

In the preceding chapter we saw how strains develop within the material base of Potter Addition's kinship system as it becomes integrated into the moral economy of lower-class life. In the course of that analysis, lower-class descent groups were isolated from one another and treated as if each constituted an undifferentiated group. Whether a relative was an affine or a consanguine or whether lineally or collaterally related to the family was not half as important as the fact that he or she could supply desperately needed aid in times of crisis. We saw that the ambivalences and antagonisms that were generated *within a single descent group* were crucial in understanding the dialectics of kinship's domestic domain.

Our focus now shifts from kinship's external system to the dynamics of its *internal system*—what Meyer Fortes (1969) calls the *politico-jural domain of kinship*. Moving from the material infrastructure to the moral interior of kinship, I will concentrate on the interaction *between kin groups* and the personal identities and group loyalties that are forged in the *war between affines*. Along with the aforementioned variable class niche and the open households of the domestic domain, the war of the affines is yet a third source of social uncertainty and ambivalence among the lower class. Before mapping the details of this internecine conflict, however, I must define more precisely the nature of the politico-jural domain of kinship.

I. THE AXIOM OF KINSHIP AMITY

In many preindustrial cultures kinship plays a dominant role in organizing society. This is so much the case, in fact, that the politico-jural domain of kinship is often synonymous with the social structure of the society itself. In such societies a politically mediated set of kinship roles is the structural mechanism by which society's various institutional sectors are integrated. In such societies kinship derives its everyday content from the political, economic, and religious life of the society. Within kinship's domain the distribution of social rights and obligations is worked out in the conflict, competition, and cooperation that occurs between corporate descent groups.

In modern class societies—those in which political, legal, and economic institutions have been structurally differentiated from the sphere of kinship—delineating the politico-jural domain is more problematic. Modern descent groups seldom assume the form of legitimate political units.[1] The state, with its established monopoly on the use of force and the right legitimately to adjudicate conflicts, has displaced corporate descent groups as the institutionalized arbiter of political and civic rights. While there is a body of family law that prescribes parent-child responsibilities, regulates family estate transfers, defines incest, and delineates the relationships and responsibilities among members of divorced families, kinship is no longer the primary vehicle by which political rights and obligations are allocated.

What, then, makes up kinship's politico-jural domain in modern social formations? What, indeed, can be included if in modern societies certain classes are excluded from full participation in society's political and economic life? For those persons and classes excluded from full and equal participation in the ritual life of the community, how can the politicolegal order be anything more than an indifferent, moral-legal backdrop like that which we find in "The Beggar's Opera"—an external code imposed from above and cynically evaded by those below? How can the politico-jural domain of lower-class kinship be anything more than an abstract set of remote dictates against which the actualities of domestic life unfold? And, finally, can lower-class kinship have a meaningful politico-jural content of its own, one that reflects the conditions of the poor themselves, or must the internal system of lower-class kinship be nothing more than an inferior approximation of hegemonic norms and practices?

Meyer Fortes's later writings on kinship can be of help in answering the above questions. In *Kinship and the Social Order* (1969), he has argued that the politicolegal functions of kinship, so prevalent in preindustrial societies, are only incidentally related to kinship as such. For him, kinship's essence lies in the *axiom of amity*, an axiom that gives kinship its unique *moral character*. That moral character is expressed in kinship's universal tendency to divide the world of the individual into two exclusive domains: kin and nonkin. The axiom of amity prescribes that deference, altruism, and generosity be extended to those who are kin, and that neutrality or enmity be displayed toward all others.

This moral partitioning of the person's *lebenswelt* is kinship's primary distinguishing trait—the one that sets it off from all other social institutions. Fortes has attempted to demonstrate the way in which this axiom operates in different kinship systems through a series of comparative analyses. In *Kinship and the Social Order* he examines a diverse number of kinship systems and treats each as if it were a "paradigmatic specimen." Though the specimens he studies display a variety of ways in which kinship's politico-jural domain can be constituted, Fortes claims that this diversity is always grounded in amity's moral and emotional claims:

> Our paradigmatic specimens confirm what is well known, that kinship concepts, institutions, and relations classify, identify, and categorize persons and groups. They show, likewise, that this is associated with rules of conduct whose efficacy comes, in the last resort, from a general principle of kinship morality that is rooted in the familial domain and is assumed everywhere to be axiomatically binding. This is the rule of prescriptive altruism which I have referred to as the principle of kinship amity and which Hiatt calls the ethic of generosity.
>
> In societies of the type we are dealing with, the actor in his status as a kinsman perceives his social universe as divided, in the first instance, into two opposed spheres of moral alignment. On one side is the sphere of kinship and the familial domain; on the other, the sphere of non-kinship. In the extreme case, this specifies all that is alien and strange and outside the nexus of normal social relations. . . . [Kinship] serves as the focal premise by reference to which the actor's social universe is polarized into a field in which the rule of amity prevails, and into its contrary, ultimately perceived as the outside world, in which it does not.
>
> *We find this pattern conspicuously in societies with cognatic kinship systems that lack a differentiated politico-jural structure.* The range of persons actually drawn into the orbit of kinship—as opposed to the sphere of strangerhood that merges with enmity—then varies with circumstances. . . . *Kin and non-kin do not, in cognatic systems of this type, constitute defined "groups," but rather an ad hoc structural polarization of allegiances for the actor.* (pp. 231–32, emphasis added)

The politico-jural domain of kinship, then, always provides the individual with a way of morally partitioning his or her immediate social universe so that he or she can effectively differentiate between those who are the legitimate recipients of deference and altruism and those who are not. It is this moral partitioning that lies at the heart of kinship's internal system of social relations.

Returning to the problem of Potter Addition's kinship system, in Fortes's concept of amity we have the means for comprehending how kinship operates in a class-based, subcultural setting. The above-mentioned polarity of "ad hoc structural allegiances" can be treated as the everyday mechanisms by which the jural interior of lower-class kinship is formed. If the axiom of amity constitutes the essence of kinship's politico-jural domain (and not some institutionalized set of political relations), then there is no need to assume that the politico-jural domain of kinship is normatively homogeneous across all classes.

In truth, all classes construct domains of kinship that *formally* bifurcate the person's *lebenswelt* into kin and nonkin. The substantive basis for that partitioning and the structure of the concrete descent groups thus generated will vary significantly by class. Members of the lower class, for example, will employ models of kinship that will often be marginal to hegemonic norms; but they will nonetheless be valid for lower-class life as such. In this latter instance, the standards used to partition the world of kin and nonkin will flow from the unique values and experiences that typify the lower-class niche.

II. MERGED AND AMALGAMATED IDENTITIES

I will assume that the axiom of amity not only allows a person morally to map the differences between kin and nonkin, but also enables Ego to differentiate qualitatively between major classes of kin as well. In Potter Addition, the major axis of differentiation along which the axiom of amity usually operates involves the distinction between a person's "blood relatives" and his or her affines, i.e., "relatives by law." I have already shown how this latter discrimination operates in the case of uxoricentrism and the husband/father's relation to the gynecocratic core. It will be recalled that in constituting the model of the uxoricentric family, I began with the economic default of the husband and reasoned that this default was at the root of the husband's jural dispossession. I must now return to that model and examine in greater detail the process by which the husband's occupational failure is transformed into jural dispossession. Why must the one lead to the other? Why, for example, does the young man's status as the head of the household not see him through the crisis and offset his stigma as a failed provider? Why can he not fall back on his status as head of household to salvage some measure of his personal self-esteem?

The process by which default is generalized from the economic to the family sphere is by no means as automatic as it first appears. Thus far, I have suggested that the young wife's psychological dependency on her mother is a crucial element in this process. I have also suggested that jural dispossession is a product of the lower-class male's social-ization. But are these explanations sufficient? The young woman is certainly tied to her mother. As we saw in the case of Sue Martin, there is an intense feeling of obligation on the wife's part toward her mother, and this feeling of obligation undoubtedly contributes to the husband's jural default. Simultaneously, the hidden injuries of class and the lower-class male's resultant lack of confidence also play a role in this process. But as useful as these explanations are, they throw little light on the structural sources of this process. For that we must turn to the kinship nexus itself and ask what there is about the structure of family and kinship roles among the lower class that promotes the jural dispossession of the husband.

My earlier analyses of the husband's jural default were rooted in the economic contingencies of lower-class life and in the social psychology of the uxoricentric family. While there is no need to abandon these findings, we must now extrapolate from them in order to understand the role that kinship plays in reproducing the structure of lower-class family life. To this end I will begin with the conjugal dyad and the ways in which kinship shapes the conjugal identities of the newly married couple.

Let us assume that in bilateral systems conjugal and kinship identities can interact in one of two ways: First, the man and woman may ex-change kinship identities, so that each spouse's kinship identity be-comes an integral part of the other's conjugal identity. When such an exchange takes place each spouse becomes integrated into the kinship universe of the other. Because each is integrated into the other's kin group, the axiom of amity is extended to affines. I will call this first type *merged conjugal identities.* The second mode of identity formation inhibits the exchange of identities. That is, upon marriage, each spouse retains his or her prior kinship loyalties and merely adds on, so to speak, his or her new conjugal identity. In this instance the merging of the new conjugal identity and the old kinship identity does not take place. In-stead, a mechanical, additive process is at the heart of this second con-stellation, which I will refer to as *amalgamated conjugal identities.* In the case of amalgamated identities the extension of amity to in-laws be-comes problematic.

Farber (1971, pp. 90–95) has suggested that these two processes of identity formation are closely correlated with class. In his study of class and kinship in the Midwest he found that what I have here called merged identities were typical of upper-strata families, while amalgam-ated identities were more typical of lower-class families. Building upon Farber's thinking, we can hypothesize that the extension of amity to one's in-laws is also associated with class. With few exceptions, we can assume that amity is usually withheld from affines in lower-class kinship settings. Completing the argument, Farber's findings on class and conjugal identities have a direct bearing upon our earlier discussion of centripetal and centrifugal kinship systems. It allows us to posit the following threefold association:

$$\frac{\text{Centripetal Kinship}}{\text{Centrifugal Kinship}} :: \frac{\text{Merged Identities}}{\text{Amalgamated Identities}} :: \frac{\text{Extension of Amity}}{\text{Withholding of Amity}}$$

According to the above set of associations, centripetal kinship will have a structural affinity for both merged conjugal identities and the extension of the axiom of amity to affines. The reasoning that leads to this assertion is as follows: Centripetal kinship systems are found most often among society's upper strata, among those very families whose domestic estates require protection, orderly expansion, and the surety that family capital will be preserved and transmitted intact from one generation to the next. Moreover, the family's cultural and social capital are constantly at risk of attenuation or status degradation, and this risk is no greater than when the children enter the marriage market. It is then that children acquire mates who, like themselves, will be responsible for the protection, expansion, and orderly transmission of the family's culture in the next generation.

At such junctures, centripetal kinship systems are always confronted with the possibility that the child's selection of a mate will be a poor one—that he or she may marry someone who will introduce novel, disruptive, or deviant norms into the family's established culture. One way to avoid this potential disaster is for the parents to supervise mate selection strictly. This would presumably maximize the chances of cultural or class-based homogamy and reduce the probability that innovative elements would be introduced into the family's culture.

Controls such as these are largely for naught, however, if the marriage is perpetually marred by tensions or ends in divorce. The possibility of marital instability would be as disruptive to estate transmission and socialization as heterogamy itself. Divorce would split and disperse the family's material and symbolic estates to such an extent that the orderly replacement of its culture might be permanently undone. Hence, centripetal kinship systems function best when they possess mechanisms for the stabilization of conjugal roles *after* the marriage has been consummated.

One such stabilizing device is the aforementioned merging of kinship identities. Such a merging would ground domestic relations in a supportive kinship nexus.[2] If the integration of kinship and conjugal identities were symmetrical, their merging would not only expand the ground for a common cultural viewpoint within the marriage, but permit the extension of kinship-based amity to affines. Merging would thus minimize conflicts between the spouses and their in-laws, and perhaps even foster future marital alliances between the two descent groups. Moreover, such a merging would ostensibly increase the marital solidarity of the couple and perpetuate the inward-looking perspective characteristic of centripetal kinship.

By contrast, underdeveloped symbolic and material estates would make merged identities both superfluous and counterproductive. If the spouses' identities were merged, then their respective kindred would have to renounce their exclusive rights to the young man and young woman's time, energy, emotional support, and material aid. In variable social and economic settings, such a ceding of resources is best avoided. By the same logic, marriage would seldom increase the material or symbolic estate of either kin group. If anything, marriage would produce little more, in the long run, than a new set of asymmetrical obligations.

It would make more sense for each spouse to keep his or her earlier kinship commitments completely separate from the identity he or she acquired upon marriage. The unity of interacting personalities ostensibly produced by merging would in this case be replaced with conjugal identities marked by bifurcated loyalties and commitments. In the case of centrifugal systems, conjugal identities would be composed of a quartet of conflicting interests. The husband would be (1) the head of the new conjugal unit, and (2) his kin group's representative to the new marriage. The wife would be (3) the head of her conjugal unit, and (4) her family's representative to the marriage. Just as the conjugal dyad is prevented from establishing closure in the domestic domain because of its uncertain economic situation, so now affinal interests keep it from achieving closure in the politico-jural domain.

Because of these amalgamated identities, the structure of the lower-class family can be seen as a *decentered aggregation of affines* surrounded by a plurality of powerful affinal interests. The husband and wife are merely in-marrying affines to their own families of procreation. It is as if the marriage itself were little more than a secondary alliance between two jealous descent groups that refuse to relinquish control over their respective assets. The descent groups define the man and woman as exclusively *their* kin and treat their marriage as if it were merely a transitory disturbance.

In light of my earlier analysis of uxoricentrism, it can be seen that amalgamated identities form a fertile seedbed for the production of uxoricentric families. Uxoricentrism is not just a reaction to the economic realities of lower-class life; it is equally the expression of a predisposing set of kinship relations that generate from within themselves the structural possibility of transforming the husband's economic default into familial default as well. The jural dispossession of the husband usually takes place within a nexus of amalgamated kinship identities. The degradation ceremonies by which this dispossession occurs, insofar as they are orchestrated by the mother-in-law, conform to the politics of the above quartet of layered identities.

Thus, while occupational default is a major precipitating stimulus of the husband's jural displacement, it is by no means the whole story. The amalgamated identities of the jural domain are equally crucial catalysts for translating occupational crisis into jural default. This point is at the heart of Mira Komarovsky's analysis of the unemployed husband's loss of authority in his family. In her study of family life during the Great Depression, Komarovsky (1940, pp. 23–64) found that an unemployed husband's familial disenfranchisement was not automatic. In only thirteen of the fifty-nine families she studied did the husband's economic default actually result in a loss of familial authority (p. 23). Unemployment was not the automatic cause of his loss of authority; it was merely the final, precipitating factor. If the relationship between the husband and his wife was built upon what Komarovsky (pp. 49–65) calls "primary grounds" (i.e., grounds of genuine marital respect and emotional closeness), then the husband's job loss seldom resulted in a loss of family authority. If, on the other hand, the conjugal dyad was "instrumentally" integrated, (i.e., sustained by little more than the woman's economic dependence upon her husband) then unemployment could become a pretext for the wife to challenge the husband's authority. The actual loss or retention of his authority, however, was ultimately mediated by the emotional tenor of the marriage itself.

Whereas Komarovsky focused upon the emotional interior of the household, I have pitched my analysis at the level of kinship's jural domain. Nonetheless, her point and mine are fundamentally the same: The character of conjugal relations is a primary determinant of how those around the husband interpret his occupational troubles. Further, I believe that when conjugal identities are amalgamated, as in the case of most lower-class couples, the instrumental basis of marital solidarity will, over time, become more prominent and the power of the primary bonds will diminish. If a couple begins and lives most of its early years in a situation in which there is a combination of economic shocks and a hostile affinal faction ready at every moment to define the husband as an outsider, then an erosion of the primary bases for marital integration is almost assured. In time, though it did not start out as such, the marriage will be reduced to a tenuous instrumental arrangement.

Given the quartet of factional interests that make up amalgamated identities, the husband's jural dispossession gives rise to a *dual movement* in kinship space. We have already examined the first of these in our analysis of uxoricentric family life—the banding together of the wife and her relatives against the husband. In conformity with the antagonistic interests that ground amalgamated identities, they will define the husband's economic default as more *his* problem than theirs. Since the wife's descent group has invested little in the husband's identity (there having been no merging of identities), it is easy for them to isolate the husband and turn him into a scapegoat. Since he had been an in-marrying interloper all along, and little of the affinal group's prestige or esteem had been invested in either his success or failure, when failure comes the wife's kin will not hesitate to isolate the intruder and cut their losses.

The second movement is that which takes place between the dispossessed husband and his effective kin. It entails the rediscovery or renewal of the bonds of solidarity that tie him to his own descent group. Just as the wife and her mother close ranks and make common cause against him, so now the fourth member of the conjugal quartet, his kinship group, enters into the unfolding marital drama and further undermines the couple's conjugal solidarity. This occurs when the young male discovers that his kin are willing to support him, no matter what. Just at the moment he is being stripped of jural legitimacy, he may find that his siblings—most especially his sisters—are willing to bring him into their households and have him play the role of a supportive uncle. Upon occasion, he may even become a male role model for his sister's children. Ironically, as one opportunity for instrumental leadership closes, another opens up.

III. AFFINAL STRUGGLES

The consequences of amalgamated identities go beyond the shaping of fragile conjugal identities. Their ramifications are felt at all levels of kinship, ranging from the concrete material exchanges and reciprocities that form the external system of kinship to the sentiments and moral dictates that order kinship's internal system. We can better appreciate the manifold ways in which affinal conflict shapes lower-class family and kinship if we turn to a series of anecdotes drawn from Mary Graham's life history. These illustrative anecdotes begin with the material concerns of the domestic domain and move progressively to the morally ordered interior of kinship's jural domain.

For the moment then, let us return to the moral economy of kinship and take up once more the issue of kinship reciprocity. This time, however, let us examine the way in which this reciprocal gift giving jurally bifurcates domestic identities along affinal lines. Again, we will have only Mary's narrative since Grant is too shy to talk of such things:[3]

I know that sometimes Grant throws it up to me for taking in "kin and stray kids." He says, "If you wouldn't do this, we'd be a lot further along in getting stuff that we really want." But I don't think that's right. Like I've told him, my family has been pretty good on the helping end. His family was always *pretty* stingy! They very seldom ever carried their load. I think that all we've ever done was feed them. [laughter] I think every week his family was here Friday, Saturday, and Sunday; we'd end up feeding them. He's got one uncle who is a downright tightwad! That man can have a hundred-dollar bill in his billfold and stand and lie as big as day, and say that he can't afford to buy his own groceries. I seen it with my own eyes.

Now I'm not saying my family is a bunch of angels—God knows! But whenever we had trouble, my family was there to help. Daddy would every once in awhile bring stuff up to us, because maybe he just felt like it. I mean, it wasn't 'cause we really needed it, but, really, Daddy and Mom helped us more than any of Grant's kin. Mom used to buy stuff and give it to us, groceries and stuff, if we really needed it, but not his family! If we needed money, we would go and borrow from my brothers. Of course, they was the only brothers that were old enough to work then. And I know we borrowed money from Jesse one time and paid him back. The next time maybe we would go to Vern and borrow money from him, and we'd pay him back. But we borrowed money from them just once or twice. And that was because, maybe, one of the kids was sick or something, and we needed medicine. Now, Aunt Mollie, on my mom's side, and Uncle Chester used to help us a lot, too. When they came out, Aunt Mollie would always stop and buy groceries whether we needed it or not, and give them to us.

Even old Grandpa, my daddy's dad, always pulled his weight—or tried to. He would come out and stay with us a week or two, and then he'd go to daddy's and stay a month, and maybe he'd go back to his home and stay. Really, Grandpa never really actually lived with hardly anybody but Dad, and then he really didn't live with Daddy. Daddy had that little garage he made into a house and he lived down there, oh, for about a year or so. Then, he moved to town and lived there about three or four years. But Grandpa Edwards was a good old grandpa. He always loved cornbread and fried corn cakes—and he helped, in his way. He always brought his cornmeal and stuff with him when he came around because he wanted his corn cakes. Corn cakes for breakfast, corn cakes and gravy for lunch, corn cakes and gravy for supper. But, if we needed anything and didn't have it, then that poor old soul was there and seen that we got it. He didn't have a lot of money because he just had his pension, but he was real good at helping. But the story with Grant's side of the family was always different. Most of the time Grant will tell you that himself, if he don't turn bull-headed.

We noted in the last chapter that Mary keeps a set of mental books as to who does their "fair share" and who does not. In retrospect, it is not difficult to see that much of Mary's accounting of reciprocities was shaped by a series of affinal discriminations. In the above passage she continues that same categorical keeping of accounts. There is not only a clear difference in how she views her relatives, as opposed to her in-laws, but it is also obvious that she stratifies her own kin in terms of their relative willingness and *ability* to reciprocate. By contrast, these latter indulgences are seldom extended to Grant's side of the family. Instead, she sees her in-laws as largely unwilling to honor any covenant of mutual generosity. Contrast this perception of Grant's people with the loving depiction of her paternal grandfather and his monomania for corn cakes. The latter evokes images of Steinbeck's Grandpa Joad and the actor Charlie Grapewin's lascivious enactment of the old man antic-ipating his first taste of California grapes. This passionate parable of the talents has no parallel in her depiction of Grant's kin.

If the ramifications of in-law antagonisms were limited only to the *material* openness of the Graham's domestic domain, then the schism might be quarantined to the irksome marauding of in-laws. The quartet of schismatic identities, however, penetrates to the very jural interior of kinship when it takes the form of kinship criticism. Which relatives can and cannot act as legitimate family critics is seldom clear. Criticism, in fact, can come from several directions at once.

We can fruitfully compare this structure of criticism with that which ideally occurs in centripetal formations. The assignment of the critic's role in the latter system is relatively unambiguous and conforms to strict rules of recruitment and succession. It is usually assigned to a relative in an ascendant generation, one whose objectivity is enhanced by being placed outside the domestic unit being critiqued. The prototype of the role of critic in centripetal systems is the upper-class paterfamilias, or the father's brother in middle-class French families (Pitts 1964). In addition to the clarity of the critic's role in centripetal systems, there is a cultural stability built into such critical processes that minimizes potential anomie. Merged identities ensure that the evaluative standards enunci-ated by the kinship critic and those held by the couple will be similar. Merged identities will not only decrease disruption caused by criticism based upon divergent values, they will also minimize communicative misunderstandings.

Contrast this depiction of centripetal criticism with that which exists in Potter Addition. Both the structure of lower-class kinship and the superfluity of strict mate selection limit the homogeneity of the family cultures involved. A conflict of divergent family traditions, while creat-ing even more of a need for clear critical input, will actually diminish the efficacy of criticism. Amalgamated identities predispose a kin group to defend its culture from the cultural criticism of in-marrying "for-eigners," so that the emergence of a legitimate family critic, one who can speak with a univocal authority to both the husband and the wife, is all but precluded.

The fact that almost any adult member of either descent group has the right to criticize an affine means that a din of criticism, often contradictory and coming from several directions at once, is the rule. This diffuse array of criticism is in fact the arrangement of which Mary Graham once ran afoul, for in what follows, her "affine's affine," of all people, is the source of critique; but worse from Mary's perspective, the woman's right to monitor and criticize her conduct seems to be upheld by Grant:

> Grant's sister-in-law, Camille, is jealous of me, always has been. It all started with a damned bit of silliness at a picnic with Grant's brother, Edgar. He tried to get me to eat something, and I didn't want to. The more he wanted me to, the more I refused. Finally, he came over and tried to make me eat it—that's when we started to rassle. Edgar is, of course, a shrimp, and I'm pretty strong, so it ended with me on top of him, making him eat the damned stuff! Everybody laughed—we almost died laughing—except Camille. She was mad as hell and for a moment showed it. She never said anything at the time, though. In fact, they would come out and see us every once in awhile and nothing was ever said one way or the other. But my sister told me that Camille had gotten mad over that incident. I never thought much about it until about a year later when I was pregnant with Marthe. We were still living out here in Potter Addition and Edgar and Camille were living two houses down from us. One day, Edgar's uncle called and asked me to go get him. They didn't have a phone at that time, so we had told them to give folks our number if they wanted to get in touch. So I went over and got Edgar. Of course, Camille wasn't home; she was working. John Graham, Grant's older brother, saw me go in and went and told Camille when she came home. He said that I was over there seeing Edgar when she wasn't home. Now, here I am, bigger than a barrel carrying Marthe. She comes over, mad as hell, saying, "That's pretty good. You come over here and fix my husband's meals and everything else when I'm not at home." I was just stunned. "Camille," I said, "I haven't been coming to your house. I very seldom even see Edgar at all." Well, she just agged and agged, and then left. When Grant gets off work that evening, here comes his sister and she tells him all this. It stirred up a mess of trouble in our marriage for a day or so, until I could make Grant see that I was in no physical condition to be doing what I was being accused of.
>
> Some years later, I found out that nothing had got settled. Edgar and Grant were working on a harvesting job about five miles west of Piedmont then. Grant would say, "Bring out some coffee and cookies or something." See, they would leave just before daybreak so they could start work as soon as it got light. I would take it out and think nothing of it. Then, after awhile, Grant was coming home and wouldn't eat supper. I asked him why. He said that Camille was bringing sandwiches and stuff

out around five o'clock every day. When she found out a few days later that I was bringing them breakfast she came over and said, "I want you to stop taking them breakfast." When I asked why, she said it was ruining Edgar's dinner. See, it was my ten o'clock cookies, not her five o'clock sandwiches that was the problem! But I held my tongue and told her, "I'll quit with the cookies if you do the same with the sandwiches." That settled it, but for a long while she wouldn't even speak to me.

That fall, they started it up all over again. We were all sitting around the table and they kept agging me on. They had done it sneaky-like all summer, but I had kept my peace. But that day, I was making applesauce. I decided enough was enough. I started talking back—having it out with them. Things got going pretty hot and heavy, and I guess we were all shouting. All of a sudden, Grant jumped up and says, "That's it, Mary, we're going to have a few words of our own. You better keep your mouth shut or you'll have the landlord asking us to move." I said, "I don't care. Its better we move than to put up with the crap I've been putting up with." Having had my say, I shut up.

But the longer I thought about it and the harder I stirred my applesauce there on the stove, the more I vowed that the next morning I would go over to Camille's and settle that mess. Well, I caught them just right. Camille was outside hanging clothes and Edgar was working in the yard on the car. I told her, "If you think I'm seeing your husband on the sly, then, by God, you two are going to start supporting me—I'm here to collect next week's grocery money!" Things just exploded: Edgar started laughing, and the more he laughed, the madder she got. The madder she got, the more he laughed. Finally, she got beet-red, sputtered something, and stomped off into the house. And you know, that's all it took. Today Camille is the best sister-in-law I've got. But see how things get started? They never forget, they just collect things and save them. Then they chip, chip, chip until you get out or have it out. I learned to have it out—that time.

In earlier chapters, we saw the severity of the problems that affinal antagonisms raised for family authority patterns. We now have another example, centering on a preposterous charge of adultery. We previously saw Mary struggling to close off her household from external, affinal criticism over the issue of raising her brother-in-law, Danny. There we saw how claims of siblingship disrupted the internal decision-making structure of the household. The fact that the Graham sibling group had as its point of political leverage not just Danny, but also Grant, attests to the depth of those undiminished sibling loyalties and their ability to disrupt conjugal solidarity.

Grant's loyalties seem tragically split in both Danny's case and in the one just reported. He seems unable to choose between being Mary's husband on the one hand, and being a brother to his siblings on the other. From Mary's perspective, Grant has acted in both instances more to mollify his siblings than to defend the autonomy of his own family.[4] His giving an inordinately high priority to his sibling's preferences has a parallel in Sue Martin's earlier admission that she might well choose her mother over Al, if push came to shove. The only difference is the locus of the interfering identity. In Sue's case the structure of solidarity and identity was vertical and filial in nature, while in Grant's case, its locus is rooted in horizontal siblingship.

The next incident in Mary's struggle with her in-laws involves, again, her perception of being deserted by Grant in favor of his brothers. This time, though, the politico-jural stakes are much higher since this controversy involves a dispute over the transmission of personal identities and the potential allegiances that bind one generation of kin to the next. It involves a controversy over Mary's first son by another man, Jerry. Just as Mary had wanted to incorporate her brother-in-law, Danny, into her nuclear family and seal off his socialization from affinal monitoring, raising him as her own, so now Grant wants to adopt Jerry, giving the young boy the Graham surname. Mary balks at this, which raises a storm of protest from her in-laws, one that is still boiling two decades later. Mary's desire to give Jerry his father's surname is seen by Grant's siblings as an insult to the Grahams as a whole:

> Even before we got married, Grant's family started spreading lies about me and my family. They told him I had been wild and that my family was trash. Of course, I was no angel growing up. Who is? But I was in no way what they were saying I was. What really made them mad was after I married Grant, he wanted to adopt Jerry. I said, "Okay, but I want Jerry to keep his daddy's name. I want him to know who his daddy was and to be proud of it." I don't think Grant liked that, but he loved me and went along. Later on, he adopted Jerry and let Jerry keep his daddy's name. His brothers and sisters went through the roof when they heard I wouldn't change Jerry's name to Graham. "Doesn't she think the Graham name is good enough for Jerry?" "What's wrong with you being Jerry's dad?" "Does she think she and Jerry's father are better than us?" Stuff like that. They tried to drag up some of my old boyfriends, to boot, and throw them up to me. Even now, Grant and his kin drags it all out ever so often. When we get in a fight, they still throw all of this up at me. It seems they just can't let it lie—always hitting you in the face with ancient history. To this day, they think I'm not a good wife and that Grant was a fool to get mixed up with me. In fact, on our wedding day one of his aunts asked him if he had got me pregnant—if that was why he was *having* to marry me!
>
> I've wondered all of these years why they have done me that way. I think I've kind of figured it out to some extent. Before our marriage, Grant kind of worshipped his older brother, John. He treated him like he was a god—bowed down to him when he spoke to him. In a lesser way, Grant was like that with all of his family. When any of them wanted money, why

Grant just unrolled the green and let 'em have it. He was stupid enough to give it to them, and would never see it again. He still does this to this day, but not often, not like he used to. But once we got married and they asked for money, they started getting told No! I told Grant we were not going to do it anymore. I think really that's why they was really against us getting married. They knew Grant would change. They were more or less jealous of me because of this. That's why they didn't like me from the start.

This anecdote goes to the very heart of my claims concerning affinal antagonisms and their expression in the amalgamated identities that make up the lower-class family. The household's penetration by effective kin groups in the form of an undiminished solidarity of siblings is indicated in Mary's resentful analysis of Grant's alleged domination by John. As far as Mary is concerned, *her problems* are caused by Grant's unaltered attachment to a set of premarital kinship loyalties. She sees Grant's alleged submission to John as being at the center of her inability to establish a domestic life free from pernicious gossip and unwarranted criticism. Moreover, it is her passionate belief that the prospects of her and Grant's marriage improving are in direct proportion to her ability to exclude his siblings from having any influence whatsoever in their family life. If she could neutralize the power of Grant's siblings, then her family would be much happier. We wager that Grant might agree, but would insist that Mary has chosen the wrong set of siblings upon which to lay the blame.

11

The Social Construction of the Kindred:
Sibling-Based Descent Groups

I. POTTER ADDITION'S DESCENT GROUPS

There are three distinct forms of kinship organization in Potter Addition. They correspond, roughly, to the three family types referred to in Chapter 7. The first is that of the founding families who first settled in the community. Though these families distance themselves from the urban mainstream by staying on the edge of city life, they are nonetheless firmly ensconced in Grand Prairie's cultural orbit. Embracing the area's dominant, patrilateral culture, their organizational core consists of a three generation line of males. The men, though dominant, are by no means uncontested autocrats in family and kinship affairs. Their wives, fitting the mold of Clay County's strong farm women, have a significant voice in everyday decision-making. The domestic power of these women notwithstanding, the men still hold an edge in family decision making and kinship affairs. For this reason, I will call this first type of kinship organization *patrilateral descent groups*.

The second descent group formation is associated with the uxoricentric family. The uterine dyad of mother/grandmother and daughter/mother-sibling forms its genealogical nucleus. Though these *uxoricentric descent groups* are common in Potter Addition, they lack the sense of self-certainty and cultural legitimacy that Clay County's dominant culture bestows upon patrilaterally organized formations. As such, uxoricentrism is a shadow institution in Clay County; isolated and left to operate unimpeded in the demiworld of Potter Addition, it is a powerful form of family and kinship organization within Potter Addition itself.

The third kinship configuration is the *sibling-based descent group*. It is predicated on the role default of both parents and the inability of either of the spouses' descent groups effectively to restore the shattered life of the family. Having no vertically organized kinship roles around which received rights and obligations can be permanently regrouped, the resulting kin group is constructed around all that is left: a horizontally organized solidarity of siblings.

I will argue in this chapter that sibling-based kinship's *minimalist assumptions* make it a fundamental structure of lower-class life and the culture of poverty. The social structure of sibling-based descent groups, their mode of integration, and the organizational challenges to which they correspond faithfully reflect the centrifugal tendencies of lower-class kinship in a way that uxoricentric kinship never can. Uxoricentric descent groups, by contrast, are more complexly mediated phenomena, and are grounded in the very structural tendencies that epitomize sibling-based descent groups. Because of this, we will discuss sibling-based descent groups first, deferring our analysis of the uxoricentric kindred to the next chapter.

II. THE BIRTH OF THE SIBLING-BASED KINDRED: THE STORY OF MARY GRAHAM

Sibling-based descent groups are formed when the jural collapse of the father is followed by the default of the mother. This happens most often when there is no mother/grandmother present to step in, support the daughter/mother, and take up the slack caused by the husband's failure. Instead, the mother becomes a sibling to her own children, and the family's mantle of leadership passes to an older child, generally a female. It then becomes that child's responsibility to preserve the integration and structure of her troubled family of orientation.[1] Even after the children grow up, marry, establish their own households, and ostensibly move through an otherwise normal family cycle, they never wholly break free of their original family of orientation. The sibling-based descent group often fuses conjugal and sibling identities to such an extent that when the siblings reach adulthood and begin their families, the latter are little more than an extension of the sibling group.

The sibling-based constellation faithfully reflects lower-class life in that it is a generationally minimal formation, with little family estate to preserve and transmit. It is a model of centrifugality, when compared to its stable, patrilateral, petit bourgeois counterpart, and appears to be without fully operative descent lines. This generational shallowness and momentary break in cultural continuity make sibling-based descent the lower limen of possible descent group formations that lower-class life can produce. Born as it is of parental default and the implosive traumas that originally forge the strong sibling bond, this culture is seldom passed on to the next generation.

Sibling-based descent groups are therefore transitional configurations. As the sibling group's members grow up and marry, the developmental cycles of their families of procreation will evolve along one of four possible paths: First, the adult woman may establish a traditional marriage along the lines of the Parsonsian prototype that we discussed earlier. Second, her marriage may transmute into an uxoricentric formation. In such situations the female sibling will not default in her conjugal role after her spouse has defaulted in his. This pattern is most visible in the nuclear families of those women who early in life "rose to the occasion" and became parents to their own siblings. The third path is that by which a male sibling raises himself by his own masculine bootstraps, so to speak, and constructs a family organized around hegemonically sanctioned, patrilateral principles. When this path is followed, it usually produces a man of outwardly heroic proportions who is all too often tragically insecure in his own masculinity. The last path repeats the double parental default that gave rise to the sibling-based descent group. Despite these divergent developmental pathways, each trajectory involves the *founding of a family tradition* from within the experiences of the individual sibling and his or her cohort, not the orderly reproduction and transmission of intact estates across generations.[2]

The process by which sibling-based descent groups originate is best grasped through a case study. We are fortunate to have Mary Graham's description of how she and her siblings synthesized their kinship universe from the shards and leavings of her parents' failed marriage. Mary and her siblings are still in the process of building a kinship tradition and are still fending off the predation of outsiders. In the following account she tells of the collapse of her parents' marriage and of her mother's struggle to preserve her family:

We moved to Grand Prairie in 1940. I was just ten years old when we moved over here on Union Street. Dad had been employed most of the time that we lived out in the country. In the winter, when farm work was slow, he cut and quartered firewood. Before the war, when things got real thin, he would work for WPA. So he always had some kind of work. By 1940, though, jobs was getting scarce and he wasn't able to make a go of it on the farm anymore. I don't remember how Dad found out about the job, but almost as soon as we arrived he got hired at United Foundry. There were seven of us by then; him, Mom, myself, my three brothers, and my sister, Mildred. Our first house was two miles south of Piedmont. Later, we moved over to Colson and finally, at the end of the school term, Dad decided to move closer to work. It was then that we moved up on Union Street in Grand Prairie, here.

I can't remember Daddy ever being without work until he quit United

Foundry and started to drive a cab. He started running around and drinking about then. Uncle Slats and him drove cab together, and Slats didn't help matters much. A lot of people blame the cab driving and Uncle Slats for Mom and Daddy's divorce, but that's wrong. To my notion they had always had trouble. Dad had always been crazy jealous of my mom. I can remember when we were kids he was jealous of any man who came to the door, but he didn't have no reason to. Before they came up here they argued. I think that it hurt us kids, all that bickering. Grandma Morris talked to us kids about it and explained it, but I know a lot of times I used to go and cry about it. The other kids really didn't understand that much because they were still small. But sometimes when you'd hear them going at it, you would be afraid that they were going to kill each other. Usually, however, most of their arguing was done while we were in school. Daddy drove cab on graveyards [i.e., late-night shifts] and never come home until the morning. By the time we got home, things were usually pretty well calmed down. Things very seldom got violent. They'd argue and bicker a lot, but I guess the first fight they ever had, where they actually hit each other, was when we kids wasn't around. They got into it and I guess Daddy slugged Mom and Mom just turned around and surprised him, she slugged him back. He sat down and bawled, "Well, Mom, you hurt me." I can remember Mom telling that story more than once.

Things kept getting worse. It got to where he would come home real late, and sometimes not at all. He wouldn't tell Mom where he had been, and she had heard enough about the wild life of the cabbies downtown where she could guess. I can remember a lot of them drank and they believed in this "running around." If you didn't have your wife with you, then you got a girlfriend. Some of them took a notion that if they wanted to take their wives, okay. If not, why they went out and got somebody else. They was all cab drivers and this was the way they played. If a woman fare didn't have enough money, well, sometimes they took it out in trade. Things just went from bad to worse for almost two years. In 1942, just after we moved out here to Potter Addition, Mom and Dad was divorced. I think they were married twenty-three years.

Mom went to work waitressing at the Olympic Cafe on Main Street, uptown, while Daddy still drove cab. A couple of months after the divorce, him and Mom started to argue over Daddy not always paying us money, and he finally quit sending it altogether. Things got so bad that a lot of times when school was out Mom would let us go and stay with her mother, Grandma Morris, so we would be sure and have something to eat. As things got worse, Mom couldn't even afford to pay the rent, so we moved over on Speer Avenue in Grand Prairie. We stayed there when I was in the eighth grade. Grandma, Aunt Opal and Uncle Stan, Mom's sister and her husband, came in at that time and helped some.

Those were bad years for Mom. It seemed the harder she worked, the more we slipped behind. She became real bitter. For one thing, Mom more or less built up a hate for Daddy and what Daddy had done. Even after she got a divorce she kept telling the boys, "Oh, he won't have nothing to do with you until after you're old enough to make a living, and then he'll want to come and live with you and have you support him." But, really, Daddy didn't want that. I don't remember Daddy ever asking anything from us kids. I really don't. I look at it this way, there's always two sides to everything. Mom done things that I know of that my brothers didn't know she did. Whether they know it or not today, I can't say. Also, I knew things that Dad done that I didn't approve of. I was always closer to Daddy than I ever was to Mom, so when he started helping again I didn't hold past grudges like the boys did.

They were bad years in other ways. Those were years when Mom should have been talking to us kids about our problems, but she just didn't want to be bothered. Really and truly! Of course, by her working and everything it was hard on Mom. I can understand better now, but then I couldn't. That was when Aunt Carlie kind of stepped in. Like when I upped and quit school she got me a job down where she worked, down at the White Line Laundry. She always gave me advice and tried to help out as much as she could. She was always good. She and Uncle Duff were always good to us and good to Mom. They helped Mom out whenever she needed anything—Mom needed money, they would loan it to her; if she needed groceries, they'd buy groceries. While Mom was working day and night to keep our family together we lived with them and, if not them, then a lot of different relatives pitched in. We stayed with Mom's mom and dad until Grandma passed away that July; Grandpa Morris died the next January, poor old man. When Grandma died we stayed with Aunt Rose and Uncle Ted. Mostly, however, Aunt Carlie and Uncle Duff kept us. They practically raised me after Grandma died. It was during that time I got so close to Aunt Carlie. She's more like a mother to me even today than my own mom. I mean, she always explained things to me. If I was in trouble or needed help, she was always there. Her and Uncle Duff were the closest to me of any of them.

For two years I and my brothers and sister were kicked from pillar to post. Finally, Mom gave up trying to keep us together. She went to Hanksville where she got a good paying job, and we went to live with Daddy and his new wife, Marie, in Crosby. I was fourteen then. Mom went to Hanksville and she worked over there. She tried to buy us kids as much as she could, but she was havin' it hard, too.

Mary's narrative is one of narrowing options. The collapse of her parents' marriage and the subsequent default of her mother make the orderly replacement of a *received* patrilateral tradition all but impossible. The death of Grandma and Grandpa Morris soon after the divorce prevents Mary's mother from moving herself and her children back home, and establishing a fledgling uxoricentric arrangement. Even when the Morrises were alive, they appear to have been ill prepared to take in Mary's mother and support her family. Consequently, the major source of aid from Mary's early adolescence until her early childbearing years comes mostly from a plethora of uncles and aunts, who, though hard-pressed, take in Mary's family for short periods of time. The mother's kin cannot, however, afford to support so large a family without risking going under financially themselves. For this reason, Mary and her siblings end up on their father and his new wife's doorstep. At that point, as impossible as it seems, things go from bad to worse:

Now Daddy and Marie only lived in a little two-room place out there at the time, so we kids fixed our beds in a garage that Daddy fixed up into a house. I don't know whose idea it was, Marie's or Dad's, but we would have to wait if we wanted anything to eat. She'd fix a meal and us kids waited until Daddy and her got through eating. If there was stuff left, we'd eat—otherwise, we'd starve. Us kids used to go out at night, steal corn, and go behind the garage and cook it after Marie went to bed and Daddy left for work. Many times we lived off of just that corn. There was also Mr. Baker, he would feel sorry for us and give us stuff out of his garden. A lot of times, Mr. Baker and his wife would fix cookies and stuff and invite us kids over. They were real nice people.

Finally, I run away from home. I had been working at this chicken place on South Dakota Avenue, called the Chicken Shack. I worked there every night, and with the money I made, I bought groceries for the kids. I didn't have much choice. Us kids were goin' without and it was starting to have its effect. We used to be pretty solidly built. Mom's still got a picture where it showed us when she took us to Daddy, and another of when she come and got us. You can see in them that we were practically skin and bones because they were starving us kids to death.

About a month after I left Crosby, one of Daddy's uncles told him a bunch of lies about me and they had me picked up and put on probation for running away from home and working under age. During the hearing, none of how Daddy and Marie were mistreating us came out. Mom asked me not to say anything about it because it could get her and Daddy in a lot of trouble, maybe even get Daddy thrown in jail. Besides, if it came out that Daddy and Marie were hurting us, she would have to take us back and she wasn't able to support us yet. She was afraid that if all of this came out in court they might put us in a foster home. So I kept quiet about why I left home and got put on probation. As part of the probation, I had to go back to Crosby. In a couple of months, though, I got tired of Crosby and asked Daddy if I could go see the probation officer and get permission to move in with his sister, Aunt Myrt. She told me that I could come and live with her and work, so I went to live with her. They told Mom, of course, because I was really in Mom's custody, but Mom okayed it for me to go live there. I was on probation for a year, but the judge told me if I was old enough to work, I was old enough to be on my own. So I went to work at John's Donut shop, up here on Main Street. The money I made went to support myself and to buy food and clothes for my brothers and sister. In September Mom came back to Grand Prairie and moved out here to Potter Addition and lived with Aunt Opal and Uncle Stan. I moved back in with her and Uncle Stan and Aunt Opal two months later, and Mom and me both went to work at the drive-in up here at Four Corners.

Mary's narrative reconstructs for us the process by which she becomes the self-appointed provider for her brothers and sister. Even as she resides in her father's house, she assumes parental functions. By stealing corn at night and cooking it for her siblings, she critiques her parent with a subtle "propaganda of the deed." Just as she conceals parental neglect from outsiders, so she compensates for that neglect. Being the oldest, she goes to work to buy food and clothing for her siblings. However, an emotional toll is levied throughout this process of forced maturation. We have had inklings of the price she has paid throughout this volume. Yet, despite this toll, *or more likely because of it,* Mary shows little rancor. Her parents' actions are acknowledged as deplorable, and yet she excuses them. Even in 1967 she is loyal to them to a fault. This is evident in the way Mary coolly relates how she "took the rap" in court rather than lose one or both of her parents. No matter how much they may have failed as parents, they are still all she has; jail for them and guardianship for her and her siblings would have meant an irrevocable loss. She holds her peace now, just as she did then, maternally granting her siblings the luxury of hating a parent who wronged them in their youth. It is obvious that despite the abuse she and her siblings have suffered, family was and still is preferable to the solicitude and kindness of strangers. In the final analysis family is all Mary has, and family is all she will ever have.

Within a year of her court appearance, Mary's mother returns from Hanksville and takes her children back. Mary, now sixteen, moves back home and a few weeks this side of her seventeenth birthday meets Jimmy Johnson:

> I met Jimmy Johnson while I was waitressing at the drive-in. He was an airman up at the air base just east of Farmer City. We started dating on the weekends and pretty soon it was obvious that we were very much in love. Mom didn't want me dating an airman because of the way they are with local girls. But she got to know him and liked him a lot more as we started dating. When he got out four months later, he moved to Grand Prairie and got a job working construction.
>
> All of that came to an end though in pretty short order when Jimmy left town. I was four months pregnant by then. Mom cared for me through the entire period that I was so sick with Jerry. She and Aunt Carlie took turns being with me when Jerry was born. I was sick and scared, and as lonely as I have ever been in my life.

We already know the rest of Mary's story: Within a year or so of Jerry's birth, Grant begins to court her, and little wonder, for she is by now a beautiful and voluptuous woman. But we also know that by the time Grant courts Mary the possibilities for alternative forms of effective kin organization have been further constricted. Mary's absorption into Grant's descent group, itself soon to be stripped of its lineal core by the early death of both his parents, is precluded. Given the nature of the affinal relations that I described in the previous chapter, the only realistic option left open to Mary is her own sibling group. Thrown back on their devices, Mary and her siblings are driven inward in order to survive.

Even now Mary is still absorbed in being a parent to her siblings. It might be assumed since she functions as a parent for her siblings that she has reinstituted a quasi-lineal structure within her sibling group. That is, she has merely exchanged places with her mother and become a mother to her siblings. Such an assumption would be incorrect. Mary will never be a sanctioning instrumental authority to her brothers and sister. She is, even now, much too desirous of their affection and approval to risk alienating them by assuming the role of a sanctioning parent. This egalitarian texture, even where one sibling has sacrificed disproportionately for the others, is the hallmark of a sibling-based kindred. It is this horizontal leveling that sets sibling-based descent groups apart from their patrilateral and uxoricentric counterparts.[3]

The aid given Mary's mother during her long struggle to keep the family together goes beyond mere financial help. It includes a bewildering array of uncles and aunts being surrogate parents to Mary and her siblings.[4] Just as Mary has taken in Danny and so many other "stray kids, stray dogs, and stray cats" over the years, so she herself was taken in by her kin when she was a child in need. Though all such acts were desperately appreciated by Mary and her siblings, the aid and advice of her Aunt Carly stand out as being of special importance to Mary and of theoretical interest to us.

I have assumed throughout that in the early evolution of the sibling-based kindred, the effective absence of the wife's mother forms the context in which mother default occurs. Now I would like to add a proviso: Under such conditions this vacuum is often filled by the mother's sister. The maternal aunt becomes a surrogate mother and much more. She not only serves as a mother by extension, but as a companion to her niece in a way the girl's mother never is. This very special relation has already been underscored by Mary. Aunt Carlie is something special—just how special is communicated in the following passage:

> *Mary:* When I was growing up, I didn't know nothing about, you know becoming a woman and all that jazz. I couldn't go and talk to Mom about it. Aunt Carlie was really more of a mother to me than Mom ever was, because I could ask Aunt Carlie and she would sit and explain things to me. But with Mom, it was

"Shut up and get out of here. How do I know?" When I got pregnant, Mom didn't find out until the latter part of December, and she wouldn't have found out even then if I hadn't of passed out at work. Aunt Carlie knew it way before Mom, and she explained everything to me.

Dave: You mean, she never explained the facts of life to you?

Mary: Mom never explained nothing to us kids. She never told me about becoming a woman—like when you start your monthly. She never told me a thing about it. When I did start, I'm telling you, I was scared. I never told Mom. I just sat and I bawled. It was Aunt Carlie that explained to me what was happening. The evening I had my first monthly I told Aunt Carlie, "I don't know what's the matter with me, whether I hurt myself or what; you come look and see. She sat and told me and explained all that to me. Then she went downstairs and jumped onto Mom. Mom had never told us any of this.

Dave: Do you think your Mom was a good mom to you?

Mary: Oh, yes. I think Mom was real good to us kids. I don't have a thing against my mom.

Dave: Yeah, but was she a *good* mom?

Mary: I think so, Dave. She tried to keep us kids together. In fact, Mom done a good job keeping us kids together after she and Dad separated.

Dave: Is that what you consider a good mom? Someone who . . .

Mary: Well, I mean, if we were sick or anything, Mom was always there to help. When I think about the first ten years of my married life, I spent half of it in the hospital. If it wasn't me, it was one of the kids, and Mom was always right there to help. Mom's helped me and Grant a lot since we've been married.

During my stay in Potter Addition, I found no male parallel to the maternal aunt and the support she provides for her niece, nor do I know of one now. To my knowledge the young man has no male relative to whom he can turn in the same way that the niece does when she seeks out her mother's sister. Men, on occasion, speak with great fondness of an uncle, but they seldom talk of him with the same intensity that characterizes the mother's sister/sister's daughter relationship. As an aside, it should be noted that this asymmetry of collateral support may be as much a product of the region and its history as it is a trait of the culture of poverty. That is, the mother's sister/sister's daughter relation is a staple of certain border state, rural-based kinship patterns. If such an asymmetrical relation is an established cultural pattern in the border states, it is obvious that this natural asymmetry becomes even more exaggerated when poverty and parental default enter the kinship equation.

III. THE BROTHER AS EX-OFFICIO FAMILY MEMBER

In Chapter 10, I talked of the double movement that generates the male's marginality to his own family of procreation and the crucial part that affinal conflict plays in shaping the internal system of lower-class kinship. I have yet to discuss that second movement in which the brother is reabsorbed into his own sibling group. When such a move occurs, it conforms to the quartet of antagonistic kinship identities that impinge upon the lower-class household. The brother is a constant ally of his sister during periods of domestic conflict. In such situations the brother balances the role of adversary to the husband with the role of "objective" kinship critic. Under the guise of the latter, however, he is first and foremost, along with his sister, representing the interests of their sibling group:

> *Mary:* Grant kind of got mad at my brothers—all of them—because when we was having trouble in fifty-six and separated he come down at Mom's and was blowing off. He was always jealous of my brothers.
>
> *Dave:* Why was he jealous of them?
>
> *Mary:* Well, Dave, if you seen our family during the years we were all home and later, whenever we would get together at Mom's it was just one big happy family. You'd sworn to God we had walked into Mom's, had only been gone an hour, and just come back. You'd swear we hadn't left home. That's just the way it always was. Grant got mad because my brothers would joke with me and say, "Hi Sis. It's been so long since we've seen you and all." When we was having the trouble in fifty-six, my brother, Vernon, told Grant, "You never treat our sister mean." Of course, he had two sisters but in one way I was the only sister, because I took care of them and meant more to them. [Mary pauses, then continues] No . . . that's one thing I'd have to say, Dave, if me and Grant ever had any trouble, I'd go to my brothers. Many a time when we've been on the warpath, all I have to do is say something to one of my brothers, and he straightens it out.
>
> *Dave:* Well, how does he straighten it out? Give me an example.
>
> *Mary:* He sits Grant down, talks to him, and asks him what's wrong. He points out where Grant is done just as much wrong, or is just as much to fault as I am. Grant is one of these guys who never really admits that he has ever done anything wrong. If he knows he's done wrong, he won't admit it. He will argue with you that he knows he's right, but Grant is just that way. In fact, every one of his brothers is that way. I don't think he's got a single brother that would ever admit that he'd done wrong.

Dave:	How about your Dad? Did he ever . . .
Mary:	A lot of times. I know when Grant was drinking a lot during that one stretch, I talked to Daddy about it, and Daddy talked to Grant. Of course, the boys were still at home, living with Dad and my stepmom at the time, and I remember the boys jumping Grant. They upheld me because I was their sister.
Dave:	When you get into little disputes like this, which is more likely to occur: Will Grant's brothers take your side or his side?
Mary:	Are you kidding? I don't think any of his relations would take my side except for one sister of his. I can remember when me and Grant was having problems because of Grant's drinking. They were butting in, and anything they would tell him he would believe. He was drinking quite a bit, but, of course, you know, his brothers weren't any help then.
Dave:	How about your own brothers? Will they pretty well stick by you?
Mary:	You better believe they'll stick by me. They always have.
Dave:	Even when they know you're wrong?
Mary:	Most generally, my brothers helped. They always try to find the bottom of it.

In this passage we have an excellent expression of the amity, affection, and solidarity that binds siblings to one another. The quartet of interests that shape the interior of the Graham household is clearly visible in that Mary is now the beneficiary of the same kind of sibling solidarity that so irked her in the preceding chapter. In assuming an ex officio leadership role in the Graham household, the mediating actions of Mary's brothers convert a domestic dispute into a confrontation between two kin groups. There is a symmetry between the brothers' intervention in this instance and Mary's earlier stories of Grant's brothers intruding into the family decision-making process. What is sibling aid from Mary's perspective can just as easily be interpreted as affinal interference from Grant's point of view, and vice versa.

IV. MINIMALIST KINSHIP

The formation of lower-class descent groups along lines of sibling solidarity is a defensive activity. Sibling-based descent groups begin with few material resources to protect or expend, and with little more than mutual affection upon which to draw. From this marginal base of affection and amity the sibling group reconstructs its kinship universe. Their kinship capital consists of a single generation's experiences and commitments, the dim memories of "better days," and the failed myths

of a moribund family tradition. Because of these minimal formal properties and the paucity of family capital involved, sibling-based descent
groups are the epitome of centrifugal kinship as it has evolved in Potter
Addition.

By stepping over the catalog of horrors and abuse in Mary's narrative,
we see a kindred being built almost from scratch. I have treated Mary's
case, as I did the Stoner-Martin family history, as paradigmatic of a
certain lower-class family and kinship type. Yet Mary's case seems so
extreme that one might question how representative and meaningful
her case history actually is. Although statistically rare, such cases are
theoretically crucial. There are other examples of such cases in the existing literature, and I myself have seen similar examples while growing
up in the Midwest. Long before taking up residence in Potter Addition,
I was acquainted with another sibling group similar to Mary's. These
siblings, too, had banded together to form a defensive constellation.
After struggling for a decade following the father's death to keep the
family together, their mother remarried and "abandoned" her thirteen
children. "Old Man Barnett," as they referred to their stepfather, had
"made a deal" with the mother. He would marry her and take her into
his new home, but he would not take her children. Since he was the
"richest man in town," Barnett could afford to rent a house on the
"other side of town," move the children into it, and support them until
they were grown. Twenty-five years after the fact, none of the children
I met—and I met ten in all—would condemn their mother for forming
this pact. Quite the contrary, they defended their abandonment. She
had supported them on her own for ten years by taking in laundry and
accepting the mincing and demeaning charity of the local churches.
Marriage to Old Man Barnett was seen by her children as her last chance
to escape future decades of back-breaking labor. As with Mary's pallid
defense of her mother as being a "good mom," they also defended their
mother. They hated the churches and the degradation they felt every
time "Christian charity" was extended to them with the same passion
with which they loved their mother and defended her. The oldest
brother, Elza, or "L.Z." as he was affectionately called, raised the
younger children for the next decade, until the youngest left home,
"hitting the rails" at the age of fourteen. Elza never married and was still
as much a parent to his brothers and sisters as he was a sibling when I
met him some forty years ago.

I bring Elza and his family up at this juncture because, despite the
sexual reversal of mothering roles, it closely resembles Mary's situation.
Though the person uniting the sibling-based kindred was a male, Elza
performed as Mary had; the oldest of the children, he was acknowledged by his brothers and sisters as being "the one who raised us all."

Elza was revered and honored by his siblings. The few times I saw him with his brothers and sisters, they were loving and deferential. But Elza had paid a price for this deference. He had never left the small Indiana hamlet in which he had been born and in which he had raised his siblings. He had never settled down and had children of his own. As was always pointed out to me by his brothers and sisters, he had "been too busy raising and taking care of us to get involved." A warm outgoing person who had been a taxicab driver most of his life, Elza loved children, and, in turn, children were attracted to this shy, understated giant of a man. He had sacrificed, it seemed, everything to raise his brothers and sisters. Part of that sacrifice had been his sexuality, for he seemed strangely androgynous in a family of hard-drinking, womanizing men who were constantly brawling in bars and fighting on union picket lines.

Elza's sacrifice was greater than I had realized in the years I knew him. Mary's sacrifice, though she never discussed it, must surely have been as great. Elza's example, gleaned many years before my fieldwork began, lends a ring of truth to Mary's case history. This intuitive sense of correctness, when buttressed by the works of Schneider and Smith (1973), Stack (1974), Anspach and Rosenberg (1972), and Brown (1952a), strengthens the claim that the sibling-based descent group is empirically real and essential to understanding the minimalist kinship associated with the culture of poverty.

After reading Mary's biographical account, the reader can readily see how lower-class kinship in the heartland resists any easy subsumption using the descriptive terminology usually associated with cognatic descent systems. The horizontal nature of group formation and integration, the temporally transitory and often nontransitive nature of the sibling-based kindred, and the fact that in the next generation its households may transmute into configurations that diverge radically from the ones that gave birth to them suggest that sibling-based descent groups are not descent groups in the conventional sense. At the same time, they *are* effective kindred in every other sense. They are operative kin groupings organized genealogically around bonds of siblingship. They honor, almost fanatically at times, the axiom of amity, and promote and protect one another's interests above all else. Concomitantly, the siblings establish boundaries between themselves and the rest of their world, lines that often cut across marriages. They also show a prescriptive enmity toward outsiders who presume too much, as in Mary's family shoot-out with Henry Curry. Sibling descent groups, in short, are creative instruments of adaptation and survival that have at their core a deep set of "blood-based" moral commitments. For all this, however, they still lack the acid test of generational depth.

But even if sibling-based descent groups lack generational depth, we cannot assume that structured patterns of kinship are absent. Mary's narratives should disabuse us of the idea that we have before us a case of familial anomie, pure and simple. In the last few chapters we have watched Mary and Grant labor mightily to secure stable relations with their kin. It is not possible to dismiss their efforts of constructing and maintaining patterns of amity as a mere foundering in chaos. While there is ongoing affinal conflict, this would seem to be a structurally based attribute of the kinship field itself. In this case, the existence of affinal conflict is not as important as the fact that the conflict is structured along stable lines of prescriptive altruism and patterns of amity.

The sibling-based descent group is thus not chaos, but a rational response to chaos. It is not the death of kinship, but its rebirth. It is the heroic response that individuals like Mary Graham make when in a halting and piecemeal fashion they fabricate an effective kindred from the sparse and bitter leavings of a collapsed family life. This is the significance of Mary's story. Her kinship universe lies somewhere between the classic bilateral descent group envisaged by Peranio (1961) and Firth (1963) and a socially disorganized aggregate. It is an occasional descent group moved one step closer to chaos, but is itself never engulfed by that chaos. It operates as a descent group might, but lacks the formal requirements of generational depth.

This last point raises another even thornier problem. If the sibling-based descent group is not a descent group in the strictest sense of the term and not an anomic aggregate, neither is it structured along conventional cognatic lines of vertical filiation. There are, to be sure, the genealogical nodes of parental filiation and the *abstract* lines by which one's ancestry can still be traced and through which bilateral stocks can be reconstructed. Shallow as these lines are, they can still be used to assemble a technical kindred and should not be derogated. But, in terms of everyday efficacy, is there an effective cognatic kindred here, or merely a group of siblings thrown together to fend for themselves as best they can?

All that seems to be *operationally intact* in Mary's kinship universe are two "empty" points of filial attachment. For what they are worth, they can be used to establish a minimal social legitimacy for making an occasional claim on kin, but little more. With few exceptions (such as Aunt Carlie) these points of attachment are operationally useless in procuring the practical means of everyday security. They are genealogical nodes in an abstract kinship space that "lead nowhere" as far as providing resources that could effectively counter the inward implosion of the collapsed family's estate. The resources are just not there in the lower class, even though the genealogical lines are intact. Certainly these kin groups are of little actual help in saving a family, and are even of less help in restoring a depleted family capital for the benefit of the next generation. With few exceptions, the vertically organized personal kindred, in cases such as Mary's, can act only for short periods and supply limited material aid and surrogacy before the kinsmen's own domestic group is threatened.

How, then, is an effective kindred constructed under these conditions? How are concrete descent groups assembled by those so young, when normal nodes of attachment have ceased to be effective conduits for recruiting senior kin and their resources? The answer, as we have seen, is that if one cannot go up the genealogical tree and thereby recruit lineals and/or collaterals from a generationally shallow stock, one must turn to what is left. *Effective personal kin* must be recruited *laterally*, from within the sibling group itself. There is, to be sure, a crucial halo of uncles and aunts who become early sources of aid and support. In a decade or so, however, these same ascending collaterals, as in Uncle Stan's and Aunt Opal's case, will become supplicants for aid. At this point the sibling core becomes an umbrellalike structure whose job it is to protect the fragile nuclear households embedded in it. In reality, it can rely on little else.

The sibling-based kindred, then, as an operational, cognatic descent formation is a largely alineal structure in its *everyday functioning*. As it and its constituent households pass through their respective developmental cycles, ascending collaterals become less and less a source of compensatory aid, while the siblings for a decade or two become one another's major source of kinship capital. With little or no lineal core surviving the trauma of parental default, and little or no inherited estate to protect or resecure for the next generation, the sibling-based descent group is the clearest material expression of centrifugal kinship that I found in Potter Addition. Its minimalist structure and its dogged adherence to the axiom of amity make it the most primordial kinship form I encountered in Potter Addition. First as children, then as adults, the siblings are integrated by a common biography and beleaguerment-born feelings of affection. Obeying the norm of prescriptive altruism, they remain one another's chief support.

At this point, the image of the *bricoleur* once again suggests itself. Like Potter Addition's housing, sibling-based descent groups are assembled from the bits and pieces of once coherent structures. Like the community's *bricoleur* housing, sibling-based descent groups are pragmatic, protective structures that clearly serve the immediate needs of those who have pieced them together. Since kinship and kinship groups are being synthesized on the spot, *not intergenerationally replicated*, and since the structure of the kindred is not so much a received tradition as an attempt to begin anew, centripetal kinship norms are superfluous in sibling-based descent groups. Salvage, not reproduction; beginning anew, not securing a revered past; these are the immediate tasks confronting Mary and her siblings as they reassemble and repair a shattered world of family and kinship.

12

Uxoricentric Descent Groups

I. THE SYNTHETIC NATURE OF UXORICENTRIC KINSHIP

Uxoricentric and sibling-based descent groups differ in how and why they come about. The crises that give birth to sibling-based kinship are those of an unpredictable and increasingly hostile niche that threatens the economic and demographic integrity of the domestic group. They are organized around the fundamental problem of reconstructing from scratch a viable kinship tradition. Their everyday preoccupations center on maintaining a functioning domestic domain. In comparison, the driving logic of uxoricentric kinship is only rarely concerned with material estates. The relative economic stability of the gynecocratic core's senior household makes uxoricentric formations better able to endure poverty's uncertain niche.

The dynamics of uxoricentric descent groups are grounded in the jural contours of uxoricentrism itself: in the husband's default, in the exclusionary structure of the gynecocratic core, and in the provincializing dialectic itself. When transported to the jural domain of kinship, these fundamentally domestic factors express themselves as conflicts over how and to whose benefits the uxoricentric kindred and its resources will be put. Will the descent group be organized vertically to meet the intergenerational, reproductive needs of the gynecocratic core, or will it be organized horizontally to serve the solidarity needs of a cohort of sisters and their families?

The analysis of the sibling-based kindred presented in Chapter 11 is crucial to understanding the structure and dynamics of uxoricentric kinship. The principles along which uxoricentric descent groups are organized contain many of the same structural assumptions that govern sibling-based descent's constructive possibilities. The two forms of kinship differ only in that uxoricentric kinship contains an *additional set of structural premises* that are located outside lower-class life itself. This set of "surplus premises" gives uxoricentric kinship its unique character.

I believe that some variant of sibling-based descent groups can be found wherever the culture of poverty emerges in capital's developmental wake. Thus the sibling-based descent groups of Potter Addition resemble the shallow, relatively undeveloped bilateral structures reported by Oscar Lewis in his studies of the *vecinidades* of Mexico City and the slums of New York City. Uxoricentric structures and their constitutive processes are another matter. They will seldom occur in other culture of poverty settings.[1] We have already seen in our analysis of provincialization how the dialectics of uxoricentric households are rooted in the class-based ambivalences of America's heartland. Uxoricentric kinship bears the unmistakable mark of a small-town, semirural, midwestern lower class struggling to gain access to the means of petit bourgeois propriety. Because uxoricentric kinship originates in a process of provincialization that honors and incorporates the heartland values of a local petit bourgeoisie, it most readily emerges in those insular situations where this class and its values still enjoy a hegemonic foothold. Concomitantly, the historical specificity of these values prevents uxoricentric kinship from having the same generalizability that I have attributed to sibling-based kinship. Because of this normative "surplus," uxoricentrism, when transplanted to an urban area or third-world context, would in all likelihood vanish as it accommodated itself to a new milieu (Riessman 1964). But left in its generative heartland context, it will continue to mirror small capital's cultural aspirations, even as gynecocratic dominance reproduces practices better suited for survival in the lower-class niche.[2] Once this is recognized, we can see uxoricentric kinship for what it is: the unification within a single structure of two radically different cultural commitments. It is neither the unmediated product of Potter Addition's lower-class niche, nor the unfettered realization of Grand Prairie's petit bourgeois ideal. On the one hand, it is conditioned by its variable class niche and, as such, exhibits many of the traits that characterize sibling-based descent formations. On the other hand, it has assimilated the centripetal tendencies characteristic of patrilateral kinship. Since this conception of uxoricentric kinship is at odds with my earlier depiction of the uxoricentric family, we must now pause briefly and attend to those differences.

In my earlier discussion of provincialization the reality and ideality of lower-class family life was framed in terms of an oscillation between uxoricentric and petit bourgeois domestic forms. Each family form was treated as the ideal typical expression of its respective class subculture, so that the dynamics occurring at the domestic level of uxoricentric family organization were in reality a dialectic rooted in the cultural con-

tradictions of class. This model is still adequate for describing the phenomenological reality of those living in uxoricentric households. The
cyclical alternations that typify uxoricentrism are defined by the actors
themselves as a choice between uxoricentric dependency and the petit
bourgeois ideal that dictates that a daughter establish an autonomous
nuclear family. Not only does this model describe the worldview that
families employ in everyday life, but the "conceptual fiction" of treating
uxoricentrism as prototypical of lower-class life helps us comprehend
the actuality of uxoricentrism. At the same time, since it is framed in
terms of the domestic roles that make up the gynecocratic core, this
approach is limited when it comes to analyzing uxoricentric descent. We
must thus find a related analytic model that goes beyond the model of
uxoricentrism's domestic domain, while preserving its essentials.

In constructing this alternative model, I will continue to treat petit
bourgeois family life and its patrilateral configurations as one of the two
poles around which the dialectics of the uxoricentric kindred revolve.
That much does not change as we move from uxoricentrism's domestic
domain to studying its descent formation. In light of the findings of
Chapter 11, however, I will no longer assume that uxoricentric domestic
life forms the second pole of that dialectical movement. That extreme is
now occupied by sibling-based descent groups. Because of this shift, our
understanding of uxoricentrism's provincializing dialectic, as it occurs at
the level of kinship, must be recast.

When interpreted against the background of kinship's politico-jural
domain, uxoricentrism's provincializing process can best be understood
as a dialectical movement between the hierarchical, generational tendencies of petit bourgeois kinship and a horizontally ordered, egalitarian solidarity of siblings. These contradictory forces express themselves
as alternating movements within a single kindred in which at one moment various kinsmen may organize themselves as if they were an *intergenerational* sodality of parents and children, and at the next, as if they
were a solidary, *intragenerational* cohort of siblings.

Uxoricentric kinship is then a dialectical unification of opposites. On
the one hand, it embraces the principles of centripetal kinship. Like the
vertically ordered structures of local petit bourgeois kinship, it expresses
itself as a *solidary lineage*. This moment in the life of the uxoricentric
descent group is manifested in the gynecocratic core's monopolization
of the family life of its members. During this phase, uxoricentric descent
groups have as their structural core the mother/grandmother, those
daughters who are momentarily her satellites, and their families. At the
other pole of kinship's dialectic, uxoricentric kinship exhibits structural
tendencies that we have thus far associated with centrifugal kinship.
Operating in opposition to the lineal commitments of the gynecocratic

core, this centrifugal counterforce is grounded in the sibling solidarity that is often found among those sisters who are momentarily "outcasts." The horizontal, egalitarian principles of solidarity that dominate sibling-based descent groups now oppose the vertical organizing principles of the gynecocratic core. Here the dialectics of uxoricentrism array a gathering of distaff sisters against the mother/grandmother and those siblings who have temporarily been drawn into her orbit.

Uxoricentric descent group organization thus encompasses two kinship options at once without being reduced to either. I will use the term *sublation* to denote how the oppositional principles of centripetal and centrifugal kinship are combined to create uxoricentric kinship. This term, used sociologically, refers not only to the originating logic of a social formation (how these contradictory social elements first come to be joined), but also to the process by which it continues to reproduce itself.

This latter, integrative aspect of sublation bears further examination, for when many sociologists use the word *integration* they refer to a series of harmonized, noncontradictory parts that are fused into an organism-like whole. When seen from this latter perspective, if there are inner antagonisms contained within this "organic entity," they are either accidental and hence transitory, or will be repressed by the self-equilibrating tendencies and adaptive needs of the social organism itself.

Integration through sublation is of a different order. It involves a *unification of opposites* that preserves the antagonistic aspects of its constituent parts even as it joins them into a structurally compatible whole. This, "dialectical integration," involves an irony that has no counterpart in organic conceptions of integration. In the case of sublation, the antagonisms between the parts are ameliorated in the process of their unification, and yet the conflict itself is still preserved within the new entity. The antagonisms which were originally properties of the parts, become relational attributes of the newly formed whole. The conditions that had previously precluded a productive synthesis of these antagonistic elements now become properties of the larger system. Once reconciled as elements of the larger whole, the parts themselves are changed. Their "presynthetic" conflicts are reconciled by being moved higher up, so to speak, in the emergent structural hierarchy. *Antagonisms at this point are transformed into mediated contradictions*. While harmonizing the antagonisms of the parts at the level of the system as a whole, sublation simultaneously preserves those antagonisms by transforming the whole itself into a dynamic unity of contradictions. The resultant structure contains within itself a set of generative tensions that provide it with an *internal source of movement*. Thereafter, there is a constant tendency for one constituent to "pull against its opposite," for one movement within the structure to set off a countermovement.

Uxoricentric kinship and its descent groups are formed by just such a sublated tension. They incorporate into themselves the antagonistic principles of other class-specific kinship formations, and in so doing form a third, autonomous, but contradictory configuration. As with all dialectically constituted structures, uxoricentric descent groups never experience these contradictions as they existed prior to their sublation. That is, uxoricentric kinship's dialectic does not reduce uxoricentrism first to patrilateral kinship and then move it to its sibling-based opposite. Instead, uxoricentrism's sublating logic endows each oppositional element with an altered social form. The substance of the previous antagonisms become possibilities that are lived within the horizon of the larger uxoricentric constellation. Each becomes an interior possibility that brackets the range of variations that uxoricentric kinship and its descent groups can take without being transformed into one or the other of their constituent components. The antagonistic principles are now experienced by those living in uxoricentric descent groups as the limiting possibilities and extremes of uxoricentrism itself. The logic of uxoricentric kinship transforms the organizational sense of patrilateral and sibling-based descent formations into an emergent set of axioms that are internal to uxoricentrism itself.[3]

As we noted earlier, the kinship commitments of Potter Addition's founding families, such as the Danielses, approximated a patrilaterally organized kindred. Similarly, the Grahams and the Edwardses were treated as the embodiment of sibling-based descent groups. The Martins and the Stoners were treated as prototypical of uxoricentric households. Within uxoricentrism's totalizing context, Mary Stoner, Sue Martin, their husbands, and Sue's siblings construct interactional patterns that conform first to one principle and then to the other. These uxoricentric alternatives are not, however, lived by the Stoners and the Martins in the exact way that they are lived by, say, the Danielses' clan, on the one hand, or the Grahams', on the other. Instead, each set of polar premises is lived as if it were a possibility of uxoricentric kinship only. Hence, petit bourgeois certitude and its strong lineal arrangements are most closely approximated within the horizon of uxoricentric descent groups when the gynecocratic core dominates its immediate circle of effective kin. When a crisis occurs and a daughter and her family turn for aid to the mother/grandmother and her gynecocratic core, the daughter and her family are integrated into an age-graded, uterine hierarchy that exhibits its own centripetal logic. Ordered along centripetal lines, uxoricentrism structurally approximates patrilateral kinship organization. During these periods of centripetality, norms of closure, accumulation, orderly replacement of gynecocratic culture, and the stabilization of joint family estates become dominant concerns of the daughter and her family. During such periods, the workings of the gynecocratic core functionally parallel those of the three-generation line of males in petit bourgeois kinship.

There are other times, however, when the mother/grandmother will raise the specter of middle-class propriety and cut a daughter loose. When this happens, the daughter and her family are not ejected from uxoricentrism lock, stock, and barrel. Instead, the daughter usually is able to join a group of distaff sisters who, like herself, have temporarily been barred from their mother's grace. The dialectics of gynecocratic domination now transform the kinship commitments of the junior females into a newfound solidarity of sisters that is arrayed against the core of mother/grandmother and dependent sisters. The daughter, suddenly "thrown out into the cold" and deprived of maternal approval and aid, restructures her effective kin group along lines similar to those of sibling-based descent groups.

The mother/grandmother's provincializing denial is comparable to the mother default that generates sibling-based kinship. But for all the heuristic value of such a comparison, it must be remembered that this denial is carried out *within uxoricentrism's horizon.* If the daughter is temporarily cut out of the prior lineal arrangement, she is still not thrown into the same lonely situation that Mary Graham has known most of her life. There is a difference between actual double parental default and its semblance in uxoricentric kinship. The alternative to being integrated into the gynecocratic core of a uxoricentric formation then is not that of being cast out of the uxoricentric formation altogether. The alternative to expressing solidarity with the uterine line is instead that the woman's new kin commitments are organized around the principle of sibling solidarity. Under the impetus of the provincializing dialectic as it operates in the domain of kinship, the logic of centripetal hierarchies is replaced with a centrifugal egalitarianism between sisters. It is at this point that the uxoricentric descent group most closely approximates its sibling-based counterpart. The major difference is that in the uxoricentric domain the shadow of a competent, senior female continues to fall across the *ressentiment-filled efforts* of the sisters to achieve sibling self-organization.

The preceding describes the dramatic breaks in continuity that periodically expose the composite structure of uxoricentric descent groups. Usually, however, the everyday organization of the uxoricentric kindred is a moving synthesis, so that the more a woman and her family become part of the gynecocratic core, the less accessible they are for being members of the distaff sibling formation. Conversely, the more embedded the woman is in her sibling group, the less available she and her family are for being recruited into the gynecocratic core. This is because provincialization at the level of kinship is predicated on two social-psychological premises: the ever-present possibility of sibling competition for the mother's favor, no matter what the daughter's current status, relative to the gynecocratic core; and the mother/grandmother's continuing ability to disrupt the sibling group's solidarity by playing off one daughter, or group of daughters, against another, and hence forming a series of ever-shifting alliances.

Multiply Sue Stoner's guilt and insecurity concerning her mother by the size of her female sibling cohort, and one has a fair approximation of the emotional limits placed on sibling solidarity at any given moment. There are few cases in which a daughter becomes so estranged that she cannot be drawn away from her sisters and returned to her mother's favor. For these reasons, the sector of the effective uxoricentric kindred that is ordered by sibling solidarity always has a variable composition and changing levels of social cohesion. The lifelong rivalry between sisters, even at the zenith of a rediscovered commonality, is never far below the surface. The most minor incident can reignite a lifetime of competition and resentment and destroy the most painstakingly reconstructed sense of sisterhood. Hence, the primary antagonisms between sisters resemble dormant geologic fault lines, which can be set off at any moment. These fault lines form the ground of gynecocratic domination, and when used by the mother/grandmother to retain control of the uxoricentric family, set off parallel provincializing movements in the organization of the uxoricentric kindred. At the level of kinship, the dyadic dependencies of uxoricentric family life are replaced by the coalition politics of the uterine triad. In this triadic scenario, provincialization is no longer just an abandonment of the daughter to the powers of a capricious niche. The withdrawal of support from one daughter is often accompanied by the drawing of a second daughter back into the gynecocratic web. Thus, the mother not only controls her daughters via provincialization at the level of household aid and interaction, but also sets in motion a "circulation of sisters" in kinship space as they move between the gynecocratic core and its peripheral sodality of sisters.

The composite nature of uxoricentric kinship is summarized in Figure 12.1. The cells on either side of the illustration represent ideal-typical models of petit bourgeois kinship and the "minimalist forms" of lower-class kinship. The center cell summarizes the composite outlines of uxoricentric kinship. The three cells are arranged so as to show the sublated composition of this third and final form of lower-class kinship.

With this schematic, my analysis of lower-class kinship is brought to a close. In these pages I have tried to show that lower-class descent groups and their logic are far from being pale replicas of bourgeois kinship configurations. They are creative responses to a singular situation: the poverty niche against which the poor daily struggle. Lower-

LOWER CLASS SIBLING-BASED KINSHIP GROUP

1. DESCENT PRINCIPLE: Solidarity of siblings. Double default of parents creates a transitory personal kindred and cognatic grouping based primarily on sibling amity.

2. DOMINANT KINSHIP NORMS: Kinship groups organized around centrifugal kinship norms. Decomposition of family and its estates obviate the need for centripetal norms. Chronic crises and need for immediate solutions predicated on minimal family resource base. Social situations created in which centrifugal norms are more conductive to the adaptation of fractured family.

3. DESCENT GROUP STRUCTURE: Alineal aggregation of siblings and their families of procreation. Effective kin group loosely integrated along horizontal lines. Siblings and their families are oriented toward the sibling who took up the role of surrogate parent.

4. FAMILY FORM: Parental household is characterized by double parental default. Siblings' families of orientation may develop in any of a number of directions: uxoricentric, traditional nuclear, or disorganized forms.

5. DOMESTIC GROUP STRUCTURE: Open household with variable demographic composition. Fusion of sibling group and the fate of the households founded by siblings. Male siblings have "ex officio" status in sisters' households as critics in times of crisis.

6. FAMILY NORMS: Permanent availability in sibling generation. As a whole or individually, members try to keep their families of procreation and their sibling-based, effective kindred intact. Diverse family cultures may develop in later stages of the developmental cycle as each sibling constructs his or her respective family culture and estate "from scratch."

UXORICENTRIC KINSHIP GROUP

1. DESCENT PRINCIPLE: Solidarity of the uterine line is the operative norm. Provincialization of family norms by mother/grandmother, however, gives rise to aperiodic, transitory formations based on the principle of sibling solidarity.

2. DOMINANT KINSHIP NORMS: Kinship groups organized around centripetal norms. Matriline attempts to construct a jurally exclusive lineage, not unlike that of the hegemonically dominant petit bourgeois model. Accumulation of family capital in the form of uterine estates is fostered and kept under the control of strong senior female.

3. DESCENT GROUP STRUCTURE: Gyneocratic collective integrated across generational lines. Uxoricentric household led by the mother/grandmother is the basic functional unit of activity and aid. Provincialization, however, allows for a structural fluctuation between the compound, uxoricentric households, holding together one senior female and the households of several daughters, and an effective kindred formed by the sisters themselves. This creates a set of transitory, dyadic relations.

4. FAMILY FORM: Uxoricentric family predominates. Again, provincialization creates a variable structure that fluctuates between compound families formed around a two or three generational uterine core, and a form of pseudo-petty bourgeois, nuclear family and household structure.

5. DOMESTIC GROUP STRUCTURE: Mother/grandmother and daughter/mother-sibling usually maintain separate households that are nonetheless structurally integrated under the mother/grandmother. Provincialization is a source of aperiodic short-run fluctuations.

6. FAMILY NORMS: Orderly replacement of the uterine family culture is the focus of family efforts. Struggle to construct family outside the control of hegemonic male culture should not obscure the fact that this is a mirror image of petit bourgeois family form, differing only in its inability to gain cultural recognition and transgenerational stability.

PETIT BOURGEOIS PATRILATERAL KINSHIP GROUP

1. DESCENT PRINCIPLE: Solidarity of the lineage. Non-default of either parent leaves the principle of patrilateral domination more or less intact. Women often have strong voice in family affairs. Filiation dominates siblingship as organizing principle.

2. DOMINANT KINSHIP NORMS: Kinship groups organized around centripetal norms. Highly stratified system of kinship roles within and between descent groups. Stratification and principle of jural exclusiveness preserves family capital and facilitates its future accumulation. Generational stratification governs pre-disposition of family assets.

3. DESCENT GROUP STRUCTURE: Effective cognatic kindred structured along principle of patrifiliation. Kin groups composed of relatively intact nuclear families that are integrated vertically by lines of agnatic kinsmen.

4. FAMILY FORM: Households of all generations characterized by relative stability. Family composed of conjugal dyad and children. Configuration of family roles grounded in traditional conceptions of age and sex differentiation, with duties assigned accordingly.

5. DOMESTIC GROUP STRUCTURE: Relatively closed household with stable demographic composition. High levels of internal differentiation with the isolated neolocal, nuclear family as the basic structural unit through which the effective kindred operates.

6. FAMILY NORMS: Family organization facilitates the orderly replacement of family culture over generations. Family estates are stable in content from generation to generation. Focus is on the preservation of symbolic and domestic estates over time. Centripetal norms and the accumulation of family capital emphasized in the ordering of family life.

Figure 12.1. Uxoricentric kinship groups and family structures as the sublation of sibling-based and patrilateral formations.

class kinship is thus not a descent into chaos, but a rational and structured response to chaos. It is not the death of kinship, as some would have it, but kinship's fragile rebirth—the halting fabrication of an effective kindred that responds under varying conditions to the bitter contingencies of lower-class life. Ultimately, it is an act of defiance by those who refuse to succumb to the hopelessness and barbarism into which our society would drive them.

II. LOWER-CLASS KINSHIP AS A WHOLE

The last half of this work has been devoted to analyzing the three basic forms of family and kinship that ordered life in Potter Addition. Our analysis has had three major divisions. First, we explored the impact that material conditions had on shaping the domestic life and kinship commitments of the poor. Second, we showed that while the structures of family life and kinship were conditioned by the material infrastructure of poverty, both had a relative historical and structural autonomy from material conditions as such. Finally, we showed how kinship structures were socially reproduced and, in times of crisis, intentionally reconstituted from the nostalgic myths, uncertain memories of times past, and the biographical sinews of a cut-off generation. This last reconstructive element is especially important for understanding the unifying dynamics of Potter Addition's world of kinship. As we have seen, the majority of Potter Additionites live out their lives in one of three basic kinship constellations: the patrilateral, the uxoricentric, or the sibling-based descent group. If circumstances force a person to abandon one of these formations (precluding, of course, a fall into familial anomie), then the probability is high that he or she will reconstruct an effective kindred that follows the contours of one of the other two. For these reasons, the forms of family and kinship in Potter Addition can be seen as a tripartite division of a self-reproducing whole. No single kinship constellation can be fully understood except in reference to the other two.

Figure 12.2 presents an idealized schematic of this holistic aspect of kinship in Potter Addition. In summarizing the major findings of this work, it depicts the various stochastic processes of substitution and transformation that ostensibly link the three kinship forms into a single system. The schematic reads from left to right and begins with the putative stability of the class niche in which a family operates. Thus, the nature of the class niche becomes a crucial bifurcation point for determining the kind of domestic arrangements and kinship groups that

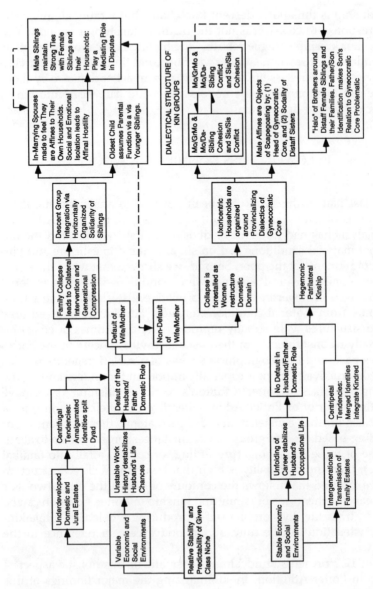

Figure 12.2. The production and reproduction of lower-class family and kinship patterns as a whole.

develop in the families of the poor and near-poor. If the niche is relatively stable and predictable, a developmental process ensues that in all likelihood will produce the classical Parsonsian family and its attendant patrilateral configuration. As we have seen, the maintenance of traditional male hegemony and the avoidance of husband default is a fundamental linchpin of Clay County's domestic culture. The processes that preempt husband default are shown in the lower left-hand branch. They include two causal complexes: one grounded in the occupational sphere, the other residing in the normative contours of kinship. This lower branch depicts the way in which a stable occupational niche and its orderly careers provide the material base by which lower-class men can normally avoid domestic default. This stable material base, when combined with centripetally structured kinship, provides the necessary grounding for patrilateral descent groups. This patrilateral alternative is the rule among many of Potter Addition's founding families. Sustained by the "poor, but good people" of Potter Addition, this kinship configuration in practice and precept is quite close to the petit bourgeois descent formations that have been the analytic foil of this work.

The reader should note that the structure and content of this lower branch are the mirror image of the upper branch, representing the process of husband default. Both branches contain a set of occupational and kinship trajectories that, when combined, create radically different outcomes. Thus the upper left-hand branch depicts the occupational dynamics that lead to husband default. Beginning with variable environments, it depicts the unstable work histories and adaptive failures that plague the husband's early work life. At the same time, a second causal branching depicts the role that lower-class kinship plays in producing husband default. The presence of this second branch emphasizes the fact that the jural domain of lower-class kinship can be neither reduced to a set of objective economic forces nor treated as a purely subjective phenomenon. In assuming that amalgamated conjugal roles constitute the lower-class nuclear family, I wish to underscore the relative autonomy of kinship as a factor in generating husband default. For this reason, Figure 12.2 depicts husband default as lying at the confluence of two paths: one occupational and economic in origin, the other located in the cultural superstructure of lower-class life.

Moving to the middle of Figure 12.2, the upper portion of the schematic treats husband default as a crucial choice point. If followed by the wife's default, it leads to either family collapse and the onset of anomie (not shown in Figure 12.2) or sets the stage for the construction of a sibling-based descent group. The top right-hand portion of Figure 12.2 summarizes the process by which sibling-based descent formations develop, while the lower portion traces the unfolding of uxoricentric descent groups and their dialectical reproduction.

Two dashed arrows at the right of the schematic run counter to the general flow of the schematic. They represent feedback loops in the developmental cycles of lower-class kinship. Both pertain to the reproduction of male marginality in the domestic domain by causes other than economic default. It will be recalled that in my analysis of the uxoricentric family, sexual stereotyping by strong female agents helped reproduce from within the domestic domain itself a potent, predisposing source of male default. The role of reproducing male superfluity through uxoricentric socialization is represented by the lower dashed arrow.

The upper right-hand arrow denotes a second set of contingencies. Lower-class kinship provides two possible paths that a husband's domestic career may take. First, the disenfranchised husband in the uxoricentric family may become an ex officio member of one or more of his sisters' households, or, as in the case of sibling-based descent groups, he can become the founder of a new patrilateral tradition. By breaking the pattern of double parental default established in his family of procreation (which called the sibling-based descent group into existence in the first place), the male sibling's household might yet approach the patrilateral norm. In order to keep the schematic in Figure 12.2 simple, this latter transformational possibility has not been depicted. It should, however, be considered as being implicit in the dashed arrow closing the sibling-based descent branch of our model.

Finally, the last feedback loop represented by dashed arrows runs between the sibling-based kinship branch and the uxoricentric branch. It represents a transformational possibility within the matrix of lower-class kinship. The female in a sibling-based descent group can conceivably found within her family of procreation a nascent uxoricentric constellation. This possibility is especially plausible in the case of those women who have already assumed a quasi-parental leadership role vis-à-vis their own siblings. This final possibility links the three lower-class kinship formations into a single transformational network. It demonstrates the speculative possibility that the three forms of kinship encountered in Potter Addition are in reality three loosely integrated alternatives of a single system.

13

Potter Addition Today

I returned to Grand Prairie in October 1991. After an absence of almost twenty years, I had come back to do research on a social history of Potter Addition. The trip was also a pretext for renewing old friendships, for Potter Addition and its people had never been far from my mind in the intervening years. In one sense I had never been away; friends still living in Grand Prairie occasionally reported to me what was happening in Potter Addition, and on several occasions I had talked by phone with Mary Graham and Lonnie Carter. We already know Mary from her narratives. Lonnie was a valued resource person and close personal friend during my stay in Potter Addition. A person of vast wit and intelligence who possessed a gift for storytelling that was legendary, he helped me understand and interpret what I saw during my fieldwork, and steered me around the usual pitfalls that plague participant-observer studies.

In my last telephone conversation with Lonnie, some three years before, he had boasted that I would not recognize Potter Addition. Sewers had finally been hooked up, the streets were paved with concrete, and a long-awaited community center had been built. A HUD-financed community improvement grant was restoring homes. HUD had even bought out Bull Gomes's junkyard, but as was befitting Bull's character, and much to the irritation of many in the community, he had delayed the entire process by haggling over a "fair price."

Thus, even before I arrived, I knew that Potter Addition had changed physically. The question uppermost in my mind, however, was "Had it changed socially and culturally as well?" Had the HUD-financed improvements also eliminated poverty in Potter Addition? And, if so, had the community's vibrant culture been compromised in the process? Along with the pain and misery of living poor, the people of Potter Addition had possessed a basic sense of personal honesty, vitality, and bawdiness that I had come to appreciate the longer I worked in the academy.

These were the thoughts and questions utmost in my mind as I drove the 180 miles that separated Grand Prairie and the metropolitan airport at which I had landed. Not surprisingly, the closer I got to Grand Prairie, the more my facade of scholarly detachment gave way to vague feelings of apprehension. The weather did not help my mood. From the moment I left the airport I had been engulfed in a steady downpour, which continued during my entire stay. As I drove in the hours just before dusk, the landscape was framed in low-lying clouds and tinted with shades of gray, gunmetal blue, and distant silhouetted blacks. As the interstate left the wooded region that lay south of Clay County and entered the prairie heartland, the gloom, low clouds, and driving rain progressively erased the details of the landscape. The houses, grain elevators, and forested groves were now reduced to silhouettes. Diminished to its bare essentials by the dusk and gloom, the prairie seemed more vast and foreboding than I had remembered. Feeling a sense of exposure and personal vulnerability I had not known in two decades gave my questions an increasingly personal tone. My curiosity as to how much Potter Addition had changed expanded to include how much I myself had changed.

I. THE CORPORATE UNIVERSITY

To understand the changes in Potter Addition requires first knowing how Grand Prairie and Clay County had changed. And that requires, in turn, understanding how the university had changed. Grand Prairie had lived and died with the university for the previous half century and, as I soon found out, this was still the case. Despite local efforts at economic diversification, Grand Prairie was still a one-industry town. The relation between higher education and corporate capital, which was just taking hold in the late fifties and early sixties, had by 1991 evolved to the point that the character of the university itself had altered. The university in Grand Prairie had become a powerful "corporate" university. It was one of a handful of large, state-funded institutions of higher education that now served a national constituency. Despite a series of setbacks in state funding and the loss of several faculty "stars" to higher bidding institutions, the university had in recent years grown and prospered. Possessing one of the most effective fund-raising foundations in the nation, and having a first-rate faculty that was famous for obtaining lucrative research grants, the university had offset many of its local funding crises. In 1990, not an untypical year according to the Grand Prairie newspaper, the university had solicited more than $120 million from corporations, the federal government, individual supporters, and various outside granting agencies.

Those running the university had spent that money well. They used it, among other things, to expand significantly the institution's physical plant and real estate holdings. This was most evident on the campuses housing the engineering and agricultural schools, and in the physical changes that had taken place in the areas immediately adjacent to the university. In two decades, the engineering campus had nearly doubled both the number of its buildings and the land area it occupied. This growth had been fueled in large part by Pentagon and other federal research funding, though several sizable bequests from individual donors had recently enriched the college's building program. The growing power of contract research and corporate bequests was equally evident on the agricultural campus. An early leader in the development of biotechnology, the agricultural school, and through it the university, had prospered from the growing connection between corporate largess and higher education.

Other evidence of the university's prosperity could be seen in the area immediately surrounding the main campus. Over the years, a nine-square-block area west of campus, once the site of off-campus student housing, had been purchased. The housing had been demolished and replaced by a new physical sciences complex, a performing arts center, and a fast-growing dormitory area. Other land had been purchased and while awaiting similar development had been given over to paid parking areas.

The university's invasion of the surrounding community signaled a major shift in the political and economic balance of power that for decades had mediated the antagonistic forces of town and gown. Those parochial conservatives who in the fifties and sixties had voiced fears that the university would some day economically overwhelm the community, and in the process consume Grand Prairie's small-town culture, by 1990 had seen their worst nightmares come true. While Grand Prairie and Clay County had traditionally profited from the university's presence, the power of the corporate university had pushed things beyond the petty struggles that had previously marked the town/gown split. By 1991 the class system of Grand Prairie itself, and the collection of occupational subcultures that enriched it, had been reorganized so as to better serve the needs of the university.

The extent of the university's hegemony can be seen in the way it has reorganized the occupational structure of the region. The two charts making up Figure 13.1 use forty years of U.S. Census data to trace the

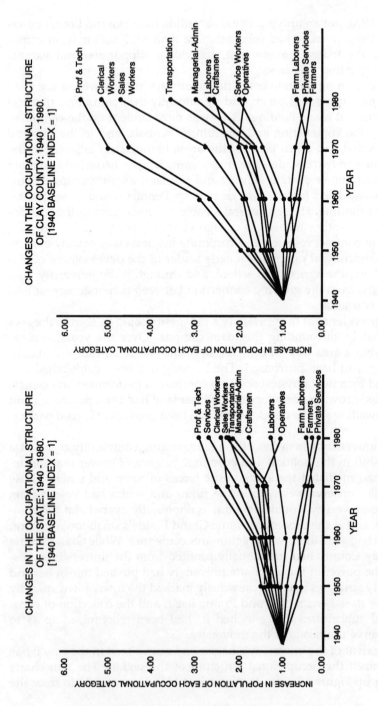

Figure 13.1. The occupational evolution of Clay County and the state.

occupational evolution of Clay County and the state. They compare the proportional rate of change in the number of persons employed in twelve occupational categories. Notice that most of the curves in Figure 13.1 slope upward as they move to the right. Such curves are said to be positively sloped, and indicate increased growth. The steeper the slope of a curve, the greater the rate of growth in that category. Conversely, when a curve slopes downward, it is negatively sloped, and represents a decreasing rate of growth. Again, the steeper the slope, the greater the rate of decline. The data in Figure 13.1 have been standardized so that state and county data can be directly compared. Thus the year 1940 is used as a baseline against which to index the forty-year redistribution of population elements among each of the twelve categories. To do this, the number of persons in each category for 1940 is divided into the figures for their respective category for that year and for each census year thereafter. This is why the index for 1940 has the value of 1.00 and all succeeding years fan out from that point.

The first findings of interest in Figure 13.1 pertain to the comparative rates of overall occupational growth for both state and county. When the two charts of Figure 13.1 are compared globally, *dramatically differing rates of increase between the occupational spheres of the state and the county as a whole* are revealed. Because the vertical axes of both charts are on the same scale, the respective rates of occupational growth as they have occurred at the county and state levels can be directly compared. Thus, the relatively greater width of the fanlike pattern of spread between them suggests that, overall, the *rate* of occupational expansion has been much greater for Clay County than for the state as a whole.

The corporate university's role in shaping this robust growth is suggested when we compare the state and county figures for two categories: professional and technical workers, and clerical workers. At the state level, these two categories, along with service occupations, make up the three fastest growing categories in the state. All three have more than doubled their relative values since 1940. In Clay County, however, these two categories have increased more than fivefold, and represent far and away the largest shift in Clay County's occupational structure. The major occupational situs from which these shifts emanate is the university. Its faculty, the support staff of technicians, and the pink-collar clerical staff make up the lion's share of these two occupational categories and their growth. When taken together, these categories account for a full 42 percent of Clay County's labor force in 1980, a surprisingly high figure for a county that earmarked some 93 percent of its land for purely agricultural uses that year. Thus, in both the absolute number of jobs generated, as well as in the relative amount of growth in Clay County's various occupational spheres, the university dominates the regional economy more than ever. It is, in fact, no exaggeration to say that the economic welfare of both the city and the county remains irrevocably tied to the growth of Grand Prairie's corporate university.

II. GRAND PRAIRIE

If I had any doubts that the university's expansion had been a stimulus to other economic changes in Grand Prairie, they were dispelled almost immediately upon my arrival. I had reserved a room at the local Holiday Inn because of its location. It lay just off the interstate on Prospect Avenue, a major north-south artery located on Grand Prairie's western edge. I knew the motel from my earlier days in Grand Prairie: It was just south of the interstate and west of the ghetto. To the north of the interstate, open farm land stretched to the horizon. At least that was how it had been. Upon my arrival I found that a large shopping complex had been erected north of the freeway. The complex was flanked on the west by Prospect Avenue, where a series of seven or eight fast-food restaurants was doing a thriving business. To the north a new warehouse district had been established, while a mixed area of warehousing and light industry had been built on its eastern boundary. The intersection of Prospect and the interstate was no longer the boundary between town and country, and Prospect Avenue had long ago ceased to be Grand Prairie's westernmost artery.

More surprises awaited me the next day. As I drove around the city, it became apparent that much of the area's retail activity had shifted from Grand Prairie's central business district to a series of shopping centers and malls that now ringed the city. Judging from the growth of these shopping areas, Grand Prairie had experienced vigorous commercial growth in the last twenty years, though, as I learned later, in the late eighties there had been a downturn. A second metamorphosis had also occurred on the city's edge. A thriving light manufacturing sector had sprung up in several places around the city. When I left Grand Prairie in the late sixties, various food processing and warehousing firms that were tied to the agricultural sector were already well established. During that same period a group of high-tech assembly plants were just beginning to locate in the area. In the seventies and eighties these new industries and several others like them had mushroomed on Grand Prairie's periphery. Many had located in Clay County specifically because of the university's presence, and the pool of intellectual capital and sophisticated facilities that were readily at hand.

Even though the county's economy had slowed in the last half of the 1980s, Clay County had still experienced a manufacturing boom. This upturn was all the more remarkable given that the state's economy, especially its manufacturing sector, had stagnated during this period. Although this stagnation was not on the same catastrophic scale as that of the so-called rust belt of the industrial Northeast, it followed the pattern described in the deindustrialization literature (Bluestone and Harrison 1982; Harrison and Bluestone 1988; Bowles, Gordon, and Weisskopf 1991).

Clay County had been a beneficiary of this pattern of industrial flight to more rural and less contentious regions. Since the gradual disappearance of the railroads and Grand Prairie's shop facilities, Clay County's industrial sector had remained largely dormant. When it finally did take off in the early seventies, it exhibited all the vigor of a newly industrializing region. Those businesses coming to Clay County tapped a set of cheap labor markets and a public sector that had barely been touched. Indications of this can be seen in Figure 13.1. By comparing state and county data on the three occupational categories usually associated with the manufacturing sector—operatives, craftsmen, and laborers—we can see that *at the state level* growth in all three categories has either leveled off or declined significantly. Since the 1940s, the relative proportion of nonagricultural laborers, for example, barely held its own relative to the growth of the other occupational categories. The same is true of operatives, a category that showed moderate growth until the 1970s, then dropped rapidly. Craftsmen have done better, but only marginally so.

The figures are dramatically different for Clay County. Though the operatives category shows parallel declines for both county and state after 1970, Clay County operatives enjoyed a higher proportionate growth. By the same token, the increase in the laborers and craftsmen categories shows a relatively robust pattern of growth in Clay County. The county's craftsmen, in fact, fare the best of the three, posting a relative increase of some 59 percent. It is significant, as we will soon see, that the occupational categories of laborers and operatives are traditionally low-skilled and low-paying occupations. Therefore, occupational growth in Clay County is greatest in the very sectors that are marked by low skill requirements and low wages.

A second set of statistics in Figure 13.1 rounds out the picture of the kinds of economic changes experienced by Clay County. The occupational categories farmers and farm laborers steadily decline at both the state and county levels. Their long-term negative slopes set them apart from the generally expansive trends in the other occupations. These declines are not surprising, however. They are mere extrapolations of the same century-long trend in agrarian capital formation we noted earlier. Moreover, the actual number of jobs lost over this period was not so large that unemployment in the agricultural sector would act as a drag on the overall growth of Clay County's economy. The growth of jobs in the manufacturing sector over the last two decades would easily have absorbed the displaced agrarians—assuming, of course, that upon leaving farming the rural emigres would seek employment in Clay County.

Yet, there is a dark side to Clay County's economic miracle. Grand Prairie and Clay County are increasingly becoming three societies: The first lives and works in some degree of relative comfort and security; the second constantly teeters on the edge of poverty, suspended between "good people" and the despairing, superfluous poor—the third society. Much of Grand Prairie's new prosperity seems to have been built upon the backs of the second class of poorly paid full-time workers. This can be seen most clearly by looking at which occupational sectors have experienced the greatest expansion. In the last three decades, job growth has occurred most rapidly in four nongovernmental, industrial sectors: agricultural services, service industries, manufacturing, and finance and banking. The first three pay the lowest average salaries in Clay County. By contrast, the sectors that traditionally paid the best wages at both the state and county levels—mining and construction—have declined over the last forty years. Since these three sectors were historical strongholds of blue-collar unionism, their decline must be seen as much in terms of shifting political contingencies as the result of some mythical mechanism that impersonally drives labor markets.

When the spectacular growth in the low-paying pink-collar category of clerical workers is considered in conjunction with the above inverse relation in the industrial sector between low wage levels and high rates of job growth in the nonunion sectors of the local job market, Clay County's commercial "renaissance" assumes a different meaning. It parallels the nationwide pattern of that *fin de siècle* economic phenomenon called Reaganomics. Clay County, like other underdeveloped rural regions, benefited greatly from the decade-long political dismantling of industrial America, the rise of high-tech industries, and the creation of low-paying service and manufacturing jobs. The role the university has played in this transformation, moreover, seems to parallel the role played by "military Keynesianism" in Reaganomics generally. The university's nonmarket funding sources, like military spending at the community levels, have formed a solid fiscal foundation from which selected, market-oriented industries have taken off and grown (Peterson 1991, pp. 31–32). Along with the stabilizing social infrastructure provided by public professionals and a white-collar work force, this non-market source of public funding has handsomely complemented the industrial portion of Clay County's economic revival. Thus, Clay County's prosperity reflects both the lighter and darker sides of the last two decades.

III. CLAY COUNTY AND ITS SMALL TOWNS

Clay County did not grow as fast as Grand Prairie, yet many of its small towns show the same outward signs of prosperity. In their case, however, affluence exacted a heavy toll in their ability to preserve their communal autonomy and character. When my fieldwork ended, Clay County was a mosaic of small-town cultures in transition. Grand Prairie was Clay County's political and financial heart, and had been for almost a century. Yet, until recently, the county seat had never been able to subordinate its villages and hamlets. The Frisian farming communities in Clay County's northeast corner, for example, largely remained closed to the many modern ideas and progressive attitudes that flowed from Grand Prairie's cosmopolitan university. Exhibiting a cultural cohesion that often verged on the xenophobic, these tightly-knit little farming hamlets preserved many of the institutions and folkways that their ancestors brought with them from northern Europe more than a century ago.

Similarly, several communities in the southeastern and southwestern townships of Clay County had been built along railroad lines or spurs that only marginally traversed the county at its corners. These villages and hamlets owed their existence to the railroads that criss-crossed Clay County in the late nineteenth century. Themselves peripheral in many ways to life in the county seat, their economic heart was the local grain elevator and the stores that served the neighboring farms. By the late twenties, these towns had hit their peak, some boasting their own banks and, in a few cases, even their own auto dealerships. Small-town life, while often circumscribed politically and economically by activities in Grand Prairie, was not dominated by Grand Prairie. As late as the 1940s, the culture of these outlying villages and hamlets was still organized by a very different set of ecological and institutional rhythms than those which regulated life in Grand Prairie. It is true, of course, that throughout the closing decades of the last century and the first third of this, Clay County's center and periphery worshiped the same civic religion, upheld the same principles of unfettered individualism and unlimited life chances, and saw the same hand of providence working to achieve a just allotment of reward and punishment among the races and classes. But that credo was always subject to local variations and loose, sometimes nearly heretical interpretations.

This changed with the demographic and commercial collapse of the small town after the second world war. It was then that Clay County's multilayered pluralism began to unravel and to reorganize itself ecologically and socially around Grand Prairie. The relative social and geographical isolation of the towns and hamlets that had been a source of parochialism and a bulwark against "outside interference," had, by the early seventies, all but evaporated. This was especially true of those towns located within about a ten-mile radius of the county seat. By this time, a web of interstate highways, laid out so that many of the small towns had their own off-ramps, was nearing completion. Criss-crossing the county and converging on Grand Prairie, this system soon converted what had once been a collection of parochial cultures into a tightly integrated web. Indeed, census data suggest that the rate of social and demographic decline of many of Clay County's villages and hamlets was often proportional to their distance from Grand Prairie. By 1990, the familiar concentric zone form of urban organization used by the Chicago School to analyze urban processes described the emergent patterns of interaction between Clay County and its urban center.

Grand Prairie now sits at the center of two distinct ecological zones. The first extends in roughly a ten-mile radius around the county seat. The second contains the remainder of the county's rural hinterlands. The demographic consequences of this ecological reordering can be seen in Figure 13.2. The populations of these villages and hamlets in the first zone have experienced explosive growth in the last ten years. More distant villages and hamlets located in the second ring have continued to stagnate demographically. Three villages in Zone I especially (Prophet City, Piedmont, and Toulon) are now an easy twenty-minute drive from Grand Prairie, and are the fastest growing residential places in the county. In the late sixties they were fast becoming bedroom communities for Grand Prairie's economic and academic elites. They have now been transformed into thriving suburban enclaves.

As Figure 13.2 shows, the villages and hamlets in this inner ring were spared the decline of their sister communities in the outer ring. In fact, in the last decade they outstripped Grand Prairie itself in terms of population increase. The price of their salvation and survival, however, has been the surrender of whatever was left of their social and cultural autonomy. Those hamlets in the second zone will be spared that fate, but only at the cost of becoming superfluous to the gathering forces that now shape Clay County.

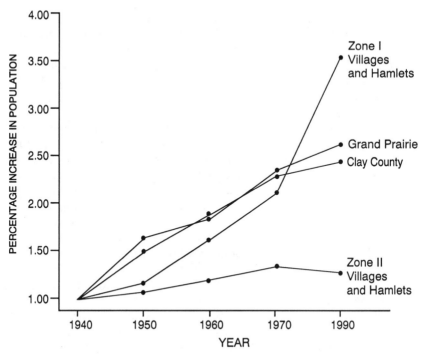

Figure 13.2. Population growth of Clay County's towns and hamlets relative to their distance from Grand Prairie.

IV. CLAY COUNTY'S FARMERS

The changes in Clay County's rural hinterland were more gradual, but no less dramatic than those overtaking Grand Prairie and its satellite communities. The land is still fabulously rich, is well cared for, and still produces a seemingly unending abundance of feed grains. As we have seen, however, agriculture in Clay County supports fewer families each year. While this trend has not changed over the last seven decades or so, there are nonetheless signs of a new emerging agrarian class in Clay County's hinterland. This new class pursues a lifestyle that is markedly different from that of their forefathers. The poor-mouthing farmers who kept their property in a state of workable disrepair to cheat the grasping tax assessor have given way in several instances to a group of wealthy farmers who are not shy about displaying their wealth. Someone touring Clay County's back roads will be surprised to see one immaculate, well-cared for farmstead after another. Newly painted barns and restored houses, some of them truly grand in appearance, testify to the pride that a new generation of self-satisfied farmers takes in itself and its craft. Respectful of tradition to a fault, but still hungry for the recognition that comes with long tenure on the land, one or two farmers have taken to an uncharacteristic form of boasting: painting on their barns, often in a gothiclike calligraphy, their family names and the year they or their forefathers began farming.

Such conspicuous status displays have been institutionalized by the Clay County Historical Society. Metal roadside placards designating "centennial farms" have been placed along the roadside in front of selected homesteads. The placards tell passersby that the families now working this particular centennial farm are descended from kin groups that have owned and worked this land for a century or more. Reading between the lines and counting back through the years, the words on the marker also tells us that those who founded these centennial farms were able to weather the cycle of depressions that shattered rural America in the 1880s and 1890s. These families also survived the agricultural crisis of the 1920s, and have yet to succumb to the agricultural depression of the 1980s.

Those holding the land today are thus descended from people who not only held on to what they built in years of crisis, but who actually expanded their holdings. The continuation of this savage pattern of survivors feeding off the misery of failed neighbors and kinsmen is seen in the data on land accumulation for the last forty years. In 1954 the average size of farms in Clay County was 208 acres, some 20.2 percent larger than the average for the state. In 1987 the average size of a farm in Clay County measured 356 acres, an increase in average size of 71.1 percent in three decades.

But land and people cannot be separated here. Rising average acreages are merely another way of talking about producers leaving the land. In 1954 Clay County had 2,847 farm operators working its land. In 1987 that figure was 1,671, a decline of 41.3 percent. The underlying dynamics of this decline can best be grasped by looking at who lost out and who stayed. In 1954, there were 1,437 operators working farms of between 180 and 499 acres. They accounted for half the farmers in the county. In 1987 the number of operators in this category fell to 549 and represented only 32.9 percent of all farm operators in the county. During this same period, 84 farms averaged between 500 and 999 acres in size in 1954; by 1984 that figure had increased fourfold, to 386. Even more telling are the data on the county's largest farms: in 1954, four farms owned between one thousand and two thousand acres, while no farm was larger than two thousand acres. In 1987, eighty-three enterprises held between one thousand and two thousand acres, while eleven exceeded two thousand acres.

We can see how these figures translate into concentrations of economic power by looking at the distribution of agricultural sales in Clay County. By breaking down the total dollar volume of agricultural sales in Clay County for any given year by the dollar size of sales per individual farm, we can obtain a rough measure of how agricultural life in Clay County is presently stratified. Thus in 1978, 455 farms (some 22 percent of the commercial farms in Clay County) had agricultural sales of one hundred thousand dollars or more. These farms accounted for fully 57 percent of Clay County's total agricultural sales. By contrast, 496 farms with sales of less than twenty thousand dollars each (the poorest quarter as measured by total sales) accounted for less that 2.0 percent of the county's agricultural sales. In less than a decade, the number of farms in 1987 with sales of one hundred thousand dollars or more were reduced to only 363. Despite this 27 percent decline, however, this category of farms raised its share of agricultural sales to 67.7 percent. Concomitantly, in that same year 489 farms (29 percent) had sales of less than twenty thousand dollars. They accounted for 1.1 percent of total agricultural sales in the county.

These patterns of capital accumulation and polarization in the agricultural sphere rival in scale the concentration and centralization of capital in America's industrial sector. Indeed, this degree of accumulation makes the designation "industrial agriculture" a fitting term for describing the structure of farming in Clay County. That most of these enterprises are still owned and worked by individual families, cooperating brothers, or fathers and sons does not alter the fact that farming in Clay County has become a truly corporate, if not oligo-polistic affair.

V. PERSISTENT POVERTY

The dominant structures of Clay County's new political economy are clear to see. Its anchoring points are agricultural production on a truly industrial scale, a corporate university with national ties, a burgeoning manufacturing and warehousing sector, and finally an ever-tightening integration of social and ecological forces around an urban core. This economy, moreover, has experienced little of the social disorganization and institutional anomie that might otherwise accompany a rapidly expanding economy. Perhaps the reason for this relatively unproblematic growth lies in the fact that Clay County's light industrial sector has taken root in a "mature community," one whose social system is firmly grounded in Grand Prairie's university-driven infrastructure and Clay County's land-based wealth.

In other circumstances, one might predict that the wealth of the land, the flow of university funding into the community, and the balanced growth of nonpolluting, light industries would generate well-being throughout all levels of local society. But as we have seen, this is not the case. The proliferation of low-paying jobs in both the public and private sectors is a key element of the region's overall prosperity. The lower blue-collar working class and its white-collar counterparts have paid a disproportionate price for the region's economic success.

Others have paid a different price: that of continuing social neglect. There is still a portion of Clay County's people who, despite the expansion of the industrial and various service sectors, have never made it out of poverty. Clay County's good times never came for these people; for them the seventies and the eighties were simply more of the same. Here are the figures: In 1970 the census reported that 2,647 families and 16,886 individuals lived below the official poverty line in Clay County. This represented 7.2 percent of Clay County's families and 10.3 percent of its population. In 1980, 2,585 families (6.9 percent of all families in Clay County) were living below the poverty line, while the total number of all persons living in poverty increased to 19,482 (13.2 percent of Clay County's population). Then there were the "near-poor," those families and persons with incomes that were 125 percent of the official poverty line. Their numbers also increased during the decade of the seventies. In Clay County, 16.7 percent of the population were below or at the 125 percent line in 1970, while in 1980 their numbers rose to 17.6 percent of the population. What is remarkable about this poverty is that it persisted during a period in which the growth and expansion I have described were in full swing.

The social profile of the poor in Clay County is not that different from that found in national poverty studies. In terms of gross numbers, more whites than blacks lived below the poverty line in Clay County. In 1970 the ratio was 4.5 to 1. In 1980 that ratio had diminished slightly to 4.4 to 1. By way of contrast, the percentage of each race living in poverty is the reverse of this picture. In 1970, 9.2 percent of whites and 31.4 percent of blacks lived below the poverty line, while 11.8 percent of whites and 26.9 percent of blacks lived in poverty in 1980. The 4 percent drop in Clay County's black poverty rate during the seventies provides little comfort considering the concomitant 2.6 percent rise in white poverty.

Most of the families in Clay County who live in poverty are not female headed, but live instead in two-parent households. Thus, in 1970, 71.1 percent of all households living below the poverty line were headed by males, while a decade later 55.5 percent were headed by males. This latter figure reflects an alarming rise in female-headed households, and underscores the emergence of a much-discussed feminization of poverty. Largely because of this, women and children—both black and white—are overrepresented in the ranks of Clay County's poor. Finally, running counter to public conceptions of the poor, most of the "official poor" are also in the ranks of the "working poor." In 1970, 72.5 percent of the heads of impoverished households in Clay County reported that they worked at some time during the preceding year. In 1980 that figure had fallen to 66.2 percent, undoubtedly presaging the area's economic troubles. Two thirds of the households, then, contain the working poor, including 64 percent of those female-headed households living in poverty. In the same year, 77 percent of those in Clay County classified by the U.S. Census as "unrelated individuals" living in poverty reported working for some unspecified period in the preceding year. Unfortunately these census figures do not report how long any of the poor in Clay County worked—household heads or unrelated individuals—nor do we know the length of time between periods of employment.

These are the data on the old-style poverty. When combined with the poverty that continuously hangs over the heads of Clay County's low-paid workers, we can construct a collective portrait of two contradictory worlds: one part of Clay County, despite its role in helping to create Clay County's economic miracle, is still poor—many living within a paycheck or two of poverty. The other world is a well-off and prospering minority of well-educated, secure families. Clay County's circumstances, moreover, are paradigmatic of other rural counties that have made the leap to prosperity in the seventies, only to see it falter in the mideighties.[1] It is against this background of the new poverty and the old that we can now answer the question, "How much have things changed in twenty years?" The answer is that poverty still exists, but is more subtly clothed than before. It is harder to find in a society that has become expert in substituting cosmetic covers for cures, but it is still there; I found it in the dry census figures that our government collects decennially. I found it also in Grand Prairie's ghetto and its fringe communities.

VI. THE CHANGING FACE OF POVERTY

Potter Addition is no longer a free-standing community, surrounded on three sides by open fields and by Salt Creek on its fourth, as it was that first day I saw it. A large, well-kept, and obviously up-scale complex of apartments and condominiums now borders the community on its western edge. This complex was on the drawing boards when I left, and was completed in the seventies. It extends from Potter Addition's western edge to Highway 111. To the north of the complex, stretching along Highway 111 to Spooner Road and the old school-house, is a new shopping center, replete with supermarket and ancillary businesses. North of Spooner Road, where beautiful fields of wheat once stretched to the interstate (with nothing beyond it as far as the eye could see), stands a series of senior citizen apartments. This housing and several more expensive complexes have jumped the interstate and are now sprawling northward to Farmer City.

The Spooner Road School, which marked the intersection of Highway 111 and Spooner Road, is still there. It houses the same roofing company it did when I first saw it. This is almost all, however, that has remained the same. Located immediately behind the old school and the shopping center, straddling both sides of the road, is a combination garage, towing service, and auto insurance agency. A sign above the towing service announces that both it and the garage belong to a cousin of Kevin Thomas. The sign also indicates that the insurance agency is somehow associated with the first two businesses. Apparently the car cult is still active and providing at least some of its devotees with an honest living. Further east, on the north side of Spooner Road, stand low-cost apartments and a series of trailer courts. On Spooner Road's south side, just beyond Potter Addition, there is still a patchwork of open fields and small stands of scrub and timber that run to the interstate. Beyond the interstate, on the other side of the Spooner Road overpass, is a pastiche of new brick "suburban homes" and older frame dwellings.

Thus, Potter Addition is no longer out in the country as it once was, and it is no longer on the leading edge of Grand Prairie's fringe. Yet, despite the evolution and outward expansion of the fringe, Potter Addition has retained much of its former marginal character. Even though an expanding Grand Prairie has leap-frogged it, Potter Addition is still an unincorporated, socially distinct community. It has never been incorporated into the city, I suspect, for three reasons: First, on the basis of people's past reactions to the subject of incorporation, Potter Addition's response would have been so fierce that the city would have risked a major embarrassment had it tried to absorb the community. Second, city officials would have had little stomach to take on a feisty community whose tax base would have contributed little to the city's revenues. And, finally, the new "business" located in lower Potter Addition made it an undesirable acquisition. Now sitting on the bank of Salt Creek, across the stream from the old Grand Prairie waste treatment plant, is a new garbage and waste disposal facility. Built in the early eighties and located in the extreme southeastern part of Potter Addition, this facility was built over the strenuous objections of many in the community. Despite this opposition, however, local officials still approved the location of this obviously pariah enterprise. This one act on the part of the city suggests that despite other changes in Potter Addition's relations with Grand Prairie, its niche's historical role in Grand Prairie's social ecology has changed very little over the years. Potter Addition and its immediate environs are still culturally defined as a legitimate dumping grounds for Grand Prairie's material and social refuse. The very idea that the city would permit this sort of business to locate in a predominantly residential area, especially one that had struggled so hard over the years to improve its reputation, is bizarre. It is little wonder that many Potter Additionites saw this as merely the latest in a long chain of affronts.

Still, the record of official dealings with Potter Addition during the seventies and eighties reveals several positive instances. Chief among these are the HUD-financed improvements and the construction of the Potter Addition Community Center. The fact that the community obtained these concessions from Clay County's and Grand Prairie's elites reveals some amount of sympathy to Potter Addition's changing needs. And there is no doubt that HUD and local matching monies have made a difference. Lonnie was right: the physical rehabilitation of the community makes it practically unrecognizable to someone who had known the old Potter Addition. Many of the shacks in upper Potter Addition are gone. So are the notorious little houses that lined King Street. Gone also is the dwelling made from the two boxcars, the house made of joined chicken coops, and the rehabilitated pigsty. Trailers or factory-built homes stand where these exotic structures once stood. Visually the old Potter Addition was a polyglot affair. Today it has a tight, clean, and healthy look. There is also a uniformity among the residences that was not a part of the old community. This uniformity is largely the result of the two-toned aluminum siding that covers many of the area's older structures. My first reaction to the ubiquity of the aluminum siding was, "They must have had one hell of a siding sale one weekend during the seventies!"

While Potter Addition looked better than I had ever seen it, I also found the new look somewhat disquieting. There is no arguing that many of the older structures needed to be brought up to code, and that the HUD-backed efforts certainly made Potter Addition a more pleasant place in which to live. Who in their right mind could argue against such progress? Yet it was with some sadness that I realized that the siding, while improving the looks of the community, had also concealed many of the telltale signs that had once provided clues to the biography of the various houses and their serial construction. Those biographies had been part of the intimate humanity and visible history of the community, but now they were gone. Displaying perhaps too much of the cynicism of our times, I also wondered to myself whether or not any of this would have occurred if some slick developer had not decided to build his or her posh complex so close to Potter Addition.

Dramatic changes other than those in housing had also altered Potter Addition's visual presence. The building that housed the Potter Addition Volunteer Fire Department now stands empty. Once a focal point of male activity and a source of community pride, the fire department has moved to new quarters some four miles further east on Spooner Road. In making the move the fire department lost its exclusive community character. True, its fine new building still bears Potter Addition's name, but the volunteer fire department is now a creature of forces much larger than the small cooperative undertaking I knew twenty years ago. It is no longer the company fabricated from practical need and throwaway equipment that had been bought or borrowed from other local fire departments. Nor is it the prideful property built out of the collective sweat of a hard-working, stigmatized community. I doubt that strangers are now dragged by residents to the new fire station the way I was, to be shown the pride of the community: "our fire department."

Another collective representation of the community is also gone. A verdant field now stands where Bull Gomes's junkyard once did. It is kept cut and trimmed by a recent retiree. With Bull's business gone, one can now stand on Potter Avenue and, instead of seeing a sea of junked automobiles, have an unimpeded view of the apartment complex. Bull himself is dead. As fate would have it, he did not have the final say in determining the how and when of his departure. One evening a fire broke out on the back of his property and burned for almost twelve hours. When it was finally extinguished, the yard, his Quonset hut, and the garage were all ashes. Miraculously, the inferno was kept from spreading to adjoining structures. Thus, Bull and his yard are gone, as are the controversies that alternately outraged and entertained the community as he stormed through our lives. As is befitting Bull's legend, there was scandal to the very end as rumors of arson spread through the community.

Two other junkyards have also shut their doors. The yard on Banks Avenue that was run on the sly as a part-time business and ace in the hole by my heavy-equipment operator neighbor is gone. It has been replaced by a small trailer park, which houses five or six trailers. Their size and condition suggest that, despite everything, lower Potter Addition is still home to yet another generation of poor. The other junkyard, the one that had been located next to Betty's Market, has been cleaned up and the old house in which its owner had lived has been torn down. A new prefabricated house has been erected in its place. This leaves only the junkyard in Potter Addition's southeast corner. It is still open and causes little trouble. Located near the new waste disposal business, it is sufficiently out of sight that it is seldom a point of controversy.

Finally, Betty's store is gone. It closed in the midseventies. Although LaRue died shortly after I left, Betty kept the store open until infirmity and illness made it impossible for her to continue. She tried to sell the store, but no one came forth to buy it and continue her nostalgic gesture toward small-town life. Consequently, she closed her doors and converted the downstairs, the former store area, into living quarters when her sickness made climbing stairs all but impossible. Frail and failing, she spent her last years in the rooms that had been formerly occupied by the store, where so much had happened to shape Potter Addition and its character.

The structure is now owned by the woman who cared for Betty in her last years. Known as a kind and giving woman throughout the community, she had always dreamed of owning her own home. Her family's poverty, however, kept it from scraping up enough money for a down payment. Betty solved that problem by making special arrangements in her will for her nurse and friend to buy her house without having to make the usual down payment. People in the community saw Betty's act as being typical of her kindness, but for all that, not exceptional. Betty's farewell gesture was simply another example of the long tradition in Potter Addition of the poor looking out for one another.

VII. CONTINUITIES IN THE CULTURE OF POVERTY

Socially, Potter Addition is still a tight little community. While it has lost many of its earlier identifying features and institutional anchorings, such as Bull's Garage, Betty's Market, and the volunteer fire department, it has retained that élan and sense of cohesiveness that always marked its culture of poverty. It is still culturally conservative in that it values and fetishizes tradition as only the socially marginal can. This is seen in the differences that still visually set the community apart from the new residential areas that now surround it. One still gets the feeling, when turning off Spooner Road onto Potter Avenue, of entering another time. This sense is derived, perhaps, from the contrast between the surrounding apartment complexes newly crowded together on their treeless planes, and the small houses of Potter Addition, each on its own lot, shaded by century-old trees.

But there is more than surface appearance at work here. Personal commitments to the past are sustained in the community by a strong set of cultural forces and motives. The details of everyday material culture still communicate, despite the cosmetic changes in appearance, the sentiments and values I encountered twenty years ago. Potter Addition is as self-consciously separate as it ever was, and it has consciously chosen to remain so. The only difference is that its residents seem less defensive about who they are and what it means to "be Potter Addition" than they were in the past.

These efforts to preserve continuity are clearly visible, for example, in the activities of the new Potter Addition Community Center. Its agenda contains a wide range of programs and services designed to meet the immediate needs of a changing community. At the same time, it is an instrument for perpetuating revered practices and protocols. It is now the agreed-upon public meeting place for various community-based groups and organizations. As such, it is but the latest solution to a sixty-year predicament. The need for a public gathering place in Potter Addition has been chronic. Early in the community's history, public gatherings were held in individual homes, usually of one of the founding families. Over time this arrangement proved unsatisfactory, since many felt uncomfortable hammering out community issues on someone else's private turf, especially when it meant disagreeing with your host. When the volunteer fire station was built, the problem of having access to a neutral public place for community meetings was solved when the community decided to attach a clubhouse onto the back of the fire station. Community meetings were held in the clubhouse for nearly two decades. This arrangement became increasingly untenable, however, when the so-called fire house faction, a group of families that had been instrumental in founding the volunteer fire department, developed interests that clashed with other groups in the community. These tensions ended when the fire department moved, but the closing of the firehouse created anew the need for a neutral meeting ground. This problem was finally solved when the Potter Addition Community Center was built, and a local woman who had remained outside the factional in-fighting of the past was appointed its director.

The community center preserves Potter Addition's need for cultural continuity in several other ways. It has taken over, for example, many of the socially integrative functions that Betty's Market fulfilled before it closed its doors. This latter fact is not surprising, since the center is currently run by one of Betty's closest friends, someone who was raised in the community, raised her own family there, and who spent endless hours during her childbearing years sitting behind the counter, keeping Betty company, and taking part in the female banter that was the very soul of Betty's establishment. The director has established an everyday routine in the community center that preserves as much as possible the social tempo and caring spirit that Betty and her store once gave to the community. Thus, coffee hours in the morning and afternoon are staples of the center's offerings, and when the administrative load permits, its director is always ready for another cup of coffee and some talk with "her regulars."

There are familial sources of cohesion and cultural continuity as well. Potter Addition is raising its fifth generation of children, and many of its adults are themselves third- and fourth-generation Potter Additionites. One of the things that surprised me most was that so many whom I had known as children twenty years ago are still living in the community, raising families, and reproducing a family tradition that in many cases was only being hammered out when I was there. Economics undoubtedly has something to do with these choices, for many of these people are only marginally better off than their parents were. At the same time, family loyalties and heartland values also play a determining role. Thus, several children are living in the houses that their parents, long dead, bought or built. Others purchased property in the area while their parents were still living and chose to raise their children where they themselves had grown up. In several instances these properties are adjacent to one another so that they form kinship enclaves. Many of these enclaves are matrilaterally structured, much as they were when I lived in the community, having at their structural core a group of solidary females. Other enclaves are made up of brothers, some of whom have purchased adjacent lots and appear to have formed male-based kinship groupings.

A particularly interesting group of young Potter Additionites consists of those who were born in Potter Addition, left the community for several years, and have now returned to put down roots. The community considers these children living proof of the old adage that Lonnie Carter often quoted in defense of Potter Addition: "People out here gripe and complain about this place all the time. But, when they do finally "up and move away," they're never really happy until they move back. They just can't wait to get back." This adage, now elevated to being a local piece of wizened folk wisdom, applies to another group, one composed of children who have left Potter Addition, but have not moved very far. They visit Potter Addition once or twice a week, and emotionally have never left Potter Addition or their parents.

A few in this latter group, however, represent something new in the life of Potter Addition and Clay County. As I noted earlier, in Potter Addition's culture of poverty some people have traditionally harbored a mixture of resentment at being driven from the land and a utopian slip of hope that some miracle might yet allow them to return. As I have reported here, this antimodernist, antiurban attitude was most clearly manifested by those adults reared in families that had been forcibly ejected from the land. The family's move to Potter Addition was a way of forestalling the final step toward cultural assimilation as long as possible. I assumed, when reporting their plight, that the long march toward assimilation would be completed by their children, as their alternatives were increasingly narrowed.

This assumption now appears to be incorrect. The migratory movement that shaped the social life of Clay County for more than seventy years—the movement from farm and hamlet to the city and its fringe—has partially reversed itself. Because of Clay County's recent economic development, several of Potter Addition's young adults have been able to settle in that handful of flourishing villages that have become bedroom communities for Grand Prairie. By taking advantage of job opportunities opening up in these outlying areas, they have successfully opted for the same familiarity and ambience of small-town life that originally attracted their parents to Potter Addition. Their jobs are no less menial nor more secure economically than those which their parents had when they were their age. And certainly the young emigres are no better or worse off than those of their age who have stayed in Potter Addition. Both groups live on the edge, much as their parents had, and many have experienced the emotional turmoil that wracked their parents' lives in the early years of marriage. Still, this generation has given renewed expression to the antimodernist discontent that they learned growing up in Potter Addition. For the moment, they have beaten the system, realizing their parent's dream in a way that the older generation could not. While they cannot return to a life of farming, they are "back in the country," and as close to the land as they can possibly get. In effect, they are reconstructing in their own generation the dream world that sustained an earlier generation of alienated emigres on the fringe.

Such moves to the country have not disrupted kinship patterns and other traditional dependencies. These booming villages and hamlets are close enough to Potter Addition for children to maintain almost daily ties with parents who have remained in Potter Addition. Thus Carol Thomas's son Kevin and his cousin have moved to Toulon and opened up a marginal well-drilling business. Others have established "blue-collar businesses" on a shoestring: sewer and septic tank services, delivery services, and the like. Displaying an affinity of lower-class males for entrepreneurialism that I noted twenty years ago, they, and several others like them, have taken advantage of the business opportunities that opened up during the eighties in Grand Prairie and its satellite communities. One can only guess how many of these businesses will be operating ten years from now.

In one or two instances entire kin groups have made the move back to small-town life. Thus, Grant and Mary Graham, perpetual farmers at heart, and small-town denizens for most of their youth, never did take to "big city life," no matter how much they tried. When two of their sons moved to Prophet City, and took with them their oldest grandchild, they sold their modest home in Potter Addition and returned to their former haunts. They now live in a small house on the edge of Prophet City. Like their children, they are as broke as they were while living in Potter Addition, but they now live across town (a five-minute drive) from their two sons and their families, and that is what counts. Grant, now nearing retirement, has an easy commute to his old job at a Grand Prairie dairy, while Mary brings in a few dollars every so often baby-sitting. On weekends you will find the Grahams in the middle of the same orchestrated chaos they lived in twenty years ago, and in which everyone in Potter Addition, at one time or another, participated. That same madness continues, ensured by the fact that Grant and Mary live within two miles of seven of their fourteen grandchildren and two of their three great-grandchildren (the remainder live in Grand Prairie and are brought out once a week or more to visit).

No matter how one looks at it, Mary's story has a happy ending, despite the fact that she will never know what most of us call economic security. She has triumphed over unbelievable odds. Constructing with her siblings a new kinship universe from scratch, nourishing it, and protecting it from outside predation, she is now its uncontested matriarch. Did I say uncontested? Well almost! In the cruelest cut of all, at least from Mary's viewpoint, two of Grant's brothers have followed his example, and moved their families to Prophet City. One lives down the block from where the Grahams live. Grant, of course, is pleased. I did not have the courage to ask Mary how the affine wars were going. Instead I bit my tongue and took heart knowing that the more the really important things in life change, the more they remain essentially the same.

VIII. THE EVOLUTION OF POTTER ADDITION'S CULTURE OF POVERTY

Not surprisingly, many of the old faces in Potter Addition are gone. Several families improved their economic circumstances enough to move to the suburbs. Their move is seen by old-timers as a lack of commitment to the community—proof that they were "never really Potter Addition in the first place." A few of the old sixties cohort remained in Potter Addition until they retired, and then moved. Two are of particular interest because they were among the very few to find their way back home. One returned to the Appalachians after retiring from the university, while the other took his family and his construction pension to the south central foothills of Tennessee. There they bought plots of land, an acre or two in size, to raise gardens on and, I would like to believe, raise a cow or a pig or two for the fun of it, while living off their retirement checks.

Finally, several who were residents during my fieldwork moved and then disappeared, so that there is no knowledge of their present whereabouts. Nancy Norris and Sarah Lane are among these. When Freida died in the early seventies, Nancy pulled up stakes and left the community. No one has heard of her or her children since. Sarah, who had moved in and out of Potter Addition many times, left for the last time shortly after I did. Like Nancy, she dropped from sight and has not been heard from. Sarah's mother remained in Potter Addition until she died sometime in the early seventies.

In twenty years, death took a ferocious toll among my old friends and neighbors. The cohort that gave so much color and character to the community, persons such as Betty, LaRue, Bull, Mary Stoner, and Freida, are no longer there to enrich Potter Addition. None of my original resource persons survived. Lonnie Carter was the last, and he died in April 1991 of cancer. Much to my everlasting regret, my last phone call to him turned out to be our last conversation. Cancer also took Sue Martin's father and her husband Al Martin, but not before Sue divorced him, thus settling the issue of whether or not Al would survive Mary Stoner's hard-bitten ways. Sue has remarried and is now living in Farmer City.

None of Potter Addition's founders are now alive. Only one or two of their children still live in the community, although several of their grandchildren still live in Potter Addition or keep in touch on a regular basis. The claims to leadership in community affairs that their families once exercised were waning in the late sixties. That erosion continued in the seventies and eighties, so that now they share power, such as it is, with certain members of the Morris and Rails clans—the bitterly poor kin groups that flooded the area during the war and immediately thereafter. The latter have proved themselves over the years to be "genuine Potter Addition" and, in a fashion typical of the social justice meted out in Potter Addition, are firmly integrated into the community and its loose governing structure.

Despite death and the various migrations in and out of Potter Addition, the most important demographic fact about Potter Addition is that over the last two decades its population has remained amazingly stable. Thus, a large proportion of the families that lived in Potter Addition twenty-five years ago are still there. Undoubtedly the mania for owning land and a home, varying degrees of economic limitation on mobility, and satisfaction with life on the fringe have stabilized residential patterns among this cohort. Because of this stability, Potter Addition is now an aging community in a county whose average age is one of the lowest in the state.

As for Potter Addition's culture of poverty, it still exists, but it has evolved as the community itself has matured. There is, to be sure, among the families who have recently moved into the community, and among the children of older established families, the same material poverty and uncertainty that gave birth to Potter Addition's culture of poverty twenty years ago. For them, poverty's uncertain niche continues to evoke the same values, beliefs, orientations, and gambits that I documented during my fieldwork. The low-wage structure of local industries and the vagaries of lower-class existence in the eighties and nineties in all likelihood will continue to create the objective foundations for this branch of the culture of poverty.

Such poverty and its cultural expression, however, are no longer the rule in Potter Addition. This does not mean that poverty and its subculture have disappeared. Rather, their expression has changed as the community itself has matured and adapted to its changing social niche. Thus, for example, in those families headed by adults aged thirty-five to sixty, working wives are now the rule. Many of the women who twenty-five years ago opted to stay home and raise children are now in the empty-nest phase of their family cycle and have gone to work. Almost all are part of that low-paid core of service workers and unskilled operatives who drive Clay County's prosperity. I suspect that this pattern is increasingly typical among those households in Potter Addition whose women are still in their childbearing years. Thus Potter Addition seems to be part of that larger pattern of rural poverty in America reported by Gorham (1992, pp. 21–39) and Flora (1992, pp. 201–14).

Such a development can mask the actual poverty rate rather than change it. Peterson (1991), for example, has shown how the dynamics of two-earner incomes helps explain the fact that while real individual income has steadily fallen since 1973, real family income has fared somewhat better. While only slightly on the increase, the latter has been able to hold its own against inflation. Thus, even when the presence of the second wage earner may technically raise a marginal family above the poverty line, it contributes little to the long-term sense of security that is the constant companion of families on the edge. I doubt, moreover, that it has done much to combat the everyday uncertainty that reaffirms at every turn the premises of the subculture of poverty.

There are those households in which poverty has disappeared, at least temporarily. In such households, the stabilizing of the husband's occupational chances in later life and the fact that the family cycle has reached the empty-nest phase brings greater economic stability. These families exemplify the longitudinal pattern in which families move in and out of poverty several times, and in some cases finally raise themselves out of poverty permanently. This cyclical pattern, one that scholars now believe describes the poverty of a great many Americans, shows

how families encounter several "spells of poverty" in one lifetime (Ellwood 1988; Sawhill 1988; Hill 1985). Needless to say, the existence of
such cycles does not vitiate the idea that these families continue to
reproduce a persistent subculture of poverty. If anything, the recurrent
nature of these cycles of poverty forces people to live with the knowledge that poverty may be only gone for the moment, but is not banished. As a result, these cycles merely affirm the worldview generated
by the subculture of poverty.

Thus, many of the people I saw living on poverty's edge as young
couples have moved into that more stable period of their occupational
lives where they are drawing steadier incomes. They are doing no more
than following a path already taken by their parents. Recall that in
earlier chapters I showed how parents were in many cases able to aid
newlyweds precisely because the parents were entering the stable years
of their occupational lives. Because of the low wage structure documented here and the continuing class characteristics of young lower-
class men and women, their parents, much as *their* parents before them,
will probably spend a significant portion of their discretionary income
helping their children make it through tough periods. That much has
not changed.

What has changed, however, is that there are now more old folks in
Potter Addition living on increasingly uncertain pensions and restricted
incomes. Statistically this form of poverty and uncertainty, augmented
by the anxiety that attends chronic illness and old age, is in the ascen-
dance in Potter Addition. Despite the fact that the aged are reputedly
the most privileged of all those groups presently threatened with poverty, such an edge is not now as great as it once was. This collective
aging of Potter Addition is apparent if one examines the changes that
have overtaken the Potter Addition Community Center in recent years.
When the center was originally proposed, the main rationale for its
construction centered on the needs of Potter Addition's young people.
Such a center was needed to combat juvenile delinquency. Indeed, at
the time there was a need for such a facility. By the time the center was
built, though, the community was at a demographic watershed in its
history. As the community aged, problems of delinquency were soon
bypassed by the problems of the elderly. The community center became
increasingly involved with the needs of Potter Addition's senior citizens. Tapping nostalgia and, again, a revered community tradition, the
center sponsors old-timey ham, beans, and cornbread suppers. Thurs-
day night bingo, a staple of fund-raising among Potter Addition's community organizations for almost fifty years, is also a popular activity in
the community. The head of the center has defined her job increasingly
as helping senior citizens, though her work is still multifaceted, and she

takes on any project that can stir the hearts of even a handful of Potter Additionites, no matter what their age.

Apropos the changing face of poverty in Potter Addition, much of the director's time is spent dealing with the material needs of the poorer senior citizens. Chief among these functions is providing a service that deals with problems of hunger and nutrition. Two or three times a month a truck is dispatched from Grand Prairie to DeSoto, more than 150 miles away, to buy groceries at a regional food center. Part of a nationwide, nongovernmental, self-help program, seniors and those on welfare pool their money and purchase their food at cut-rate prices. They, of course, are not allowed to buy anything they want. Their choice is limited to those government commodities currently being distributed, and whatever groceries or produce the regional organization has been able to buy at bulk prices. Sometimes, people are unhappy about the offerings available, but the diets of the poor can always accommodate themselves to what is available and affordable. This much, too, has not changed.

This then is what I found upon my return to Grand Prairie and Potter Addition. The county is prospering as never before, both on and off the farm. There are few poor farmers in Clay County anymore, because only rich families can now afford to cultivate the land. The university is still a preeminent institution of higher learning. At the same time it is increasingly at risk, with each passing year, of becoming a great academic shell, which under the aegis of corporate America will become a prospering research park that wraps itself in the sacred mantle of humane learning. It has already become a triumph of marketing, one that sells the talents of its intellectuals year-round and the strength and grace of its athletes on crisp autumn afternoons.

Poverty still exists in Clay County, but in an altered form. It is now masked so as not to offend certain sensibilities, but continues to live in the interstices of Clay County's institutional life, lodged somewhere between the "disinterested learning" of professional academics, the low wages that fuel Clay County's economic renaissance, and the bountiful harvests of a rich land. Potter Addition is still there, older, less rowdy and colorful, and in some ways a bit too sedate for my tastes. It is still held hostage by that quiet, often desperate peonage that is the continuing hallmark of poverty's uncertain way of life. The same age-old protean struggle against need in a land of plenty that I recorded twenty years ago is still being waged, though often on different terms than I first recorded. But above all, the people of Potter Addition have managed to endure. Physically, they are older and more frayed around the edges than they were twenty years ago, not unlike myself. Spiritually, they still exhibit the intelligence and abandon, the same protective cynicism and wicked humor that they have always had. They have also developed that peculiar sense of self that poor people acquire once they know that they will never get what they deserve from the system, but that by hook or by crook they will get more than the law allows a poor person to have. That much has not changed in Potter Addition.

14

Potter Addition and its Poverty

I. POVERTY, SYSTEM, AND SOCIAL REPRODUCTION

My analysis of poverty has been organized around four recurring motifs. The first maintains that while poverty *originates* in the structural contradictions of capitalist production, it is *culturally reproduced* by the poor. Having the intelligence and cunning to cope with poverty, but not the political wherewithal to abolish it, the poor have little choice but to construct a way of life that enables them to deal with poverty's chaotic niche. Although claiming that the poor culturally reproduce their poverty, this work is opposed to the preachments of right-wing ideologues who attempt to absolve the system by blaming the poor for their impoverished condition. This work also opposes those who view the poor as passive victims of the system. In that the culture of poverty is a necessary requirement for capital's systemic reproduction, the poor are active, indeed necessary, agents in capital's social reproduction. Thus any attempt to eliminate poverty must not concentrate on reforming the poor, but on changing the generative contradictions of the capitalist mode of production.

The second motif pertains to the culture of poverty itself. The culture of poverty is not, as many social scientists claim, an inferior replica of the dominant culture. It possesses a logic all its own, one grounded in the life world of the lower class. For that reason, that logic is best judged using criteria that are internal to lower-class life itself. In Potter Addition's case, cultural reproduction proceeds according to the materialistic logic of the *bricoleur,* and is opposed to the formalized bureaucratic rationality of an urban-based, *fin de siècle* America. As we saw in the early chapters of this volume, this *bricolage style* has its roots in the petty mode of production that flourished in America's agricultural heartland prior to the second world war. Those who take this approach have for generations prided themselves on their pragmatism and "make-do-with-nothing" way of life. In earlier days, as now, *bricolage* was often combined with a smugness and a festering ressentiment that allowed marginal farmers and handymen to glory in their ability to "cheat the system" and "live better than the law allowed."

Valued for its character-building effects, perceived as a time-tested way of coping with everyday adversity, preserved during the long march from the land, and nostalgically adapted to a new nexus of urban need, *bricolage* and its protocols provide Potter Addition's culture of poverty with its unique style. In the opening chapters of this work we saw how Potter Addition's material infrastructure was formed using the *bricoleur*'s worldview and method. This spirited worldview was also capable of fomenting ideological resistance. Its mixture of nostalgia, instrumentality, and muted disdain for "doing things by the book" was at the base of the countercultural claims and defenses that permeated Potter Addition's occupational worldview. Its dissenting potential was attested to in the activities of the car cult and agrarian leisure practices. Both culture complexes could be transformed at a moment's notice into subterranean vehicles of ideological self-defense. The process of familial provincialization also followed the reconstitutive logic of the *bricoleur*. Families often synthesized the hegemonic values of local elites with those validated by lower-class praxis to produce the domestic dialectic of uxoricentric domination. Finally, there was Mary Graham's poignant, piecemeal construction of her sibling-based kin group as she struggled to bring coherence to the shattered remnants of her family universe. In each case, the reconstitutive logic of the *bricoleur*, the ability of the poor to piece together a coherent life from the remains and leavings of "respectable society," formed the recurrent interpretive focus of this work.

The third motif revolved around the claim that subcultures of poverty are pathological in their content. As we have seen, Potter Addition's subculture of poverty does deviate from the dominant norms of Clay County. Far from being pathological, however, Potter Addition's culture of poverty actually *complements* the operation of Clay County's and Grand Prairie's dominant culture and facilitates its functioning. This work has documented the many ways in which the "normal" and "deviant" in Clay County and Grand Prairie form a set of interdependent and mutually reinforcing oppositions. We witnessed, for example, the many ways in which the poor worked the moral and material interstices of public life. This mining of public culture's interstices and contradictions not only contributed to Potter Addition's alternative economy, it was a crucial part of the normal process of commodity production and exchange in the local community. These patterned evasions of public culture, therefore, were in actuality necessary reproductive elements in the local economy and its social system. Furthermore, as we have seen, these evasions and informal indulgences significantly shaped and softened the harsher aspects of Potter Addition's everyday poverty. We thus concluded that, given the ease with which Potter Addition's citizens finessed institutionalized power, its poverty was part of a *larger symbiotic process* from which the poor, their bosses, and their alleged cultural betters all significantly benefited.

The final organizing theme concerns the methodological and ontological role that dialectics played in Potter Addition's poverty. From the opening discussion of the "ecological theory of classes," through the analysis of provincialization and kinship reciprocity, to the dissection of the structure and dynamics of uxoricentric kinship, I have argued that the ontology of Potter Addition's culture of poverty is dialectically constituted. The dialectical patterns themselves discussed in this work shared three attributes: First, their dialectical constitution was real in that they were not mechanically constituted or abstractly deduced, but emerged from the real-life predicaments of life in Potter Addition. Second, each dialectic was historically grounded. Each drew its expressive substance and inner motion from the sociohistorical contradictions of Clay County's heartland culture. Finally, the emergent dialectics were usually nonprogressive in nature. That is, the contradictions did not resolve themselves at a higher level of sociocultural integration. Instead, reflecting the social and political impotence of the poor, their material predicament, and the reproductive realities of late capitalism, the dialectics of lower-class life took the form of a series of cyclic repetitions.

This circularity was demonstrably the case in the provincializing dialectic that regulated uxoricentrism's domestic domain. The same nonprogressive and concrete dialectic was similarly underscored as we located Potter Addition's world of kinship midway between the centripetal kinship structures of Clay County's Frisian farmers and the centrifugally oriented collectivities of Grand Prairie's black lumpen proletariat. And, finally, it was the dynamic that drove uxoricentric kinship as it alternated between the vertical integration of generations and the horizontal unities of sibling solidarity.

In summary, then, these four motifs—the social construction of poverty, the spirit of *bricolage* that regulates its construction, the symbiotic nexus in which poverty's material and cultural reproduction occurs, and the dialectical structuring of the subculture of poverty itself—have emerged as the organizing principles of Potter Addition's everyday poverty. Set in the context of Marxist political economy, these motifs have been useful in making interpretive sense of the historically specific forms of poverty that I encountered in this heartland community.

II. NECESSARY AND SURPLUS POVERTY:
ALTERNATIVE PATHS TO POVERTY

Throughout this work I have assumed that the *basic* strategies the poor employ in coping with their poverty have not altered in twenty-five years. This does not mean that we do not know more about poverty now than we did then. We do. Nor does it mean that the economic and political sources of poverty have not changed. Over the last twenty-five years many new paths to poverty have emerged, some of which are so novel that scholars have been forced to speak of the "new poor." (Gorham 1992, pp. 22–23; Flora 1992, pp. 201–7). The paths themselves are diverse: There is the plight of the newly discovered working poor (Ellwood 1988, pp. 81–127; Duncan 1992), the growing isolation and desperation of the so-called black underclass (Wilson 1987; Ellwood, 1988, pp. 89–230), the trend toward the feminization of poverty (Ehrenreich and Piven 1984; Goldberg and Kremen 1986; Humphries 1983), and, finally, deindustrialization—that new phase of the class war that levels entire regions (Bluestone and Harrison 1982; Harrison and Bluestone 1988).

As disturbing as these new forms of poverty are, there is nothing in the literature on the new poor and their everyday plight that requires me to revise the ethnographic interpretations offered here. How poor people cope today with poverty's uncertainty is substantially the same as it was twenty or thirty years ago. The subculture of poverty is still constructed and operates with the same rationality that it did in the sixties, even as its tactical details are molded to fit different sociohistorical contexts. The basic adaptive character of the culture of poverty remains the same.

What has changed, however, are the ways in which people are being *driven* into poverty. In the last three decades late capitalism has faced an unparalleled series of accumulation crises. In its attempts to resolve these problems structurally, it has resurrected old poverties and fabricated startling new ways of making people poor. Thus, while there are many unanswered questions about the new poor and their poverty, this much seems clear: The new poverty and the old differ significantly in their structural origins, but for all that they are both a product of the same class struggle. Although they represent different phases of that struggle, their paths converge in the generation of superfluous populations.[1]

The two paths to poverty differ chiefly in terms of the mechanisms by which they impoverish their victims. To appreciate this, we must distinguish conceptually between the old poverty and the new poverty. The old poverty is the one Marx discovered in his analysis of the contradictions of capitalist production and its so-called laws of motion. This type of poverty is still with us. It has its roots, as always, in the creation of industrial reserve armies. As such it is a permanent attribute of a market-oriented system of production for private profit. As we have argued, this poverty is a necessary consequence of the orderly and ever more efficient operation of capital's productive forces. For as long as capitalist relations are allowed to organize a society's productive forces, industrial reserve armies of the unemployed and subemployed will continue to be a part of the social landscape. For this reason, this poverty can be said to be a *necessary poverty*.

The new poverty, in contrast, is largely a *surplus poverty*. It is not an unintended consequence of capital's productive apparatus, but occurs during periods of crisis when the power of the state is used to redefine politically the legal rights and cultural obligations that make up class boundaries. It is invoked in times of crisis, and is the product of conscious political decisions on the part of society's policymaking elites. During such periods the taxing powers, fiscal activity, and mediating functions of the state are used by the ruling elites either to redistribute society's wealth directly or to redefine class boundaries politically so that the higher orders will benefit. Such actions usually shore up old hegemonic patterns of domination in order to protect a temporarily destabilized elite or to pave the way for a new ascendant class fraction. In the latter case new forms of exploitation and oppression are politically endorsed, and new forms of wealth are generated. This new political edge also leads simultaneously to the diminution of the powers of other class fractions. Thus, especially in times of crisis, the politically engineered advance of one group often entails a zero-sum impoverishment of previously protected populations, who get deprived of their former political and economic privileges.

The two paths to poverty, then, differ essentially in that one originates in the policymaking domain while the other is a function of ongoing economic contradictions. In either case the production of superfluity is a class-mediated act. In applying this distinction, however, we must not reify it. We must not lose sight of the fact that in a capitalist social system the two paths are intimately related and reinforcing. In capitalist social formations economic conflicts are always politically mediated affairs, just as political institutions and the struggles that shape them are grounded in a class-mediated nexus of economic conflict. Even with this proviso, it is obvious that a great many of the new poor are the victims of surplus poverty. In most instances when scholars speak of the new poverty, they have in mind the state-engineered path to poverty that originates in the political abrogation of long-standing class compromises (Harrison and Bluestone 1988; Duncan and Sweet 1992; Deavers and Hoppe 1992; Harvey 1989).

In recent years, for example, surplus poverty has been generated by a fiscal restructuring of the welfare state that has altered its system of distributing social wages and benefits. On the one hand, state-supported social costs and transfer payments, which were once considered to be a basic civic right by most Americans, have been either eliminated or made the subject of annual bargaining (Piven and Cloward 1982). At the same time there has been a radical downward shifting of the tax burden. Hence, the power of the state has been systematically used to provide the upper classes with undue advantages in those situations where their interests have come into conflict with their working- and lower-class adversaries.

Reaganomics, of course, is but the latest example of the use of state power in times of crisis to redraw class boundaries and, in doing so, to create increased levels of poverty. This has been documented by progressive scholars such as Harrison and Bluestone (1988), Ellwood (1988), Harvey (1989), Peterson (1991), and Bowles, Gordon, and Weisskopf (1991), not to speak of the flood of occasional papers and periodic reports issued by such organizations as the University of Wisconsin's Institute for Research on Poverty and the Washington-based Center on Budget and Policy Priorities.

Interestingly enough, one of the most cogent critiques and documentations of the use of the state during the Reagan years to channel society's wealth upwards, while new forms of poverty were created below, comes from the pen of the well-known conservative, Kevin Phillips. He has recently developed these themes in his much discussed *The Politics of Rich and Poor* (1990), where he draws a parallel between the populist era, which saw the sacking of the nation by the robber barons of the Gilded Age, the "Roaring Twenties," and the Reagan eighties. In such periods the political and economic elites of the era used state apparatuses to enrich themselves at the expense of the common man's impoverishment. The erstwhile framer of the Republicans' "southern strategy," and the current foe of the Reaganite "parvenus," supports his analysis with a wide range of statistical sources that document the nation's growing class inequality. More importantly, in discussing wealth and poverty in America, he has—to the distress of many conservative ideologues—documented the reemergence of class forces in America.[2]

Two decades of eroding social consciousness and crisis have combined with the step-by-step dismantling of the welfare state to create surplus poverty. A generation of deindustrialization and Rust Belt politics at home, which was little more than a conscious policy of fostering domestic unemployment in order to open up cheap out-sourcing labor markets abroad, has had its predictable effects. In Chapter 13 we saw how surplus poverty has come to Clay County in the form of low wages and the swelling of the ranks of the working poor.

Despite recent rationalizations that the emergence of a "new world order" requires Americans to tolerate poverty at home, or that the requirements of international competition in a capitalist world system demand that Americans scale down their lifelong expectations, informed observers know that surplus poverty is neither natural nor inevitable. It is no more a necessary price of progress than the creation of industrial reserve armies is the natural price of our enjoying the benefits of industry. Instead, surplus poverty is the price that is exacted from the many, to sustain a system of accumulation that benefits the few. When the contours of the class struggle are symmetrical, this price can be minimized. When it is as one-sided as it has been in recent years, however, the price the poor must pay increases dramatically.[3]

III. THE DENIAL OF CLASS

After more than a decade of silence, poverty is once again a subject of controversy in the United States. In marked contrast to the debate of the 1960s, however, this new discourse is grounded in a set of assumptions that effectively ignores or denies any explanatory role to class dynamics. When the term *class* is used at all, it generally denotes different income groups. Moreover, this denial of class is a fundamental background assumption of the debate, for all parties appear to have agreed on its exclusion.

This new denial of class also carries with it an implicit denial of the current debate's historic roots in the 1960s. Most of the individuals involved in the present discussion are reluctant to examine the historical antecedents of their ideas, as well as the social ferment that shaped them. It would be easy to dismiss this amnesia as a postmodernist disdain for all forms of historical narrative. But this is not the case, for historical commentaries on poverty and social policy have been recently attempted. What is being excluded from these commentaries, however, is an analysis of class and a review of the debate as it was framed in the sixties.

Two examples will suffice to show what I mean. Charles Murray's *Losing Ground* (1984, pp. 3–49) begins with a fanciful reconstruction of the history of America's welfare system from the New Deal to the Great Society. Drawing on the disingenuous ideology of the Reagan eighties, the neoconservative Murray poses as the "caretaker" of the New Deal and its orthodoxies. As was done by Reaganites throughout the decade, Murray misinterprets and then misappropriates the New Deal and its welfare reforms, so that he can use them to attack the social programs formulated during the Kennedy and Johnson years. Deconstructing the New Deal in a manner similar to that employed by neoconservative historians when they appeal to the "intentions of the founding fathers" to justify their own present-day interpretations of constitutional law, Murray uses the alleged intentions of those who framed New Deal welfare institutions to critique the policies of the Kennedy and Johnson administrations. As might be expected, the Kennedy administration receives special criticism. According to Murray, it was during this period that the abstract theories and elite wisdom of Camelot's intellectuals betrayed the New Deal, replacing its "equality of opportunity" agenda with their own "equality of outcome" goals.

I will not waste time challenging this interpretation. Suffice to say that there are alternative accounts of the New Deal and its intentions concerning welfare policy that are both more balanced and more plausible.[4] What is of interest to us, however, is his tactic of denying the class roots of poverty. By using a demonology that blames the liberal Washington elite and its hanger-on intellectuals for betraying the New Deal and creating the current "welfare mess," he is able to ignore the social ferment at the bottom of our society that gave rise to both New Deal legislation (see Bernstein 1971, pp. 92–126, 217–318) and the welfare programs of the sixties.

This tactic is not innocent. If Murray did not downplay the structural sources that gave rise to the social discontent of the 1930s and the 1960s, he would have to examine the unfolding contradictions of capitalist society itself. This he does not want to do. As he informs his readers early in his work, the one thing that he wants to avoid in his analysis is an explanation of poverty that blames the system (Murray 1984, pp. 24–40). Taking a page from Malthus, he places blame on the state and insists that it was the welfare programs themselves that caused the rising poverty rates of the last two decades.

A second example of the denial of class and a failure to come to grips with the structural ferment and ideas of the 1960s is found in Nicholas Lemann's *The Promised Land* (1991). Lemann's ostensibly liberal analysis of black poverty during the great migration from Mississippi to Chicago in the 1940s has repeated many of Murray's errors. Like Murray, Lemann believes the federal government failed to stem the rising tide of poverty during the 1960s because its welfare policies were fatally flawed. Sandwiched between a series of beautifully written family histories that document the lives of the black migrants before, during, and after their move north are two chapters, "Washington" and "Chicago," in which Lemann attacks the nation's social policies (1991, pp. 109–306). Fleshing out Murray's neoconservative reading of the war on poverty, Lemann mounts an especially virulent assault on the political philosophy that undergirded the Community Action projects. He suggests that these projects were doomed to fail because their idealistic goals were not consistent with the realities of contemporary urban life. By using the testimony of former poverty warriors from the Kennedy and Johnson administrations, Lemann reveals that cynical opportunism, gullibility, liberal guilt, and bureaucratic infighting were the driving forces behind the War on Poverty. According to Lemann, it was these human foibles and the corrupt logic embodied in radical political action that eventually defeated the efforts of utopian radicals and Potomac intellectuals alike.

Once again I will not quibble over the merits of this biased reconstruction. As before, better accounts of the programs that Lemann attacks have been written (for example, see Katz 1989, pp. 9–78). Even if we were to agree on the banality and opportunism of those who ran Camelot and the Great Society, Lemann could still not explain the causes of the poverty he so elegantly documents in his life histories. Nor could he plausibly account for the downfall of the programs for which he has such scorn. This is because Lemann, like Murray, is loath to acknowledge the role that those at the bottom of society played in pushing the national and local politicians to act. Katz, in fact, while not referring specifically to either Murray or Lemann, sums up their position and exposes the weakness of their account as he outlines the evolution of conservative poverty policy in the late seventies and eighties:

> By default, intellectual as well as political initiative passed to conservatives, who searched for explanations for continued poverty amid affluence that could justify reducing government aid to cities and social benefits to individuals. In the process, conservative thought about poverty and social welfare passed through two stages and entered a third in the years between the mid-1970s and the late 1980s. It began by denying that poverty remained a real problem. As this argument lost plausibility, conservatives updated some very old ideas that blamed both poor people themselves and the misguided, if well-intentioned, interventions of government.
>
> By the late 1980s, as conditions worsened, only the most intransigent conservatives could disagree that government played a critical role in the alleviation of poverty and social disorganization, and conservative writers increasingly subordinated the libertarian implications of free-market philosophy to a new authoritarianism. The result was a refurbished conservatism that justified big government by advocating the extension of its control over the behavior of millions of Americans. By emphasizing the obligations of the poor instead of their entitlement to public benefits, the appeal of the new authoritarianism diffused beyond conservative circles; in Congress, it even became the intellectual foundation of a bipartisan approach to welfare reform. (1989, p. 125)

As I have said, *all parties* have consented to this silence. Even liberals and New Age radicals have found it to their advantage either to ignore the dynamics of class or to redefine class in terms of income groupings. When denying class, the liberals in particular must walk a perilous tightrope. On the one hand, to prove the need for a more equitable social order, they must denounce the "malefactors of great wealth." If they go too far in this direction, however, they risk adopting elements of a critical class analysis and may, sooner or later, drift into calling for a profound restructuring of the social order. On the other hand, the further their justification for the welfare state moves away from the class nexus, the closer their ideology and policies move toward either blaming individuals or official malice for the existence of social problems—the hallmark of neoconservative thought. Whenever possible, the best strategy for liberals is to deny the role class plays in shaping the nation's institutional life. For most liberals, models of class and class conflict are as objectionable today as they were three decades ago. The old specters of populism and class war still haunt the pluralistic democracy they envisioned in the sixties. This may, in fact, explain the distorted and historically inaccurate account of populism that for more than four decades has been the staple of many political scientists and sociologists.[5]

The same denial of class often characterizes New Age radicalism. Some feminists, for example, employ a social ontology that emphasizes gender antagonisms as the driving force of history, while either ignoring or downplaying the importance of class struggle. This puts them at odds with Marxist analysis. In its more extreme form, this ontology has generated feminist theories that are designed to supplant Marxist class analysis with a theory of gender oppression (Palmer 1990, pp. 3–87, 145–87). Needless to say, this denial of class has created both confusion and consternation among the ranks of those who refer to themselves as feminist Marxists. In its more constructive moments, however, the feminist perspective augments and enriches our understanding of poverty. It continually reminds both scholars and the informed public, as we have enunciated repeatedly in this volume, that poor women carry a social burden that is radically different from that which poor men must carry.

In a similar vein, recent analyses of race and the lived experiences of minority groups in America have also greatly enriched our understanding of the racially specific contours of poverty. Many of those committed to an analysis of race and its impact upon society, however, have also practiced a denial of class. Some scholars, for example, seem to fear that a class-based analysis showing that the black middle classes have made significant professional and economic progress in recent years, while the plight of the black urban underclass has worsened, could undercut the resolve of national leaders to eradicate racial inequality in America. Understandably, there is a growing division among poverty scholars over the relative efficacy of class-based as opposed to discrimination-based explanations of poverty. Perhaps most notably, William Julius Wilson's studies of race, class, and poverty (1978, 1988) have drawn considerable fire for arguing that black poverty is increasingly more a class problem than it is one of discrimination.

The denial of class, then, in various guises on both the right and the left, has generated attempts to explain poverty using criteria narrower than those employed in a Marxist class analysis. This denial has often led to systematic misrepresentations concerning the theories of poverty and policy innovations that emerged out of the poverty debate of the sixties. These misrepresentations have then been put forth as reality to a new generation of poverty scholars, who understandably dismiss them out of hand. Despite recent efforts to rehabilitate such ideas as "internal colonialism," "the culture of poverty," and "community action," there is still little interest among an entire generation of scholars in establishing a conceptual dialogue between the sixties and the present. As Katz (1989, pp. 64–65) has argued, the rejection of the internal colonialism model as a means of explaining the persistence of black poverty was ultimately rejected as much for its Marxist grounding as for any specific flaw in the argument itself. I have made a similar argument in explaining the fate of the subculture of poverty concept over the last two decades. I suspect that the radical Marxist critique implicit in Lewis's theory is the reason that those presently claiming liberal or reformist credentials have in general been willing to let neo-conservative scholars misappropriate Lewis's seminal concept (see, for example, Himmelfarb 1983, pp. 369–70). They know that, if they are going to achieve their dream of instituting universal welfare entitlements within existing class arrangements, explosive issues such as the strengths of the poor and their communities, the reality of cultural pluralism, and the demand of the sixties that the poor be given the right of self-determination are issues better left dormant.

Finally, the same evasion of class has contributed greatly, I believe, to how contemporary poverty scholars regard the demise of the Community Action programs. One of the goals of these programs was to use Federal monies and expertise politically to give the poor more bargaining power vis-à-vis local authorities. In many cases these efforts were too successful. Once the poor actually became involved in these programs, they began to make loud and embarrassing demands that the local elites were neither willing nor able to meet (Katz 1989, pp. 95–101). That clamor ended when the Green Amendment emasculated the dissent by requiring that local leaders be given power over such programs. Once this was done, the dangers of "maximum feasible participation" were effectively ended.

The failure to establish a dialogue between the present and the past is even more distressing when we realize that our contemporary denial of class carries with it a denial of the poor themselves. During the sixties those who endorsed class explanations of poverty often used Lewis's vision of the poor to defend them from the puritanical desire of reformers to "improve" them. Among those scholars there was a deep, some would charge overly romantic, conviction that the poor had gleaned from a lifetime of exploitation and need, a knowledge and way of life that insulated them from the hypocrisies of bourgeois culture. Those scholars believed, in effect, that the poor—despite all efforts at their brutalization—had retained the virtues of compassion and self-sacrifice that had all but disappeared in the more affluent classes.

In the late fifties and early sixties many who endorsed this populist image were part of a vital left culture that was only then succumbing to decades of persecution. Some had had intimate contact with ethnic, religious, or regional subcultures that demonstrated a humanity and collective sense of caring that they thought superior to the commercial hegemony that daily produced greater increments of affluence and alienation. Others came to the same conviction via bohemianism or a lifelong commitment to radical politics. In the latter case, an intelligentsia, often with deep roots in Trotskyism, Debsian socialism or submerged populist cultures, had made the virtues of the poor the grounding premise of a lifetime of political resistance. For them, Lewis's subculture of poverty thesis was little more than an extension of their political ideology, one that always demanded that social action and social theory be dialectically grounded in an open dialogue with those who understood exploitation firsthand. It was from the example of the poor and the working class that these teachers had been taught.

This was the everyday ideological nexus that had been endorsed by more than four generations of radicals. It was, indeed, this prescientific and pretheoretic nexus that predisposed many radicals, including Lewis, to respect the way of life of the lower orders—warts and all. This is why for many poverty researchers in the sixties it was only natural to listen attentively to those at the bottom and to learn from them. Those who had suffered at the bottom of society, though often uneducated, at times bigoted, and at times unbelievably cruel, nonetheless possessed creative powers that could be found nowhere else. While these views concerning the poor were often tinged with romanticism, those who had dedicated their lives to serving the working class and the poor knew full well that the lower orders were both virtuous and talented, and also flawed. They also believed that the lower orders were the most likely candidates for building an egalitarian society.

It was that ambivalent sense of awe and dismay at what the working class and the poor were, and what they and we could be that recommended Lewis's work to many of us in that decade of ferment and hope. It was this noncondescending necessity that we treat the poor as equals, the feeling that we could learn much from the uneducated and stigmatized, that premised the research efforts of many scholars in the sixties. That approach to poverty often seems to get lost in the present poverty debate. Too many times the poor are treated as little more than a statistical caricature constructed out of the latest multivariate techniques. At other times they are the subject of poor bashing by conservatives. In either case, when seen through the lens of contemporary social science, the poor seem little more than a figment of the policy planner's imagination, one that reduces living humans to abstract baskets of standard market commodities. While we will probably not let these mythologized abstractions starve, neither will we feel the need to let them speak to us in their own voices or to collaborate with them in constructing their own futures.

IV. THE QUESTION OF PATHOLOGY

One final irony typifies the poverty debate of the last few years. Even as social scientists deny class and the poor, and study poverty from what appears to be a safe distance, they are continuously being schooled in the *possibility* of their own academic superfluity. The uncertainty of life in Potter Addition, once so remote, now elicits disturbing echoes in our own lives. We are learning what the people of Potter Addition discovered long ago: No one is safe and secure in an economic system that survives periodically by cannibalizing its vital parts. Through a bitter twist of fate, the hermeneutic that once encouraged social scientists to approach the poor and their poverty as if they were a world apart is evaporating in a world of "gypsy moth" professors (an industrial reserve army, if there ever was one), the erosion of tenure, economic exigency, the commodification of knowledge, the industrialization of the conditions under which knowledge is produced, and the increasing deskilling and proletarianization of the professorate. We are no longer strangers to the sense of superfluity that was once reserved for only the disreputable and undeserving poor.

The same process that produced the present age of diminished expectations has resurrected the necessity that all Americans be reschooled in the economic fear that drove earlier generations. Having been reintroduced to the ever-present threat of their own fall into superfluity, many Americans cloak their fear in a newfound moralizing that has transformed past compassion for the poor into a hatred for those who have already fallen. This fear, now turned to hatred, is often at the center of what Michael Lewis (1978) calls the "calculus of estrangement." He elegantly sets forth what that calculus is, and how we have been schooled in it:

> If the anger, militance, and cynicism of the disinherited confirm the liberals' doubts and convert them into moralists, this conversion in turn only increases the anger, militance, and cynicism of the disinherited. From their point of view, those who professed friendship and sympathy have now shown their true colors. The sympathy must appear to have been false, the professions of friendship nothing short of hypocritical. Those among the disinherited who may have been willing to give the liberals the benefit of the doubt, those who may have been willing to excuse the inadequacy of their efforts as good-faith inadequacy, are no longer willing to do so. Those whose anger merely smoldered are now inflamed with rage; those who merely flirted with militance are now convinced of its necessity; those who might have been saved from cynicism are now en-crusted in it. For the moralists, both long standing and newly converted, this quantum increase in the alienation of the disinherited is but further evidence of their reprehensible character, further evidence that they are the problem and that their lowly estate is but the just desert of their moral default. The calculus, at this point, will have run its dialectical course. The estrangement between the good solid citizens and the disinherited will be complete and very probably irreversible.
>
> If such a calculus in fact does unfold as I have just projected, the culture of inequality will indeed change, but it will change in a way promising an increasingly troubled existence for most of us. If the calculus of estrange-ment runs its projected course, the character of the individual-as-central sensibility will become increasingly one-dimensional. Success and failure, together with inequalities of perquisite and status, will be seen more and more as the just correlates of individual morality and immorality. Whereas in the present success and failure are interpreted by some (the liberals) as functions of competence on the one hand and incompetence on the other, if the calculus runs its course the pure moralistic interpretation espoused by the conservatives will become virtually the only credible manifestation of the individual-as-central sensibility. The liberals, despairing at the hostility of the disinherited, will have been won over to the moralism of the conservatives, and their present construction of the sensibility, their present emphasis on competence and deficiency explanations for incom-petence, will have been discredited and relegated to history. (pp. 195–96)

In one sense, this calculus of estrangement is nothing new. The cycle by which liberal, egalitarian reform gives way to radical schism and ends in the estrangement and cultural reaction of the middle strata is periodically played out in class-based societies that are ruled by a democratic ethos. In its most recent incarnation, begun in the late sixties and continuing to this day, it is the vehicle by which the fear and sub-rosa ressentiment of the nonpoor express themselves in a virulent form of scapegoating. Even the social sciences have not been immune to this ressentiment and scapegoating. As we have already noted, it surfaced in the area of poverty research itself during the 1980s, when reactionary dogmas were pawned off as scientific certainties and were used to guide national policy.

In refusing the claims of these latest theoretical expressions of the calculus of estrangement, I believe that the standing question that poverty poses cannot be framed in terms of eliminating poverty while staying within capital's horizon. It cannot be, as most contemporary pronouncements would have it, a question of how to raise one group out of poverty by reprogramming its behavior. Such programs overlook the same cruel fact: If some are to prosper and flourish under capital's auspices, others must remain in poverty. If it is not *that* group living in poverty and reproducing a way of life something akin to Potter Addition's, then some other group will have to take its place. Other people will have to become the object of fear and scapegoating—accused of living pathological lives, and hence truly deserving of their poverty.

I do not deny, of course, that pathology exists among the poor. I have noted many individual cases of pathology in this work. I have also documented instances in which early pathologies were overcome and converted into strengths in later life—for example, the women of Potter Addition. If in their youth they are often uncertain, weak, or rebellious hell-raisers, in their mature years they are often something quite different. From among those who survive those early trials of daughter/ mother-siblingship, there often emerges an emotionally solid, verbally articulate, and clear-headed adult. By the time these women become mother/grandmothers, they possess an aggressiveness and intelligence that makes them much more than Lucy Parsons's (1969, pp. 167–73) "slave's slave." If they are battered by the hidden injuries of class, or carry with them an ineradicable guilt for having failed their parents in adolescence, or are now living down a promiscuous past, or still seem to have learned little when it comes to men, mothers, or children, they can also be hard, uncompromising, and compassionate champions of their grandchildren and passionate defenders of their community. This was underscored again and again on my return to Potter Addition.

Contemporary commentators who insist on treating poverty and its subculture as merely pathological seem to have missed the fact that such people live shut off from us, ready to make their communities better places to live. They also miss the fact that such women and their male counterparts, if given the resources and the chance to act, can be a valuable resource for social renewal. They are a latent cadre that could be used to renew poor communities—if renewal along democratic lines is really what we want. Indeed, if the untapped capacity of the Martins, the Stoners, and the Walshes of our world to move heaven and earth for the betterment of themselves and their grandchildren is ignored, then one has little choice but to portray poor communities as Nicholas Lemann (1986) has done: as decapitated bodies whose intellect, morality, and will have fled to the suburbs.

On the basis of my experiences in Potter Addition, I must reject this type of collective stereotyping of the poor and their communities. In countering imageries such as those raised by Lemann and others, I would merely refer the reader to Mary Stoner and Freida Walsh, and the strong, aggressive mastery that each exercised over her crumbling environment. I would invite the reader to review Sue Martin's and Mary Graham's narratives once again, and have him or her note that lying beneath the grammatical flaws of everyday speech there is a depth of intelligence and degree of verbal skills that has taken flight among all but the very best of our all-too-conventional, all-too-bourgeois university students.

It seems safe to predict that if the resources and political opportunities that opened up twenty years ago were to emerge once again, these women and men could be organized into such effective and mean-tempered advocates that we might well need a dozen or more Green Amendments to quell their demands for social change and social justice. Were this to happen again, then the prevailing myth of the 1970s turned big lie in the 1980s could be laid to rest. That lie, now turned litany, is that the antipoverty programs were well funded, were allowed to operate for a sufficient length of time, and were free enough from parochial restraints to prove their interventionist efficacy, and that when they failed, they fell of their own weight and illogic. If we wish to test that lie, along with our resolve to create a society of equals, I wager that the poor we have encountered in these pages would be more than willing to call our hand.

There is yet another problem with explanations that equate pathology with the subcultural practices of the poor. They overlook the fact that the alleged and real pathologies of poor persons are more often than not *our* pathologies as well. The pathologies of the poor may seem larger and more bizarre than ours. It may even be true that the frequency of deviance is greater among the poor than among other classes. But this instance does not warrant the conclusion that the poor as a group have a monopoly on vice and pathology and that their poverty springs from that pathology. Whether the "sick person" drifts into lower-class communities because of a "disease" contracted elsewhere in the class structure or merely succumbs to it because of a life of grinding poverty, the pathology and its symptoms reflect not just the class niche, but the contradictions of the larger social order of which that niche is a part.

When properly understood, the pathology of the poor tells us not only of the impact of a life of need upon a person, it tells us something about the sicknesses that haunt us all. Insofar as the subculture of poverty incorporates into itself the hegemonic norms of the larger culture, adapting them to the particular needs of its niche, it also assimilates the contradictions of the hegemonic classes. The pathologies we so readily recognize among the poor are often little more than our own sicknesses, distorted and rendered garish by the stresses and strains of material need and radical uncertainty.

I have tried to communicate this viewpoint throughout. The distortion of social relations and the pettiness induced by kinship reciprocity practiced under the conditions of extreme material need have their counterparts in other classes who also have "deadbeat" kin who cannot be shaken for love nor money. The poignant struggle of mother against daughter, the internal contradictions of male socialization, the exclusion of the son-in-law, the jealousy of affines, the shrewishness of mothers destroying their daughters, the destruction of sons and daughters at the hands of those who love them, daughters spending the rest of their lives trying to repay and appease their mothers for youthful transgressions, and the heroism and perseverance of people building a life from practically nothing should strike a resonant chord somewhere in each of our own genealogies.

There is in the stories of the Norris, Graham, and Stoner clans a family resemblance to the strength and weaknesses of those heartland bourgeoisies whom Edgar Lee Masters, Theodore Dreiser, and Sinclair Lewis so ambivalently inscribed in their poetry and fiction. There is in the lives of Potter Additionites that same proprietary darkness and gothic undercurrent of panicky normalcy that Sherwood Anderson in his *Winesberg Ohio* called "grotesqueries." There is the same cruel acting out of morality plays in Potter Addition that one finds in Grand Prairie—plays that glory in perversity, even as they puritanically denounce it—scenarios that reaffirm eternal verities that no longer count. These morality plays, imbued with a complex spirit of loving intimacy and unwarranted cruelty, draw their subject matter and actors from the community itself. They have as their centerpieces, whether it be in Potter Addition or Grand Prairie, sotten aunts, closeted uncles, out-of-wedlock pregnancies, adulterous mates, bastard offspring, and families ruined by scandal and drink.

Each class has its own *chiaroscuro* of light and dark, which it combines into its own singular and explosive unity, as it taps the common pool of virtue and vice that binds humans together. Because they are part of the same dynamic social whole, each class shares its pathologies with every other class. And even as it shares its own special sicknesses with other classes, each hones its own special pathology so as to make it vengefully appropriate to its niche. Each class subculture is, hence, that fusion of cultural strengths and weaknesses that give it its unique style and identity. Once this is realized, the entire neo-Malthusian, moralizing enterprise can be scrapped and replaced with a more correct axiom: The structure and culture of poverty, as riddled with pathology as it may or may not be, cannot be reduced to individual pathology. It is, instead, an assemblage of well-honed mechanisms that enable the poor to survive a class niche that would otherwise destroy them. Within the admitted, but insignificant husks of individual pathologies there is an irreducible body of adaptive cultural content that many poor persons embrace and practice. Before we ask them to jettison what they have so painstakingly forged, we might well reexamine their culture and ours and ask if we do them or ourselves any favor by demanding that they emulate us.

Notes

Chapter 1

1. The antipoverty movement in America is now old enough to have its own history. It has been written by Michael B. Katz, and is entitled *The Undeserving Poor: From the War on Poverty to the War on Welfare* (1989). It is a thorough and politically balanced work. It not only traces the shifts in intellectual style that occurred during this period, but also attempts to make its own analytic and philosophical contribution to the newly emerging poverty debate of the late 1980s and 1990s.

2. Recent studies of white, nonethnic poverty have concentrated on American southerners. They fall into three groupings. First, there are the studies of southern life. Prominent among these are works on the Appalachian Highlander. Harry Caudill's *Night Comes to the Cumberlands* (1962), Jack Weller's *Yesterday's People* (1965), and James Brown's (1952a, 1952b, 1952c) Beech Creek Monographs deal with the region's history and culture. A second group of studies by Schwarzweller (Brown, Schwarzweller, and Mangalum 1963; Schwarzweller and Brown 1967; Schwarzweller and Seegar 1967) has investigated Appalachian migrants and the factors effecting their adjustment to northern, urban life. Killian's (1953, 1970, pp. 91–119) earlier research on the adjustment of southern whites in Chicago was a ground-breaking work in this area. In the late 1960s a new series of studies documented the tribulations of displaced southerners and the New Left's attempts to organize poor white immigrants. Todd Gitlin and Nanci Hollander's powerful tract, *Uptown: Poor Whites in Chicago* (1970), and Joseph Harwood's doctoral dissertation, *Work and Community Among Urban Newcomers: A Study of the Social and Economic Adaptations of Southern Migrants in Chicago* (1966), typify this trend in politically oriented community studies. Finally, there is a handful of participant-observer studies that construct the everyday world of poor whites. Two works are of special note here. Joseph T. Howell's *Hard Living on Clay Street* (1973) describes in the grittiest of ethnographic detail the daily struggles of white, lower blue-collar working-class families. Janet M. Fitchen's *Poverty in Rural America: A Case Study* (1981) is an especially valuable account of poverty in a small, rural community.

Chapter 2

1. This liberal reawakening can best be seen in three recent works. First, William Julius Wilson's *The Truly Disadvantaged: the Inner City, the Underclass, and*

Public Policy (1987) is self-consciously a policy-oriented work. It attempts to refute in no uncertain terms the conservative claims of Charles Murray's *Losing Ground* (1984), while taking up the sociological problem of race and poverty, which liberals abandoned in the early 1970s. Providing counterarguments to conservative ideologues, he develops an analysis of poverty and ends his work with a series of policy recommendations that propose an active expansion of existing welfare state entitlements. William Julius Wilson relied heavily on the findings reported in David T. Ellwood's *Poor Support: Poverty in the American Family* (1988). This work is devoted to explaining the various reasons persons descend into poverty and in delineating the needs of poor people by the type of household in which they reside. He thus differentiates between the programmatic needs of two-parent households in which one or both adults work, single-parent households headed by women, inner-city black households, etc. In each case, he prescribes a mixture of economic and welfare reforms that would meet the needs of various impoverished households. Finally, Michael B. Katz's *The Undeserving Poor: From the War on Poverty to the War on Welfare* (1989) provides us with the best overview of American poverty to date. A history of the antipoverty movement from the 1960s to the present, the later chapters attempt to develop a set of liberally oriented philosophical and sociological justifications for restructuring and expanding the liberal welfare state apparatus.

2.   For a summary and critical review of the nature and limits of orthodox economic models of poverty, see David M. Gordon's *Theories of Poverty and Underemployment* (1972, pp. 25–43, 97–110).

3.   The fact that capitalism produces poverty and wealth simultaneously is, for Marx, its essential feature. In light of this, *Capital, Volume 1* ([1867] 1970) can be read as a cumulative series of analyses, each devoted to illuminating a different aspect of *the social structure of capitalist production*. These analyses culminate in Chapter 25, "The General Law of Capitalist Accumulation"(pp. 612–713). In this chapter Marx singles out the political economy of Thomas Malthus for a withering critique, asserting that Malthus's ahistorical treatment of population dynamics is little more than a crude and reified apology for capitalism. Countering Malthus, Marx argues that the phenomenon of overpopulation has little to do with differential rates of population growth and food production. Rather, modern poverty for Marx is a sociohistorical attribute of the capitalist mode of production. Poverty is no more rooted in nature than are the classes that structure capitalism itself. Having been constructed by collective human praxis, poverty, like classes themselves, can be eliminated by concerted, collective action.

4.   Unlike latter-day "neo-Malthusians," who see poverty as a relation between natural population increase and the marginal productivity of land, labor, and machines, radical theory locates poverty's origins in the historically specific social organization of capitalist production. In "historicizing poverty," radical theory separates itself from those reified accounts that treat poverty as natural and in some degree inevitable. The historical specificity of capitalist poverty, as opposed to earlier forms of poverty, is directly spelled out by Marx when he confronts Malthusian political economy:

> With the magnitude of social capital already functioning, and the degree of its increase, with the extension of the scale of production, and the mass of the labourers set in motion, with the development of the productiveness of their labour, with the greater breadth and fulness (*sic*) of all sources of wealth, there is also an extension of the scale on which greater attraction of labourers by capital is accompanied by their greater repulsion; the rapidity of the change in the organic composition of capital, and in its technical form increases, and an increasing number of spheres of

production becomes involved in this change, now simultaneously, now alternately. The labouring population therefore produces, along with the accumulation of capital produced by it, the means by which itself is made relatively superfluous, is turned into a relative surplus-population; and it does this to an always increasing extent. This is a law of population peculiar to the capitalist mode of production; and in fact every special historic mode of production has its own special laws of population, historically valid within its limits alone. An abstract law of population exists for plants and animals only, and only in so far as man has not interfered with them. ([1867] 1970, pp. 630–32)

5. I have already directed the reader's attention to Marx's discussion of the origins of the industrial reserve army in *Capital, Volume 1*. He again takes up this subject in a more developed form in *Capital, Volume 3* (211–67) when he discusses the tendency of the rate of profit to fall and enumerates the social factors that offset that tendency. An excellent update and critical interpretation of this aspect of Marx's work can be found in David Harvey's *The Limits of Capital* (1982, pp. 159–89, 300–7).

6. The term "absolute surplus population" is used by James O'Connor (1974, p. 32) to refer to surplus populations formed in the early phases of labor's formal subordination to capital. It refers to the process by which early capitalist manufacture defeats domestic labor and its traditional productive mode. The result parallels the impact of relative surplus value in that it also creates a surplus population from among the ranks of those who once gained their livelihood from a productive mode that has since been bypassed.

7. Marx's treatment of this subject in the concluding section of *Capital, Volume 1* ([1867] 1970) entitled "The So-Called Primitive Accumulation," is seminal. The amount of subsequent scholarship in this area has been so vast as to defy easy summary. I will thus list only the chief works I have found useful in preparing this chapter: J. L. and Barbara Hammond's *The Village Laborer* (1970), E. P. Thompson's *The Making of the English Working Class* (1966), Craig Calhoun's *The Question of Class Struggle: Social Foundations of Popular Radicalism During the Industrial Revolution* (1982), and Maurice Dobb's classic, *Studies in the Development of Capitalism* (1947, pp. 123–220).

8. It was often the sons, not the displaced fathers, who eventually filled the ranks of the newly forming industrial proletariat. Such a pattern is not restricted to the past or to the England of industrialism's first blush. In the 1960s, I met several unemployed miners in Appalachia who were "sticking it out" rather than move north, waiting for the mines to reopen so that they could work for two more years, say, and then qualify for the United Mine Workers (UMW) pension plan. Certainly this pattern, or something similar to it, is being repeated in the present "rust belt." In these areas, workers who are too old to start over and who refuse to leave an area in which their families have been rooted for generations stay put, hoping against hope for the reopening of the mills. [See Barry Bluestone and Bennett Harrison's *The Deindustrialization of America* (1982) for a general discussion of America's latest foray into the creation of new surplus populations.]

9. See Chapter 3, "The Rise of the Democratic Family," of Steven Mintz and Susan Kellogg's *Domestic Revolutions: A Social History of American Family Life* (1988) for a general historical account of the evolving relationship between the structure of the family and its domestic domain and the changing labor needs of industrial capitalism as they unfolded in the United States.

10. Those working with the segmented labor market model are emphatic in asserting that their work should not be confused with the simple core versus

periphery dichotomy. While their researches are partially grounded in the dual-economy concept, they maintain that there can be no simple isomorphism established between core and periphery on the one hand, and primary and secondary labor markets on the other. Corporate capital, they argue, has its own supply of low-skilled, insecure, and poorly paid labor segments. These workers are part of the "subordinate primary segment." Rounding out this triadic distinction are the *secondary* jobs attached to small, peripheral capital. When seen from this tripartite perspective, it is obvious that secondary labor and subordinate primary labor, while not identical, share many traits. For a recent discussion of this triadic conception of labor markets, see David M. Gordon, Richard Edwards, and Michael Reich's *Segmented Work, Divided Workers* (1982, pp. 1–17, 165–239).

11.   Critically oriented sociology has recently been inundated with a series of revisionist texts whose "postmodern" analyses of "postindustrial" society assert that late capitalism has finally resolved its economic contradictions through political means. Though taking up widely differing themes, these analyses purport to show that class antagonisms and the relations of capitalist production that in the past generated class conflict have now been superseded by other sources of oppression such as race and gender. Such analyses also maintain that Marxist political economy has also become analytically passe, and must now be replaced by more pluralistic forms of social and economic analysis. This position is now being challenged by many on the left who feel that the postmodernists have exaggerated the degree and nature of structural change that capitalism has undergone since the end of the second world war. Thus, in the last year or so, a series of countercritiques (Harvey 1989; Callinicos 1990; Palmer,1989; Harvey and Reed 1990) have begun to surface that challenge the thesis that capitalism has changed to such an extent that Marxist analysis is no longer useful in understanding the dynamics of late capitalist society. Each work has sought either to reaffirm the validity of Marxist theory and its analytic relevance for studying postmodern phenomena, to affirm the need for critical theory to return to its Marxist foundations, or to assert the need to return to the premises of classical Marxist political economy in order to make sense of the social and cultural contradictions of capital itself.

12.   Richard Levins and Richard Lewontin (1985, pp. 65–84) in discussing the interaction of organisms and their environment within the context of evolutionary theory have suggested a parallel position in their discussion of ecological "adaptation" and its role in natural selection. They conclude that organism and ecological niche are correlative and, of necessity, codefining entities. To describe an environment independently of the organisms that inhabit it or to analyze an organism's attributes independently of the environment in which it lives, as though the two develop independently of each other, is conceptually dubious. Adaptation is not just a matter of a preformed organism adapting at ever greater levels of perfection to a constant habitat, it is a mutual transformation of the one by the other, so that the reality of the one is a precarious balance and function of the other.

13.   It was only as my fieldwork progressed and as I worked in subsequent years on this project that I became aware that the theme of uncertainty and its role in shaping the conduct of those living in poverty was a consistent, if underemphasized theme in much of the literature. It is first and foremost an integral part of Karl Marx's analysis of capitalist society. His critique of capitalism's anarchy of production has as one of its major foci the instability that capitalist

social relations injects into the lives of all classes. In *Capital* he not only documents how the use of machinery increases labor's productivity and leads to a revolutionizing of the means of production, but he also demonstrates how this process perpetually destabilizes traditional craft communities and the lives of its inhabitants:

> Modern Industry never looks upon and treats the existing form of a process as final. The technical basis of that industry is therefore revolutionary, while all earlier modes of production were essentially conservative. By means of machinery, chemical processes and other methods, it is continually causing changes not only in the technical basis of production, but also in the functions of the labourer, and in the social combinations of the labour-process. At the same time, it thereby also revolutionizes the division of labour within the society, and incessantly launches masses of capital and of work people from one branch of production to another. But if Modern Industry, by its very nature, therefore necessitates variation of labour, fluency of function, universal mobility of the labourer, on the other hand, in its capitalistic form, it reproduces the old division of labour with its ossified particularizations. We have seen how this absolute contradiction between the technical necessities of Modern Industry, and the social character inherent in its capitalistic form, dispels all fixity and security in the situation of the labourer; how it constantly threatens, by taking away the instruments of labour, to snatch from his hands his means of subsistence, and, by suppressing his detail-function, to make him superfluous. We have seen, too, how this antagonism vents its rage in the creation of that monstrosity, an industrial reserve army, kept in misery in order to be always at the disposal of capital; in the incessant human sacrifices from among the working-class, in the most reckless squandering of labour-power, and in the devastation caused by a social anarchy which turns every economic progress into a social calamity. ([1867] 1970, Volume 1, pp. 486–87)

The theme of uncertainty in the lives of those who live in capitalist society was underscored by the British socialist and educator, R. H. Tawney (1920). He analyzed not just productive techniques, as Marx had, but argued that private property is an institutionalized mechanism that acts as a psychic buffer for the few against the inherent uncertainty of capitalist social relations:

> To the small investors, who are the majority of property-owners, though owning only an insignificant fraction of the property in existence, its meaning is simple. It is not wealth or power, or even leisure from work. It is safety. They work hard. They save a little money for old age, or for sickness, or for their children. They invest it, and the interest stands between them and all that they dread most. Their savings are of convenience to industry, the income from them is convenient to themselves. "Why," they ask, "should we not reap in old age the advantage of energy and thrift in youth?" And this hunger for security is so imperious that those who suffer most from the abuses of property, as well as those who, if they could profit by them, would be least inclined to do so, will tolerate and even defend them, for fear lest the knife which trims dead matter should cut into the quick. . . .
> This need for security is fundamental, and almost the gravest indictment of our civilization is that the mass of mankind are without it. Property is one way of organizing it. It is quite comprehensible therefore, that the instrument should be confused with the end, and that any proposal to modify it should create dismay. In the past, human beings, roads, bridges and ferries, civil, judicial and clerical offices, and commissions in the army have all been private property. . . .
> In fact, however, property is not the only method of assuring the future, nor, when it is the way selected, is security dependent upon the maintenance of all the

rights which are at present normally involved in ownership. In so far as its psychological foundation is the necessity for securing an income which is stable and certain, which is forthcoming when its recipient cannot work, and which can be used to provide for those who cannot provide for themselves, what is really demanded is not the command over the fluctuating proceeds of some particular undertaking, which accompanies the ownership of capital, but the security which is offered by an annuity. Property is the instrument, security is the object, and when some alternative way is forthcoming of providing the latter, it does not appear in practice that any loss of confidence, or freedom or independence is caused by the absence of the former. (pp. 72–74)

Contemporary sociological literature is sprinkled with numerous references to uncertainty and unpredictability and their relation to lower-class conduct and social organization. Dorothy Nelkin (1969, 1970) uses the fact that migrant workers live lives of chronic uncertainty to show that behavior that might otherwise be deemed irrational and self-destructive is both reasonable and eufunctional in stabilizing the everyday life of the migrant work crews and their members. See also the monograph she has written with senior coauthor, William H. Freidland, *Migrant: Agricultural Workers in America's Northeast* (1971).

At the level of recent sociological theory, two works have dealt extensively with the role that uncertainty and unpredictability play in lower-class life. First, S. M. Miller's (1965) four-fold typology of the American lower-class identifies two concrete sources of unpredictability in lower-class life. By distinguishing between (1) stable and unstable family configurations, and (2) secure and insecure economic existences, he is able to differentiate between what he calls the "stable poor," "the unstable poor," "the strained," and "the copers." Second, Cohen and Hodges (1963), in a much neglected article, have explored the role that unpredictability plays in shaping the cultural orientations of the poor. In the following passage they summarize their position—that lower-lower-class (LL in the following passage) life is an orderly, collective solution to economic and social uncertainty:

The task of the LL is to evolve a way of life that will reduce his insecurity and enhance his power in ways that do not depend on achievement in the universalistic sector and on command of a rich and sophisticated variety of perspectives. He can do this by forming a network of relationships, with people similarly circumstanced, that is in some ways like a mutual insurance scheme. People linked by such a network provide one another with a sense of status and worth, and also with aid and support in time of need, without regard to fluency, leverage or merit in the formally organized world of work and among the anonymous incumbents of public bureaucracies. Such a network differs from a conventional insurance scheme in that the kinds of benefits to which one is entitled are not specified in advance by any kind of contract or enumeration but consist broadly of "help in time of trouble"; it differs also in that one's contributions to the scheme are not specified with respect to kind, quantity or periodicity but consist of "doing whatever he can" whenever another is in need. If one has a sufficiently extensive network of such relationships, and he has honored his obligations in the past, there is probably someone to whom he can turn if he should ever need help in paying for an operation, meeting burial expenses, finding a place to live, evading a process server, or putting up the children until he is "back on his feet." Title to these benefits is not tied to incumbency of specific roles, approaches through prescribed channels, or conformity to legalistic requirements. On the contrary, the relationships are valued precisely because they are not hedged about by such conditions. In sum, the distinguishing characteristics of such relationships are that they are diffuse, reciprocal, durable, and particularistic. They will define for us a "solidary" relationship.

The LL will tend to move, so far as possible, within such a world of solidary familiars. Within this world he can move with some confidence, some security, some sense of trust, and with dignity. Outside this world he feels weak, uncertain, disparaged and distrustful. The tendency to classify people as either inside or outside this network of particularistic solidarities will, therefore, have a peculiar saliency for the LL. (pp. 307–8)

This passage summarizes not only their own perspective, but is central to the reproductive paradigm of poverty that I am developing here. Finally, in a work whose subject matter closely parallels ours, Schneider and Smith (1973, pp. 25–27) have depicted lower-class values in terms of their preoccupation with security, as opposed to upper-class norms of rationality based upon universal norms.

14. The most thorough account of Lewis's subculture of poverty concept, the way it developed and changed over the years, the occasional misgivings and ambivalence that Lewis himself had over the idea, and the political interpretations others attributed to it is admirably set out in Susan M. Rigdon's *The Culture Facade: Art, Science, and Politics in the Work of Oscar Lewis* (1988).

15. The cultural ecology model admirably accommodates those critics of the culture of poverty concept who insist upon treating culture as if it were a wholly normative domain—one devoid of material, class-based or other practical elements. Ulf Hannerz (Valentine et al. 1969, p. 186) has suggested that just such a cultural ecology approach to the culture of poverty concept would meet many of Valentine's (1968) idealist criticisms of Lewis's work. As to the plausibility of joining ecological and Marxist models of society into a coherent synthesis, see Amos Hawley's "Human Ecological and Marxist Theories" (1984).

16. I have retained these traits from Lewis's original list, even though I oppose their uncritical use in characterizing all empirical instances of the culture of poverty. Their inclusion in my own reproductive model of poverty is predicated on the inclusion of the sociological parameters of class-based degradation ceremonies (Garfinkel 1955) that generate these traits.

17. For a general discussion of the concept of sedimentation, see Peter Berger and Thomas Luckman's, *The Social Construction of Reality: A Treatise on the Sociology of Knowledge* (1966, pp. 67–72).

Chapter 3

1. In order to ensure the anonymity of the community, proper names have been made up, such as "Clay County" for the name of the original county. The same is true with the name Potter Addition. As to other aspects of ethnographic detail—statistical data, the titles of reports and documents, etc.—I have reported them as I found them, as accurately as possible. In a similar move, the names of all persons contained herein are fictitious. Finally, in order to protect the identity of those who aided in this study, certain details of the original narrative have been altered. I have been careful to ensure that in all instances such changes do not alter the sociological sense of the materials being presented.

2. The rural-urban fringe lies between the city proper and its rural hinterland. Because of its location it exhibits social and ecological characteristics that

are a mixture of rural and urban society. The sociological study of the fringe has fallen from favor in recent years. Perhaps as Robert C. Angell (Queen and Carpenter 1953, pp. 119–20) has suggested, it has become the victim of that larger, artificial division of labor that separates rural sociology from the rest of the profession. Despite this fall from grace, however, research into the structure and function of the fringe represents an area of solid accomplishment. Walter Firey's "Ecological Considerations in Planning for Rurban Fringes" (1946) is not only a classic statement on the sociological significance of the rural-urban fringe, it is also an excellent description of the general attributes of that fringe as a distinct ecological entity. The research of Noel Gist (1952) and Richard Kurtz and Joel Smith (1961) has elaborated upon Firey's original work and increased our understanding of the fringe's structure and dynamics. Finally, the 1952 Joint Symposium of the American Sociological Association and the Rural Sociological Society (Queen and Carpenter 1953) provides us with an excellent overview of the subject.

3. In addition to the culturally composite nature of fringe life, Firey (1946, p. 419) posits a relationship between the economics of mixed land use patterns and the class composition of the fringe. He sees a tendency of such areas to attract, over time, lower-class populations. His later work on the cultural determinants of land use in certain areas of Boston (Firey 1947) undoubtedly supersedes the econometric explanations of his earlier work, but by no means replaces it entirely. The two works when taken together, provide the groundwork for a single model of fringe dynamics and evolution.

4. For a more detailed treatment of the nature of this double migratory movement, see Myles Rodehaver's "Fringe Settlement as a Two-Directional Movement" (1947).

5. W. J. Spillman (1918) gave one of the first formulations of the agricultural ladder thesis at the Thirty-first Annual Meeting of the American Economic Association. This paper was part of a symposium devoted to investigating the high rates of farm tenancy that were then just emerging in the heartland. The symposium's overall theme was articulated by Richard T. Ely and Charles J. Galpin (1918), who defended tenancy as a normal developmental phase of the land tenure process. For a critical appraisal of the agricultural ladder thesis, see Shu-Ching Lee's (1947) article on the subject.

6. Many households in the community remained relatively free of vermin, but only by dint of an unending struggle on the part of homeowners. In some of the student housing rentals that encircled the University in Grand Prairie, infestation was as bad and often worse than anything I encountered in Potter Addition.

7. The way in which the material and symbolic aspects of a community actually shape the identities of those who live in it, though crucial to the understanding of the structure and functioning of modern communities, has not been given a systematic interpretation until very recently. David Hummon's *Commonplaces: Community Ideology and Identity in American Culture* (1990) in correcting this oversight, has gathered together and interpreted the widely dispersed references to this topic in the literature and attempted to bring to it some theoretical order. Working from this interpretive base, he has attempted to delineate empirically the factors that determine personal identity in various communal settings.

8. For a period, some children were sneaking down to Betty's at night to steal empty pop bottles. They would return them the next day for the deposit

and buy candy with the proceeds. This practice stopped when Betty and LaRue began storing their empty bottles in a locked shed. Much to the irritation of the owner of the junkyard next door, who also had a soft-drink machine, the children then shifted their nighttime raids to his premises and continued to underwrite their candy purchases at Betty's Market. This was a source of tension between the Stanses and the junkyard owners during my stay in Potter Addition.

9. Oscar Lewis has noted that such demoralization need not be a universal trait of the subculture of poverty. When a community is homogeneous in its composition and physically segregated from its parent community (by barriers such as a ghetto wall, say) or is spatially isolated from that community (as in the case of Potter Addition), then common consciousness and a community élan often emerge among those living in poverty.

10. Bryan Palmer's *Descent into Discourse: The Reification and the Writing of Social History* (1990) surveys the various kinds of problems that arise when abstract, theoretical categories, such as the Marxist conception of class and class conflict, are used to interpret the historical record. Since the ideographic facts that express the historical specifics of class and class conflict seldom fit hand in glove with the constructs being employed, many historians have despaired of ever finding classes and their antagonisms in the historical data themselves. This has led some historians to abandon altogether the concept of class as a way of ordering the historical record, and turn, instead, to categories like age and gender. Palmer is critical of such self-interested "despairings," however, and holds that while sociological conceptions of class may serve to sensitize the researcher as to what to look for in the historical record when trying to trace the dynamics of class and class conflict, such constructs cannot be too rigidly or too literally applied. The actual historical constitution of classes and their relations often draw from radically different (and often contradictory) social formations. This is especially true in those instances where there is a conjunction of one mode of production with another, or transition to one from another. Our solution to this predicament is essentially Palmer's: The details of the historical and ethnographic record should always be given precedence over any theoretically derived model. The conception and definition of class, say, employed in a work should emerge from the data itself. In this way a dialectic of theory and fact is more easily sustained.

Chapter 4

1. These occupations would correspond to what segmented-labor-market analysts call the "subordinate primary segment" of Grand Prairie's labor force. The greater job security and stability of life-style of these workers make them socially and culturally marginal to both the secondary working class of Potter Addition, as well as the more secure members of Grand Prairie's primary labor force. This marginality was often reflected by the way the people holding these jobs were regarded by others in the community. Often hailing from the families that originally settled the area and hence firmly ensconced in the community's leadership cohort, these people were often subjected to the kind of occasional jealousies and pettiness that so often work to level status differences in small communities.

2.   The occupational values manifested in the jack-of-all-trades orientation should not be written off as just so much sour grapes. These occupational values are neither a reaction formation to the larger culture nor a spiteful inversion of its values. Harry Braverman (1974), drawing from his own biography, has reminded us of the characteristic values and pride of craft that so often enrich working-class life. He has also reminded us in his discussion of Taylorism that academics possess the same occupational biases and blind spots that they attribute to the working class and the poor. After all, Schmidt, the "thick-headed Dutchman" whose intellect Frederick Taylor so demeaned, even as he taught him to load pig iron more efficiently, had built his own house from scratch. As Braverman notes, not many of us could boast of such an achievement. A more recent expression of this pride in work and achievement and its role in sustaining working-class radicalism can be found in Norman Best's autobiographical work, *A Celebration of Work* (1990).

3.   See Joseph T. Howell's *Hard Living on Clay Street* (1973, pp. 344–45) for comments concerning the attractiveness that owning one's own business has for lower-class males.

Chapter 5

1.   My decision to restrict this analysis to Potter Addition's males does not assume that women are indifferent or immune to the injuries of class. Rather, such a decision is grounded in the real differences that work plays in shaping male and female identities. As we shall see in later chapters, the family and household often form a parallel arena of ideological challenge for women and their peer group.

2.   I have been cautious in my claims concerning class consciousness in Potter Addition. This is because any such consciousness is in its earliest stages of formation and may indeed never "mature" into the kind of fully formed political awareness that social scientists usually refer to when discussing issues of class consciousness. As the consciousness of a "class-in-itself," the nascent subjectivity embodied in the car cult and agrarian leisure activities is only in the first stages of defining individual problems as collective ones. There is not yet, and may never be, the self-confident assertiveness, requisite self-confidence, and political assuredness that we usually associate with a "class-for-itself."

Chapter 6

1.   It should be noted that if Figure 6.1 were technically correct, the diagram would have to be given a slight upward slope. Such a positive slope would represent the tendency toward long-term price inflation. The relative position of the resource curve and the budget lines to one another would, however, retain their same *relative* positions.

2.   As Schneider and Lysgaard (1953) originally observed when they coined the term *deferred gratification pattern*, the idea has taken many forms and has been used for both descriptive and pejorative purposes. In its latter usage it can prejudicially denote the alleged lack of restraint, and hence immorality, of people and classes that do not exhibit this behavior. By defining deferred gratifica-

tion as a problem of "impulse control," the term is rendered all but useless for sociological purposes. I have never believed the term to be applicable to lower-class conduct in this psychological sense, and in the contemporary context I see little difference between the so-called "spontaneity" and "sexual honesty" of the new narcissistic professional classes and the lower classes' "inability to practice impulse control." Thus, in what follows I will treat deferred gratification as a *subcultural pattern*, one that has little if anything to do with the alleged "looser" sexual and emotional life of the lower orders of society. Instead, I will ask, as Schneider and Lysgaard originally did, under what social circumstances so-called deferred gratification patterns become a reasonable strategy by which to guide one's conduct, and under what conditions the absence of such a pattern is compatible with individual adaptation and the general reproductive needs of the person's class niche.

3.   This terminology is taken from Robert K. Merton's essay, "The Self-Fulfilling Prophecy," published in his *Social Theory and Social Structure* (1968b, pp. 475–90).

4.   As odd as this logic at first seems, it appears not to be an isolated instance. Brown has reported an almost verbatim rationale of the one just reported, but this time from a Kentucky mountain schoolteacher who fears being the object of a leveling-inspired retaliation:

> One schoolteacher remarked that he didn't dare fix his house the way he and his wife really wanted it even though they could afford to do so, because he knew the people in the neighborhood would be jealous of him, would think he was getting too far ahead of them, and would as a result not rehire him. (1952c, p. 34)

The situations and motives are, admittedly, somewhat different in that tax avoidance and internal community censure are not entirely comparable. Yet in both cases we see that fears of economic retaliation prevent persons from improving their property. It should also be noted that once such a rationale is scripted by the better-off property owners in Potter Addition, others who are destitute and cannot afford to keep up their homes can also adopt this argument in order to save face. In such cases a straightforward account in one instance becomes a dissembling facade erected by a proud, but financially pressed head of household who wants to escape the stigmatic poverty label. It is at this point that such reasoning openly becomes a protective ideological gambit for avoiding degradation in the eyes of others.

5.   I would like to suggest that the labor theory of value is a "natural" pretheoretic stance of the working-class *lebenswelt*. That is, it is apparent that Marx, in theoretically constructing his labor theory of value, gave the workers a powerful instrument of ideological critique. With it they could expropriate the Lockean defense of private property for their own ends. It is also reasonable to assume, however, that while in certain instances Marx's ideas filtered downward to workers and that over time became refined elements of an already existing common stock of proletarian knowledge, Marx also assimilated the worldview of those whom he sought to represent.

The very ease with which the working class embraces a labor theory of value and takes up the militant left rhetoric of class struggle in times of conflict (often just to scare the bejesus out of the boss, and watch him squirm) suggests that much of Marxist thought has "always been there," as the organic worldview of the working class. In the last two decades this, in fact, has become the working assumption of most radical historians who write "history from the bottom up." While workers may not always have at their command the conceptual refinements or vocabulary to talk of their life world with the same coherence that a labor theory of value might, their jobs and the conditions of their labor may be such that the concrete specifics of work provide a "natural bracketing" of experience that makes the Marxist labor theory of value and its associated doctrine of labor's exploitation axiomatic for interpreting work and its everyday antagonisms.

6.   The concept of a moral economy, like that of a natural economy, has been used to characterize precapitalist economic relations and to contrast them to the instrumental rationality of industrial capitalism. The meaning of the term, as I use it here, is taken from two articles by E. P. Thompson: "The Moral Economy of the English Crowd in the Eighteenth Century" (1971), and "Patrician Society, Plebeian Culture" (1974). Both posit the existence of a value system among the lower orders that was grounded in tradition and resistant to the "progressive" ideas of a newly emerging capitalist order. The premises of the moral economy have traditionally been the property of the commoners. Composed of increasingly archaic ideas of fairness, just price, and the right of people to secure life's necessities, even when it went against property rights and market principles, the moral economy is ethically juxtaposed to the new, ascendant market logic of the time.

When I use this term in reference to Potter Addition, I am not suggesting that this archaic ethos has survived untouched by almost two centuries of radical change. Rather I am contending that modern social and cultural systems contain within them the sublated contradictions and residues of earlier historical struggles. There is no question that nineteenth-century capitalism early on removed the moral economy from its privileged cultural position. But so many of the defeats that industrial capitalism dealt the lower classes in that earlier period were premised upon incorporating into its very structure certain of the cultural presuppositions of the defeated classes. Thus the ideological juxtaposition of fair price to market price, while vanquished from the standard economic wisdom of our day, survives in the "nonrational" domain of lower-class culture. Delegitimized and banished from public discourse, and relegated to the shadowy realm of "exogenous variables" by economists, such ideas are left to operate in the shadowy recesses of institutional life. Allowed to gestate in those institutional recesses, each new generation rediscovers and interpretively implements the very folk wisdom that formal scholarship denies.

7.   This theme has been extensively treated from the viewpoint of political economy in James O'Connor's *The Fiscal Crisis of the State* (1973), and from a slightly different vantage point by Jurgen Habermas in *Legitimation Crisis* (1975).

Chapter 7

1.   While not addressing the distribution of family forms in America directly, David Riesman makes a similar observation concerning the geographical distribution of the character types he developed in *The Lonely Crowd* (1961). He notes that the other-directed character type most adapted to the organizational life of large firms is more likely to settle in the large, urban centers of both coasts, notably in the suburbs. By comparison, the inner-directed character type pre-

dominates in the rural and small town settings of the United States (p. 32). He in fact sees his character types mechanically distributed throughout this country, superimposed at times in a nonintegrated fashion, one upon the other: "These character types, like geological or archeological strata, pile one on top of the other, with outcroppings of submerged types here and there" (p. 32). Historically and socially, Grand Prairie and Clay County form one of those largely submerged, cultural "outcroppings."

2. I will assume for the moment, without going into detail as to the reasons for it, that the one more or less follows the other automatically. I will later have to expand upon and qualify this provisional assumption when I take into account Mira Komarovsky's (1940) research on the effect that unemployment has upon the husband's exercise of family authority.

3. It should not be surprising to discover that in the late 1960s the modern women's movement had had little impact upon most of the area's women. Feminism's latest revival was, of course, only in its social and political infancy when I was doing the fieldwork for this study. Still it is safe to speculate that its programs and ideology had little to do with the needs of most lower-class women. Even Planned Parenthood was a dirty word in many of the community's households. It was seen as a snobbish organization based on antifamily and child-hating values. While these perceptions can be contested, the recent history of the women's movement—its inability to mobilize poor and working-class women to its cause, and, until recently, its tendency to downgrade childbearing and child-raising roles—would seem to suggest ample reasons why Potter Addition might remain indifferent, and at times hostile to one of the most significant social movements of recent decades.

The chasm created by conflicting class interests and class subcultures, especially as they relate to the perceived importance of traditional family life in shaping the focal interests of women, seems to place limits upon cross-class female solidarity. These issues have been taken up by Jane Humphries (1977) in her sensitive and well-reasoned article, "Class Struggle and the Persistence of the Working-Class Family."

Chapter 8

1. See Jean-Paul Sartre's *Being and Nothingness* (1966, pp. 301–15) for a discussion of the "other" as an object whose reality lies solely in the self-construction of the Ego through his or her "project." Here I have in mind the possibility of the son becoming the project of the mother and grandmother during the formative years of the young man's life. While outside the immediate interests of this work, it would seem instructive to compare this class-specific otherness of the lower-class male with the allegedly ontological otherness of the woman that Simone DeBeauvoir posits in *The Second Sex* (1953).

2. This analytic approach is by no means new. It has been effectively deployed by E. R. Leach (1954) in his classic analysis of the ideological structure of Chin political life. It has also been used by sociologists. The idea that individuals in their everyday activities reconcile contradictory normative prescriptions and in doing so create viable social structures is a central premise of much of Weberian action theory. One of its clearest applications is found in Reinhard Bendix's (1964, pp. 127–74) study of bureaucratic behavior and its dilemmas. Both

Leach and Bendix see social structure as an *ambivalent synthesis*, which emerges when actors are required to apply, mutually exclusive rules in a single institutionalized setting. In the present work we have merely applied the same analytic approach to the study of lower-class families.

3. The unhappy consciousness metaphor should not be seen as a case of the emergence of deviant norms or social disorganization among the lower classes. It is instead an example of the dialectical constitution of family values in which a compromise family form attempts to accommodate two distinct and often contradictory class-based, normative systems. The lower-class family, in the last analysis, is no more contradictory in its value composition than is, say, the petit bourgeois family. The two forms are merely the expressions of different sets of contradictions. The contradictions animating the petite bourgeoisie, for example, were roughly blocked out by Engels ([1884] 1971, pp. 66–74) as arising from the antagonisms between the natural emotions that ideally integrate the members of the bourgeois family and the destruction of that solidarity by capital's need to pass on property from one generation to the next. Much later, Max Horkheimer (1972, pp. 47–128), various members of the Frankfurt school [see Martin Jay (1973, pp. 113–42) and Mark Poster (1980)] explored the role that the family plays in the rise and reproduction of the authoritarian personality. In these latter instances the subjective and political contradictions of traditional family life have been explored so that critical Marxism has effectively expanded upon Engels's economic-based models.

4. In relation to this issue, see Janet Fitchen's (1981) observations concerning the differences in the trauma associated with the transitional strains of each sex's role. Brown (1952b) has noted the same asymmetrical tendencies by which male roles seem to be more discontinuous than those of their female counterparts in Appalachian culture.

Chapter 9

1. The remainder of this volume follows the paradigm of kinship analysis first developed by Meyer Fortes (1958, 1969). I will, however, employ a second set of terms, which George C. Homans used in his work *The Human Group* (1950). The terms coined by Fortes, the *domestic domain of kinship* and the *politico-jural domain of kinship*, will be used more or less interchangeably with Homans's parallel terminology concerning the external system of group life and its internal system. The terms *domestic domain* and *external system*, despite the radically different problematics from which they are drawn, are for all intents and purposes similar in their behavioral and structural referents. There is somewhat less fit between the concepts *internal system* and *politico-jural domain of kinship*, because of the differing levels of structural specificity at which each scholar works. Homans's behaviorism gives him a penchant for focusing upon concrete, interpersonal interactions, while Fortes's explanation of kinship's political mapping is predisposed toward the more comprehensive level of institutional functioning.

The jural domain/domestic domain dichotomy, contrasting as it does the material and adaptive moments of kinship with its moral, integrative moments, is similar to Homans's dichotomous distinction between the external system of a group and its internal system. The external system of a group's social organization is concerned with the productive role performances by which the group ensures its material survival and ecological adaptation. In the group's external system of social relations, we find activities and sentiments centering on the group's economic and ecological needs. The internal system consists of the norms, rules, practices, and sentiments that emerge during the group's adaptive activities. This internal system, while grounded in the material praxis of the group, is an elaboration of those prior productive roles, and through internal elaboration becomes autonomous of the external system's determination. Taking on a life of their own, the values and norms that make up the internal system feedback upon and alter the conditions of the external system's activities and social relations.

Homans's internal system is in many ways parallel to Fortes's politico-jural domain of kinship. Both authors seem to have similar social phenomena as the object of their analysis. Both are interested in concrete groups, their interactional interiors, and how these interiors are generalized so as to integrate the group into a larger set of social and cultural relations. Both seem to have in the back of their minds the base/cultural superstructure model of dialectical materialism. Both also wish to argue (contra mechanical Marxism) for the relative autonomy of the cultural superstructure, i.e., respectively, the politico-jural domain of kinship, or the human group's emergent internal system of values and sentiments.

2. The contrast between the supposedly rigid prescriptive norms of unilineal systems and the fluid role requirements of bilateral kinship has been exaggerated to the point of parody, and is now largely discredited. Fortes's discussion of complementary filiation suggests that the strict exclusion of one lineage in unilineal systems and the all-embracing power allocated to the other is softened significantly by a set of complementary rights being inherited from the subordinate lineage. Concomitantly, Peranio's (1961) discussion of the so-called utrolateral form of filiation shows that the open nature of bilateral kinship has a wide enough range of variation that it can approximate in the exclusivity of its role allocations the alleged either/or structure of unilineal descent systems.

3. In this society there are times when the person approaches the periphery of his or her kin group and finds that it is not clear where and how lines of demarcation should be drawn. There is often uncertainty as to what kinship terms and formal operators mean, just as there is no sure consensus as to how one "counts kin." In the former case, for example, there is confusion in the public mind as to what is exactly meant by second, third, fourth, cousins, etc., while the operator for cousinship, once, twice, or thrice removed is by no means clearly formulated in the minds of many. In other cases, people are often not sure whether one's affines and one's "affine's affines" should be regarded as part of one's kindred. Many women in Potter Addition, for example, considered as kin anyone to whom they could trace a genealogical relation, no matter how winding or how many affinal ties had to be traversed. It is also not clear in popular consciousness how many genealogical lines can be counted laterally before one stops being related to someone.

4. Jack Goody in his ground-breaking work *The Development of the Family and Marriage in Europe* (1983) has attempted to trace historically the process by which progressively constricting definitions of collaterality became part of the political struggle between Church and corporate kinship groups during the medieval and early modern periods of European history.

5. Farber assumes that kinship systems are the unalloyed expression of ei-

ther centripetal or centrifugal norms, but not both simultaneously. My approach, as seen in the analysis of uxoricentrism, treats family and kinship structures as the dynamic synthesis of contradictory norms and tendencies. His model and my interpretation may not, however, be as far apart as might first appear. This can be seen in a statement drawn from his 1975 article, concerning the oppositional tendencies of the two, and the implication for individual social action that such antagonism entails, Farber writes:

> However, one can perceive kinship as having dual functions, (a) promoting special interests of members in the system of stratification *and* (b) furthering the common interests which weld the population into a coherent society. Given two competing functions of kinship, the principles which meet the requirements of one function tend to oppose those which are consistent with the other function. There are, accordingly, two coexistent systems of kinship possible, each with its own internally consistent structure and its own justifications for conduct related to marriage, residence, property rights, interaction between generations, ties to affines, and the like. Because of the conflicting characteristics of these two systems, people are forced to choose from among competing alternatives. If we assume that in societies norms tend toward mutual consistency, then any society will gravitate toward one extreme or the other. (1975, p., 886)

6. This uncharacteristic weighing of the equality of favors being transferred is contrary to the spirit of the amital norms that ideally bind kinsmen to one another. Hence, Fortes writes:

> What the rule posits is that "kinfolk" have irresistible claims on one another's support and consideration in contradistinction to "nonkinsmen," simply by reason of the fact that they are kin. Kinsfolk must ideally share—hence the frequent invocation of brotherhood as the model of generalized kinship; and they must, ideally, do so without putting a price on what they give. Reciprocal giving between kinsfolk is supposed to be done freely and not in submission to coercive sanctions or in response to contractual obligations. This is the Tallensi ideal of proper kinship behavior. An example from more recent ethnography refers to the Plateau Tonga. In hunger years, says Colson, they "still walk many miles to beg from kinsmen. . . . These may grumble, but so long as anything remains in their granaries . . . , they are likely to divide with their indigent relatives." (1969;238)

7. The tendency to allow one's irritation at being exploited to go unvoiced over the years may be lodged in the sense of embarrassment that one feels in bringing up "money matters" with those to whom one is supposed to be intimately related. While the lower class by no means has a monopoly on such embarrassments, Muir and Weinstein (1962) have suggested that there are clear class differences in how persons regulate and monitor the extension of "social credit" to others. Thus they write:

> [L]ow-SES [socioeconomic status] respondents were unlikely to cut off social credit, while high-SES subjects were likely to do so. . . . Again, high-SES subjects were likely to feel especially willing to do favors "in return," while the majority of low-SES respondents reported that this made no difference. . . . These results may be summarized by suggesting that low-SES subjects, although conscious of, and "internally" affected by, social obligations, do not feel that they should be a factor in the pattern of future exchanges. This pattern, in turn, might be termed "modified altruism," in that one gives when able, expecting others to do the same. It is

compatible with the concept of "mutual aid" ascribed to the lower classes, especially since exchanges appeared to be family centered. . . . By contrast, the middle-class pattern more closely paralleled the financial transaction, in that expectation of specific repayment was clearly indicated. These respondents, to a great extent, *consciously* used an economic model, with business like norms, in their sociable interaction. (pp. 537–38)

If the authors are correct, the instrumental rationality and insertion of economic norms into rules governing intrafamilial altruism among middle-class kin preempts any long-term asymmetry from developing. The "unconditioned" mutual aid of the lower classes on the other hand may contribute to eventual stress between kin and friends alike. The norm of "modified altruism," as it becomes a rule among a kindred, limits the abuses of mutual aid among middle strata, so that any extended cycle of reciprocity has built into it a set of internal checks. In this case, relations may be less emotionally intense or all encompassing, but because of that very "coolness" they may also be less vulnerable to crises. By contrast, the lower -SES groupings, possessing a culture that rejects such accounting as being unseemly, are more ready (or compelled) to give aid and less likely to voice displeasure. In such circumstances the disjunction between perceived obligation and the absence of a cultural convention that sanctions the weighing of such requests by referring to the balance of past exchanges may create a relational time bomb that first creates ambivalence between kin, and then gives birth to patterns of schism and disaffiliation.

Chapter 10

1. There are, of course, significant exceptions to this rule. In the ranks of the upper class, kinship is still a strong regulating force, and is the basis for several political dynasties. The most visible are families such as the Roosevelts and Kennedys, who, in their respective ways, have fabricated kinship estates of high office based in varying degrees upon some notion of aristocratic service. Economic empires, despite the Du Ponts and their ilk, seem to be a fading phenomenon; of interest, however, is the use of business bureaucracies to facilitate the operation of transgenerational kinship estates. Thus, Collier and Horowitz (1976) have shown how "Room 5600," the administrative seat of the Rockefeller corporate empire, has exercised discretionary powers more than once over the Rockefeller wealth—powers that in earlier generations would have been the prerogative of the paterfamilias. [Recall especially Collier and Horowitz's (1976, pp. 556–75) discussion of the alienation of the Rockefeller cousins and their unsuccessful struggle to direct the Rockefeller millions in political directions opposed by the administrative guardians of the Rockefeller estate.]
2. The idea that kinship identities are exchanged upon marriage has been extensively explored by Farber in *Comparative Kinship Systems* (1968). He attempts through the use of formal models to differentiate kinship systems on the basis of (1) the extent to which kinship identities are exchanged, (2) the types of estate elements being exchanged, and (3) the number of generations over which identity transfers last. Of special interest to students of American kinship is his modeling and analysis of Western American and Biblical kinship systems and their geographical distribution in nineteenth century America (pp. 23–46).
3. As I have already noted, who tells these stories is crucial. This is especially

so in kinship systems with fluid descent group boundaries and conjugal units constituted of amalgamated kinship identities. If Grant were to speak up, I am sure that a radically different bill of particulars would be raised. In families built upon amalgamated conjugal identities and still influenced by strong residual premarital kinship commitments, the husband and wife may live in different social realities, even as they cohabit the same household.

4. The antagonistic relation between husband/wife solidarity, on the one hand, and their integration into their respective sibling groups, on the other, finds various degrees of confirmation in the literature. Graham Allen (1977), for example, found in a study of twenty-three British households that a dislike for a sibling's spouse diminished the feelings of closeness between that sibling and his brothers and sisters. Farber (1971), in a study already cited, found among lower-class subjects that when a male Ego maintained close relations with his sister, it was usually accompanied by an estrangement from his wife and children. Rosenberg and Anspach (1973) subsequently disputed Farber's general findings concerning sibling solidarity as a feature of working-class kinship, but reported nonetheless that sibling solidarity seemed to increase when the marital bond was undergoing stress or had actually dissolved:

> [S]ibling solidarity appears to be more prevalent when the conjugal bond has been disrupted, it may be one of the ways in which kinship becomes operative in a compensatory manner, rather than the focal kinship relation itself. (p. 112)

Indirect support for the tension between conjugal relations and sibling solidarity has been reported by Sonya Salamon (1982) in her study of a predominantly Irish-American rural community, Finnegan. Salamon found that sibling solidarity in Finnegan was a primary structural motif around which cooperative agricultural efforts between brothers were organized. The effectiveness of the sibling-based venture, however, was limited by the emergence of the desire on the part of each brother to pass on his estate to his own children. As Salamon notes:

> The sibling cooperative groups that tend to last longest in Finnegan are those in which one or more of the partners remained unmarried, and, therefore, do not experience a rivalry based on the needs of both partners' children. A similar pattern, interestingly enough, was observed in other ethnic communities. Because the Irish have an ideal for the manner in which a sibling team should work, they have a basis for keeping an agreement functioning longer than do other ethnic groups. The siblings, who are part of such an arrangement, try to make it work until the demands of their own children force a dissolution. (p. 361)

Expanding on this, she writes:

> Their arrangement was satisfactory until the brothers' children matured. They found it difficult to incorporate the children into the joint operation; rivalry based on concern for the welfare of one's own children interfered. Each brother has a large family, and, as one remarked about the number of his nieces and nephews, "I have 50 of those." Each brother is willing to help his own sons, but not those of his siblings. So the joint operation is beginning to break up, by mutual agreement, as the brothers buy machinery separately, store and sell their grain individually, but still pool their labor. One of the brothers has two sons who are beginning to replicate the developmental cycle. They have teamed up to pool labor and capital in a joint operation, not seeming to consider as viable potential cooperators their

cousins (uncles' children), perhaps because they are likely competitors for land. (pp. 362–63)

One can, of course, object that what is involved here is not a spouse-sibling antagonism, but an antagonism between the principle of sibling solidarity and the so-called transgenerational unity of the lineage. Yet such an argument does not rule out the possibility of the males in a given sibling group being confronted by their wives and sons as the mother and son struggle to ensure their rights of inheritance against the claims of the older sibling group.

Less ambiguous is James Brown's (1952b) observation. In his study of kinship in three Kentucky mountain communities he has singled out the sibling-spouse opposition as a distinct source of kinship-based tensions. As he notes:

> Like the parent-child relationship, the sibling-sibling relationship also tended to be weakened as the conjugal relationship was strengthened. . . . Analysis . . . makes three points clear: (1) the antagonisms practically always arose after the siblings had grown and had families of their own; (2) many of these controversies centered around the spouse of one or the other, or perhaps both, of the siblings— that is, the old relationship of siblings is changed by the new relationships formed with spouses at marriage; (3) very often these antagonisms centered around "class differences." (pp. 12–14)

The presence of these traits is especially significant for my argument, since Brown is reporting findings on a population that in many ways is ethnically similar to the people of Potter Addition. The fact that his communities are not poverty communities in the strictest sense of the term is also important, since it allows us to situate Potter Addition and its kinship system in a more sharply focused regional and ethnic context. The presence of similar kinship structures in a Kentucky mountain community, one not necessarily possessing a bona fide culture of poverty, suggests that affinal conflict as a property of kinship in Potter Addition may be both a class and an ethnically conditioned phenomenon—an Appalachian or "foothills" culture pattern that has been retained and adapted to the social needs of the class niche into which many entered upon leaving the land.

Chapter 11

1. While not dealing with mother default proper, James Brown (1952b) has noted in his study of Appalachian farm families that a tendency exists in which older sisters assume a mothering role vis-à-vis her younger siblings. He writes:

> In many cases, an older sister took charge of the younger children, and as a consequence a younger child sometimes developed feelings toward his older sister much like those toward his mother, and the older sister, in turn, sometimes developed maternal feelings toward the younger brother or sister. (p. 38)

Brown's work confirms not only this point, but other findings of this work as well. It suggests above all else, that the kinship configurations of Potter Addition are more than mere class phenomena. The parallels in Brown's work and ours suggest that the family and kinship patterns of Potter Addition are rooted in (1) variable environments, and (2) in folkways that are unique to southern, rural culture in general, and the hill country of the border states in particular. This suggests that Potter Addition's lower-class kinship is constructed in response to the class-based challenges of lower-class life, but is grounded in cultural traditions that were transported to Grand Prairie during migration.

2. This is most assuredly correct for the first two developmental possibilities, and possibly for the third as well. It might well be argued that in some families even double-parental default may become a family tradition. Such a family tradition, however, because it requires the reconstruction of family life anew in each sibling cohort, must be seen as the limiting instance in which a family's culture can be reproduced in an orderly manner.

3. The expressive foundations of sibling solidarity and its attendant emphasis upon egalitarianism among siblings stand in stark contrast to the authoritarian and instrumental norms that regulate lineage relations. This is the central finding of Elaine Cummings and David M. Schneider's "Sibling Solidarity: A Property of American Kinship" (1961). In the analyses of various of Farber's works, we have seen how this same contrast can be applied to an understanding of class and kinship and how centrifugally structured kinship can have an expressive affinity for kinship organized along sibling lines. Elmora Matthews, in her *Neighbors and Kin* (1965, pp. 125–38), has used this opposition to contrast vertical and horizontal modes of descent group integration in a Tennessee Ridge community. Her work and the earlier efforts of James Brown (1952c) both underscore the centrality of sibling sentiment and attachment in structuring kinship among Southern, rural whites of various classes. These latter two pieces of research, given that they are working with populations that are demographically and ethnically similar to the population roots of Potter Addition, lend significant support to my interpretation of Mary Graham's kinship system.

4. At this moment, an aside seems appropriate in that the names of Uncle Stan and Aunt Opal have emerged once again. Recall that this is the same couple who ate the Grahams out of house and home. The appearance of their names in this new context, as having provided food and shelter at a vulnerable moment in the frightened, young girl's development, exposes a source of reciprocity's emotional binding power that has hitherto gone unnoticed. It casts a new light on the nature of the past favors Mary may have been repaying all these years. It might explain Mary's remarkable forbearance in the face of the exploitation she has endured at the hands of these loved ones. I showed earlier how Mary had maintained the relationship long after any perceived norm of balance or equity had evaporated. I was somewhat puzzled at the time as to why Mary would remain in such a relationship when its rewards were so asymmetrically tilted against her. Her latest biographical account may provide a partial answer. Theories of reciprocity reflect the enlightenment roots of the social sciences in that they usually conceptualize reciprocity as a relation taking place between rational, consenting *adults*. In Mary's case, the history of reciprocities passing between her and Uncle Stan and Aunt Opal begins not as one of jural equals, but as a one-sided series of prestations between adults and a frightened young girl. The "first gifts" were given by loving adults upon whom, as a quite vulnerable child, Mary was suddenly dependent. The nature of these early gifts, weighted by the potency and scarring potential of fear-laden, youthful dependency, may have been so psychologically potent that in later years Mary's subjective ledger of gifts given and gifts received may never be fully balanced and capable of being closed emotionally. If Mary's case is representative of a certain type of lower-

class relation between kin, then the power of kinship reciprocity's hold on persons, as well as its later consequences for kinship's external system, may spring in part from nonrational elements associated with the age and authority hierarchies in which these acts of binding gift giving first occurred. With unstable family life-styles rampant and rates of divorce among lower-class families high, being taken in by adult relatives is probably a frequent event. Consequently, each new generation of lower-class individuals may be recruited at an early age into emotionally charged networks of reciprocal exchange that entail a lifetime of unredeemable debt. Because of these nonrational contexts, when these older kin are in need, a "lifetime of help" may back up their request for reciprocal aid. No matter how outlandish their request or how "unfair" this particular history of reciprocity has become, the request will be grudgingly honored.

Chapter 12

1. This is not to say that uxoricentrism cannot be found beyond the confines of Potter Addition. There are many similarities between uxoricentrism and the so-called black matriarchy. This might suggest that current expressions of the black matriarchy are themselves rooted as much in class mechanisms as they are in the dynamics of racial oppression. Such an observation is consistent with William Julius Wilson's writings on class, race and poverty (1978, 1987).

2. In emphasizing the historical and cultural specificity of uxoricentrism, I do not wish to imply that sibling-based descent groups are any less the product of local cultural and historical forces than uxoricentrism. It will be recalled that earlier I noted that sibling-based descent groups possessed features that might very well be derived from border state kinship patterns. At the same time, the minimalist structure of the sibling-based system, no matter what its cultural origins, was such as to make it structurally congruent with the variable class niche. In Chapter 11 that congruence was important for the argument being put forth concerning centrifugal kinship and the lower-class niche. Similarly, the culturally composite nature of uxoricentric kinship groups is the key to understanding uxoricentrism's unique place in the life of Potter Addition.

3. In earlier chapters I depicted this antagonism as being concretely and historically expressed in the localized polar extremes of Frisian centripetality versus black lumpen proletariat centrifugality. Without abandoning that descriptive opposition, I wish to recast that dialectic so that it is now internal to the structures of uxoricentric kinship itself.

Chapter 13

1. I was able to confirm this fact shortly after completing this chapter. A volume entitled *Poverty Rural in America* (1992), edited by Cynthia M. Duncan, provides one of the most complete and updated discussions of rural poverty now available. The articles in that volume, working with both national and regional data, reveal economic and social trends over the last thirty years that are very similar to those which I found in Clay County.

Chapter 14

1. While this is not the place for an in-depth examination of the dialectical relation between necessary and surplus poverty, a brief comment on the interaction of the two is in order. I assume that once a politically driven, surplus poverty is created and institutionalized, it is integrated into capital's larger social formation. In time this new source of poverty becomes part of the sedimented foundations of the new social order, i.e., it becomes part of the necessary poverty upon which the new social formation and its division of labor is predicated. The same logic would suggest that social formations evolve and, in doing so, "slough off" vestigial relations. When this happens, those prior paths to poverty associated with them may also be altered or disappear altogether.

2. Phillips's book is, in fact, a comparative study of three "capitalist blowouts," or "hey day periods" in the last century or so: the Gilded Age, the Roaring Twenties, and the Reagan eighties (Phillips 1990, pp. 52–74). True to his conservative credo, however, Phillips stops short of carrying out a full-blown analysis based on class struggle. In fact, he never succeeds in identifying the mechanisms that create these waves of wealth and poverty, and that periodically set the rich and poor against each other. Instead he takes refuge in a somewhat rambling discussion of recurrent historical cycles. He is never clear, however, as to what causes these cycles, though he does allude to Schumpeter's depiction of capitalism as creative destruction, to the ubiquitous Leontief cycles, and finally to "the similar moods and circumstances" that preceded the three periods of capitalist blowout in recent American history. In short, theory is not Phillips's strong suit in this work, though his weaving together of statistics on wealth and poverty is a useful compendium. Less successful is his attempt to dissociate Nixonian cloth coat Republicanism from the upstart Reaganite parvenus, especially when we remember that the "Checkers" speech was made by Nixon to explain a slush fund set up for him by wealthy southern Californians, many of whom could themselves have been described in the fifties as "parvenus."

3. Apropos of this idea of a new politically generated surplus poverty, Bowles, Gordon, and Weisskopf (1991, 1992) have approached this problem from a particularly different slant. They suggest that two explanations—one political and polemical in nature, the other economic and technical—can be used to explain Reaganomics and the new poverty. The first explanation is summarized quite nicely when they write:

> The superficially most obvious answer is that [the right wing] may not have been fighting the war they had proclaimed. The right may not have even cared about the long-term health of the U.S. economy or the well-being of the majority of the people. They may have sought, instead, to concentrate power and wealth in the hands of the wealthiest families and the major U.S. corporations—preferring a larger slice of a smaller pie—rather than to take their chances with the kinds of policies that would have been required to revitalize the U.S. economy. If redistribution was their objective, the battles they fought—for higher interest rates, for weaker unions, for less regulation of business, for lower taxes on the affluent, and for larger military expenditures—were not won in vain. The answer has simplicity to recommend it: it assumes that right-wing forces knew what they were doing, and they got for their troubles more or less what they set out to get. They won their war. (1991, p. 5)

The alternative to this "simplistic account," one that they endorse is as follows:

A quite different answer—and the one toward which we incline—is that they did indeed seek to reverse the economic decline they inherited from the 1960s and 1970s, but that they failed in this objective because the policy package they adopted was ill-suited for the job. Whatever the objectives of the right-wing economic policy, their dismal macroeconomic record and its buy- now/pay-later character may be attributed to five major short-comings. These shortcomings suggest that the logic of right-wing economics—its reliance on trickle-down economics, the discipline of the whip, the invisible hand, and the global big stick—was fundamentally flawed. (p. 5)

The position that the reader must accept one or the other of these explanations overlooks the fact that both are equally correct. If we approach Reaganomics as a piece of class ideology, then it is clear that both accounts are compatible. The reactionary premises that the corporate rich should once again assume their "natural leadership role" after a fifty-year political absence and that class differences in wealth and power should parallel "differences in natural ability" are consistent with the pronouncement of ultraconservative ideologues from the 1950s on. The idea that the five-point program (which the authors rightfully criticize) should be the vehicle for such a restoration, no matter how ill-informed it appeared then or appears now, fits perfectly with their ideological propensities. Ideology, however, is seldom able to produce anything other than self-deception, and here the right wing was no different. From their neo-Malthusian mount they could look down and see the growing inequality and misery of the poor and rationalize it as the just price of their brave new world. When that theory faltered and their economic instruments failed them, like most ruling classes in a decaying context they used their waning political advantage to take whatever was not nailed down, and ran—all the while bemoaning the natural imperfectability of man and society. When seen from this perspective, the two alternatives form complementary halves of a single historical act. Thus, this passage sums up many of the ideas I have put forth here concerning surplus poverty.

4.   I have in mind the works of Irving Bernstein, especially the last two volumes of his labor history trilogy, *Turbulent Years* (1971) and *A Caring Society* (1985). In both volumes he traces the various conflicting political and economic movements that shaped the thirties, as well as the organizations and personalities that clashed over the legislative content of the New Deal's welfare system. In doing so, he demonstrates that the outcome of the Social Security controversy was the product of an unstable compromise, not the consensually validated work of reasoned men and women. To make this ephemeral compromise a standard by which to measure the adequacy of all future welfare programs is at best a highly dubious venture. Domhoff's (1990, pp. 29–64) work on the role that the power elite played in shaping the original Social Security Act, though approached quite differently, reinforces the impression that class and regional conflicts were instrumental in shaping the Social Security Act's final form.

5.   The myth of the fifties that allowed the "vital center" of liberalism to demure, equally, the extremism of both the left and the right, was built on a double distortion:equating all forms of Marxism with Soviet orthodoxy on the one hand, while on the other equating right-wing nativism and McCarthyite extremism with "populism." In so doing the liberal center could pose as the only rational alternative in American politics, a political golden mean flanked on both sides by totalitarian extremes. Thus populism was equated with xenophobic, anti-Semitic, and a culturally regressive know-nothingism. We now know that

nothing could be farther from the truth. Thanks to such works as Lawrence Goodwyn's *Democratic Promise: The Populist Movement in America* (1974) and Gene Clanton's *Populism: The Humane Preference in America* (1991), this is beginning to change. American populism is now recognized as a progressive form of American radicalism that challenged the excesses of a nascent, monopoly capitalism with innovative forms of economic cooperation and political resistance.

References

Agee, James and Walker Evans. 1960. *Let Us Now Praise Famous Men, Three Tenant Families*. Boston: Houghton Mifflin.

Allen, George. 1977. "Sibling Solidarity." *Journal of Marriage and the Family* 39: 177–84.

Anspach, Donald and George S. Rosenberg. 1972. "Working-Class Matricentricity." *Journal of Marriage and the Family* 34:437–42.

Averitt, Robert T. 1968. *The Dual Economy: The Dynamics of American Industry Structure*. New York: Norton.

Bendix, Reinhard. 1964. *Nation-Building and Citizenship*. New York: John Wiley and Sons.

Bendix, Reinhard and Bennet Berger. 1959. "Images of Society and Problems of Concept Formation in Sociology." Pp. 92–120 in *Symposium on Sociological Theory*, edited by Lewellyn Gross. New York: Harper and Row.

Berger, Peter and Thomas Luckmann. 1966. *The Social Construction of Reality: A Treatise on the Sociology of Knowledge*. Garden City, New York: Doubleday.

Bernstein, Irving. 1971. *Turbulent Years: A History of the American Worker, 1933–1941*. Boston: Houghton Mifflin.

———. 1985. *A Caring Society: The New Deal, the Worker, and the Great Depression*. Boston: Houghton Mifflin.

Best, Norman. 1990. *A Celebration of Work*. Lincoln: University of Nebraska Press.

Bluestone, Barry and Bennett Harrison. 1982. *The Deindustrialization of America: Plant Closing, Community Abandonment, and the Dismantling of Basic Industry*. New York: Basic Books.

Bowles, Samuel, David M. Gordon, and Thomas E. Weisskopf. 1991. "Right-Wing Economics Backfired. *Challenge* 34:4–9.

———. 1992. "No Quick Fixes: An Economic Strategy for Progressives." *Nation* 254:145–54.

Braverman, Harry. 1974. *Labor and Monopoly Capital: The Degradation of Work in the Twentieth Century*. New York: Monthly Review Press.

Brown, James Stephen. 1952a. "The Conjugal Family and the Extended Family Group." *American Sociological Review* 17:297–305.

———. 1952b. "The Farm Family in a Kentucky Mountain Neighborhood." Kentucky Agricultural Experiment Station Bulletin 587. Lexington: University of Kentucky.

———. 1952c. "The Family Group in a Kentucky Mountain Farming Community." Kentucky Agricultural Experiment Station Bulletin 588. Lexington:
University of Kentucky.

Brown, James Stephen, Harry K. Schwarzweller, and Joseph Mangalum. 1963.
"Kentucky Mountain Migration and the Stem-Family, an American Variation on a Theme by LePlay." Rural Sociology 28:48–69.

Calhoun, Craig Jackson. 1982. The Question of Class Struggle: Social Foundations of
Popular Radicalism During the Industrial Revolution. Chicago: University of
Chicago Press.

———. 1983. "The Radicalism of Tradition, Community Strength or Venerable
Disguise and Borrowed Language?" American Journal of Sociology 88:886–914.

Callinicos, Alex. 1990. Against Postmodernism: A Marxist Critique. New York: St.
Martin's Press.

Caudill, Harry. 1962. Night Comes to the Cumberlands: A Biography of a De-
pressed Area. Boston: Little, Brown.

Chinoy, Ely. 1955. Automobile Workers and the American Dream. New York: Doubleday.

Clanton, Gene. 1991. Populism: The Humane Preference in America, 1890–1900.
Boston: Twayne Publishers.

Cohen, Albert K. and Harold M. Hodges. 1963. "Characteristics of the Lower
Blue Collar Class." Social Problems 10:305–34.

Collier, Peter and David Horowitz. 1976. The Rockefellers: An American Dynasty.
New York: Holt, Rinehart and Winston.

Coser, Lewis. 1965. "The Sociology of Poverty; to the Memory of Georg Simmel." Social Problems 13:140–48.

———. 1969. "Unanticipated Conservative Consequences of Liberal Theorizing." Social Problems 16:263–72.

Cummings, Elaine and David M. Schneider. 1961. "Sibling Solidarity: A Property of American Kinship." American Anthropologist 63:498–507.

Davenport, William. 1959. "Nonunilinear Descent and Descent Groups." American Anthropologist 61:557–72.

Deavers, Kenneth L. and Robert A. Hoppe. 1992. "Overview of the Rural Poor
in the 1980s." Pp. 3–20 in Rural Poverty in America, edited by Cynthia M.
Duncan. New York: Auburn House.

DeBeauvoir, Simone. 1953. The Second Sex. New York: Knopf.

Della Fava, L. Richard. 1980. "The Meek Shall Not Inherit the Earth." American
Sociological Review 45:955–71.

Department of Housing and Urban Development. 1980. Clay County Community
Development: The Potter Addition Improvement Project. Grand Prairie: Clay
County Development Office.

Dobb, Maurice. 1947. Studies in the Development of Capitalism. New York: International Publishers.

Domhoff, G. William. 1990. The Power Elite and the State: How Policy Is Made in
America. Hawthorne, NY: Aldine de Gruyter.

Duncan, Cynthia M. (ed.). 1992. Poverty in Rural America. New York: Auburn
House.

Duncan, Cynthia and Stephen Sweet. 1992. "Introduction: Poverty in Rural America." Pp. xix–xxvii in *Poverty in Rural America*, edited by Cynthia H. Duncan. New York: Auburn House.

Ehrenreich, Barbara and Frances Fox Piven. 1984. "The Feminization of Poverty." *Dissent* 162–70.

Ellwood, David T. 1988. *Poor Support: Poverty in the American Family*. New York: Basic Books.

Ely, Richard T. and Charles J. Galpin. 1918. "Tenancy as an Ideal System of Landownership." *American Economic Review* 9:180–212.

Engels, Frederick. [1884] 1971. *The Origins of the Family, Private Property, and the State*. New York: International Publishers.

Farber, Bernard. 1964. *Family, Organization and Interaction*. San Francisco: Chandler.

_____. 1968. *Comparative Kinship Systems: A Method of Analysis*. New York: John Wiley and Sons.

_____. 1971. *Kinship and Class: A Midwestern Study*. New York: Basic Books.

_____. 1975. "Bilateral Kinship: Centrifugal and Centripetal Types of Organization." *Journal of Marriage and the Family* 37:871–88.

_____. 1981. *Conceptions of Kinship*. New York: Elsevier.

Firey, Walter. 1946. "Ecological Consideration in Planning for Rurban Fringes." *American Sociological Review* 11:411–21.

_____. 1947. *Land Use in Central Boston*. Cambridge, MA: Harvard University Press.

Firth, Raymond. 1963. "Bilateral Descent Groups, an Operational View." Pp. 22–27 in *Studies in Kinship and Marriage: Dedicated to Brenda Z. Seligman on Her 80th Birthday*, edited by I. Schapera. London: Royal Anthropological Institute of Great Britain and London.

Fitchen, Janet M. 1981. *Poverty in Rural America: A Case Study*. Boulder, CO: Westview Press.

Flora, Cornelia Butler. 1992. "The New Poor in Midwestern Farming Communities." Pp. 201–14 in *Rural Poverty in America*, edited by Cynthia M. Duncan. New York: Auburn House.

Fortes, Meyer. 1958. "Introduction." Pp. 1–14 in *The Developmental Cycle in Domestic Groups*, edited by Jack Goody. Cambridge: Cambridge University Press.

_____. 1969. *Kinship and the Social Order. The Legacy of Lewis Henry Morgan*. Chicago: Aldine.

Freeman, J.D. 1955. *Iban Agriculture, a Report on the Shifting Cultivation of Hill Rice by the Iban of Sarawak*. London: Her Majesty's Stationery Office.

Freidland, William H. and Dorothy Nelkin. 1971. *Migrant: Agricultural Workers in America's Northeast*. New York: Holt, Rinehart and Winston.

Gans, Herbert J. 1962. *The Urban Villagers: Group and Class in the Life of Italo-Americans*. New York: Free Press of Glencoe.

_____. 1968. "Culture and Class in the Study of Poverty: An Approach to Anti-Poverty Research." Pp. 201–28 in *On Understanding Poverty: Perspectives from the Social Sciences*, edited by Daniel P. Moynihan. New York: Basic Books.

Garfinkel, Harold. 1955. "Conditions of Successful Degradation." *American Journal of Sociology* 61:420–24.

Gist, Noel. 1952. "Ecological Decentralization and Rural-Urban Relationships." *Rural Sociology* 7:328–35.

Gitlin, Todd and Nanci Hollander. 1970. *Uptown: Poor Whites in Chicago.* New York: Harper Colophon.

Goldberg, Gertrude S. and Eleanor Kremen. 1986. "The Feminization of Poverty: Only in America?" *Sociological Forum* 1:3–12.

Goodwyn, Lawrence. 1976. *Democratic Promise: The Populist Movement in America.* New York: Oxford University Press.

Goody, Jack. 1983. *The Development of the Family and Marriage in Europe.* Cambridge: Cambridge University Press.

Gordon, David M. 1972. *Theories of Poverty and Underemployment: Orthodox, Radical, and Dual Labor Market Perspectives.* Lexington, MA: Lexington Books.

Gordon, David M., Richard Edwards, and Michael Reich. 1982. *Segmented Work, Divided Workers: The Historical Transformation of Labor in the United States.* Cambridge: Cambridge University Press.

Gorham, Lucy. 1992. "The Growing Problem of Low Earnings in Rural Areas." Pp. 21–40 in *Rural Poverty in America,* edited by Cynthia M. Duncan. New York: Auburn House.

Gouldner, Alvin. 1960. "The Norm of Reciprocity: A Preliminary Statement." *American Sociological Review* 25:161–78.

Gramsci, Antonio. 1971. *Selections from the Prison Notebooks of Antonio Gramsci.* New York: International Publishers.

Habermas, Jurgen. 1975. *Legitimation Crisis.* Boston: Beacon Press.

Hammond, J.L. and Barbara Hammond. 1970. *The Village Laborer, 1760–1832: A Study in the Government of England before the Reform Bill.* New York: Harper and Row.

Harrington, Michael. 1984. *The New American Poverty.* New York: Holt, Rinehart and Winston.

Harrison, Bennett and Barry Bluestone. 1988. *The Great U-Turn: Corporate Restructuring and the Polarization of America.* New York: Basic Books.

Harvey, David. 1982. *The Limits of Capital.* Chicago: University of Chicago Press.

———. 1989. *The Condition of Postmodernity: An Enquiry into the Origins of Cultural Change.* Oxford: Basil Blackwell.

Harvey, David L. and Michael Reed. 1990. "The Limits of Synthesis: Some Comments on Habermas' Recent Sociological Writings." *International Journal of Politics, Culture and Society* 4(3):345–70.

Harwood, Joseph. 1966. "Work and Community among Urban Newcomers: A Study of the Social and Economic Adaptation of Southern Migrants in Chicago." Dissertation submitted to the Department of Sociology, University of Chicago.

Hawley, Amos. 1950. *Human Ecology: A Theory of Community Structure.* New York: Roland Press.

———. 1984. "Human Ecological and Marxist Theories." *American Journal of Sociology* 89:904–17.

Hill, Martha S. 1985. "The Changing Nature of Poverty." *Annals of the American Association of Political and Social Sciences* 479:31–47.

Himmelfarb, Gertrude. 1984. *The Idea of Poverty: England in the Early Industrial Age.* New York: Knopf.

Homans, George C. 1950. *The Human Group.* New York: Harcourt, Brace and World.

Horkheimer, Max. 1972. "Authority and Family." Pp. 47–128 in *Max Horkheimer, Critical Theory: Selected Essays* (Matthew J. O'Connell, transl.). New York: Herder and Herder.

Howell, Joseph T. 1973. *Hard Living on Clay Street: Portraits of Blue Collar Families.* Garden City, NJ: Doubleday/Anchor.

Hummon, David. 1990. *Commonplaces: Community Ideology and Identity in American Culture.* Albany: State University of New York Press.

Humphries, Jane. 1977. "Class Struggle and the Persistence of the Working-Class Family." *Cambridge Journal of Economics* 1:241–58.

———. 1983. "The "Emancipation" of Women in the 1970s and 1980s: From the Latent to the Floating." *Capital and Class* 20:6–28.

Jay, Martin. 1973. *The Dialectical Imagination: A History of the Frankfurt School and the Institute for Social Research, 1923–1950.* Boston: Little, Brown.

Jensen, Arthur R. 1969. "How Much Can We Boost I.Q. and Academic Achievement?" *Harvard Educational Review* 33:1–123.

Katz, Michael B. 1989. *The Undeserving Poor: From the War on Poverty to the War on Welfare.* New York: Pantheon.

Killian, Lewis M. 1953. "The Adjustment of Southern White Immigrants to Northern Urban Norms." *Social Forces* 32:66–70.

———. 1970. *White Southerners.* New York: Random House.

Kohn, Melvin L. 1969. *Class and Conformity: A Study in Values.* Homewood, IL: Dorsey Press.

Komarovsky, Mira. 1940. *The Unemployed Man and His Family, the Effect of Unemployment upon the Status of the Man in Fifty Nine Families.* New York: Dryden Press for the Institute for Social Research.

Kozol, Johnathan. 1978. *Children of the Revolution: A Yankee Teacher in the Cuban Schools.* New York: Delta Books.

Kurtz, Richard A. and Joel Smith. 1961. "Social Life in the Rural-Urban Fringe." *Rural Sociology* 26:24–38.

Lasch, Christopher. 1978. *The Culture of Narcissism: American Life in an Age of Diminishing Expectations.* New York: W. W. Norton.

Leach, E.R. 1954. *Political Systems of Highland Burma: A Study of Kachin Social Structure.* Boston: Beacon Press.

Lemann, Nicholas. 1986. "The Origins of the Underclass." *Atlantic Magazine* 258(June):31–55, 259(July):54–68.

———. 1991. *The Promised Land: The Great Black Migration and How It Changed America.* New York: Knopf.

Levi-Strauss, Claude. 1963. *Structural Anthropology.* New York: Basic Books.

———. 1969. *The Elementary Structures of Kinship.* Boston: Beacon Press.

Levins, Richard and Richard Lewontin. 1985. *The Dialectical Biologist.* Cambridge, MA: Harvard University Press.

Lewis, Michael. 1978. *The Culture of Inequality*. Amherst: University of Massachusetts Press.

Lewis, Oscar. 1964. "The Culture of Poverty." Pp. 149–73 in *Explosive Forces in Latin America*, edited by John Jay TePaske and Sidney Nettleson Fisher. Columbus: Ohio State University Press.

———. 1966. *La Vida: A Puerto Rican Family in the Culture of Poverty—San Juan and New York*. New York: Random House.

———. 1968. "The Culture of Poverty." Pp. 187–200 in *On Understanding Poverty, Perspectives from the Social Sciences*, edited by Daniel P. Moynihan. New York: Basic Books.

Liebow, Elliot. 1967. *Talley's Corner: A Study of Negro Street Corner Men*. Boston: Little, Brown.

Lukacs, Georg. [1922] 1971. *History and Class Consciousness: Studies in Marxist Dialectics*. Cambridge, MA: MIT Press.

Malthus, Thomas Robert. [1872] 1960. "Book IV: Of our future prospects respecting the removal or mitigation of the evils arising from the principle of population." Pp. 477–594 in *An essay on the principle of population, or, A view of its past and present effects on human happiness; with an inquiry into our prospects respecting the future removal or mitigation of the evils which it occasions*, edited by Gertrude Himmelfarb. New York: Modern Library.

Marx, Karl. [1867] 1964. *The Economic and Philosophical Manuscripts of 1844*. New York: International Publishers.

———. [1867] 1970. *Capital: A Critique of Political Economy*. New York: International Publishers.

Matthews, Elmora M. 1965. *Neighbors and Kin: Life in a Tennessee Ridge Community*. Nashville, TN: Vanderbilt University Press.

Matza, David. 1966. "The Disreputable Poor." Pp. 289–302 in *Class, Status and Power: Social Stratification in Comparative Perspective*, edited by Reinhard Bendix and Seymour Martin Lipset. New York: Free Press.

Merton, Robert K. 1968a. "Social Structure and Anomie." Pp. 185–214 in *Social Theory and Social Structure*, (2nd ed.). New York: Free Press.

———. 1968b. *Social Theory and Social Structure*, (2nd ed.). New York: Free Press.

Miller, S. M. 1965. "The American Lower Classes: A Typological Approach." Pp. 22–39 in *New Perspectives on Poverty*, edited by Arthur B. Shostack and William Gomberg. Englewood Cliffs, NJ: Prentice Hall.

Miller, Walter. 1958. "Lower Class Culture as a Generating Milieu of Gang Delinquency." *Journal of Social Issues* 14:5–19.

———. 1968. "The Elimination of the American Lower Class as National Policy: A Critique of the Ideology of the Poverty Movement of the 1960's." Pp. 260–315 in *On Understanding Poverty: Perspectives from the Social Sciences*, edited by Daniel P. Moynihan. New York: Basic Books.

Mintz, Steven and Susan Kellog. 1988. *Domestic Revolutions: A Social History of American Family Life*. New York: Free Press.

Muir, Donald E. and Eugene A. Weinstein. 1962. "The Social Debt: An Investigation of Lower-Class and Middle-Class Norms of Obligation." *American Sociological Review* 27:532–39.

Murray, Charles. 1984. *Losing Ground: American Social Policy, 1950–1980*. New York: Basic Books.

Nelkin, Dorothy. 1969. "A Response to Marginality: The Case of Migrant Farm Workers." *British Journal of Sociology* 20:375–89.

———. 1970. "Unpredictability and Life Style in a Migrant Labor Camp." *Social Problems* 17:449–56.

Newton, Jan. 1977. "Economic Rationality of the Poor." *Human Organization* 36:50–61.

O'Connor, James. 1973. *The Fiscal Crisis of the State*. New York: St. Martin's Press.

———. 1974. *The Corporation and the State*. New York: St. Martin's Press.

Orshansky, Molly. 1965. "Counting the Poor: Another Look at the Poverty Profile." Pp. 42–81 in *Poverty in America*, edited by Louis A. Ferman, Joyce A. Kornbluh and Alan Haber. Ann Arbor: University of Michigan Press.

Orwell, George. 1958. *The Road to Wigan Pier*. New York: Harcourt, Brace, Jovanovich.

Palmer, Bryan. 1990. *Descent into Discourse: The Reification of Language and the Writing of Social History*. Philadelphia: Temple University Press.

Parsons, Lucy E. 1969. "Speech of Lucy E. Parsons." Pp. 167–72 in *The proceedings of the founding convention of the I.W.W.* New York: Merit Publishers.

Parsons, Talcott. 1949. "The Social Structure of the Family." Pp. 241–74 in *The Family: Its Function and Destiny*, edited by Ruth Nanda Anshen. New York: Harper and Brothers.

———. 1951. *The Social System*. New York: Free Press.

Parsons, Talcott and Robert Bales, in collaboration with James Olds, Morris Zelditch, Jr., and Phillip E. Slater. 1955. *Family, Sociology and Interaction Process*. New York: Free Press.

Pehrson, Robert W,. 1954. "Bilateral Kin Groupings as a Structural Type." *University of Manila Journal of East Asiatic Studies* 3:199–202.

Peranio, Roger. 1961. "Descent, Descent Line and Descent Group in Cognatic Social Systems." Pp. 93–113 in *Symposium: Patterns of Land Utilization and Other Papers. Proceedings of the 1961 Annual Meeting of the American Ethnological Society*, edited by Viola Garfield. Seattle: University of Washington Press.

Peterson, Wallace C. 1991. "The Silent Depression." *Challenge* (July–August): 29–34.

Phillips, Kevin. 1990. *The Politics of Rich and Poor, Wealth and the American Electorate in the Reagan Aftermath*. New York: Random House.

Pilcher, William W. 1972. *The Portland Longshoremen: A Dispersed Urban Community*. New York: Holt, Rinehart and Winston.

Pitts, Jesse. [1963] 1964. "The Case of the French Bourgeoisie." Pp. 545–50 in *The Family: Its Structure and Functions*, edited by Rose L. Coser. New York: St. Martin's Press. [Originally pp. 249–54 in *In Search of France*, edited by Stanley Hoffman et al. Cambridge, MA: Harvard University Press.]

Piven, Frances Fox and Richard A. Cloward. 1982. *The New Class War: Reagan's Attack on the Welfare State and Its Consequences*. New York: Pantheon.

Polanyi, Karl. 1944. *The Great Transformation: The Political and Economic Origins of our Times*. Boston: Beacon Press.

Poster, Mark. 1980. *Critical Theory of the Family*. New York: Seabury Press.

Queen, Stuart A., and David B. Carpenter. 1953. "The Sociological Significance of the Rural-Urban Fringe: From the Urban Point of View." Paper presented at the joint session of the American Sociological Society and the Rural Sociological Society, Atlantic City, New Jersey, September 3, 1952. *Rural Sociology* 18:102–7.

Riesman, David (with Nathan Glazer and Reuel Denny). 1961. *The Lonely Crowd: A Study of the Changing American Character*. New Haven, CT: Yale University Press.

Riessman, Frank. 1964. "Low-Income Culture: The Strengths of the Poor." *Journal of Marriage and the Family* 26:417–21.

Rigdon, Susan M. 1988. *The Culture Facade: Art, Science, and Politics in the Work of Oscar Lewis*. Urbana: University of Illinois Press.

Rodehaver, Myles W. 1947. "Fringe Settlement as a Two-Directional Movement." *Rural Sociology* 12:49–57.

Rodgers, Harrell. 1982. *The Cost of Human Neglect: America's Welfare Failure*. Armonk, NY: M. E. Sharpe.

Rosenberg, George S. and David F. Anspach. 1973. "Sibling Solidarity in the Working Class." *Journal of Marriage and the Family* 35:108–13.

Salamon, Sonya. 1980. "Ethnic Differences in Farm Family Land Transfers." *Rural Sociology* 45:290–308.

_____. 1982. "Sibling Solidarity as an Operating Strategy in Illinois Agriculture." *Rural Sociology* 47:349–68.

Salamon, Sonya and Kathleen K. Markan. 1984. "Incorporation and the Family." *Journal of Marriage and the Family* 46:167–78.

Salamon, Sonya and Shirley M. O'Reilly. 1979. "Family Land and Developmental Cycles Among Illinois Farmers." *Rural Sociology* 44:525–42.

Sartre, Jean-Paul. 1966. *Being and Nothingness: A Phenomenological Essay on Ontology*. New York: Washington Square Press.

Sawhill, Elizabeth. 1988. "Poverty in the U.S.: Why Is It So Persistent?" *Journal of Economic Literature* 26:1073–119.

Schneider, David M. and Raymond T. Smith. 1973. *Class Differences and Sex Roles in American Kinship and Family Structure*. Englewood Cliffs, NJ: Prentice Hall.

Schneider, Louis and Sverre Lysgaard. 1953. "The Deferred Gratification Pattern: A Preliminary Study." *American Sociological Review* 18:142–49.

Schwarzweller, Harry K. and James S. Brown. 1967. "Social Class Origins, Rural-Urban Migration, and Economic Life Chances: A Case Study." *Rural Sociology* 32:5–19.

Schwarzweller, Harry K. and John F. Seegar. 1967. "Kinship Involvement: A Factor in the Adjustment of Rural Migrants." *Journal of Marriage and the Family* 29:662–71.

Scott, Marvin B. and Stanford Lyman. 1968. "Accounts." *American Sociological Review* 33:46–62.

Sen, Amartaya. 1978. "On the Labor Theory of Value: Some Methodological Issues." *Cambridge Journal of Economics* 2:175–90.

_____. 1981. "Ingredients of Famine Analysis: Availability and Entitlements." *Quarterly Journal of Economics* 96:433–64.

_____. 1990. "Food Entitlements and Economic Chains." Pp. 374–86 in *Hunger in History: Food Shortage, Poverty, and Deprivation*, edited by Lucille Newman. London: Basil Blackwell.

Sennett, Richard C. and Jonathan Cobb. 1972. *The Hidden Injuries of Class*. New York: Knopf.

Shu-Ching, Lee. 1947. "The Theory of the Agricultural Ladder." *Agricultural History* 21:53–61.

Simmel, Georg. 1950. "The Stranger." Pp. 402–8 in *The Sociology of Georg Simmel*, edited by Kurt H. Wolf. New York: Free Press.

_____. [1908] 1965. "The Poor." *Social Problems* 13:118–39.

Spillman, W. J. 1918. "The Agricultural Ladder." *American Economic Review* 9: 171–79.

Stack, Carol B. 1974. *All Our Kin: Strategies for Survival in a Black Community*. New York: Harper and Row.

Steinbeck, John. 1939. *The Grapes of Wrath*. New York: Modern Library.

Steward, Julian H. 1955. *Theory of Culture Change: The Methodology of Multilinear Evolution*. Urbana: University of Illinois Press.

Suttles, Gerald. 1968. *The Social Order of the Slum, Ethnicity, and Territory in the Inner City*. Chicago: University of Chicago Press.

Sweezy, Paul. 1942. *The Theory of Capitalist Development*. New York; Monthly Review Press.

Tawney, R. H. 1920. *The Acquisitive Society*. New York: Harcourt, Brace, Jovano-vich.

Thompson, E. P. 1966. *The Making of the English Working Class*. New York: Random House.

_____. 1971. "The Moral Economy of the English Crowd in the Eighteenth Century." *Past and Present* 50:76–135.

_____. 1974. "Patrician Society, Plebeian Culture." *Journal of Social History* 7: 382–405.

_____. 1978. *The Poverty of Theory and Other Essays*. New York: Monthly Review Press.

Tickameyer, Ann R. 1992. "The Working Poor in Rural Labor Markets: The Example of the Southeastern United States." Pp. 41–62 in *Rural Poverty in America*, edited by Cynthia M. Duncan. New York: Auburn House.

Tumin, Melvin. 1953. "Some Principles of Stratification: A Critical Analysis." *American Sociological Review* 18:387–93.

Valentine, Charles A. 1968. *Culture and Poverty: Critique and Counter-Proposals*. Chicago: University of Chicago Press.

Valentine, Charles A., Catherine H. Brendt, Ethel Boissevain, John H. Bushnell, Peter Carstens, Thomas Gladwyn, Ulf Hannerz, V. K. Kochar, Eleanor Leacock, Oscar Lewis, William Mangin, David Matza, Margaret Mead, Walter B. Miller, and Daniel P. Moynihan. 1969. "Book Review: Culture and Poverty: Critique and Counter-Proposals. *Current Anthropology* 10:183–201.

Veblen, Thorstein. 1948. *The Portable Veblen*, edited by Max Lerner. New York: Viking Press.

Weller, Jack. 1965. *Yesterday's People: Life in Contemporary Appalachia*. Lexington: University of Kentucky Press.

West, James. 1945. *Plainville, U.S.A.* New York: Columbia University Press.

Wilensky, Harold L. 1961. "Orderly Careers and Social Participation: The Impact of Work History on Social Integration in the Middle Mass." *American Sociological Review* 26:521–39.

Wilson, William Julius. 1978. *The Declining Significance of Race: Blacks and Changing American Institutions*. Chicago: University of Chicago Press.

———. 1987. *The Truly Disadvantaged: The Inner City, the Underclass and Public Policy*. Chicago: University of Chicago Press.

Wolf, Eric R. 1966. "Kinship, Friendship, and Patron-Client Relations in Complex Societies." Pp. 1–22 in *The Social Anthropology of Complex Societies*, edited by Michael Banton. London: Tavistock.

Young, Michael and Peter Willmott. 1957. *Family and Kinship in East London*. Harmondsworth, Middlesex, England: Penguin.

Author Index

Subject Index